Fourth Workshop on e-Commerce and NLP 2021 (ECNLP 4)

Held online due to COVID-19

Bangkok, Thailand
6 August 2021

ISBN: 978-1-7138-3373-4

Printed from e-media with permission by:

Curran Associates, Inc.
57 Morehouse Lane
Red Hook, NY 12571

Some format issues inherent in the e-media version may also appear in this print version.

Association for Computational Linguistics
209 N. Eighth Street
Stroudsburg, Pennsylvania 18360

Phone: 1-570-476-8006
Fax: 1-570-476-0860

acl@aclweb.org

Additional copies of this publication are available from:

Curran Associates, Inc.
57 Morehouse Lane
Red Hook, NY 12571 USA
Phone: 845-758-0400
Fax: 845-758-2633
Email: curran@proceedings.com
Web: www.proceedings.com

ECNLP 4

The Fourth Workshop on e-Commerce and NLP

Proceedings of the Workshop

August 6, 2021
Bangkok, Thailand (online)

Introduction

It is our great pleasure to welcome you to the Fourth Workshop on e-Commerce and NLP (ECNLP).

This workshop focuses on intersection of Natural Language Processing (NLP) and e-Commerce. NLP and information retrieval (IR) have been powering e-Commerce applications since the early days of the fields. Today, NLP and IR already play a significant role in e-Commerce tasks, including product search, recommender systems, product question answering, machine translation, sentiment analysis, product description and review summarization, and customer review processing. With the exploding popularity of chatbots and shopping assistants – both text- and voice-based – NLP, IR, question answering, and dialogue systems research is poised to transform e-Commerce once again.

The ECNLP workshop series was designed to provide a venue for the dissemination of late-breaking research results and ideas related to e-commerce and online shopping, as well as a forum where new and unfinished ideas could be discussed. After three successful editions since 2019, we are happy to host ECNLP 4 at ACL 2021 and once again bring together researchers from both academia and industry.

We have received a larger number of submissions than we could accept for presentation. ECNLP 4 received 34 submissions of long and short research papers. In total, ECNLP 4 featured 21 accepted papers (62% acceptance rate). The selection process was competitive and we believe it resulted in a balanced and varied program that is appealing to audiences from the various sub-areas of e-Commerce.

We would like to thank everyone who submitted a paper to the workshop. We would also like to express our gratitude to the members of the Program Committee for their timely reviews, and for supporting the tight schedule by providing reviews at short notice.

We hope that you enjoy the workshop!

The ECNLP Organizers June 2021

Organizers:

Shervin Malmasi (Amazon, USA)
Surya Kallumadi (Lowe's Companies, Inc., USA)
Nicola Ueffing (eBay Inc, Germany)
Oleg Rokhlenko (Amazon, USA)
Eugene Agichtein (Emory University, USA)
Ido Guy (eBay Inc, Israel)

Program Committee:

Ali Ahmadvand
Federico Bianchi
Eliot Brenner
David Carmel
Giuseppe Castellucci
Lei Chen
Young-joo Chung
Marcus Collins
Pradipto Das
Besnik Fetahu
Ciro Greco
Ido Guy
Ajinkya Kale
Sudipta Kar
Mladen Karan
Tracy Holloway King
Srijan Kumar
Wai Lam
Yitong Li
Weihua Luo
Amita Misra
Emerson Paraiso
Arushi Prakash
Julia Reinspach
Oleg Rokhlenko
Raksha Sharma
Venkat Srinivasan
Sinduja Subramaniam
Jacopo Tagliabue
Liling Tan
Irina Temnikova
Xiaoting Zhao

Table of Contents

BERT Goes Shopping: Comparing Distributional Models for Product Representations

Federico Bianchi
Bocconi University
Milano, Italy
f.bianchi@unibocconi.it*

Bingqing Yu
Coveo
Montreal, CA
cyu2@coveo.com

Jacopo Tagliabue
Coveo AI Labs
New York, United States
jtagliabue@coveo.com†

Abstract

Word embeddings (e.g., word2vec) have been applied successfully to eCommerce products through *prod2vec*. Inspired by the recent performance improvements on several NLP tasks brought by contextualized embeddings, we propose to transfer BERT-like architectures to eCommerce: our model – *Prod2BERT* – is trained to generate representations of products through masked session modeling. Through extensive experiments over multiple shops, different tasks, and a range of design choices, we systematically compare the accuracy of *Prod2BERT* and *prod2vec* embeddings: while *Prod2BERT* is found to be superior in several scenarios, we highlight the importance of resources and hyperparameters in the best performing models. Finally, we provide guidelines to practitioners for training embeddings under a variety of computational and data constraints.

1 Introduction

Distributional semantics (Landauer and Dumais, 1997) is built on the assumption that the meaning of a word is given by the contexts in which it appears: word embeddings obtained from co-occurrence patterns through *word2vec* (Mikolov et al., 2013), proved to be both accurate by themselves in representing lexical meaning, and very useful as components of larger Natural Language Processing (NLP) architectures (Lample et al., 2018). The empirical success and scalability of *word2vec* gave rise to many domain-specific models (Ng, 2017; Grover and Leskovec, 2016; Yan et al., 2017): in eCommerce, *prod2vec* is trained replacing words in a sentence with product interactions in a shopping session (Grbovic et al., 2015), eventually generating vector representations of the products. The key intuition is the same underlying *word2vec* – you can tell a lot about a product by the company it keeps (in shopping sessions). The model enjoyed immediate success in the field and is now essential to NLP and Information Retrieval (IR) use cases in eCommerce (Vasile et al., 2016a; Bianchi et al., 2020).

As a key improvement over *word2vec*, the NLP community has recently introduced *contextualized representations*, in which a word like *play* would have different embeddings depending on the general topic (e.g. a sentence about *theater* vs *soccer*), whereas in *word2vec* the word *play* is going to have only one vector. Transformer-based architectures (Vaswani et al., 2017) in large-scale models - such as BERT (Devlin et al., 2019) - achieved SOTA results in many tasks (Nozza et al., 2020; Rogers et al., 2020). As Transformers are being applied outside of NLP (Chen et al., 2020), it is natural to ask whether we are missing a fruitful analogy with product representations. It is *a priori* reasonable to think that a pair of sneakers can have different representations depending on the shopping context: is the user interested in buying these shoes because they are running shoes, or because these shoes are made by her favorite brand?

In *this* work, we explore the adaptation of *BERT*-like architectures to eCommerce: through extensive experimentation on downstream tasks and empirical benchmarks on typical digital retailers, we discuss advantages and disadvantages of contextualized embeddings when compared to traditional *prod2vec*. We summarize our main contributions as follows:

1. we propose and implement a BERT-based contextualized product embeddings model (hence, **Prod2BERT**), which can be trained with online shopper behavioral data and produce product embeddings to be leveraged by

*Federico and Bingqing contributed equally to this research.

†Corresponding author.

Proceedings of the 4th Workshop on e-Commerce and NLP (ECNLP 4), pages 1–12

downstream tasks;

2. we benchmark Prod2BERT against *prod2vec* embeddings, showing the potential accuracy gain of contextual representations across different shops and data requirements. By testing on shops that differ for traffic, catalog, and data distribution, we increase our confidence that our findings are indeed applicable to a vast class of typical retailers;

3. we perform extensive experiments by varying hyperparameters, architectures and fine-tuning strategies. We report detailed results from numerous evaluation tasks, and finally provide recommendations on how to best trade off accuracy with training cost;

4. we share our code[1], to help practitioners replicate our findings on other shops and improve on our benchmarks.

1.1 Product Embeddings: an Industry Perspective

The eCommerce industry has been steadily growing in recent years: according to U.S. Department of Commerce (2020), 16% of all retail transactions now occur online; worldwide eCommerce is estimated to turn into a $4.5 trillion industry in 2021 (Statista Research Department, 2020). Interest from researchers has been growing at the same pace (Tsagkias et al., 2020), stimulated by challenging problems and by the large-scale impact that machine learning systems have in the space (Pichestapong, 2019). Within the fast adoption of deep learning methods in the field (Ma et al., 2020; Zhang et al., 2020; Yuan et al., 2020), product representations obtained through *prod2vec* play a key role in many neural architectures: after training, a product space can be used directly (Vasile et al., 2016b), as a part of larger systems for recommendation (Tagliabue et al., 2020b), or in downstream NLP/IR tasks (Tagliabue and Yu, 2020). Combining the size of the market with the past success of NLP models in the space, investigating whether Transformer-based architectures result in superior product representations is both theoretically interesting and practically important.

Anticipating some of the themes below, it is worth mentioning that our study sits at the intersection of two important trends: on one side, neural models typically show significant improvements at large scale (Kaplan et al., 2020) – by quantifying expected gains for "reasonable-sized" shops, our results are relevant also outside a few public companies (Tagliabue et al., 2021), and allow for a principled trade-off between accuracy and ethical considerations (Strubell et al., 2019); on the other side, the rise of multi-tenant players[2] makes sophisticated models potentially available to an unprecedented number of shops – in this regard, we design our methodology to include *multiple* shops in our benchmarks, and report how training resources and accuracy scale across deployments. For these reasons, we believe our findings will be interesting to a wide range of researchers and practitioners.

2 Related Work

Distributional Models. *Word2vec* (Mikolov et al., 2013) enjoyed great success in NLP thanks to its computational efficiency, unsupervised nature and accurate semantic content (Levy et al., 2015; Al-Saqqa and Awajan, 2019; Lample et al., 2018). Recently, models such as BERT (Devlin et al., 2019) and RoBERTa (Liu et al., 2019) shifted much of the community attention to Transformer architectures and their performance (Talmor and Berant, 2019; Vilares et al., 2020), while it is increasingly clear that big datasets (Kaplan et al., 2020) and substantial computing resources play a role in the overall accuracy of these architectures; in our experiments, we explicitly address robustness by *i)* varying model designs, together with other hyperparameters; and *ii)* test on multiple shops, differing in traffic, industry and product catalog.

Product Embeddings. Prod2vec is a straightforward adaptation to eCommerce of *word2vec* (Grbovic et al., 2015). Product embeddings quickly became a fundamental component for recommendation and personalization systems (Caselles-Dupré et al., 2018; Tagliabue et al., 2020a), as well as NLP-based predictions (Bianchi et al., 2020). To the best of our knowledge, *this* work is the first to explicitly investigate whether Transformer-based architectures deliver higher-quality product representations compared to non-contextual embeddings. Eschauzier (2020) uses Transformers on cart

[1] Code available at `https://github.com/vinid/prodb`

[2] As an indication of the market opportunity, in the space of AI-powered search and recommendations we recently witnessed Algolia (Techcrunch, 2019a) and Lucidworks raising 100M USD (Techcrunch, 2019c), Coveo raising 227M CAD (Techcrunch, 2019b), Bloomreach raising 115M USD (Techcrunch, 2021).

co-occurrence patterns with the specific goal of basket completion – while similar in the masking procedure, the breadth of the work and the evaluation methodology is very different: as convincingly argued by Requena et al. (2020), benchmarking models on unrealistic datasets make findings less relevant for practitioners outside of "Big Tech". Our work features extensive tests on real-world datasets, which are indeed representative of a large portion of the mid-to-long tail of the market; moreover, we benchmark several fine-tuning strategies from the latest NLP literature (Section 5.2), sharing – together with our code – important practical lessons for academia and industry peers. The closest work in the literature as far as architecture goes is *BERT4Rec* (Sun et al., 2019), i.e. a model based on Transformers trained end-to-end for recommendations. The focus of *this* work is not so much the gains induced by Transformers in sequence modelling, but instead is the quality of the representations obtained through unsupervised pre-training – while recommendations are important, the breadth of *prod2vec* literature (Bianchi et al., 2021b,a; Tagliabue and Yu, 2020) shows the need for a more thorough and general assessment. Our methodology helps uncover a tighter-than-expected gap between the models in downstream tasks, and our industry-specific benchmarks allow us to draw novel conclusions on optimal model design across a variety of scenarios, and to give practitioners actionable insights for deployment.

3 Prod2BERT

3.1 Overview

The Prod2BERT model is taking inspiration from BERT architecture and aims to learn context-dependent vector representation of products from online session logs. By considering a shopping session as a "sentence" and the products shoppers interact with as "words", we can transfer masked language modeling (MLM) from NLP to eCommerce. Framing sessions as sentences is a natural modelling choice for several reasons: first, it mimics the successful architecture of *prod2vec*; second, by exploiting BERT bi-directional nature, each prediction of a masked token/product will make use of past and future shopping choices: if a shopping journey is (typically) a progression of intent from exploration to purchase (Harbich et al., 2017), it seems natural that sequential modelling may capture relevant dimensions in the underlying vocabulary/catalog. Once trained, Prod2BERT becomes capable of predicting masked tokens, as well as providing context-specific product embeddings for downstream tasks.

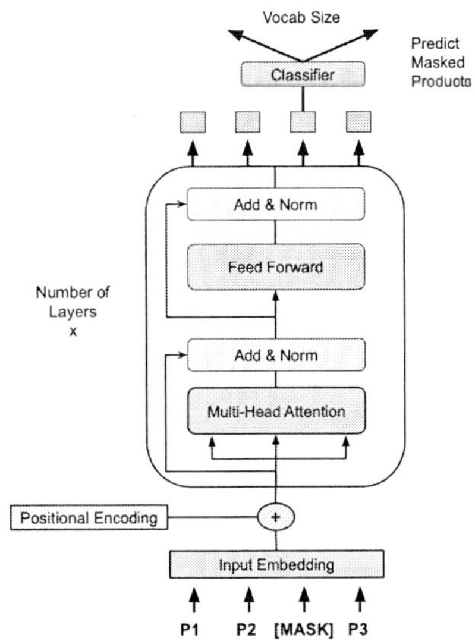

Figure 1: Overall architecture of Prod2BERT pre-trained on MLM task.

3.2 Model Architecture

As shown in Figure 1, Prod2BERT is based on a transformed based architecture Vaswani et al. (2017), emulating the successful BERT model. Please note that, different from BERT's original implementation, a white-space tokenizer is first used to split an input session into tokens, each one representing a product ID; tokens are combined with positional encodings via addition and fed into a stack of self-attention layers, where each layer contains a block for multi-head attention, followed by a simple feed forward network. After obtaining the output from the last self-attention layer, the vectors corresponding to the masked tokens pass through a softmax to generate the final predictions.

3.3 Training Objective

Similar to Liu et al. (2019); Sun et al. (2019), we train Prod2BERT from scratch with the MLM objective. A random portion of the tokens (i.e., the product IDs) in the original sequence are chosen for possible replacements with the *MASK* token; and the masked version of the sequence is fed into the model as input: Figure 2 shows qualitatively the relevant data transformations, from the original

Figure 2: Transformation of sequential data, from the original data generating process – i.e. a shopping session –, to telemetry data collected by the SDK, to the masked sequence fed into Prod2BERT.

shopping session, to the telemetry data, to the final masking sequence. The target output sequence is exactly the original sequence without any masking, thus the training objective is to predict the original value of the masked tokens, based on the context provided by their surrounding unmasked tokens. The model learns to minimize categorical cross-entropy loss, taking into account only the predicted masked tokens, i.e. the output of the non-masked tokens is discarded for back-propagation.

3.4 Hyperparameters and Design Choices

There is growing literature investigating how different hyperparameters and architectural choices can affect Transformer-based models. For example, Lan et al. (2020) observed diminishing returns when increasing the number of layers after a certain point; Liu et al. (2019) showed improved performance when modifying masking strategy and using duplicated data; finally, Kaplan et al. (2020) reported slightly different findings from previous studies on factors influencing Transformers performance. Hence, it is worth studying the role of hyperparameters and model designs for Prod2BERT, in order to narrow down which settings are the best given the specific target of our work, i.e. *product representations*. Table 1 shows the relevant hyperparameter and design variants for Prod2BERT; following improvement in data generalization reported by Liu et al. (2019), when $duplicated = 1$ we augmented the original dataset repeating each session 5 times.[3] We set the embedding size to 64 after preliminary optimizations: as other values offered no improvements, we report results only for one size.

Parameter	Values
# epochs [*e*]	10, 20, 50, 100
# layers [*l*]	4, 8
masking probability [*m*]	0.15, 0.25
duplicated [*d*]	1, 0

Table 1: Hyperparameters and their ranges.

4 Methods

4.1 Prod2vec: a Baseline Model

We benchmark Prod2BERT against the industry standard *prod2vec* (Grbovic et al., 2015). More specifically, we train a CBOW model with negative sampling over shopping sessions (Mikolov et al., 2013). Since the role of hyperparameters in *prod2vec* has been extensively studied before (Caselles-Dupré et al., 2018), we prepare embeddings according to the best practices in Bianchi et al. (2020) and employ the following configuration: $window = 15$, $iterations = 30$, $ns\_exponent = 0.75$, $dimensions = [48, 100]$. While *prod2vec* is chosen because of our focus on the quality of the learned representations – and not just performance on sequential inference *per se* – it is worth nothing that kNN (Latifi et al., 2020) over appropriate spaces is also a surprisingly hard baseline to beat in many practical recommendation settings. It is worth mentioning that for both *prod2vec* and Prod2BERT we are mainly interested in producing a dense space capturing the latent similarity between SKUs: other important relationships between products (substitution (Zuo et al., 2020), hierarchy (Nickel and Kiela, 2017) etc.) may require different embedding techniques (or extensions, such as interaction-specific embeddings (Zhao et al., 2020)).

4.2 Dataset

We collected search logs and detailed shopping sessions from two partnering shops, **Shop A** and **Shop B**: similarly to the dataset released by Requena et al. (2020), we employ the standard definition of "session" from Google Analytics[4], with a total of five different product actions tracked: *detail*, *add*, *purchase*, *remove*, *click*[5]. Shop A and Shop B are

[3] This procedure ensures that each sequence can be masked in 5 different ways during training.

[4] `https://support.google.com/analytics/answer/2731565?hl=en`

[5] Please note that, as in many previous embedding studies (Caselles-Dupré et al., 2018; Bianchi et al., 2020), action

Shop	Sessions	Products	50/75 *pct*
Shop A	1,970,832	38,486	5, 7
Shop B	3,992,794	102,942	5, 7

Table 2: Descriptive statistics for the training dataset. pct shows 50th and 75th percentiles of the session length.

mid-sized digital shops, with revenues between 25 and 100 millions USD/year; however, they differ in many aspects, from traffic, to conversion rate, to catalog structure: Shop A is in the sport apparel category, whereas Shop B is in home improvement. Sessions for training are sampled with undisclosed probability from the period of March-December 2019; testing sessions are a completely disjoint dataset from January 2020. After pre-processing[6], descriptive statistics for the training set for Shop A and Shop B are detailed in Table 2. For fairness of comparison, the exact same datasets are used for both Prod2BERT and *prod2vec*.

Testing on fine-grained, recent data from *multiple* shops is important to support the internal validity (i.e. "is this improvement due to the model or some underlying data quirks?") and the external validity (i.e. "can this method be applied robustly across deployments, e.g. Tagliabue et al. (2020b)"?) of our findings.

5 Experiments

5.1 Experiment #1: Next Event Prediction

Next Event Prediction (NEP) is our first evaluation task, since it is a standard way to evaluate the quality of product representations (Letham et al., 2013; Caselles-Dupré et al., 2018): briefly, NEP consists in predicting the next action the shopper is going to perform given her past actions. Hence, in the case of Prod2BERT, we mask the last item of every session and fit the sequence as input to a pre-trained Prod2BERT model[7]. Provided with the model's output sequence, we take the top K most likely values for the masked token, and perform comparison with the true interaction. As for *prod2vec*, we perform the NEP task by following industry best practices (Bianchi et al., 2020): given a trained *prod2vec*, we take all the before-last items in a session to construct a session vector by average pooling, and use kNN to predict the last item[8]. Following industry standards, *nDCG@K* (Mitra and Craswell, 2018) with $K = 10$ is the chosen metric[9], and all tests ran on $10,000$ testing cases (test set is randomly sampled first, and then shared across Prod2BERT and *prod2vec* to guarantee a fair comparison).

5.1.1 Results

Model	Config	**Shop A**	**Shop B**
Prod2BERT	$e = 10, l = 4,$ $m = 0.25, d = 0$	0.433	0.259
Prod2BERT	$e = 5, l = 4,$ $m = 0.25, d = 1$	**0.458**	**0.282**
Prod2BERT	$e = 10, l = 8,$ $m = 0.25, d = 0$	0.027	0.260
Prod2BERT	$e = 100, l = 4,$ $m = 0.25, d = 0$	0.427	0.255
Prod2BERT	$e = 10, l = 4,$ $m = 0.15, d = 0$	0.416	0.242
prod2vec	$dimension = 48$	<u>0.326</u>	0.214
prod2vec	$dimension = 100$	0.326	<u>0.218</u>

Table 3: *nDCG@10* on NEP task for both shops with Prod2BERT and *prod2vec* (**bold** are best scores for Prod2BERT; <u>underline</u> are best scores for *prod2vec*).

Table 3 reports results on the NEP task by highlighting some key configurations that led to competitive performances. Prod2BERT is significantly superior to *prod2vec*, scoring up to 40% higher than the best *prod2vec* configurations. Since shopping sessions are significantly shorter than sentence lengths in Devlin et al. (2019), we found that changing masking probability from 0.15 (value from standard BERT) to 0.25 consistently improved performance by making the training more effective. As for the number of layers, similar to Lan et al. (2020), we found that adding layers helps only up until a point: with $l = 8$, training Prod2BERT with more layers resulted in a catastrophic drop in model performance for the smaller Shop A; however, the

type is not considered when preparing session for training.

[6]We only keep sessions that have between 3 and 20 product interactions, to eliminate unreasonably short sessions and ensure computation efficiency.

[7]Note that this is similar to the word prediction task for cloze sentences in the NLP literature (Petroni et al., 2019).

[8]Previous work using LSTM in NEP (Tagliabue et al., 2020b) showed some improvements over kNN; however, the differences cannot explain the gap we have found between *prod2vec* and Prod2BERT. Hence, kNN is chosen here for consistency with the relevant literature.

[9]We also tracked *HR@10*, but given insights were similar, we omitted it for brevity in what follows.

Model	Time A-B	Cost A-B
prod2vec	4-20	0.006-0.033$
Prod2BERT	240-1200	48.96-244.8$

Table 4: Time (minutes) and cost (USD) for training one model instance, per shop: *prod2vec* is trained on a *c4.large* instance, Prod2BERT is trained (10 epochs) on a *Tesla V100 16GB* GPU from *p3.8xlarge* instance.

same model trained on the bigger Shop B obtained a small boost. Finally, duplicating training data has been shown to bring consistent improvements: while keeping all other hyperparameters constant, using duplicated data results in an up to 9% increase in *nDCG@10*, not to mention that after only 5 training epochs the model outperforms other configurations trained for 10 epochs or more.

While encouraging, the performance gap between Prod2BERT and *prod2vec* is consistent with Transformers performance on sequential tasks (Sun et al., 2019). However, as argued in Section 1.1, product representations are used as input to many downstream systems, making it essential to evaluate how the learned embeddings generalize outside of the pure sequential setting. Our second experiment is therefore designed to test how well contextual representations transfer to other eCommerce tasks, helping us to assess the accuracy/cost tradeoff when difference in training resources between the two models is significant: as reported by Table 4, the difference (in USD) between *prod2vec* and Prod2BERT is several order of magnitudes.[10]

5.2 Experiment #2: Intent Prediction

A crucial element in the success of Transformer-based language model is the possibility of adapting the representation learned through pre-training to new tasks: for example, the original Devlin et al. (2019) fine-tuned the pre-trained model on 11 downstream NLP tasks. However, the practical significance of these results is still unclear: on one hand, Li et al. (2020); Reimers and Gurevych (2019) observed that sometimes BERT contextual embeddings can underperform a simple GloVe (Pennington et al., 2014) model; on the other, Mosbach et al. (2020) highlights catastrophic forgetting, vanishing gradients and data variance as important factors in practical failures. Hence, given the range of downstream applications and the active debate on transferability in NLP, we investigate how Prod2BERT representations perform when used in the *intent prediction* task.

Intent prediction is the task of guessing whether a shopping session will eventually end in the user adding items to the cart (signaling purchasing intention). Since small increases in conversion can be translated into massive revenue boosting, this task is both a crucial problem in the industry and an active area of research (Toth et al., 2017; Requena et al., 2020). To implement the intent prediction task, we randomly sample from our dataset 20,000 sessions ending with an add-to-cart actions and 20,000 sessions without add-to-cart, and split the resulting dataset for training, validation and test. Hence, given the list of previous products that a user has interacted with, the goal of the intent model is to predict whether an add-to-cart event will happen or not. We experimented with several adaptation techniques inspired by the most recent NLP literature (Peters et al., 2019; Li et al., 2020):

1. *Feature extraction (static)*: we extract the contextual representations from a target hidden layer of pre-trained Prod2BERT, and through average pooling, feed them as input to a multi-layer perceptron (MLP) classifier to generate the binary prediction. In addition to alternating between the first hidden layer (*enc_0*) to the last hidden layer (*enc_3*), we also tried concatenation (*concat*), i.e. combining embeddings of all hidden layers via concatenation before average pooling.
2. *Feature extraction (learned)*: we implement a linear weighted combination of all hidden layers (*wal*), with learnable parameters, as input features to the MLP model (Peters et al., 2019).
3. *Fine-tuning*: we take the pre-trained model up until the last hidden layer and add the MLP classifier on top for intent prediction (*fine-tune*). During training, both Prod2BERT and task-specific parameters are trainable.

As for our baseline, i.e. *prod2vec*, we implement the intent prediction task by encoding each product within a session with its *prod2vec* embeddings, and

[10]Costs are from official AWS pricing, with 0.10 USD/h for the *c4.large* (https://aws.amazon.com/it/ec2/pricing/on-demand/), and 12,24 USD/h for the *p3.8xlarge* (https://aws.amazon.com/it/ec2/instance-types/p3/). While obviously cost optimizations are possible, the "naive" pricing is a good proxy to appreciate the difference between the two methods.

Model	*Method*	Shop	Accuracy
Prod2BERT	*enc_0*	*Shop B*	**0.567**
Prod2BERT	*enc_3*	*Shop B*	0.547
Prod2BERT	*concat*	*Shop B*	0.553
Prod2BERT	*wal*	*Shop B*	0.543
Prod2BERT	*fine-tune*	*Shop B*	0.560
prod2vec	-	*Shop B*	0.558
Prod2BERT	*enc_0*	*Shop A*	0.593
prod2vec	-	*Shop A*	**0.602**

Table 5: Accuracy scores in the intent prediction task (best scores for each shop in **bold**).

feeding them to a LSTM network (so that it can learn sequential information) followed by a binary classifier to obtain the final prediction.

5.2.1 Results

From our experiments, Table 5 highlights the most interesting results obtained from adapting to the new task the best-performing Prod2BERT and *prod2vec* models from NEP. As a first consideration, the shallowest layer of Prod2BERT for feature extraction outperforms all other layers, and even beats concatenation and weighted average strategies[11]. Second, the quality of contextual representations of Prod2BERT is highly dependent on the amount of data used in the pre-training phase. Comparing Table 3 with Table 5, even though the model delivers strong results in the NEP task on Shop A, its performance on the intent prediction task is weak, as it remains inferior to *prod2vec* across all settings. In other words, the limited amount of traffic from Shop A is not enough to let Prod2BERT form high-quality product representations; however, the model can still effectively perform well on the NEP task, especially since the nature of NEP is closely aligned with the pre-training task. Third, fine-tuning instability is encountered and has a severe impact on model performance. Since the amount of data available for intent prediction is not nearly as important as the data utilized for pre-training Prod2BERT, overfitting proved to be a challenging aspect throughout our fine-tuning experiments. Fourth, by comparing the results of our best method against the model learnt with *prod2vec* embeddings, we observed *prod2vec* embeddings can only provide limited values for intent estimation and the LSTM-based model stops to improve very quickly; in contrast, the features provided by Prod2BERT embeddings seem to encode more valuable information, allowing the model to be trained for longer epochs and eventually reaching a higher accuracy score. As a more general consideration – reinforced by a qualitative visual assessment of clusters in the resulting vector space –, the performance gap is *very small*, especially considering that long training and extensive optimizations are needed to take advantage of the contextual embeddings.

[11]This is consistent with Peters et al. (2019), which states that inner layers of a pre-trained BERT encode more transferable features.

6 Conclusion and Future Work

Inspired by the success of Transformer-based models in NLP, *this* work explores contextualized product representations as trained through a BERT-inspired neural network, *Prod2BERT*. By thoroughly benchmarking Prod2BERT against *prod2vec* in a multi-shop setting, we were able to uncover important insights on the relationship between hyperparameters, adaptation strategies and eCommerce performances on one side, and we could quantify for the first time quality gains across different deployment scenarios, on the other. If we were to sum up our findings for interested practitioners, these are our highlights:

1. Generally speaking, our experimental setting proved that pre-training Prod2BERT with Mask Language Modeling can be applied successfully to sequential prediction problems in eCommerce. These results provide independent confirmation for the findings in Sun et al. (2019), where BERT was used for in-session recommendations over academic datasets. However, the tighter gap on downstream tasks suggests that Transformers' ability to model long-range dependencies may be more important than pure representational quality in the NEP task, as also confirmed by human inspection of the product spaces (see Appendix A for comparative t-SNE plots).

2. Our investigation on adapting pre-trained contextual embeddings for downstream tasks featured several strategies in feature extraction and fine-tuning. Our analysis showed that feature based adaptation leads to the peak performance, as compared to its fine-tuning counterpart.

3. Dataset size *does* indeed matter: as evident from the performance difference in Table 5, Prod2BERT shows bigger gains with the largest amount of training data available. Considering the amount of resources needed to train and optimize Prod2BERT (Section 5.1.1), the gains of contextualized embedding may not be worth the investment for shops outside the top 5k in the Alexa ranking[12]; on the other hand, our results demonstrate that with careful optimization, shops with a large user base and significant resources may achieve superior results with Prod2BERT.

While our findings are encouraging, there are still many interesting questions to tackle when pushing Prod2BERT further. In particular, our results require a more detailed discussion with respect to the success of BERT for textual representations, with a focus on the differences between words and products: for example, an important aspect of BERT is the tokenizer, that splits words into subwords; this component is absent in our setting because there exists no straightforward concept of "sub-product" – while far from conclusive, it should be noted that our preliminary experiments using categories as "morphemes" that attach to product identifiers did not produce significant improvements. We leave the answer to these questions – as well as the possibility of adapting Prod2BERT to even more tasks – to the next iteration of this project.

As a parting note, we would like to emphasize that Prod2BERT has been so far the largest and (economically) more significant experiment run by *Coveo*: while we *do* believe that the methodology and findings here presented have significant practical value for the community, we also recognize that, for example, not all possible ablation studies were performed in the present work. As Bianchi and Hovy (2021) describe, replicating and comparing some models is rapidly becoming prohibitive in term of costs for both companies and universities. Even if the debate on the social impact of large-scale models often feels very complex (Thompson et al., 2020; Bender et al., 2021) – and, sometimes, removed from our day-to-day duties – Prod2BERT gave us a glimpse of what unequal access to resources may mean in more meaningful contexts. While we (as in "humanity we") try to find a solution, we (as in "authors we") may find temporary solace knowing that good ol' *prod2vec* is still pretty competitive.

[12]See https://www.alexa.com/topsites.

7 Ethical Considerations

User data has been collected by *Coveo* in the process of providing business services: data is collected and processed in an anonymized fashion, in compliance with existing legislation. In particular, the target dataset uses only anonymous uuids to label events and, as such, it does not contain any information that can be linked to physical entities.

References

Samar Al-Saqqa and Arafat Awajan. 2019. The use of word2vec model in sentiment analysis: A survey. In *Proceedings of the 2019 International Conference on Artificial Intelligence, Robotics and Control*, pages 39–43.

Emily M. Bender, Timnit Gebru, Angelina McMillan-Major, and Shmargaret Shmitchell. 2021. On the dangers of stochastic parrots: Can language models be too big? In *Proceedings of the 2021 ACM Conference on Fairness, Accountability, and Transparency*, FAccT '21, page 610–623, New York, NY, USA. Association for Computing Machinery.

Federico Bianchi, Ciro Greco, and Jacopo Tagliabue. 2021a. Language in a (search) box: Grounding language learning in real-world human-machine interaction. In *Proceedings of the 2021 Conference of the North American Chapter of the Association for Computational Linguistics: Human Language Technologies*, pages 4409–4415, Online. Association for Computational Linguistics.

Federico Bianchi and Dirk Hovy. 2021. On the gap between adoption and understanding in nlp. In *Findings of the Association for Computational Linguistics: ACL-IJCNLP 2021*. Association for Computational Linguistics.

Federico Bianchi, Jacopo Tagliabue, and Bingqing Yu. 2021b. Query2Prod2Vec: Grounded word embeddings for eCommerce. In *Proceedings of the 2021 Conference of the North American Chapter of the Association for Computational Linguistics: Human Language Technologies: Industry Papers*, pages 154–162, Online. Association for Computational Linguistics.

Federico Bianchi, Jacopo Tagliabue, Bingqing Yu, Luca Bigon, and Ciro Greco. 2020. Fantastic embeddings and how to align them: Zero-shot inference in a multi-shop scenario. In *Proceedings of the SIGIR 2020 eCom workshop, July 2020, Virtual Event, published at http://ceur-ws.org (to appear)*.

Hugo Caselles-Dupré, Florian Lesaint, and Jimena Royo-Letelier. 2018. Word2vec applied to recommendation: hyperparameters matter. In *Proceedings of the 12th ACM Conference on Recommender Systems, RecSys 2018, Vancouver, BC, Canada, October 2-7, 2018*, pages 352–356. ACM.

Mark Chen, Alec Radford, Rewon Child, Jeffrey Wu, Heewoo Jun, David Luan, and Ilya Sutskever. 2020. Generative pretraining from pixels. In *Proceedings of the 37th International Conference on Machine Learning, ICML 2020, 13-18 July 2020, Virtual Event*, volume 119 of *Proceedings of Machine Learning Research*, pages 1691–1703. PMLR.

Jacob Devlin, Ming-Wei Chang, Kenton Lee, and Kristina Toutanova. 2019. BERT: Pre-training of deep bidirectional transformers for language understanding. In *Proceedings of the 2019 Conference of the North American Chapter of the Association for Computational Linguistics: Human Language Technologies, Volume 1 (Long and Short Papers)*, pages 4171–4186, Minneapolis, Minnesota. Association for Computational Linguistics.

Ruben Eschauzier. 2020. ProdBERT: Shopping basket completion using bidirectional encoder representations from transformers. In *Bachelor's Thesis*.

Mihajlo Grbovic, Vladan Radosavljevic, Nemanja Djuric, Narayan Bhamidipati, Jaikit Savla, Varun Bhagwan, and Doug Sharp. 2015. E-commerce in your inbox: Product recommendations at scale. In *Proceedings of the 21th ACM SIGKDD International Conference on Knowledge Discovery and Data Mining, Sydney, NSW, Australia, August 10-13, 2015*, pages 1809–1818. ACM.

Aditya Grover and Jure Leskovec. 2016. node2vec: Scalable feature learning for networks. In *Proceedings of the 22nd ACM SIGKDD International Conference on Knowledge Discovery and Data Mining, San Francisco, CA, USA, August 13-17, 2016*, pages 855–864. ACM.

Matthieu Harbich, Gaël Bernard, P. Berkes, B. Garbinato, and P. Andritsos. 2017. Discovering customer journey maps using a mixture of markov models. In *SIMPDA*.

Jared Kaplan, Sam McCandlish, Tom Henighan, Tom B Brown, Benjamin Chess, Rewon Child, Scott Gray, Alec Radford, Jeffrey Wu, and Dario Amodei. 2020. Scaling laws for neural language models. *arXiv preprint arXiv:2001.08361*.

Guillaume Lample, Alexis Conneau, Marc'Aurelio Ranzato, Ludovic Denoyer, and Hervé Jégou. 2018. Word translation without parallel data. In *6th International Conference on Learning Representations, ICLR 2018, Vancouver, BC, Canada, April 30 - May 3, 2018, Conference Track Proceedings*. OpenReview.net.

Zhenzhong Lan, Mingda Chen, Sebastian Goodman, Kevin Gimpel, Piyush Sharma, and Radu Soricut. 2020. ALBERT: A lite BERT for self-supervised learning of language representations. In *8th International Conference on Learning Representations, ICLR 2020, Addis Ababa, Ethiopia, April 26-30, 2020*. OpenReview.net.

Thomas K Landauer and Susan T Dumais. 1997. A solution to plato's problem: The latent semantic analysis theory of acquisition, induction, and representation of knowledge. *Psychological review*, 104(2):211.

Sara Latifi, Noemi Mauro, and D. Jannach. 2020. Session-aware recommendation: A surprising quest for the state-of-the-art. *ArXiv*, abs/2011.03424.

Benjamin Letham, Cynthia Rudin, and David Madigan. 2013. Sequential event prediction. *Machine learning*, 93(2-3):357–380.

Omer Levy, Yoav Goldberg, and Ido Dagan. 2015. Improving distributional similarity with lessons learned from word embeddings. *Transactions of the Association for Computational Linguistics*, 3:211–225.

Bohan Li, Hao Zhou, Junxian He, Mingxuan Wang, Yiming Yang, and Lei Li. 2020. On the sentence embeddings from pre-trained language models. In *Proceedings of the 2020 Conference on Empirical Methods in Natural Language Processing (EMNLP)*, pages 9119–9130, Online. Association for Computational Linguistics.

Y. Liu, Myle Ott, Naman Goyal, Jingfei Du, Mandar Joshi, Danqi Chen, Omer Levy, M. Lewis, Luke Zettlemoyer, and Veselin Stoyanov. 2019. RoBERTa: A robustly optimized BERT pretraining approach. *ArXiv*, abs/1907.11692.

Yifei Ma, Balakrishnan (Murali) Narayanaswamy, Haibin Lin, and Hao Ding. 2020. Temporal-contextual recommendation in real-time. In *KDD '20: The 26th ACM SIGKDD Conference on Knowledge Discovery and Data Mining, Virtual Event, CA, USA, August 23-27, 2020*, pages 2291–2299. ACM.

Laurens van der Maaten and Geoffrey Hinton. 2008. Viualizing data using t-sne. *Journal of Machine Learning Research*, 9:2579–2605.

Tomas Mikolov, Kai Chen, Gregory S. Corrado, and Jeffrey Dean. 2013. Efficient estimation of word representations in vector space. *CoRR*, abs/1301.3781.

Bhaskar Mitra and Nick Craswell. 2018. An introduction to neural information retrieval. *Foundations and Trends® in Information Retrieval*, 13(1):1–126.

Marius Mosbach, Maksym Andriushchenko, and D. Klakow. 2020. On the stability of fine-tuning bert: Misconceptions, explanations, and strong baselines. *ArXiv*, abs/2006.04884.

Patrick Ng. 2017. dna2vec: Consistent vector representations of variable-length k-mers. *ArXiv*, abs/1701.06279.

Maximilian Nickel and Douwe Kiela. 2017. Poincaré embeddings for learning hierarchical representations. In *Advances in Neural Information Processing Systems 30: Annual Conference on Neural Information Processing Systems 2017, December 4-9, 2017, Long Beach, CA, USA*, pages 6338–6347.

Debora Nozza, Federico Bianchi, and Dirk Hovy. 2020. What the [MASK]? making sense of language-specific BERT models. *arXiv preprint arXiv:2003.02912*.

Jeffrey Pennington, Richard Socher, and Christopher Manning. 2014. GloVe: Global vectors for word representation. In *Proceedings of the 2014 Conference on Empirical Methods in Natural Language Processing (EMNLP)*, pages 1532–1543, Doha, Qatar. Association for Computational Linguistics.

Matthew E. Peters, Sebastian Ruder, and Noah A. Smith. 2019. To tune or not to tune? adapting pretrained representations to diverse tasks. In *Proceedings of the 4th Workshop on Representation Learning for NLP (RepL4NLP-2019)*, pages 7–14, Florence, Italy. Association for Computational Linguistics.

Fabio Petroni, Tim Rocktäschel, Sebastian Riedel, Patrick Lewis, Anton Bakhtin, Yuxiang Wu, and Alexander Miller. 2019. Language models as knowledge bases? In *Proceedings of the 2019 Conference on Empirical Methods in Natural Language Processing and the 9th International Joint Conference on Natural Language Processing (EMNLP-IJCNLP)*, pages 2463–2473, Hong Kong, China. Association for Computational Linguistics.

Ann Pichestapong. 2019. Website personalization: Improving conversion with personalized shopping experiences.

Nils Reimers and Iryna Gurevych. 2019. Sentence-BERT: Sentence embeddings using Siamese BERT-networks. In *Proceedings of the 2019 Conference on Empirical Methods in Natural Language Processing and the 9th International Joint Conference on Natural Language Processing (EMNLP-IJCNLP)*, pages 3982–3992, Hong Kong, China. Association for Computational Linguistics.

Borja Requena, Giovanni Cassani, Jacopo Tagliabue, Ciro Greco, and Lucas Lacasa. 2020. Shopper intent prediction from clickstream e-commerce data with minimal browsing information. *Scientific Reports*, 2020:16983.

Anna Rogers, Olga Kovaleva, and Anna Rumshisky. 2020. A primer in BERTology: What we know about how BERT works. *Transactions of the Association for Computational Linguistics*, 8:842–866.

Statista Research Department. 2020. Global retail e-commerce sales 2014-2023.

Emma Strubell, Ananya Ganesh, and Andrew McCallum. 2019. Energy and policy considerations for deep learning in NLP. In *Proceedings of the 57th Annual Meeting of the Association for Computational Linguistics*, pages 3645–3650, Florence, Italy. Association for Computational Linguistics.

Fei Sun, Jun Liu, Jian Wu, Changhua Pei, Xiao Lin, Wenwu Ou, and Peng Jiang. 2019. Bert4rec: Sequential recommendation with bidirectional encoder representations from transformer. In *Proceedings of the 28th ACM International Conference on Information and Knowledge Management, CIKM 2019, Beijing, China, November 3-7, 2019*, pages 1441–1450. ACM.

Jacopo Tagliabue, Ciro Greco, Jean-Francis Roy, Bingqing Yu, Patrick John Chia, Federico Bianchi, and Giovanni Cassani. 2021. Sigir 2021 e-commerce workshop data challenge.

Jacopo Tagliabue and Bingqing Yu. 2020. Shopping in the multiverse: A counterfactual approach to in-session attribution. *ArXiv*, abs/2007.10087.

Jacopo Tagliabue, Bingqing Yu, and Marie Beaulieu. 2020a. How to grow a (product) tree: Personalized category suggestions for eCommerce type-ahead. In *Proceedings of The 3rd Workshop on e-Commerce and NLP*, pages 7–18, Seattle, WA, USA. Association for Computational Linguistics.

Jacopo Tagliabue, Bingqing Yu, and Federico Bianchi. 2020b. The embeddings that came in from the cold: Improving vectors for new and rare products with content-based inference. In *RecSys 2020: Fourteenth ACM Conference on Recommender Systems, Virtual Event, Brazil, September 22-26, 2020*, pages 577–578. ACM.

Alon Talmor and Jonathan Berant. 2019. MultiQA: An empirical investigation of generalization and transfer in reading comprehension. In *Proceedings of the 57th Annual Meeting of the Association for Computational Linguistics*, pages 4911–4921, Florence, Italy. Association for Computational Linguistics.

Techcrunch. 2019a. Algolia finds $110m from accel and salesforce.

Techcrunch. 2019b. Coveo raises 227m at 1b valuation.

Techcrunch. 2019c. Lucidworks raises $100m to expand in ai finds.

Techcrunch. 2021. Bloomreach raises $150m on $900m valuation and acquires exponea.

Neil C. Thompson, Kristjan Greenewald, Keeheon Lee, and G. Manso. 2020. The computational limits of deep learning. *ArXiv*, abs/2007.05558.

Arthur Toth, L. Tan, G. Fabbrizio, and Ankur Datta. 2017. Predicting shopping behavior with mixture of rnns. In *eCOM@SIGIR*.

Manos Tsagkias, Tracy Holloway King, Surya Kallumadi, Vanessa Murdock, and Maarten de Rijke. 2020. Challenges and research opportunities in ecommerce search and recommendations. In *SIGIR Forum*, volume 54.

U.S. Department of Commerce. 2020. U.s. census bureau news.

Flavian Vasile, Elena Smirnova, and Alexis Conneau. 2016a. Meta-prod2vec: Product embeddings using side-information for recommendation. In *Proceedings of the 10th ACM Conference on Recommender Systems, Boston, MA, USA, September 15-19, 2016*, pages 225–232. ACM.

Flavian Vasile, Elena Smirnova, and Alexis Conneau. 2016b. Meta-prod2vec: Product embeddings using side-information for recommendation. In *Proceedings of the 10th ACM Conference on Recommender Systems, Boston, MA, USA, September 15-19, 2016*, pages 225–232. ACM.

Ashish Vaswani, Noam Shazeer, Niki Parmar, Jakob Uszkoreit, Llion Jones, Aidan N. Gomez, Lukasz Kaiser, and Illia Polosukhin. 2017. Attention is all you need. In *Advances in Neural Information Processing Systems 30: Annual Conference on Neural Information Processing Systems 2017, December 4-9, 2017, Long Beach, CA, USA*, pages 5998–6008.

David Vilares, Michalina Strzyz, Anders Søgaard, and Carlos G'omez-Rodr'iguez. 2020. Parsing as pretraining. *ArXiv*, abs/2002.01685.

Bo Yan, Krzysztof Janowicz, Gengchen Mai, and Song Gao. 2017. From itdl to place2vec: Reasoning about place type similarity and relatedness by learning embeddings from augmented spatial contexts. In *Proceedings of the 25th ACM SIGSPATIAL International Conference on Advances in Geographic Information Systems*, SIGSPATIAL '17, New York, NY, USA. Association for Computing Machinery.

Fajie Yuan, Xiangnan He, Alexandros Karatzoglou, and Liguang Zhang. 2020. Parameter-efficient transfer from sequential behaviors for user modeling and recommendation. In *Proceedings of the 43rd International ACM SIGIR conference on research and development in Information Retrieval, SIGIR 2020, Virtual Event, China, July 25-30, 2020*, pages 1469–1478. ACM.

Han Zhang, Songlin Wang, Kang Zhang, Zhiling Tang, Yunjiang Jiang, Yun Xiao, Weipeng Yan, and Wenyun Yang. 2020. Towards personalized and semantic retrieval: An end-to-end solution for e-commerce search via embedding learning. In *Proceedings of the 43rd International ACM SIGIR conference on research and development in Information Retrieval, SIGIR 2020, Virtual Event, China, July 25-30, 2020*, pages 2407–2416. ACM.

Xiaoting Zhao, Raphael Louca, Diane Hu, and Liangjie Hong. 2020. The difference between a click and a cart-add: Learning interaction-specific embeddings. In *Companion Proceedings of the Web Conference 2020*, WWW '20, page 454–460, New York, NY, USA. Association for Computing Machinery.

Zhen Zuo, L. Wang, Michinari Momma, W. Wang, Yikai Ni, Jianfeng Lin, and Y. Sun. 2020. A flexible large-scale similar product identification system in e-commerce.

A Visualization of Session Embeddings

Figures 3 to 6 represent browsing sessions projected in two-dimensions with t-SNE (van der Maaten and Hinton, 2008): for each browsing session, we retrieve the corresponding type (e.g. shoes, pants, etc.) of each product in the session, and use majority voting to assign the most frequent product type to the session. Hence, the dots are color-coded by product type and each dot represents a

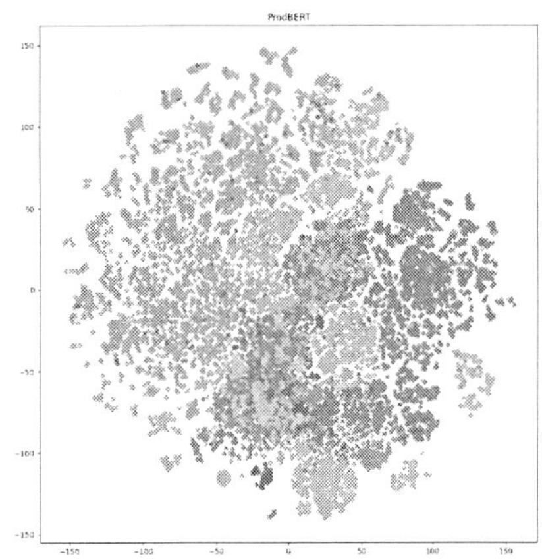

Figure 3: T-SNE plot of browsing session vector space from Shop A and built with the first hidden layer of pre-trained Prod2BERT.

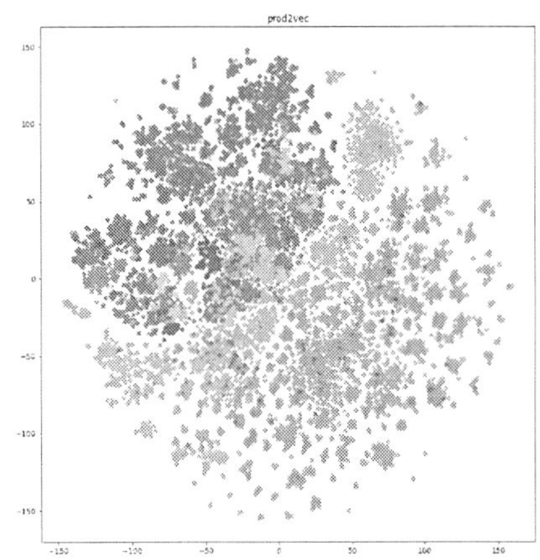

Figure 4: T-SNE plot of browsing session vector space from Shop A and built with *prod2vec* embeddings.

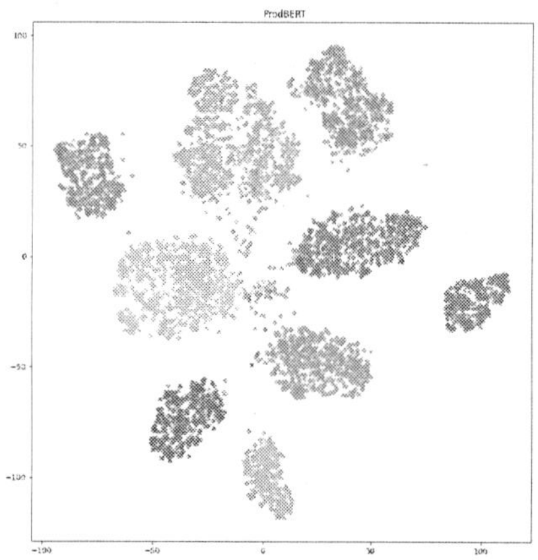

Figure 5: T-SNE plot of browsing session vector space from Shop B and built with the first hidden layer of pre-trained Prod2BERT.

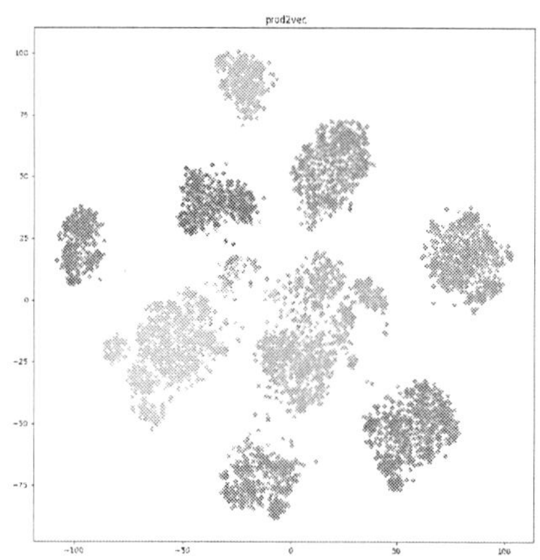

Figure 6: T-SNE plot of browsing session vector space from Shop B and built with *prod2vec* embeddings.

unique session from our logs. It is easy to notice that, first, both contextual and non-contextual embeddings built with a smaller amount of data, i.e. Figures 3 and 4 from Shop A, have a less clear separation between clusters; moreover, the quality of Prod2BERT seems even lower than *prod2vec*, as there exists a larger central area where all types are heavily overlapping. Second, comparing Figure 5 with Figure 6, both Prod2BERT and *prod2vec* improve, which confirms Prod2BERT, given enough pre-training data, is able to deliver better separations in terms of product types and more meaningful representations.

Attribute Value Generation from Product Title using Language Models

Kalyani Roy
IIT Kharagpur, India
kroy@iitkgp.ac.in

Pawan Goyal
IIT Kharagpur, India
pawang@cse.iitkgp.ac.in

Manish Pandey
Carnegie Mellon University
manish.pandey@west.cmu.edu

Abstract

Identifying the value of product attribute is essential for many e-commerce functions such as product search and product recommendations. Therefore, identifying attribute values from unstructured product descriptions is a critical undertaking for any e-commerce retailer. What makes this problem challenging is the diversity of product types and their attributes and values. Existing methods have typically employed multiple types of machine learning models, each of which handles specific product types or attribute classes. This has limited their scalability and generalization for large scale real world e-commerce applications. Previous approaches for this task have formulated the attribute value extraction as a Named Entity Recognition (NER) task or a Question Answering (QA) task. In this paper we have presented a generative approach to the attribute value extraction problem using language models. We leverage the large-scale pretraining of the GPT-2 and the T5 text-to-text transformer to create fine-tuned models that can effectively perform this task. We show that a single general model is very effective for this task over a broad set of product attribute values with the open world assumption. Our approach achieves state-of-the-art performance for different attribute classes, which has previously required a diverse set of models.

1 Introduction

Product attributes and their values play an important role in e-commerce platforms. There are hundreds of thousands of products sold online and each type of product has a different set of attributes. These attributes help customers search for products, compare the relevant items and purchase the product of their choice. While details of a product can be found both in its title as well as its description, commonly, the title includes important attributes of the product. Everyday many new products are added to the product catalogue often with new at-

Figure 1: An example of a product with its title, attributes and values. There is no value for the attribute 'Fingerboard Material' and it is represented as NULL.

tributes types and values. However, attribute information is often sparse, noisy and incomplete with missing values. For example, Figure 1 shows a product with its description and attribute value pairs available on the website. It contains attribute values for *Brand Name*, *Type* etc., but there are missing attributes, such as "Dual-coil" for *Pickup Type*, "6" for *Strings* etc. Given the wide diversity of products and new products constantly emerging, it is important that attribute value extraction works with the *open world assumption*, i.e., values for the attributes not seen before.

Earlier work (Ghani et al., 2006; Chiticariu et al., 2010; Gopalakrishnan et al., 2012) for attribute value extraction use a rule based approach with the help of a domain specific seed dictionary to identify the key phrases. Other work have formulated this as named entity recognition (NER) problem (Putthividhya and Hu, 2011; More, 2016). However, these approaches do not work under the open world assumption. More recently, various neural network based approaches have been proposed and applied to sequence tagging model for attribute value extraction. Huang et al. (2015) is the first to apply the BiLSTM-CRF model for sequence tagging. Zheng et al. (2018) propose an end-to-end tagging model using BiLSTM, CRF and attention without any dic-

Proceedings of the 4th Workshop on e-Commerce and NLP (ECNLP 4), pages 13–17
August 5, 2021.

tionary or hand-crafted features. Most of these approaches create separate models for different attributes. Also, for each attribute a, they have one set of tags to denote beginning (B_a) and inside (I_a) of that attribute. Hence, these methods are not scalable for large set of attributes and these models can not identify emerging values for unseen attributes. Recent works (Xu et al., 2019; Wang et al., 2020) have set up this task as question answering (QA) task. Question answering in machine reading comprehension (MRC) selects a span of text from the given context to answer the question. Xu et al. (2019) considers product title as context, attribute as query, and proposes to find the attribute value using only global set of BIO tags. Although the sequence tagging models (Zheng et al., 2018; Xu et al., 2019) achieve promising result, they do not work well for discovering new attributes values.

In contrast to past extractive or classification based approaches, we have taken a generative approach to identify attribute values. Text generation using language models has several applications in real-world tasks such as text-editing, article writing, sentence completion, etc. Text infilling aims to fill the missing part of a given sentence. Motivated by their success as well as to leverage the large scale pretraining of the language models, we formulate the attribute value extraction as an instance of text infilling task as well as an answer generation task. We utilize Infilling by Language Modeling (ILM) (Donahue et al., 2020) for the infilling approach and we fine-tune Text-to-Text Transfer Transformer (T5) (Raffel et al., 2020) as an answer generation task. We summarize the main contribution of this work as follows:

- We propose a language modeling approach for attribute value extraction.
- We empirically demonstrate that this approach achieves state-of-the-art results on discovering new attribute values.

2 Problem Statement

In this section, we formally define the problem of attribute value generation. Given a product context $T = (w_1^t, w_2^t, ..., w_m^t)$ and its attribue $A = (w_1^a, w_2^a, ..., w_n^a)$, our goal is to generate the value $V = (w_1^v, w_2^v, ..., w_e^v)$. For example, the context of the product in Figure 1 is "ammoon Electric Guitar 6 String Solid Wood Brims 23 Frets Basswood Body Dual-coil Pickup Tremolo & Rhythm Control with Pickguard". Consider the two attributes *Type* and *Fingerboard Material*. We want to generate the value "Electric Guitar" for the attribute *Type* and NULL for the attribute *Fingerboard Material* as this attribute is not present in the context.

Attributes	Train	Valid	test
All	76,970	10,996	21,991
Brand Name	7,969	1,095	2,348
Material	2,824	373	752
Color	735	112	197
Category	662	86	206

Table 1: Statistics of the AV-109K dataset and its four frequent attributes

In this work, first, we formulate this problem as a (i) *text infilling* task and then as an (ii) *answer generation* task. For *text infilling*, we combine the context, T, attribute, A, and the value, V, in a sentence as "T. A is V." where the attribute value V is masked as blank. Our objective is to generate the missing span in this sentence to predict this value. Let the incomplete sentence be $\tilde{S} = (w_1^s, w_2^s, ..., w_p^s)$. Our model outputs the best attribute value sequence $\tilde{V}$ by learning the distribution $\tilde{V} = P(V|\tilde{S})$. In the *answer generation* approach, our aim is to generate V as the answer, considering T as the context and A as the question.

3 Experimental Setup

3.1 Dataset

We have used publicly available dataset[1] which is collected from Sports & Entertainment category of AliExpress (Xu et al., 2019). This dataset contains 110,484 examples. Each example contains a triple, i.e., context as product title, an attribute and its value. We preprocessed the dataset to handle noisy data, and removed triples with empty values and triples with '-', '/' as value. This led to a dataset comprising of 109,957 triples which we refer to as AV-109K. There are 2,157 unique attributes and 11,847 uniques values in this dataset. Also, not all the attributes have a value in the context and these are represented as NULL. There are 21,401 such triples in AV-109K. We randomly split the data into 7:1:2 ratio, i.e., we randomly select 76,970 triples as training set, 10,996 triples as validation set, and the remaining 21,991 triples as the test set.

[1] `https://raw.githubusercontent.com/lanmanok/ACL19_Scaling_Up_Open_Tagging/master/publish_data.txt`

Method	$EM(\%)$	$P(\%)$	$R(\%)$	$F_1(\%)$
SUOTag	68.88	70.81	71.31	71.06
ILM	81.14	83.35	83.38	83.37
T5	**81.35**	**83.89**	**83.75**	**83.82**

Table 2: Performance comparison on the AV-109K dataset

To further examine the model's ability to generate values for unseen attributes, we select five attributes with relatively low frequency ($< 0.1\%$) in the dataset: *Frame Color*, *Lenses Color*, *Shell Material*, *Wheel Material* and *Product Type* and the number of triples for these attributes are 108, 62, 36, 23, and 523, respectively. All the triples with these attributes are included in the test set. From the remainder of the dataset, we pick 10% as validation set and the rest as the training set. We refer to this dataset as AV-zero.

3.2 Evaluation Metrics

To evaluate the models, we use the *Exact Match* (EM) metric on the generated values where the whole sequence of the value must match. Since values can contain more than one tokens and models may generate tokens in any order, we have also computed average bag of word precision, recall and F_1 score as our evaluation measure which are denoted as P, R and F_1, respectively. Let N be the size of the dataset, $V = \{v_1, v_2, .., v_N\}$ be the gold standard values, $G = \{g_1, g_2, ..., g_N\}$ be the generated values, and $|v_i \cap g_i|$ denotes the bag of words overlap between the gold standard and the generated values corresponding to the ith triple. The computation of P and R is shown below:

$$P = \frac{1}{N}\sum_{i=1}^{N}\frac{|v_i \cap g_i|}{|g_i|} \qquad R = \frac{1}{N}\sum_{i=1}^{N}\frac{|v_i \cap g_i|}{|v_i|}$$

3.3 Baselines

We compare our models with BiLSTM-CRF (Huang et al., 2015) and SUOTag (Scaling Up Open Tag) (Xu et al., 2019)[2].

- **BiLSTM-CRF** (Huang et al., 2015) is considered to be the state-of-the-art sequence tagging model for NER tasks. It uses the word embedding from pretrained BERT model and applies a BiLSTM layer over it to the contextual representation. Finally a Conditional Random Fields (CRF) (Lafferty et al., 2001) layer is applied over this BiLSTM.

- **SUOTag** (Xu et al., 2019) uses two separate BiLSTMs over the BERT based pretrained word embeddings to represent the context and attribute. Then, it applies a cross attention between these two representations followed by a CRF layer.

[2]AVEQA (Attribute Value Extraction via Question Answering) (Wang et al., 2020) is also a recent work that could potentially be a baseline, but we could not get the numbers as the code was not publicly available.

	Models	SUOTag	ILM	T5
NULL	Precision (%)	41.73	75.25	**77.32**
	Recall (%)	**93.10**	78.99	74.09
	$F_1(\%)$	57.63	**77.07**	75.67
EM(%) when attributes appear in context		28.86	**61.11**	54.57
EM(%) when attributes does not appear in context		69.53	81.22	**81.78**
Values having multiple words EM (%)		47.00	62.74	**62.96**
Numerical values		43.24	66.56	**72.06**

Table 3: Performance of models on AV-109K dataset in different scenarios.

3.4 Implementation Details

All the models are implemented with PyTorch (Paszke et al., 2019). We train each model for 5 epochs. The model that performs the best on the validation set is used for evaluating the test set. The minibatch size is fixed to 32. We use AdamW optimizer and a learning rate of 5e-5. We use pretrained GPT-2 small (Radford et al., 2019) model to train ILM and we use the validation set perplexity of the model on the masked token. We fine-tune T5-Base for the answer generation framework.

3.5 Results and Discussion

We conduct experiments on different settings to (1) explore the scalability on large attribute set, (2) compare the performance on four frequent attributes, and (3) examine the model's ability to discover new attributes.

Table 2 reports the performance on the AV-109K dataset. Since BiLSTM-CRF requires to tag each of the attributes a with separate B_a and I_a tags, it is not suitable for a large attribute set. So, we did not consider this model. The overall result shows that both ILM and T5 have the capability to a handle large number of attributes. Next, we examine the models for various interesting cases such as (a) when the values are NULL, (b) when the attributes appear in the context vs. when the attributes do not appear in the context, (c) when the values contain multiple words, and (d) when value has numerical

Attributes	Model	$EM(\%)$	$P(\%)$	$R(\%)$	$F_1(\%)$
Brand Name	BiLSTM-CRF	85.77	80.99	86.37	83.59
	SUOTag	91.05	92.53	92.35	92.44
	ILM	94.72	94.93	94.89	94.91
	T5	**94.97**	**95.35**	**95.29**	**95.32**
Material	BiLSTM-CRF	65.03	65.20	67.08	66.13
	SUOTag	68.09	72.21	72.36	72.28
	ILM	**85.24**	88.59	**88.10**	**88.34**
	T5	84.57	**88.94**	87.48	88.20
Color	BiLSTM-CRF	42.64	40.74	42.64	41.67
	SUOTag	42.64	43.15	43.09	43.12
	ILM	75.63	80.29	79.8	80.04
	T5	**76.65**	**80.63**	**81.02**	**80.82**
Category	BiLSTM-CRF	48.06	51.25	50.08	50.66
	SUOTag	52.43	56.55	55.26	55.90
	ILM	**79.13**	81.56	**81.96**	**81.76**
	T5	74.27	**81.67**	80.18	80.92

Table 4: Performance comparison of different models on four frequent attributes.

data. The details are summarized in Table 3. ILM performs better than other models in identifying triples having NULL values. Specifically, language models give a much better precision in this case. There are 19.26% NULL values in AV-109K, but SUOTag predicts 43.83% data as NULL. Hence, it has such high recall. There are very few triples where the attributes appear in the context - only 1.50% in train dataset and 1.59% in test dataset. So, when the attribute appears in the context, the performance of all the models is poor in comparison with when the attribute does not appear in the context. In the AV-109K dataset, there are 4,058 triples whose value consist of multiple words. T5 performs the best in finding the values having more than one word. There are 8.5% numerical data in the test set and T5 gives much better results than other models in identifying them.

The second experiment is conducted on the four most frequent attributes of the AV-109K dataset. Table 4 shows the result. T5 performs better than other models in *Brand Name* and *Color*. For *Material* and *Category*, ILM has the best performance. We have looked into the predictions of the values in these two categories and found that T5 is not correctly identifying the NULL values. On closer look at the dataset, we find that most of those NULL values are incorrectly annotated, e.g., "new 1pcs Golf Sports Mens Right Left Hand Golf Gloves Sweat Absorbent Microfiber Cloth Soft Breathable Abrasion Gloves" - the material of this product is microfiber, but it is annotated as NULL. T5 has predicted the category as Bicycle Saddle for the title "INBIKE Soft Wide Bicycle Saddle Comfortable Bike Seat Vintage Bicycle Leather Saddle Pad", but the annotation is NULL. Although T5 has identified the correct value of the attribute, it is marked as incorrect due to faulty annotation.

Attributes	Model	$EM(\%)$	$P(\%)$	$R(\%)$	$F_1(\%)$
Frame Color	SUOTag	71.30	71.76	72.22	71.99
	ILM	69.44	69.44	69.44	69.44
	T5	**74.07**	**74.07**	**74.07**	**74.07**
Lenses Color	SUOTag	64.52	64.52	64.52	64.52
	ILM	67.74	67.74	67.74	67.74
	T5	**69.35**	**69.35**	**69.35**	**69.35**
Shell Material	SUOTag	30.56	41.2	52.78	46.28
	ILM	47.22	59.72	72.22	65.38
	T5	**58.33**	**68.06**	**77.78**	**72.59**
Wheel Material	SUOTag	47.83	52.90	60.87	56.60
	ILM	69.57	69.57	69.57	69.57
	T5	**78.26**	**78.26**	**78.26**	**78.26**
Product Type	SUOTag	20.84	21.63	21.8	21.71
	ILM	**57.17**	**68.84**	**68.59**	**68.72**
	T5	52.20	62.01	64.15	63.06

Table 5: Performance comparison of different models on AV-zero for identifying values of unseen attributes.

The last experiment is performed on AV-zero dataset. Table 5 shows the result of discovering values of five new attributes. ILM is the best in identifying "Product Type". The value of most of the "Product Type" is *Fishing Float*, but T5 either predicted the product type to be NULL or the type of the float, e.g., Luminous Fishing Float, Ice Fishing Float, etc. For the remaining three attributes, T5 outperforms other models.[3] Both T5 and ILM perform better than SUOtag in discovering unseen attribute values.

4 Conclusion

In this work, we present a formulation to generate product attribute values as (i) an instance of text infilling task and (ii) as an answer generation task. We show that we can leverage GPT-2 based and T5 text-to-text transformer models for this task. The models achieve strong results over a broad set of attributes. T5 performs better at multi-word values, and ILM is better at predicting null values. Additionally, our approach outperforms the state-of-the-art models for discovering new attribute values.

[3] We would like to note that in Table 5, for some of the attributes, all the evaluation metrics are identical. This occurs because for those attributes, the predicted value is a single token.

References

Laura Chiticariu, Rajasekar Krishnamurthy, Yunyao Li, Frederick Reiss, and Shivakumar Vaithyanathan. 2010. Domain adaptation of rule-based annotators for named-entity recognition tasks. In *Proceedings of the 2010 Conference on Empirical Methods in Natural Language Processing*, pages 1002–1012, Cambridge, MA. Association for Computational Linguistics.

Chris Donahue, Mina Lee, and Percy Liang. 2020. Enabling language models to fill in the blanks. In *Proceedings of the 58th Annual Meeting of the Association for Computational Linguistics*, pages 2492–2501, Online. Association for Computational Linguistics.

Rayid Ghani, Katharina Probst, Yan Liu, Marko Krema, and Andrew Fano. 2006. Text mining for product attribute extraction. *SIGKDD Explor. Newsl.*, 8(1):41–48.

Vishrawas Gopalakrishnan, Suresh Parthasarathy Iyengar, Amit Madaan, Rajeev Rastogi, and Srinivasan Sengamedu. 2012. Matching product titles using web-based enrichment. In *Proceedings of the 21st ACM International Conference on Information and Knowledge Management*, CIKM '12, page 605–614, New York, NY, USA. Association for Computing Machinery.

Zhiheng Huang, Wei Xu, and Kai Yu. 2015. Bidirectional lstm-crf models for sequence tagging. *arXiv preprint arXiv:1508.01991*.

John D. Lafferty, Andrew McCallum, and Fernando C. N. Pereira. 2001. Conditional random fields: Probabilistic models for segmenting and labeling sequence data. In *Proceedings of the Eighteenth International Conference on Machine Learning*, ICML '01, page 282–289, San Francisco, CA, USA. Morgan Kaufmann Publishers Inc.

Ajinkya More. 2016. Attribute extraction from product titles in ecommerce. *arXiv preprint arXiv:1608.04670*.

Adam Paszke, Sam Gross, Francisco Massa, Adam Lerer, James Bradbury, Gregory Chanan, Trevor Killeen, Zeming Lin, Natalia Gimelshein, Luca Antiga, et al. 2019. Pytorch: An imperative style, high-performance deep learning library. In *Advances in neural information processing systems*, pages 8026–8037.

Duangmanee Putthividhya and Junling Hu. 2011. Bootstrapped named entity recognition for product attribute extraction. In *Proceedings of the 2011 Conference on Empirical Methods in Natural Language Processing*, pages 1557–1567, Edinburgh, Scotland, UK. Association for Computational Linguistics.

Alec Radford, Jeffrey Wu, Rewon Child, David Luan, Dario Amodei, and Ilya Sutskever. 2019. Language models are unsupervised multitask learners. *OpenAI Blog*, 1(8):9.

Colin Raffel, Noam Shazeer, Adam Roberts, Katherine Lee, Sharan Narang, Michael Matena, Yanqi Zhou, Wei Li, and Peter J Liu. 2020. Exploring the limits of transfer learning with a unified text-to-text transformer. *Journal of Machine Learning Research*, 21(140):1–67.

Qifan Wang, Li Yang, Bhargav Kanagal, Sumit Sanghai, D. Sivakumar, Bin Shu, Zac Yu, and Jon Elsas. 2020. Learning to extract attribute value from product via question answering: A multi-task approach. In *Proceedings of the 26th ACM SIGKDD International Conference on Knowledge Discovery & Data Mining*, KDD '20, page 47–55, New York, NY, USA. Association for Computing Machinery.

Huimin Xu, Wenting Wang, Xin Mao, Xinyu Jiang, and Man Lan. 2019. Scaling up open tagging from tens to thousands: Comprehension empowered attribute value extraction from product title. In *Proceedings of the 57th Annual Meeting of the Association for Computational Linguistics*, pages 5214–5223, Florence, Italy. Association for Computational Linguistics.

Guineng Zheng, Subhabrata Mukherjee, Xin Luna Dong, and Feifei Li. 2018. Opentag: Open attribute value extraction from product profiles. In *Proceedings of the 24th ACM SIGKDD International Conference on Knowledge Discovery and Data Mining*, KDD '18, page 1049–1058, New York, NY, USA. Association for Computing Machinery.

ASR Adaptation for E-commerce Chatbots using Cross-Utterance Context and Multi-Task Language Modeling

Ashish Shenoy **Sravan Bodapati** **Katrin Kirchhoff**
Amazon AWS AI, USA
{ashenoy, sravanb, katrinki}@amazon.com

Abstract

Automatic Speech Recognition (ASR) robustness toward slot entities are critical in e-commerce voice assistants that involve monetary transactions and purchases. Along with effective domain adaptation, it is intuitive that cross utterance contextual cues play an important role in disambiguating domain specific content words from speech. In this paper, we investigate various techniques to improve contextualization, content word robustness and domain adaptation of a Transformer-XL neural language model (NLM) to rescore ASR N-best hypotheses. To improve contextualization, we utilize turn level dialogue acts along with cross utterance context carry over. Additionally, to adapt our domain-general NLM towards e-commerce on-the-fly, we use embeddings derived from a finetuned masked LM on in-domain data. Finally, to improve robustness towards in-domain content words, we propose a multi-task model that can jointly perform content word detection and language modeling tasks. Compared to a non-contextual LSTM LM baseline, our best performing NLM rescorer results in a content WER reduction of 19.2% on e-commerce audio test set and a slot labeling F1 improvement of 6.4%.

1 Introduction

Task-oriented conversations in voice chatbots deployed for e-commerce usecases such as shopping (Maarek, 2018), browsing catalog, scheduling deliveries or ordering food are predominantly short-form audios. Moreover, these dialogues are restricted to a narrow range of multi-turn interactions that involve accomplishing a specific task (Mari et al., 2020). The back and forth between a user and the chatbots are key to reliably capture the user intent and slot entities referenced in the spoken utterances. As shown in previous works (Irie et al., 2019; Parthasarathy et al., 2019; Sun et al., 2021), rather than decoding each utterance independently, there can be benefit in decoding these utterances based on context from previous turns. In the case of grocery shopping for example, knowing that the context is "what kind of laundry detergent?" should help in disambiguating "pods" from "pause". Another common aspect in e-commerce chatbots is that the speech patterns differ among sub-categories of usecases (Eg. shopping clothes vs ordering fast food). Hence, some chatbot systems allow users to provide pre-defined grammars or sample utterances that are specific for their usecase (Gandhe et al., 2018). These user provided grammars are then predominantly used to perform domain adaptation on an n-gram language model. Recently (Shenoy et al., 2021) showed that these can be leveraged to bias a Transformer-XL (TXL) LM rescorer on-the-fly.

While there has been extensive previous work on improving contextualization of TXL LM using historical context, none of the approaches utilize signals from a natural language understanding (NLU) component such as turn level dialogue acts. This paper investigates how to utilize dialogue acts along with user provided speech patterns to adapt a domain-general TXL LM towards different e-commerce usecases on-the-fly. We also propose a novel multi-task architecture for TXL, where the model jointly learns to perform domain specific slot detection and LM tasks. We use perplexity (PPL) and word error rate (WER) as our evaluation metrics. We also evaluate on downstream NLU metrics such as intent classification (IC) F1 and slot labeling (SL) F1 to capture the success of these conversations. The overall contributions of this work can be summarized as follows :

- We show that a TXL model that utilizes turn level dialogue act information along with long

Proceedings of the 4th Workshop on e-Commerce and NLP (ECNLP 4), pages 18–25
August 5, 2021.

span context helps with contextualiziation and improves WER and IC F1 in e-commerce chatbots.

- To improve robustness towards e-commerce domain specifc slot entities, we propose a novel TXL architecture that is jointly trained on slot detection and LM tasks which significantly improves content WERR and SL F1.
- We show that adapting the NLM towards user provided speech patterns by using BERT on domain specific text is an efficient and effective method to perform on-the-fly adaptation of a domain-general NLM towards e-commerce utterances.

2 Related Work

Incorporating cross utterance context has been well explored with both recurrent and non-recurrent NLMs. With LSTM NLMs, long span context is usually propogated without resetting hidden states across sentences or using longer sequence lengths (Xiong et al., 2018a; Irie et al., 2019; Khandelwal et al., 2018; Parthasarathy et al., 2019). In (Xiong et al., 2018b), along with longer history, information about turn taking and speaker overlap is used to improve contextualization in human to human conversations. With transformer architecture based on self attention (Vaswani et al., 2017) (Dai et al., 2019) showed that by utilizing segment wise recurrence Transformer-XL (TXL) (Dai et al., 2019) is able to effectively leverage long span context while decoding. More recently, improving contextualization of the TXL models included adding a LSTM fusion layer to complement the advantages of recurrent with non-recurrent models (Sun et al., 2021). (Shenoy et al., 2021) incorporated a non-finetuned masked LM fusion in order to make the domain adaptation of TXL models quick and on-the-fly using embeddings derived from customer provided data and incorporated dialogue acts but only with an LSTM based LM. While (Sunkara et al., 2020) tried to fuse multi-model features into a seq-to-seq LSTM based network. In (Sharma, 2020) cross utterance context was effectively used to perform better intent classification with e-commerce voice assistants.

For domain adaptation, previous techniques explored include using an explicit topic vector as classified by a separate domain classifier and incorporating a neural cache (Mikolov and Zweig, 2019; Li et al., 2018; Raju et al., 2018; Chen et al., 2015). (Irie et al., 2018) used a mixture of domain experts which are dynamically interpolated. It is also shown in (Liu et al., 2020), that using a hybrid pointer network over contextual metadata can also help in transcribing long form social media audio. Joint learning NLU tasks such as intent detection and slot filling have been explored with RNN based LMs in (Liu and Lane, 2016) and more recently in (Rao et al., 2020), where they show that a jointly trained model consisting of both ASR and NLU tasks interfaced with a neural network based interface helps incorporate semantic information from NLU and improves ASR that comprises a LSTM based NLM. In (Yang et al., 2020) tried to incorporate joint slot and intent detection into a LSTM based rescorer with a goal of improving accuracy on rare words in an end-to-end ASR system.

However, none of the previous work utilize dialogue acts with a non-recurrent based LM such as Transformer-XL nor optimize towards improving robustness of in-domain slot entities. In this paper we experiment and study the impact of utilizing dialogue acts along with a masked language model fusion to improve contextualization and domain adaptation. Additionally, we also propose a novel multi-task architecture with TXL LM that improves the robustness towards in-domain slot entity detection.

3 Approach

A standard language model in an ASR system computes a probability distribution over a sequence of words $W = w_0, ..., w_N$ auto-regressively as:

$$p(W) = \prod_{i=1}^{N} p(w_i|w_1, w_2, ..., w_{i-1}) \quad (1)$$

In our experiments, along with historical context, we condition the LM on additional contextual metadata such as dialogue acts :

$$p(W) = \prod_{i=1}^{N} p(w_i|w_1, w_2, ..., w_{i-1}, c_1, c_2, ..., c_k) \quad (2)$$

Where $c_1, c_2, ...c_k$ are the turn based lexical representation of the contextual metadata. For baseline, we use a standard LSTM LM as summarized below :

$$\begin{aligned} embed_i &= E_{ke}^T w_{i-1} \\ c_i, h_i &= LSTM(h_{i-1}, c_{i-1}, embed_i) \quad (3) \\ p(w_i|w_{<i}) &= Softmax(W_{ho}^T h_i) \end{aligned}$$

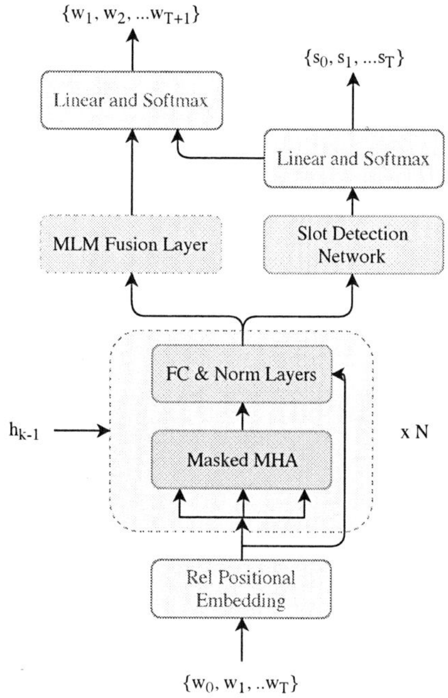

Figure 1: Transformer-XL language model architecture jointly trained with slot detection task with an optional MLM fusion layer

Utterance	i	want	my	shoes	delivered	to	seattle	next	thursday
Annotation	O	O	O	SLOT	O	O	SLOT	SLOT	SLOT

Figure 2: Example utterance with slots annotated

where $embed_i$ is a fixed size lower dimensional word embedding and the LSTM outputs are projected to word level outputs using W_{ho}^T. A $Softmax$ layer converts the word level outputs into final word level probabilities.

3.1 Transformer-XL based NLM

Although recurrent language models help in modeling long range dependencies to certain extent, they still suffer from the fuzzy far away problem (Khandelwal et al., 2018). Vanilla transformer LMs on the other hand use fixed segment lengths which leads to context fragmentation. To address these limitations and model long range dependencies, TXL models add segment-level recurrence and use a relative positional encoding scheme (Dai et al., 2019). Hence we choose to use a TXL LM directly. The cached hidden representations from previous segments helps contextual information flow across segment boundaries. If $s_k = [w_{k,1}, ..., w_{k,T}]$ and $s_{k+1} = [x_{k+1,1}, ..., x_{k+1,T}]$ are two consecutive segments of length T and h_k^n is the n-th layer hidden state produced for the k-th segment s_k, then, the n-th layer hidden state for segment s_{k+1} is produced as follows:

$$\begin{aligned} \tilde{h}_{k+1}^{n-1} &= [SG(h_k^{n-1}) \circ h_{k+1}^{n-1}] \\ q_{k+1}^n, k_{k+1}^n, v_{k+1}^n &= \tilde{h}_{k+1}^{n-1} W_q^{\mathsf{T}} \\ h_{k+1}^n &= TL(q_{k+1}^n, k_{k+1}^n, v_{k+1}^n) \end{aligned} \tag{4}$$

where $SG(.)$ stands for stop gradient and TL stands for Transformer Layer. To carry over context from previous turns, we train and evaluate the model by concatenating all the turns, including the bot responses, in a single conversation session. The model is trained with a cross entropy objective as defined below :

$$\mathbf{L_{LM}} = -\frac{1}{T}\left[\sum_{i=1}^{T} log(P(w_i \mid w_{<i}, s_{<i}))\right] \tag{5}$$

During inference time, we cache a fixed length hidden representation from previous segments. We also use the generated bot responses to perform a forward pass and carry over the context to the next user turn.

3.2 Slot detection and language modeling multi-task learning

To make the our domain-general model robust to e-commerce specific slot entities, we propose a multi-task learning approach to training the TXL LM. We train our models on both LM and slot detection tasks. Similar to slot filling, slot detection is a sequence classification task that involves predicting if a word, w_i at time step i is a domain specific slot entity. We use a separate slot detection network, consisting of a simple multi-layer perceptron, and use the final layer hidden representation from the TXL network as inputs to the network. Figure 2 shows an example utterance with the slot annotations. Formally, let $s = (s_0, s_1, ..., s_T)$ be the slot label sequence, corresponding to a word sequence $w = w_0, w_1, ..., w_T$ in the k-th segment. We model the slot label output s_t as a conditional distribution over input word sequence up to time step t, $w_{\leq t}$ similar to (Liu and Lane, 2016) :

$$\begin{aligned} h_k^n &= TL(q_k^n, k_k^n, v_k^n) \\ p(s_t|w_{\leq t}) &= SlotLabelDist(h_t^n) \end{aligned} \tag{6}$$

We use a cross-entropy training objective for the

slot detection task as below :

$$\mathbf{L_{SD}} = -\frac{1}{T}\left[\sum_{i=1}^{T} log(P(s_i \mid w_{\leq i}))\right] \quad (7)$$

To incorporate this semantic information about the word from previous time step into the NLM, we use the logits from the slot detection network to condition the probability distribution of the next word in the sequence as shown in Figure 1.

The total loss is then computed using a linear combination of LM and slot detection losses:

$$\mathbf{L_{total}} = \mathbf{L_{LM}} + \alpha_{SD}\mathbf{L_{SD}} \quad (8)$$

where α_{SD} is the weight for the slot detection loss.

3.3 Transformer-XL LM conditioning on dialogue acts

Dialogue acts (DA) in a conversation represent the intention of an utterance and is intended towards capturing the action that an agent is trying to accomplish (Austin, 1975). An example conversation snippet with DA is shown in Table 1. DA classification is typically performed in a separate component that is part of a downstream NLU system and consumes the outputs generated by ASR. The classified DA is an important contextual signal that provides hints about the type of speech pattern that can be expected in the next turn. We utilize these signals to train our TXL models. Specifically, we augment the training data with the dialogue act information prefixed to the user turns and surround them with explicit <dialogue_act> tags. The expectation is that the TXL LM learns the usage patterns associated with different dialogue acts and this information should help narrow down the search space for the model to content words relevant to the current dialogue context.

3.4 Domain adaptation using contextual semantic embeddings

In production chatbots, it is common for bot developers to provide example speech patterns, in the form of sample sentences or explicit grammars, which can then be used to bias the n-gram language models in a ASR system (Gandhe et al., 2018). This pre-defined set of speech patterns is a useful source of contextual information that can be also used to bias NLMs as well. As demonstrated in (Shenoy et al., 2021), pretrained masked language

Actor	Utterance	Dialogue Act
Bot	how can i help you today	general-welcome
User	hi i want to track my online shopping order	inform-intent
Bot	sure! what is the order number?	request
User	my order number is abcdef	inform
Bot	your order is scheduled to be delivered tomorrow	inform
User	thanks	thank-you
Bot	do you need help with anything else?	req-more

Table 1: A sample user bot conversation snippet showing example dialogue acts.

models (MLM) such as BERT, can be used to derive a fixed size semantic representation from this lexical information. Large pretrained MLMs are gaining widespread popularity and are considered as powerful language learners (Radford et al., 2016; Brown et al., 2020). However, the sentence or document embeddings derived from such an MLM without finetuning on in-domain data is shown to be inferior in terms of the ability to capture semantic information that can be used in similarity related tasks (Reimers and Gurevych, 2019). Instead of using the [CLS] vector to obtain sentence embeddings, in this paper we take the average of context embeddings from last two layers as these are shown to be consistently better than using [CLS] vector (Reimers and Gurevych, 2019; Li et al., 2020).

We use a simple fusion method as experimented in (Shenoy et al., 2021) where the hidden state from the last layer of the TXL decoder is concatenated with the BERT derived embedding. This is then followed by a single projection layer with a non-linear activation function σ, such as $sigmoid$.

$$g_t = \sigma(W[h_t^{TXL}; e^{MLM}] + b) \quad (9)$$

Where h_t^{TXL} is the hidden state from the last transformer decoder and e^{MLM} is the BERT derived embedding from in domain sample utterances. The intuition here is that the model learns to associate the domain specific BERT derived embedding with the occurrences of jargon specific to that domain. Thus providing different BERT vectors derived from different domain texts should allow the model to adapt towards such domains on-the-fly.

	Model	Retail				Fastfood			
		CWERR	IC F1	SL F1	p-value	CWERR	IC F1	SL F1	p-value
1	Non-contextual LSTM	–	–	–	–	–	–		
2	TXL	1.0%	0.5%	0.4%	0.083	12.3%	0.4%	0.9%	**0.048**
3	+ Dialogue Acts (DA)	1.2%	1.2%	1.3%	0.057	14.4%	1.0%	1.2%	**0.041**
4	+ Joint Slot Detection (SD)	4.3%	2.0%	3.3%	**0.046**	16.3%	0.9%	2.1%	**0.015**
5	+ Joint SD + DA	8.6%	2.1%	3.3%	**0.048**	17.3%	1.3%	2.7%	**0.009**
6	+ BERT Fusion	6.4%	2.8%	2.3%	**0.030**	18.2%	1.8%	4.8%	**0.004**
7	+ BERT Fusion + DA	9.6%	2.9%	2.7%	**0.023**	19.2%	1.7%	4.8%	**0.004**
8	+ Joint SD + DA + BERT Fusion	11.8%	3.8%	4.3%	**0.037**	19.2%	2.1%	6.4%	**0.002**

Table 2: ASR and NLU improvements on two e-commerce sub-domains : Retail and Fastfood. CWERR - Content Word Error Reduction, IC F1 - Relative Intent Classification F1 Improvement, SL F1 - Relative Slot Labeling F1 Improvement, MPSSWE p-value test on WERR where significant improvements are in bold

Model	$\mathbf{PPLR}_{gen}$	$\mathbf{PPLR}_{ecom}$
TXL	–	
+ Dialogue Acts (DA)	3.4%	9.9%
+ Joint Slot Detection (SD)	8.5%	11.4%
+ BERT Fusion (BF)	16.3%	23.3%
+ Joint SD + DA	9.8%	13.0%
+ BF + DA	21.5%	25.3%
+ BF + DA + Joint SD	21.0%	25.8%

Table 3: Relative perplexity reduction (PPLR) from the various TXL models on a general domain eval set (PPL_{gen}) and on e-commerce domain eval set (PPL_{ecom}).

4 Experimental Setup

4.1 Dataset

We required task-oriented dialogue datasets with actor, dialogue acts and the slot entities annotated. Since no single dataset was large enough to train a reliable language model, we used a combination of Schema-Guided Dialogue Dataset (Rastogi et al., 2019), MultiWOZ 2.1 (Eric et al., 2019; Budzianowski et al., 2018), MultiDoGo (Peskov et al., 2019) along with anonymized in-house datasets that belong to two e-commerce usecases : retail and fastfood delivery. The final LM training data consisted of 260k training samples, 56k validation and evaluation samples and around 9.9 million running words. We used a vocabulary of size 25k. We evaluated our models on anonymized in-house 8kHz close-talk audio. These audio comprised of task-oriented conversations with multiple speakers and acoustic conditions representative of real world usage and belonged to the same two usecases mentioned above. The average number of turns in the audio dataset was 5.

4.2 ASR setup and NLM setup

We used a hybrid ASR model comprising of a regular-frame-rate (RFR) model trained on cross-entropy loss, followed by sMBR (Ghoshal and Povey, 2013). The first pass LM we used was a domain-general Kneser-Ney (KN) (Kneser and Ney, 1995) smoothed 4-gram model estimated on a weighted mix of datasets spanning multiple domains. The final vocabulary size of the n-gram LM was 500k words. All our NLM rescorers used a 4-layer Tranformer-XL[1] decoder, each of size 512 with 4 attention heads. The input word embedding size was 512. We used a segment and memory length of 25. During model training we applied a dropout rate of 0.3 to both the slot detection network and TXL. For the slot detection layer we used a 3 layer MLP and used the final layer hidden representation from the TXL as the output. To obtain the BERT embedding from in-domain speech patterns, we finetune huggingface[2] pretrained BERT mode on the retail and fastfood text corpus. The derived BERT embedding size used was 768. During inference, we extract n-best hypothesis with `n<=50` from the lattice generated by the first pass ASR model. We rescored the n-best hypothesis by multiplying the acoustic score with the acoustic scale and adding it to the scores obtained from the TXL rescorer. We used a fixed α_{SD} of 0.8 for the slot detection loss.

5 Results and Discussion

Table 3 summarizes the relative perplexity reductions (PPLR). Since we are optimizing our models to improve on the e-commerce domain specific con-

[1]https://github.com/kimiyoung/transformer-xl
[2]https://github.com/huggingface/transformers

tent words we directly report the relative content word error rate reductions (CWERR) in Table 2 along with the relative impact on the downstream NLU tasks of IC and SL. For computing CWERR, we remove all the stop words comprising of commonly used function words, such as conjunctions and prepositions from the transcriptions and evaluate only on content words. We also report statistical significance of our CWER improvements using matched pairs sentence segment word error test (MPSSWE). All the WER numbers are relative to a non-contextual LSTM baseline. The gap in the performance between the two domains we tested on is reflective of the underlying training corpus distribution, which has more text belonging to the fastfood domain.

Perplexity gains indicate effective domain adaptation We report both general domain and e-commerce domain PPLR. Overall, the contextualization and domain adaptation techniques help with the PPL dropping in both cases. The jointly trained model on in-domain slot detection however clearly helps more in the e-commerce case. Moreover, since we used BERT that was finetuned on e-commerce text we again see larger gains in the domain specific testset when compared to the general domain testset (23.3% vs 16.3%).

Using system dialogue acts improves intent detection: From our experiments that train the TXL LMs with dialogue act information, it is clear that dialogue acts helps with relatively marginal gains in PPL (3.4% on generic and 9.9% on e-commerce) and WER (1.2% Retail, 14.4% Fastfood). When compared to other techniques we explored, we see that the impact on intent classification was higher in proportion to the gain in WER, which indicates that dialogue acts are valuable contextual signals to help with intent conveying phrases.

Slot detection loss yields improvements on domain specific content words: Rows 4 and 5 of Table 2 report the content WERR, IC and SL F1s that we obtain by incorporating the joint LM and slot detection (SD) loss. As expected, the multitask model improves on the content words significantly (1.2% to 4.3% on Retail, 12.3% to 16.3% on Fastfood). This WER improvement also carries over to a higher SL F1 improvement, but a relatively small IC F1 improvement. This is again indicative that the improvements are mainly on recognition of in-domain slot entities and the auxiliary function words that are important to recognize intents do not benefit as much.

Domain adaptation using BERT fusion provides maximum gains: Rows 6 and 7 in Table 2 illustrate the performance of the TXL LM that incorporates the BERT embedding fusion layer. Compared to the model trained with joint slot detection loss, BERT fusion model performs better on all ASR and the NLU metrics. It is evident from the results that the BERT embeddings that are derived from different user provided text helps the model effectively adapt to the domain that the embedding was derived from. The gains are amplified when complemented with the dialogue acts ability to improve on intent carrying words and the joint slot detection model leading to a WERR improving from 12.3% to 19.2% on the fastfood domain and 1% to 11.8% on the retail domain. This also carries over to an improvement on IC and SL F1 of 3.8%, 4.3% on retail and 2.1%, 6.4% on fastfood.

6 Conclusion

In this paper we explored different ways to robustly adapt a domain-general Transformer-XL NLM to rescore N-best hypotheses from a hybrid ASR system for task-oriented e-commerce speech conversations. We demonstrated that Transformer-XL LM trained with turn level dialogue acts benefits intent classification by improving the recognition of content words. Additionally, we show that using semantic embeddings derived from a masked language model finetuned on e-commerce domain can be effectively used to adapt a domain-general TXL LM for e-commerce domain utterance rescoring task. Finally, we introduced a new TXL training loss function to jointly predict content words along with language modeling task, this when combined with BERT fusion and dialogue acts, amplifies the WER, IC F1 and SL F1 gains. We have also shown these improvements to be statistically significant. Future work can look at integrating these methods into an end-to-end ASR system for both rescoring task and first pass LM fusion.

References

John Langshaw Austin. 1975. How to do things with words.

Tom B. Brown, Benjamin Mann, Nick Ryder, Melanie Subbiah, Jared Kaplan, Prafulla Dhariwal, Arvind Neelakantan, Pranav Shyam, Girish Sastry, Amanda Askell, Sandhini Agarwal, Ariel Herbert-Voss,

Gretchen Krueger, Tom Henighan, Rewon Child, Aditya Ramesh, Daniel M. Ziegler, Jeffrey Wu, Clemens Winter, Christopher Hesse, Mark Chen, Eric Sigler, Mateusz Litwin, Scott Gray, Benjamin Chess, Jack Clark, Christopher Berner, Sam McCandlish, Alec Radford, Ilya Sutskever, and Dario Amodei. 2020. Language models are few-shot learners.

Pawel Budzianowski, Tsung-Hsien Wen, Bo-Hsiang Tseng, Iñigo Casanueva, Stefan Ultes, Osman Ramadan, and Milica Gasic. 2018. Multiwoz - A large-scale multi-domain wizard-of-oz dataset for task-oriented dialogue modelling. *CoRR*, abs/1810.00278.

X. Chen, T. Tan, Xunying Liu, Pierre Lanchantin, M. Wan, Mark J. F. Gales, and Philip C. Woodland. 2015. Recurrent neural network language model adaptation for multi-genre broadcast speech recognition. In *Interspeech 2015, Dresden, Germany, September 6-10, 2015*, pages 3511–3515. ISCA.

Zihang Dai, Zhilin Yang, Yiming Yang, Jaime Carbonell, Quoc Le, and Ruslan Salakhutdinov. 2019. Transformer-XL: Attentive language models beyond a fixed-length context. In *Proceedings of the 57th Annual Meeting of the Association for Computational Linguistics*, pages 2978–2988, Florence, Italy. Association for Computational Linguistics.

Mihail Eric, Rahul Goel, Shachi Paul, Abhishek Sethi, Sanchit Agarwal, Shuyang Gao, and Dilek Hakkani-Tür. 2019. Multiwoz 2.1: Multi-domain dialogue state corrections and state tracking baselines. *CoRR*, abs/1907.01669.

Ankur Gandhe, Ariya Rastrow, and Björn Hoffmeister. 2018. Scalable language model adaptation for spoken dialogue systems. In *SLT Workshop 2018, Athens, Greece*, pages 907–912. IEEE.

Arnab Ghoshal and Daniel Povey. 2013. Sequencediscriminative training of deep neural networks. In *in Proc. INTERSPEECH*.

Kazuki Irie, Shankar Kumar, Michael Nirschl, and Hank Liao. 2018. Radmm: Recurrent adaptive mixture model with applications to domain robust language modeling. In *IEEE International Conference on Acoustics, Speech, and Signal Processing*, pages 6079–6083, Calgary, Canada.

Kazuki Irie, Albert Zeyer, Ralf Schlüter, and Hermann Ney. 2019. Training language models for long-span cross-sentence evaluation. In *ASRU Singapore*, pages 419–426. IEEE.

Urvashi Khandelwal, He He, Peng Qi, and Dan Jurafsky. 2018. Sharp nearby, fuzzy far away: How neural language models use context. In *Proceedings of the 56th Annual Meeting of the Association for Computational Linguistics (Volume 1: Long Papers)*, pages 284–294, Melbourne, Australia. Association for Computational Linguistics.

Reinhard Kneser and Hermann Ney. 1995. Improved backing-off for m-gram language modeling. In *ICASSP*, pages 181–184. IEEE Computer Society.

Bohan Li, Hao Zhou, Junxian He, Mingxuan Wang, Yiming Yang, and Lei Li. 2020. On the sentence embeddings from pre-trained language models. In *Proceedings of the 2020 Conference on Empirical Methods in Natural Language Processing (EMNLP)*, pages 9119–9130, Online. Association for Computational Linguistics.

Ke Li, Hainan Xu, Yiming Wang, Daniel Povey, and Sanjeev Khudanpur. 2018. Recurrent neural network language model adaptation for conversational speech recognition. In *Interspeech, Hyderabad, India, 2-6 September 2018*, pages 3373–3377.

Bing Liu and Ian Lane. 2016. Joint online spoken language understanding and language modeling with recurrent neural networks. In *Proceedings of the 17th Annual Meeting of the Special Interest Group on Discourse and Dialogue*, pages 22–30, Los Angeles. Association for Computational Linguistics.

Da-Rong Liu, Chunxi Liu, Frank Zhang, Gabriel Synnaeve, Yatharth Saraf, and Geoffrey Zweig. 2020. Contextualizing ASR lattice rescoring with hybrid pointer network language model. In *Interspeech 2020, 21st Annual Conference of the International Speech Communication Association, Virtual Event, Shanghai, China, 25-29 October 2020*, pages 3650–3654. ISCA.

Yoelle Maarek. 2018. Alexa and Her Shopping Journey. In *Proceedings of the 27th ACM International Conference on Information and Knowledge Management*, page 1. ACM.

Alex Mari, Andreina Mandelli, and René Algesheimer. 2020. The evolution of marketing in the context of voice commerce: A managerial perspective. In *HCI in Business, Government and Organizations - 7th International Conference, HCIBGO 2020, Held as Part of the 22nd HCI International Conference, HCII 2020, Copenhagen, Denmark, July 19-24, 2020, Proceedings*, volume 12204 of *Lecture Notes in Computer Science*, pages 405–425. Springer.

Tomas Mikolov and Geoffrey Zweig. 2019. Context dependent recurrent neural network language model. In *SLT*, pages 234–239. IEEE.

Sarangarajan Parthasarathy, William Gale, Xie Chen, George Polovets, and Shuangyu Chang. 2019. Long-span language modeling for speech recognition. *CoRR*, abs/1911.04571.

Denis Peskov, Nancy Clarke, Jason Krone, Brigi Fodor, Yi Zhang, Adel Youssef, and Mona Diab. 2019. Multi-domain goal-oriented dialogues (MultiDoGO): Strategies toward curating and annotating large scale dialogue data. In *Proc EMNLP-IJCNLP*, pages 4526–4536.

Alec Radford, Luke Metz, and Soumith Chintala. 2016. Unsupervised representation learning with deep convolutional generative adversarial networks.

Anirudh Raju, Behnam Hedayatnia, Linda Liu, Ankur Gandhe, Chandra Khatri, Angeliki Metallinou, Anu Venkatesh, and Ariya Rastrow. 2018. Contextual language model adaptation for conversational agents. In *Interspeech, Hyderabad, India*, pages 3333–3337. ISCA.

Milind Rao, Anirudh Raju, Pranav Dheram, Bach Bui, and Ariya Rastrow. 2020. Speech to semantics: Improve ASR and NLU jointly via all-neural interfaces. In *Interspeech 2020, 21st Annual Conference of the International Speech Communication Association, Virtual Event, Shanghai, China, 25-29 October 2020*, pages 876–880. ISCA.

Abhinav Rastogi, Xiaoxue Zang, Srinivas Sunkara, Raghav Gupta, and Pranav Khaitan. 2019. Towards Scalable Multi-domain Conversational Agents: The Schema-Guided Dialogue Dataset. *arXiv e-prints*, page arXiv:1909.05855.

Nils Reimers and Iryna Gurevych. 2019. Sentence-BERT: Sentence embeddings using Siamese BERT-networks. In *Proceedings of the 2019 Conference on Empirical Methods in Natural Language Processing and the 9th International Joint Conference on Natural Language Processing (EMNLP-IJCNLP)*, pages 3982–3992, Hong Kong, China. Association for Computational Linguistics.

Arpit Sharma. 2020. Improving intent classification in an E-commerce voice assistant by using inter-utterance context. In *Proceedings of The 3rd Workshop on e-Commerce and NLP*, pages 40–45, Seattle, WA, USA. Association for Computational Linguistics.

Ashish Shenoy, Sravan Bodapati, Monica Sunkara, Srikanth Ronanki, and Katrin Kirchhoff. 2021. Adapting long context nlm for asr rescoring in conversational agents.

G. Sun, C. Zhang, and P. C. Woodland. 2021. Transformer language models with lstm-based cross-utterance information representation.

Monica Sunkara, Srikanth Ronanki, Dhanush Bekal, Sravan Bodapati, and Katrin Kirchhoff. 2020. Multimodal semi-supervised learning framework for punctuation prediction in conversational speech. In *Interspeech 2020, Shanghai, China, 25-29 October 2020*, pages 4911–4915. ISCA.

Ashish Vaswani, Noam Shazeer, Niki Parmar, Jakob Uszkoreit, Llion Jones, Aidan N Gomez, Ł ukasz Kaiser, and Illia Polosukhin. 2017. Attention is all you need. In *Advances in Neural Information Processing Systems*, volume 30, pages 5998–6008.

W. Xiong, L. Wu, Fil Alleva, Jasha Droppo, Xuedong Huang, and Andreas Stolcke. 2018a. The microsoft 2017 conversational speech recognition system. In *ICASSP, Calgary, Canada*, pages 5934–5938. IEEE.

Wayne Xiong, Lingfeng Wu, Jun Zhang, and Andreas Stolcke. 2018b. Session-level language modeling for conversational speech. In *Proceedings of the 2018 Conference on Empirical Methods in Natural Language Processing*, pages 2764–2768, Brussels, Belgium. Association for Computational Linguistics.

Chao-Han Huck Yang, Linda Liu, Ankur Gandhe, Yile Gu, Anirudh Raju, Denis Filimonov, and Ivan Bulyko. 2020. Multi-task language modeling for improving speech recognition of rare words. *CoRR*, abs/2011.11715.

Turn-Level User Satisfaction Estimation in E-commerce Customer Service

Runze Liang[1], Ryuichi Takanobu[1], Fenglin Li[2], Ji Zhang[2], Haiqing Chen[2], Minlie Huang[1]

[1]CoAI Group, DCST, IAI, BNRIST, Tsinghua University, Beijing, China

[2]DAMO Academy, Alibaba Group, Hangzhou, China

{liangrz20, gxly19}@mails.tsinghua.edu.cn, aihuang@tsinghua.edu.cn

{fenglin.lfl, zj122146, haiqing.chenhq}@alibaba-inc.com

Abstract

User satisfaction estimation in the dialogue-based customer service is critical not only for helping developers find the system defects, but also making it possible to get timely human intervention for dissatisfied customers. In this paper, we investigate the problem of user satisfaction estimation in E-commerce customer service. In order to apply the estimator to online services for timely human intervention, we need to estimate the satisfaction score at each turn. However, in actual scenario we can only collect the satisfaction labels for the whole dialogue sessions via user feedback. To this end, we formalize the turn-level satisfaction estimation as a reinforcement learning problem, in which the model can be optimized with only session-level satisfaction labels. We conduct experiments on the dataset collected from a commercial customer service system, and compare our model with the supervised learning models. Extensive experiments show that the proposed method outperforms all the baseline models.

1 Introduction

Task-oriented dialogue systems have been widely studied recently (Gao et al., 2019; Zhang et al., 2020), and many have been widely deployed to real-world applications, such as intelligent assistants and customer service in industry. However, due to the limitation of model capability, the system may fail to understand the intent of users or complete the task, which makes it common for users to become dissatisfied with the system (Kiseleva et al., 2016b; Lopatovska et al., 2019).

In this paper, we focus on the problem of user satisfaction estimation (Chowdhury et al., 2016; Kiseleva et al., 2016a) in E-commerce customer service, where users may ask for E-commerce transactions, claim a refund or make a complaint to the customer service. An actual E-commerce customer service may serve thousands of users simultaneously, many of whom may feel dissatisfied, more or less. It is imperative to offer manual service to those users who are exhibiting signs of dissatisfaction. Nevertheless, the manual service resources are usually limited. Therefore, estimating user satisfaction can help us assign manual service priority to the users by sorting the ongoing dialogues with satisfaction scores.

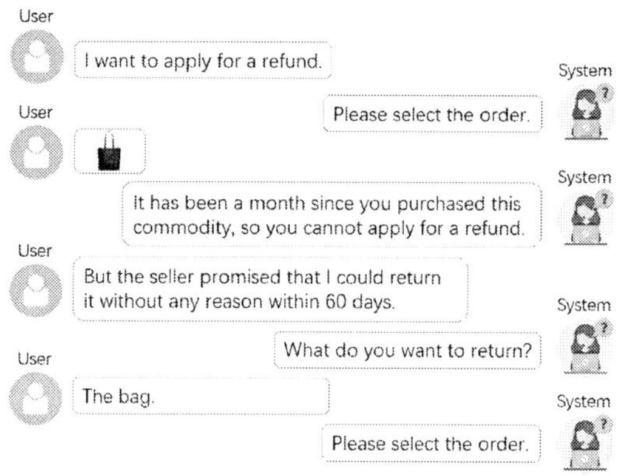

Figure 1: A dialogue example in E-commerce customer service where the system cannot understand the user's intent, thereby making the user dissatisfied.

Ideally, the satisfaction score estimation and sorting process should be in a timely and turn-level manner. Take Figure 1 for an example. In the first two turns[1], the system responses are consistent with the user utterances. Therefore, the satisfaction score until the second turn should be high, and the user should not be allocated human service. But in the third turn, the system seems to ask a weird question instead of responding to the special situation the user encounters. Therefore, the satisfaction score until the third turn should be lower than that until the second turn. And after the fourth turn,

[1]In this work, a turn consists of a pair of a user utterance and a system utterance.

Proceedings of the 4th Workshop on e-Commerce and NLP (ECNLP 4), pages 26–32
August 5, 2021.

the satisfaction score should get even lower since the system still responds improperly. Whether the user will be offered human resources in the third and the fourth turn is determined by the rank of the satisfaction score among all the ongoing dialogues.

However, in actual scenario we can only collect the satisfaction labels for the whole dialogue sessions through user feedback (Park et al., 2020), because asking the users to provide turn-level feedback will lead to poor user experience. Consequently, most of the existing works only tackle the session-level satisfaction prediction problem, where they can only predict the satisfaction label after the whole session finishes, lacking the ability to adjust the satisfaction score as the dialogue proceeds.

To address this problem, we formalize the turn-level user satisfaction estimation as a reinforcement learning problem. With carefully designed actions and reward function, we can optimize the turn-level satisfaction estimator with only session-level satisfaction labels.

To summarize, we utilize reinforcement learning to achieve turn-level satisfaction estimation in E-commerce customer service when only the session-level labels are available. Extensive experiments verify the effectiveness of our method.

2 Related Work

User satisfaction estimation for dialogue systems has been an important research topic over the past decades. Most of the existing work focused on the session-level user satisfaction estimation (Jiang et al., 2015; Hashemi et al., 2018; Park et al., 2020). Walker et al. (1997) first proposed PARADISE framework, which can estimate the user satisfaction in spoken dialogue systems through a task success measure and dialogue-based cost measures. Yang et al. (2010) extended the PARADISE framework by an item-based collaborative filtering model. Some works on user satisfaction estimation focused on extracting useful features from user-system interaction (Kiseleva et al., 2016a; Sandbank et al., 2018). Others modeled a dialogue as a sequence of dialogue actions (Jiang et al., 2015) or utterances (Hashemi et al., 2018; Choi et al., 2019). However, these methods can predict user satisfaction only after the dialog is completed, which can not be adopted in an E-commerce customer service scenario where timely satisfaction estimation is preferred.

While some works also addressed the turn-level online satisfaction estimation, they needed turn-level human annotations (Ultes et al., 2017; Bodigutla et al., 2020). These methods are not scalable in terms of annotation costs due to the large volumes of user data in E-commerce. Choi et al. (2019) used elaborate rules to generate turn-level satisfaction labels and trained the model in a supervised manner, but rules do not generalize well to the rapid growth of new data in a commercial system. Recently, Kachuee et al. (2020) suggested a self-supervised contrastive learning approach to use unlabeled data and transfer to user satisfaction prediction with labeled data, but the size of labeled data is still very large.

In our work, we propose to leverage reinforcement learning to achieve turn-level user satisfaction estimation. Only requiring session-level labels, our model is more suitable for industrial E-commerce customer service than existing methods.

3 User Satisfaction Estimation

We formally define the task in our work as follows: the tth turn of a dialogue, denoted by $\mathcal{T}_t$, consists of user request $\mathcal{T}_t^u$ and system response $\mathcal{T}_t^s$. Each dialogue d contains a few turns, namely $d = (\mathcal{T}_1, \mathcal{T}_2, ..., \mathcal{T}_T)$, and we estimate the satisfaction score sc_t of a user at each turn $\mathcal{T}_t$ $(t = 1, 2, ..., T)$.

We now describe the proposed method in detail, which consists of three components: dialogue encoder, satisfaction score estimator, and reinforcement learning module. Figure 2 shows the overview of the proposed method.

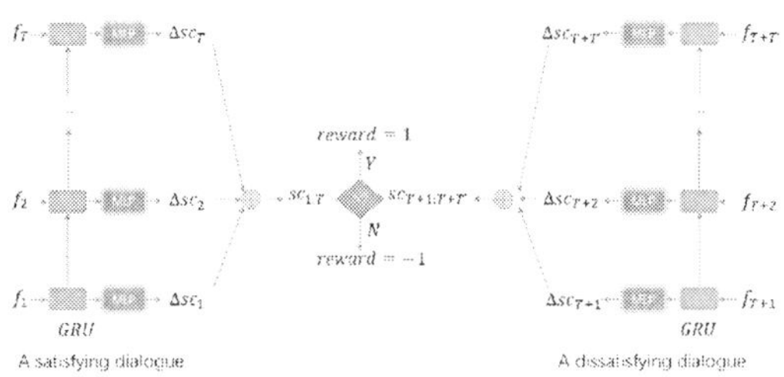

Figure 2: The overview of the proposed method.

3.1 Dialogue Encoder

Following (Choi et al., 2019), we extract features from each turn and model a dialogue as a sequence of features, such as turn index and input channel[2]. Suppose there are m features and we

[2]See Appendix A for details

denote the one-hot vector for the jth feature in turn $\mathcal{T}_t$ as f_t^j. Then the feature for the tth turn is $f_t = [f_t^1; f_t^2; ...; f_t^m]$.

For better understanding of natural languages, we use BERT (Devlin et al., 2019) to encode the pair of user and system utterances at each turn, and apply it as a part of the input features f_t.

Then, we use the gated recurrent units (GRU) (Chung et al., 2014) to get the hidden state h_t of the dialogue history up to the tth turn:

$$h_t = GRU(h_{t-1}, f_t) \tag{1}$$

3.2 Satisfaction Score Estimator

For satisfaction score estimation, our insight is that a the degree of a user's **dissatisfaction** will accumulate if he/she encounters successive improper system response (where the satisfaction score is negative and decreases over time), or can be relieved by a satisfactory reply (where the satisfaction score increases). Therefore, it is natural to predict the **increment** of user satisfaction score, not only because it is in line with the intuition that users who experience more dis-satisfactory turns are more likely to give up interacting with the system, but also the predicted increment of user satisfaction score can be regarded as the actions in reinforcement learning (see Section 3.3 for details).

Formally, having encoded the dialogue, we first predict the **increment** of user satisfaction score Δsc_t with a multilayer perceptron (MLP):

$$\Delta sc_t = MLP(h_t) \tag{2}$$

Then, we sum up the increments of user satisfaction score to get the user satisfaction score up to the tth turn:

$$sc_{1:t} = sc_{1:t-1} + \Delta sc_t = \sum_{\tau=1}^{t} \Delta sc_\tau \tag{3}$$

3.3 Reinforcement Learning Module

To optimize the satisfaction score estimator, we sample a pair of a **satisfying dialogue** (where the user is satisfied with the system at the session level) and a **dissatisfying dialogue** and compare the two predicted satisfaction scores. Our key insight is that although it is hard to directly assign each turn with the absolute value of satisfaction, the predicted satisfaction score of satisfying dialogue must be **higher than** that of the dissatisfying dialogue. We model the satisfaction score estimator as an agent assigning increment of satisfaction score to each turn given the dialogue context, and the aforementioned fact can be utilized to design the reward signal in reinforcement learning setting.

Formally, the training set $\mathcal{D}$ is split into satisfying dialogues $\mathcal{S_D}$ and dissatisfying dialogues $\overline{\mathcal{S_D}}$. In each episode of reinforcement learning, we randomly sample a satisfying dialogue $d \in \mathcal{S_D}$ with T turns and a dissatisfying dialogue $d' \in \overline{\mathcal{S_D}}$ with T' turns. Then the satisfaction score estimator is regarded as the agent, and predicts the increment of satisfaction score of each turn for d and d' successively. Thus, the length of an episode is $T + T'$.

For the first turn of satisfying dialogue (i.e., the 1st time step), the state is initialized with the features of the first turn (of satisfying dialogue). The rest states of the satisfying dialogue (i.e., the 2rd $\sim$ Tth time steps) are updated by the features of current turn and GRU hidden states encoding features of history turns (of satisfying dialogue). Similarly, for the first turn of dissatisfying dialogue (i.e., the $(T+1)$th time step), the state is reinitialized with the features of the first turn (of dissatisfying dialogue). The rest states of the dissatisfying dialogue (i.e., the $(T+2)$th $\sim$ $(T+T')$th time steps) are also updated by features of current turn and GRU hidden states encoding features of history turns (of dissatisfying dialogue). Formally, the state is defined as:

$$s_t = \begin{cases} f_t (t = 1, T+1) \\ [h_{t-1}; f_t] (t \neq 1, T+1) \end{cases} \tag{4}$$

The action $a_t = \Delta sc_t$ is sampled from the policy $\pi(a_t|s_t) \sim \mathcal{N}(MLP(GRU(s_t)), \sigma^2)$, where σ is a hyper-parameter. The rewards r_t for each time step t are all 0 except the Tth and $(T+T')$th step. The rewards for these two steps are 1 if the agent predicts $sc_{1:T} > sc_{T+1:T+T'}$, and -1 otherwise.

Let the expectation of return $J(\pi_\theta) = \mathbb{E}_{\pi_\theta}[\sum_{t=1}^{T} \gamma^{t-1} r_t] + \mathbb{E}_{\pi_\theta}[\sum_{t=T+1}^{T+T'} \gamma^{t-T-1} r_t]$, where the policy is parameterized by θ, and γ denotes the discount rate. Following the REINFORCE (Williams, 1992) algorithm, the gradient of the expectation of return can be calculated as follows:

$$\nabla_\theta J(\pi_\theta) = \mathbb{E}_{\pi_\theta}[(\sum_{t=1}^{T} \gamma^{t-1} r_t) \sum_{t=1}^{T} \nabla_\theta \log \pi_\theta(a_t|s_t)] + \mathbb{E}_{\pi_\theta}[(\sum_{t=T+1}^{T+T'} \gamma^{t-T-1} r_t) \sum_{t=T+1}^{T+T'} \nabla_\theta \log \pi_\theta(a_t|s_t)] \tag{5}$$

4 Experimental Setting

4.1 Dataset

The dataset in this experiment is sampled from a commercial customer service system, where users communicate with the intelligent assistant about the E-commerce transactions, such as claiming a refund and requesting a receipt. The users are allowed to request manual service during the dialogue if they feel dissatisfied with the automatic system. The dataset contains 1294 dialogue sessions in total, 840 and 454 of which are labeled as satisfying and dissatisfying, respectively.

4.2 Evaluation Metric

We aim at deploying our satisfaction estimator to online services, where thousands of dialogues are handled simultaneously. As the manual service resources are limited, we need to sort the ongoing dialogues by the satisfaction scores estimated by our model, and allocate manual service resource to the least satisfied users.

To evaluate the model in this scenario, we use the Area Under the Receiver Operating Characteristic Curve (AUC) (Fawcett, 2006) as the evaluation metric. In our scenario, AUC equals the probability that the satisfaction score of a randomly sampled satisfying dialogue is higher than the score of a randomly sampled dissatisfying dialogue.

4.3 Baseline

We compare our model with the following baselines: (1) DeepFM (Guo et al., 2017) which combines the factorization machine and deep neural network. (2) ConvSAT (Choi et al., 2019) which uses bidirectional LSTMs to encode the context history for each turn, and also utilizes the behaviour signals.

We train the baseline models using session-level labels with supervised learning, then treat the sub-dialogue (i.e., the first n turns of dialogue history) as a whole dialogue session to estimate turn-level user satisfaction during evaluation. We also add an augmented variant of supervised learning: we augment the training set with turn-level labels by directly copying the session-level labels as the training signals of the sub-dialogues.

5 Experiment Results

5.1 Turn-Level Satisfaction Estimation

To investigate how well the model can estimate user satisfaction in a timely manner, we first compare the AUC of each model with different number of **remaining turns** n, where we predict the satisfaction score n turns before the end of each dialogue (i.e., we predict $sc_{1:T-n}$ for a dialogue with T turns). In this way, we can test whether our model is capable of estimating the user's satisfaction tendency before a dialogue finishes or fails.

Figure 3 shows the AUC of satisfaction estimation with respect to remaining turns. Our proposed method outperforms all other methods with all remaining turns. And the improvement of our proposed method over the other methods increases as the number of remaining turns grows. The reason is that the distribution of incomplete dialogues differs from the complete ones. Since the supervised learning model only learns to score the complete dialogues during the training period, it cannot properly score the incomplete ones during the test period. In contrast, since the reinforcement learning model learns to make turn-level estimation during the training time, its estimation performance is much better than that of supervised learning model when the number of remaining turns is large. Augmenting the training data with sub-dialogues benefits the supervised learning process, but the performance is still worse than the reinforcement learning.

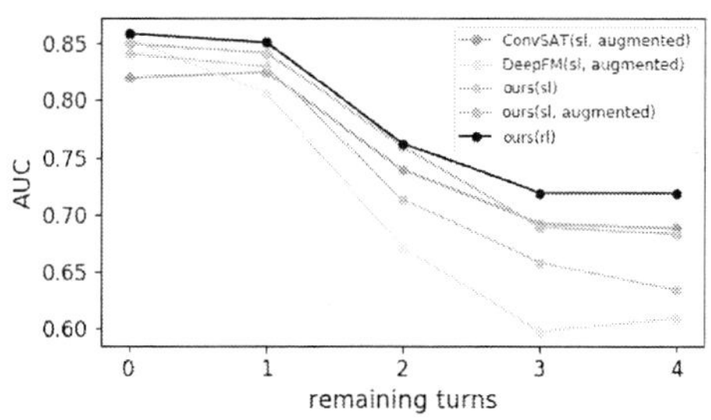

Figure 3: AUC of satisfaction estimation with different remaining turns.

To verify the effectiveness of each feature in dialogue encoding, we conduct ablation study. We remove one feature in each experiment, and the model makes satisfaction estimation with access to the complete dialogues in the test set.

The results of ablation study are shown in Table 1. The model with all the features have the best performance, indicating that every feature is useful for making satisfaction estimation.

Setting	AUC
Ours(rl)	0.859
w/o input channel	0.841
w/o turn index	0.831
w/o utterance	0.826
w/o frequence	0.791
w/o user intent	0.783

Table 1: AUC of satisfaction score.

5.2 Model Behaviour Analysis

To understand the behaviour of our proposed model, we draw the distribution of satisfaction score predicted by our model up until each specific turn. As shown in Figure 4, at the first few turns, the absolute value of satisfaction score is usually small, as users usually express their demands in the beginning with no satisfaction tendency. When the dialogue continues, the dialogues will exhibit more clues about satisfaction or dissatisfaction. Therefore, the predicted satisfaction scores go up (or down) in the satisfying (or dissatisfying) dialogues as depicted by orange (or blue) figures. This verifies the ability of distinguishing the dissatisfying dialogues from the satisfying ones by our method.

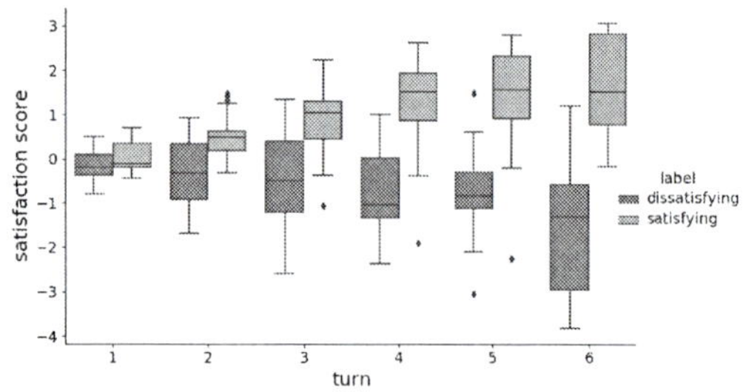

Figure 4: The distribution of satisfaction score estimated by our model up until each specific turn.

6 Conclusion

We present a reinforcement learning method to estimate turn-level satisfaction scores with only session-level labels. We verify that our model can effectively estimate satisfaction scores of customer service dialogues. In the future work, we will explore algorithms for retraining the customer service system with the help of user satisfaction estimator.

Acknowledgments

This work was partly supported by the NSFC projects (Key project with No. 61936010 and regular project with No. 61876096). This work was also supported by the Guoqiang Institute of Tsinghua University, with Grant No. 2019GQG1 and 2020GQG0005.

References

Praveen Kumar Bodigutla, Aditya Tiwari, Spyros Matsoukas, Josep Valls-Vargas, and Lazaros Polymenakos. 2020. Joint turn and dialogue level user satisfaction estimation on mulit-domain conversations. In *Proceedings of the 2020 Conference on Empirical Methods in Natural Language Processing: Findings*, pages 3897–3909.

Jason Ingyu Choi, Ali Ahmadvand, and Eugene Agichtein. 2019. Offline and online satisfaction prediction in open-domain conversational systems. In *Proceedings of the 28th ACM International Conference on Information and Knowledge Management*, pages 1281–1290.

Shammur Absar Chowdhury, Evgeny A Stepanov, and Giuseppe Riccardi. 2016. Predicting user satisfaction from turn-taking in spoken conversations. In *Interspeech*, pages 2910–2914.

Junyoung Chung, Caglar Gulcehre, Kyunghyun Cho, and Yoshua Bengio. 2014. Empirical evaluation of gated recurrent neural networks on sequence modeling. In *NIPS 2014 Workshop on Deep Learning*.

Jacob Devlin, Ming-Wei Chang, Kenton Lee, and Kristina Toutanova. 2019. Bert: Pre-training of deep bidirectional transformers for language understanding. In *NAACL-HLT 2019: Annual Conference of the North American Chapter of the Association for Computational Linguistics*, pages 4171–4186.

Tom Fawcett. 2006. An introduction to roc analysis. *Pattern Recognition Letters*, 27(8):861–874.

Jianfeng Gao, Michel Galley, and Lihong Li. 2019. Neural approaches to conversational ai. *Foundations and Trends® in Information Retrieval*, 13(2-3):127–298.

Huifeng Guo, Ruiming Tang, Yunming Ye, Zhenguo Li, and Xiuqiang He. 2017. Deepfm: a factorization-machine based neural network for ctr prediction. In *Proceedings of the 26th International Joint Conference on Artificial Intelligence*, pages 1725–1731.

Seyyed Hadi Hashemi, Kyle Williams, Ahmed El Kholy, Imed Zitouni, and Paul A. Crook. 2018. Measuring user satisfaction on smart speaker intelligent assistants using intent sensitive query embeddings. In *Proceedings of the 27th ACM International Conference on Information and Knowledge Management*, pages 1183–1192.

Jiepu Jiang, Ahmed Hassan Awadallah, Rosie Jones, Umut Ozertem, Imed Zitouni, Ranjitha Gurunath

Kulkarni, and Omar Zia Khan. 2015. Automatic online evaluation of intelligent assistants. In *Proceedings of the 24th International Conference on World Wide Web*, pages 506–516.

Mohammad Kachuee, Hao Yuan, Young-Bum Kim, and Sungjin Lee. 2020. Self-supervised contrastive learning for efficient user satisfaction prediction in conversational agents. *arXiv preprint arXiv:2010.11230*.

Julia Kiseleva, Kyle Williams, Ahmed Hassan Awadallah, Aidan C. Crook, Imed Zitouni, and Tasos Anastasakos. 2016a. Predicting user satisfaction with intelligent assistants. In *Proceedings of the 39th International ACM SIGIR conference on Research and Development in Information Retrieval*, pages 45–54.

Julia Kiseleva, Kyle Williams, Jiepu Jiang, Ahmed Hassan Awadallah, Aidan C. Crook, Imed Zitouni, and Tasos Anastasakos. 2016b. Understanding user satisfaction with intelligent assistants. In *Proceedings of the 2016 ACM on Conference on Human Information Interaction and Retrieval*, pages 121–130.

Irene Lopatovska, Katrina Rink, Ian Knight, Kieran Raines, Kevin Cosenza, Harriet Williams, Perachya Sorsche, David Hirsch, Qi Li, and Adrianna Martinez. 2019. Talk to me: Exploring user interactions with the amazon alexa. *Journal of Librarianship and Information Science*, 51(4):984–997.

Dookun Park, Hao Yuan, Dongmin Kim, Yinglei Zhang, Matsoukas Spyros, Young-Bum Kim, Ruhi Sarikaya, Edward Guo, Yuan Ling, Kevin Quinn, et al. 2020. Large-scale hybrid approach for predicting user satisfaction with conversational agents. *arXiv preprint arXiv:2006.07113*.

Tommy Sandbank, Michal Shmueli-Scheuer, David Konopnicki, Jonathan Herzig, John Richards, and David Piorkowski. 2018. Detecting egregious conversations between customers and virtual agents. In *NAACL HLT 2018: 16th Annual Conference of the North American Chapter of the Association for Computational Linguistics: Human Language Technologies*, volume 1, pages 1802–1811.

Stefan Ultes, Pawel Budzianowski, Inigo Casanueva, Nikola Mrksic, Lina Maria Rojas-Barahona, Pei-Hao Su, Tsung-Hsien Wen, Milica Gasic, and Steve J Young. 2017. Domain-independent user satisfaction reward estimation for dialogue policy learning. In *Interspeech*, pages 1721–1725.

Marilyn A. Walker, Diane J. Litman, Candace A. Kamm, and Alicia Abella. 1997. Paradise: A framework for evaluating spoken dialogue agents. In *Proceedings of the 35th Annual Meeting of the Association for Computational Linguistics*, pages 271–280.

Ronald J. Williams. 1992. Simple statistical gradient-following algorithms for connectionist reinforcement learning. *Machine Learning*, 8(3):229–256.

Zhaojun Yang, Baichuan Li, Yi Zhu, Irwin King, Gina Levow, and Helen Meng. 2010. Collaborative filtering model for user satisfaction prediction in spoken dialog system evaluation. In *2010 IEEE Spoken Language Technology Workshop*, pages 472–477.

Zheng Zhang, Ryuichi Takanobu, Qi Zhu, Minlie Huang, and Xiaoyan Zhu. 2020. Recent advances and challenges in task-oriented dialog systems. *Science China Technological Sciences*, 63(10):2011–2027.

A Implementation details

The dataset is split into training set (70%), vadidation set (15%) and test set (15%). In all experiments, the dimension of GRU output vector is 32. Each MLP is a two-layer neural network, whose hidden size is 32 and the activation function is ReLU. We use Adam as the optimizer and the learning rate is 0.0001. The batch size is 4, and the discount rate for reinforcement learning is 1. The extracted features for each dialogue turn is listed in Table 2.

Feature	Explanation
Turn index	The index of the current turn in a dialogue session. Each turn consists of a pair of user and system utterances. The dimension is 10 (1, 2, ..., 9, $\geq$10).
Frequence	How many times the (exactly) same question has been proposed by other users in one month on the system. We manually divide the scope of frequence into 8 disjoint intervals, and the dimension is therefore 8.
Input channel	The channel for each turn that users input through (e.g., keyboard and shortcut button). The dimension is 6.
User intent	The detected user intent for each turn (e.g., making a complaint and claiming a refund). The dimension is 10.

Table 2: Extracted features for each turn.

B Case Study

To better understand the turn-level satisfaction estimation behaviour of our model, we conduct case study. We sample two dialogue cases from the test set and display their contents as well as the satisfaction **increment** Δsc_t estimated by our model for each turn. It is worth noting that in this E-commerce customer service, the system might respond in rich text format, including tables, images and links. In such case, the system response will be represented by the title of the knowledge (e.g., *Knowledge*: Why I'm not eligible for the quick refund?).

turn	user utterance	system response	user input channel	Δsc_t
1	12345678 (order number)	How can I help you with this order?	order selection	-0.176
2	Why don't I get the quick refund?	*Knowledge*: Why I'm not eligible for the quick refund?	keyboard	0.250
3	Manual service.	Please describe your question, and I will help you.	keyboard	-0.861
4	Manual service, please.	I guess you might be interested in our other services.	keyboard	-0.598

Table 3: A dialogue in which the user is dissatisfied.

turn	user utterance	system response	user input channel	Δsc_t
1	87654321 (order number)	How can I help you with this order?	order selection	-0.176
2	What can I do if the seller won't refund me?	*Knowledge*: What can I do if the seller won't refund me?	knowledge recommendation	0.375
3	After applying for a refund, what if the seller doesn't react?	*Knowledge*: After applying for a refund, what if the seller doesn't react?	knowledge recommendation	0.522
4	The seller declined to refund me.	*Knowledge*: What can I do if the seller declines to refund me?	shortcut	0.365

Table 4: A dialogue in which the user is satisfied.

Table 3 shows a dialogue case where the user is **dissatisfied**. At the first turn, the user selects the order. Since it is common for users to select order in the first turn, the absolute value of the estimated satisfaction increment is small. This suggests that our model finds no clear satisfaction or dissatisfaction tendency of the user. In the second turn, the user raises a question about the quick refund. Since this is a common question and system responds with relevant knowledge, our model predicts a positive satisfaction increment (i.e., the user is likely to be more satisfied). However, in the third turn, the user asks for manual service, which usually indicates that the user is dissatisfied with the content of the last response. Therefore, our model predicts a negative satisfaction increment with large absolute value, showing that the user might become quite dissatisfied with the automatic system. At the fourth turn, the user continues asking for manual service, and therefore our model continues predicting a negative satisfaction increment with large absolute value.

Table 4 illustrates a dialogue case where the user is **satisfied**. At the first turn, the user also selects the order, and therefore the absolute value of the predicted satisfaction increment is small. In the following turns, the user consecutively clicks the knowledge recommendation links and shortcut buttons in the user interface. This is a good phenomenon because the user can conveniently get the desired information through simple clicks, without the need for typing the questions through the keyboard. Hence, our model keeps making estimation of positive satisfying increment, showing the belief that the user is satisfied.

The above cases illustrate that our proposed model can make reasonable turn-level satisfaction estimation in various situations, verifying the effectiveness and great interpretability of our reinforcement learning method.

Campaign Keyword Augmentation via Generative Methods

Haoran Shi, Zhibiao Rao, Yongning Wu, Zuohua Zhang, Chu Wang
Amazon.com Inc
Seattle, Washington, USA
{haoransh, zhibiar, yongning, zhzhang, chuwang}@amazon.com

Abstract

Keyword augmentation is a fundamental problem for sponsored search modeling and business. Machine generated keywords can be recommended to advertisers for better campaign discoverability as well as used as features for sourcing and ranking models. Generating high-quality keywords is difficult, especially for cold campaigns with limited or even no historical logs; and the industry trend of including multiple products in a single ad campaign is making the problem more challenging. In this paper, we propose a keyword augmentation method based on generative seq2seq model and trie-based search mechanism, which is able to generate high-quality keywords for any products or product lists. We conduct human annotations, offline analysis, and online experiments to evaluate the performance of our method against benchmarks in terms of augmented keyword quality as well as lifted ad exposure. The experiment results demonstrate that our method is able to generate more valid keywords which can serve as an efficient addition to advertiser selected keywords.

1 Introduction

Sponsored search has proved to be an efficient and inspiring way of connecting shoppers with interesting products. Advertisers have the freedom to provide a list of targeting keywords with associated bidding prices to the ad platform, so that their ad campaigns can match to shopper queries either lexically or semantically. The quantity and quality of targeting keywords are fundamental to the performance of the ad campaign: insufficient keywords can hardly get the campaigns with enough exposure; and low-quality ones will match shopper queries with irrelevant ads, leading to low conversion and damages to customer experiences.

Efficient and optimal keyword selection is challenging and time consuming because it requires deep understanding of the ad industry as well as the sponsored search platform. Furthermore, an ad campaign used to be designed for a single product traditionally, but ads with richer information start to appear in the recent years. Nowadays, an ad campaign can contain multiple products, brand stores, or even rich media contents. Consequently, the keyword selection task becomes even more crucial and challenging for advertisers campaign creation and management.

In this paper, we present an end-to-end machine learning solution to generate keywords for ad campaigns. The method applies to single-product campaigns as well as campaigns with any number of products. It only relies on product information like product titles, hence efficient on newly created campaigns without any performance logs in the past. We conduct offline and online experiments on the proposed method and observe significant improvements over traditional statistical methods in terms of keyword quality. Specifically, we highlight our contributions as the following:

- We propose an end-to-end solution for keyword generation. It can be applied to recommendation of high-quality keywords for advertisers as well as semantic augmentation for better ad exposure.
- The keyword generation method relies on product metadata but not historical performance data of ad. Therefore, the method applies to tail or newly-created campaigns.
- Our method is able to handle single-product-campaign as well as multi-product-campaign by leveraging semantic meanings of each product in the latent space.
- The quality and superiority of the generated keywords are validated by human audits, offline analysis as well as online experiments.

Proceedings of the 4th Workshop on e-Commerce and NLP (ECNLP 4), pages 33–37
August 5, 2021. ©2021 Association for Computational Linguistics

2 Related Work

Considerable research work has been devoted to keyword augmentation techniques because of its important applications in information retrieval, indexing, and digital library management. The majority of existing work focuses on processing documents with statistical information including term co-occurrence and frequency (Campos et al., 2020). In particular, Rose et al. (2010) proposed RAKE to split the document into candidate phrases by word delimiters and calculate their scores with co-occurrence counts. Ravi et al. (2010) first applied statistical machine translation model for keyword candidate generation and ranking. With rapid development of deep learning models, neural machine translation has surpassed statistical translation in many benchmarks, where recurrent neural networks (RNNs) and gating mechanisms are popular building blocks to model sequence dependencies and alignments (Hochreiter and Schmidhuber, 1997; Cho et al., 2014). However, extracting high-quality and diverse keywords from short document like ad campaigns remains a difficult problem due to the lack of context.

Query expansion for improved product or ad discovery, as an application of keyword augmentation, is crucial to e-commerce search engines and recommender systems. He et al. (2016) applies LSTM architecture to rewriting query into web document index space. However, the long tail distribution of the query space hinders the deployment of complicated generative models. It is well known that infrequent queries account for a large portion of the e-commerce daily queries. In Lian et al. (2019), a lightweight neural network for infrequent queries is trained, incurring even more engineering burdens for deployment. It also proposed the method of using trie-based search to normalize the decoding in the constrained semantic space, which is further investigated in Chen et al. (2020).

Expanding advertiser bidding keywords is another growing research area. Qiao et al. (2017) applies keyword clustering and topic modeling to retrieve similar keywords and Zhou et al. (2019) conducts keywords expansion in the constrained domains through neural generative models. In addition, Zhang et al. (2014) formulates the keyword recommendation problem as a mixed integer optimization problem, where they collect candidate keywords whose relevance score to the ad group exceed a threshold and handle the keyword selection problem by maximizing revenue. Such methods rely on the quality of advertiser bidding keywords. Campaigns with sub-optimal or misused keywords may suffer significantly.

3 Methods

In this section, we present our products-to-keyword framework and algorithm for campaign keyword augmentation. The framework is compatible with any seq2seq components with encoders and decoders. Given an ad campaign C including a set of products $\{p_1, p_2, \ldots, p_n\}$, our goal is to generate a list of relevant keywords $\{k_1, k_2, \ldots, k_m\}$. We will describe how we generate keywords for each product first and later generalize to ad campaigns with multiple products.

3.1 Dataset and Preprocessing

We choose to use organic search click data for model training, which includes the pairs of queries and clicked products in search log. Compared to sponsored search data, it can guide the model to generate more keywords than existing ads system as shown in Lian et al. (2019). We lowercase shopper queries and product titles, and then apply pretrained T5 tokenizer (Raffel et al., 2020) for tokenization. Note that the vocabulary space for shopper queries and product titles are ever-growing, but the subword encoding space is stable. Therefore, subword tokenization is an efficient method to handle the out-of-vocabulary issue which hurts the fluency of generated queries.

3.2 Modeling

In the following, we use $X = [x_1, x_2, ...x_L]$ to denote tokenized product title whose length is L. Let θ be the trainable model parameters, and $Q = [q_0, q_1, q_2, \ldots, q_S]$ as the padded tokenized target query, where q_0 is the special start token and q_S the special end token. For training, we feed the model with the product title X and the first s query token $Q_{<s} = [q_0, q_1, \ldots, q_{s-1}]$, to predict the next query token q_s, where $1 \leq s \leq S$.

We adopt the seq2seq model training with teacher forcing, where multi-layer Gated Recurrent Units (GRU) are used in the encoder and the decoder (Cho et al., 2014). The encoder transforms the tokenized sequence into the latent space with an embedding layer and a GRU encoder. Then the decoder transforms the latent vector back to a predicted distribution over token vocabulary given all previously decoded tokens as inputs. The token embedding layer for the encoder and the decoder are shared. We use cross entropy loss to maximize the likelihood of the model generating the correct next token for each training data point $(X, Q_{<s}, q_s)$. The objective function is written as

$$L(\theta) = -\sum_{s=1}^{S} \log\ p(q_s|X, Q_{<s}; \theta))). \quad (1)$$

3.3 Keyword Generation

Intuitively, the desired generated keywords should be diverse to accommodate different aspects of the products, and relevant to promote the products to right shoppers. In the model inference phase, the encoding is the same as in training, while in decoding process beam search is usually used for larger search space. However, standard beam search will generate similar sequences with minimal diversity. To resolve this issue, we build the trie T_Q on all tokenized queries in our training dataset to normalize the decoding. Specifically in the i-th decoding step, the decoder outputs the probability of $p(q_s|X, Q_{<s}$ over the vocabulary. Then we extract all children nodes of $Q_{<s}$ in the trie and keep those with highest probability in the candidate beam for future decoding. In this way, it is guaranteed that the generated sequence exists in the canonical query space as a path traversal in the trie ending with the special end token. We define such queries as valid queries since they reflect the word selection of shoppers. The prebuilt Trie and the inference workflow for one product title is illustrated in Figure 1 and 2 respectively.

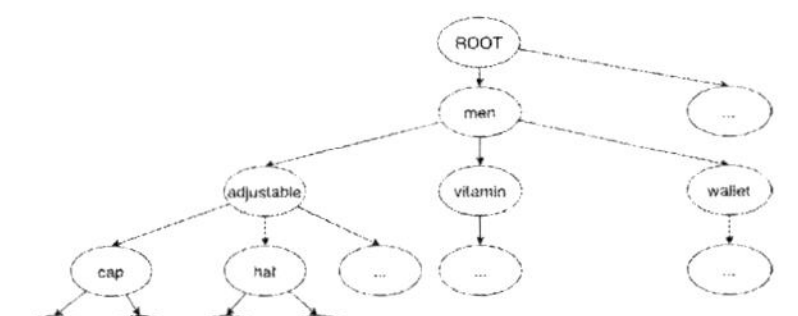

Figure 1: An illustration of the Trie built on queries

Now we discuss the handling of multiple products within one campaign. A naive solution is to generate keywords for each product, and then aggregate all generated keywords. Alternatively, we propose to encode each product title into the latent space, and apply the decoder to the averaged title encodings. These two methods are denoted as Generation by Keyword Aggregation (G-KA) and Generation by Hidden State Mixing (G-HSM).

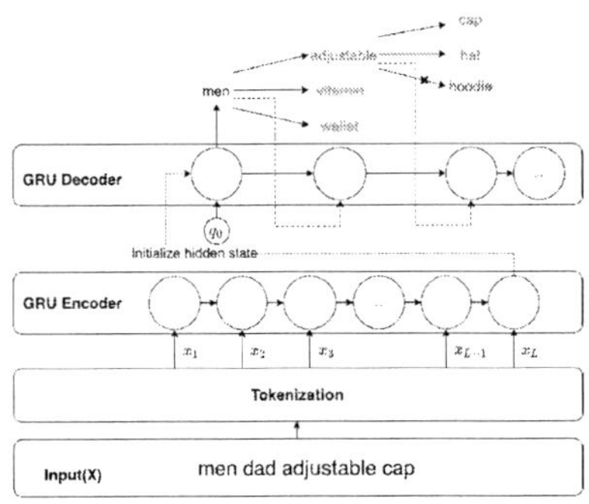

Figure 2: An illustration of the keyword generation process. Tokens in red color with strikethrough line are removed by beam search, and "men adjustable hoodie" is pruned by the query trie. Details of the encoder/decoder are omitted.

4 Experiments

In this section, we compare the performance of the proposed methods with empirical study. In Section 4.1, we explain how we collect our experimental data including training, validation, and testing; then we introduce benchmarking methods and parameter setup in Section 4.2; evaluation metrics are explained in Section 4.3; and eventually in Section 4.4, we illustrate experimental results.

4.1 Data Preparation

We collect query-product pairs in search click logs from September 2020 to March 2021. To reduce the noise, we apply a series of filtering: 1) remove stop-words in queries and product titles; 2) remove tokens with non-alphanumeric characters; 3) remove pairs with empty query or title; 4) remove query-product pairs with less than 1024 clicks.

In total, we collect 6.2M pairs of queries and products, where more than 95% of the queries have less than or equal to 6 tokens. We split them into training set (5.2M) and validation set (1M). To prevent frequent queries dominating the result and encourage diversity, we normalize the weight of all pairs to the same for training stage.

For testing, we use cold campaigns to benchmark the keyword augmentation model performance, which are campaigns with less than 100 impressions from January 2021 to March 2021. Since we use organic search log for training, there is no overlap between training and testing data.

4.2 Benchmarks and Parameters Setup

The benchmark methods include heuristics based on search log as well as trending keyword generation methods. We use ADV to denote targeting keywords provided by advertisers, and OS to denote keywords generated by organic search logs heuristically. More specifically, we extract those queries which lead to the click of the campaign products in organic search, and collect those distinct queries as keywords for the campaign. We also include RAKE in our comparison which is a popular open-sourced keyword extraction algorithm based on lexical co-occurrence statistics. To achieve better extraction performance, we run RAKE on the concatenation of all product titles in the campaign, and keep the keywords with length between 2 and 6. In addition, we compare the two variants of our proposed solutions, G-KA and G-HSM:

- G-KA: We select top 8 generated queries with lowest perplexity from each product.
- G-HSM: We select top 3 products in terms of sales in each campaign and averaged their latent encodings for decoding. We select top 8 generated queries for each campaign too.

For both variants, the encoder and decoders are 6-layer GRUs with 256 hidden dimensions, and the beam search size is set as 20. We choose the model with the lowest loss on the validation dataset.

4.3 Evaluation Method

We sample 1500 keyword-campaign pairs from each method for human annotations. Each campaign will be associated with a landing page URL including all targeted products. Three different auditors are assigned to label each pair as exactly relevant, partially relevant, and irrelevant. We take the majority decision as the final label of each pair. For simplicity, we merge exactly relevant and partially relevant labels, and report the ratio of relevance for different methods. To evaluate whether the generated keywords are able to effectively promote ad exposures, we calculate the total traffics incurred by generated keywords as a metric, and report the median total traffics as the Exposure column of Table 1. We also report the median value of the number of generated keywords for each method as the Count column, and use Exposure divided by Count to evaluate the traffic incurred by each individual keyword.

In addition, we conduct online A/B testing by enriching the campaign keywords with generated results from G-KA for ad sourcing and comparing with the existing system in terms of total ad impressions. All other components in the system, including relevance and ranking logics, are consistent for control and treatment.

4.4 Results and Analysis

Table 1 illustrates the performance of different methods in terms of the number of generated keywords, relevance ratio and exposure. For the testing campaigns without many impressions, advertisers bid on a few relevant keywords which lead to poor ad exposures. Such impression shortage issue is one of the motivations for our work, and we use this method as the baseline.

RAKE is able to extract relevant keywords from the product titles, but their exposure is quite low. Such results indicate vocabulary gap exists a between product titles and shopper queries. Organic search connects the products to the relevant queries but the amount of queries are much fewer than the baseline. Intuitively, this is because advertisers are aware of historical queries related to their products.

G-KA and G-HSM provide a moderate number of keywords with ads exposure much larger than baseline (+1665% and +2194%), though the relevance rate are lower than standard baseline. The boost of Exposure/Count also demonstrates the effectiveness of the proposed keyword generation methods with seq2seq learning framework and trie-based decoding. In addition, the G-HSM shows superiority over G-KA in terms of keyword relevancy and validity.

In our online experiment, our model increases ad impressions by 5.3%, which demonstrates the contribution from the proposed keyword augmentation methods. Note that relevance and ranking logics are the same for both control and treatment groups. Only augmented keywords not covered by existing advertiser selected keywords with good quality are able to yield additional ad exposures.

5 Conclusion and Future Work

In this paper, we formulate the sponsored search keyword augmentation task as a seq2seq learning problem in the constrained space. We present a general framework which incorporates seq2seq architecture and trie-based pruning for query generation from product titles. We compare the proposed method with baselines and other existing methods, and show that our method is able to generate relevant keywords which bring up the campaign exposure significantly. In the future, we would like to

Method	Count	Relevance	Exposure	Exposure/Count
ADV	12	97.8%	baseline	baseline
RAKE	9	93.1%	-71.66%	-62.22%
OS	2	98.1%	+192.4%	+1654%
G-KA	19	78.1%	+1665%	+1015%
G-HSM	8	88.3%	+2194%	+3341%

Table 1: Performance comparison.

explore more structured decoding strategies combined with trie to improve the generation quality, and take more factors into account when generating keywords including long-tail keywords and keyword competitiveness.

Acknowledgments

We would like to thank to Hongyu Zhu, Weiming Wu, Barry Bai, Hirohisa Fujita for their help to set up the online A/B testing, and all the reviewers for their valuable suggestions.

References

Ricardo Campos, Vítor Mangaravite, Arian Pasquali, Alipio Jorge, Célia Nunes, and Adam Jatowt. 2020. Yake! keyword extraction from single documents using multiple local features. *Information Sciences*, 509:257–289.

Pinzhen Chen, Nikolay Bogoychev, Kenneth Heafield, and Faheem Kirefu. 2020. Parallel sentence mining by constrained decoding. In *Proceedings of the 58th Annual Meeting of the Association for Computational Linguistics*, pages 1672–1678.

Kyunghyun Cho, Bart Van Merriënboer, Caglar Gulcehre, Dzmitry Bahdanau, Fethi Bougares, Holger Schwenk, and Yoshua Bengio. 2014. Learning phrase representations using rnn encoder-decoder for statistical machine translation. *arXiv preprint arXiv:1406.1078*.

Yunlong He, Jiliang Tang, Hua Ouyang, Changsung Kang, Dawei Yin, and Yi Chang. 2016. Learning to rewrite queries. In *Proceedings of the 25th ACM International on Conference on Information and Knowledge Management*, pages 1443–1452.

Sepp Hochreiter and Jürgen Schmidhuber. 1997. Long short-term memory. *Neural computation*, 9(8):1735–1780.

Yijiang Lian, Zhijie Chen, Jinlong Hu, Kefeng Zhang, Chunwei Yan, Muchenxuan Tong, Wenying Han, Hanju Guan, Ying Li, Ying Cao, et al. 2019. An end-to-end generative retrieval method for sponsored search engine–decoding efficiently into a closed target domain. *arXiv preprint arXiv:1902.00592*.

Dandan Qiao, Jin Zhang, Qiang Wei, and Guoqing Chen. 2017. Finding competitive keywords from query logs to enhance search engine advertising. *Information & Management*, 54(4):531–543.

Colin Raffel, Noam Shazeer, Adam Roberts, Katherine Lee, Sharan Narang, Michael Matena, Yanqi Zhou, Wei Li, and Peter J. Liu. 2020. Exploring the limits of transfer learning with a unified text-to-text transformer. *Journal of Machine Learning Research*, 21(140):1–67.

Sujith Ravi, Andrei Broder, Evgeniy Gabrilovich, Vanja Josifovski, Sandeep Pandey, and Bo Pang. 2010. Automatic generation of bid phrases for online advertising. In *Proceedings of the third ACM international conference on Web search and data mining*, pages 341–350.

Stuart Rose, Dave Engel, Nick Cramer, and Wendy Cowley. 2010. Automatic keyword extraction from individual documents. *Text mining: applications and theory*, 1:1–20.

Ying Zhang, Weinan Zhang, Bin Gao, Xiaojie Yuan, and Tie-Yan Liu. 2014. Bid keyword suggestion in sponsored search based on competitiveness and relevance. *Information processing & management*, 50(4):508–523.

Hao Zhou, Minlie Huang, Yishun Mao, Changlei Zhu, Peng Shu, and Xiaoyan Zhu. 2019. Domain-constrained advertising keyword generation. In *The World Wide Web Conference*, pages 2448–2459.

Personalized Entity Resolution with Dynamic Heterogeneous Knowledge Graph Representations

Ying Lin[*], Han Wang, Jiangning Chen, Tong Wang, Yue Liu, Heng Ji, Yang Liu, Premkumar Natarajan
Amazon Alexa AI
{linzying,wnghn,cjiangni,tonwng,jihj,yangliud,premknat}@amazon.com

Abstract

The growing popularity of Virtual Assistants poses new challenges for Entity Resolution, the task of linking mentions in text to their referent entities in a knowledge base. Specifically, in the *shopping* domain, customers tend to mention the entities implicitly (e.g., "organic milk") rather than use the entity names explicitly, leading to a large number of candidate products. Meanwhile, for the same query, different customers may expect different results. For example, with "add *milk* to my cart", a customer may refer to a certain product from his/her favorite brand, while some customers may want to re-order products they regularly purchase. Moreover, new customers may lack persistent shopping history, which requires us to enrich the connections between customers through products and their attributes. To address these issues, we propose a new framework that leverages personalized features to improve the accuracy of product ranking. We first build a cross-source heterogeneous knowledge graph from customer purchase history and product knowledge graph to jointly learn customer and product embeddings. After that, we incorporate product, customer, and history representations into a neural reranking model to predict which candidate is most likely to be purchased by a specific customer. Experiment results show that our model substantially improves the accuracy of the top ranked candidates by 24.6% compared to the state-of-the-art product search model.

1 Introduction

Given an entity mention as a query, the goal of entity resolution (or entity linking) (Ji and Grishman, 2011) is to link the mention to its corresponding entry in a target knowledge base (KB). In an academic shared task setting, an entity mention is usually a name string, which can be a person, organization or geo-political entity in a news context, and the KB is usually a Wikipedia dump with rich structured properties and unstructured text descriptions. State-of-the-art entity resolution methods can achieve higher than 90% accuracy in such settings (Ji and Grishman, 2011; Ji et al., 2015; Agarwal and Bikel, 2020), and they have been successfully applied in hundreds of languages (Pan et al., 2017) and various domains such as disaster management (Zhang et al., 2018a) and scientific discovery (Zheng et al., 2014; Wang et al., 2015). Therefore, we tend to think entity resolution is a solved problem in academia. However, in industry, with the rise in popularity of Virtual Assistants (VAs) in recent years, an increasing number of customers now rely on VAs to perform daily tasks involving entities, including shopping, playing music or movies, calling a person, booking a flight, and managing schedules. The scale and complexity of industrial applications presents the following unique new challenges.

Unpopular majority. There is a massive number of new entities emerging every day. The entity resolver may know very little about them since very few users interact with them. Handling these tail entities effectively requires the use of property linkages between entities and shared user interests. Similarly, there might be many new users with limited interaction history, and we need to infer their interests from other users who have interacted with similar entities.

Large number of ambiguous variants. When interacting with VAs, users tend to use short and less informative utterances with the expectation that the VAs can intelligently infer their actual intentions. This raises the need for *personalization* when resolving the entities. In the *shopping* domain, this problem is even more challenging as customers typically use implicit entity mentions

[*] This work was done when the first author was on an internship at Amazon Alexa AI.

Proceedings of the 4th Workshop on e-Commerce and NLP (ECNLP 4), pages 38–48
August 5, 2021.

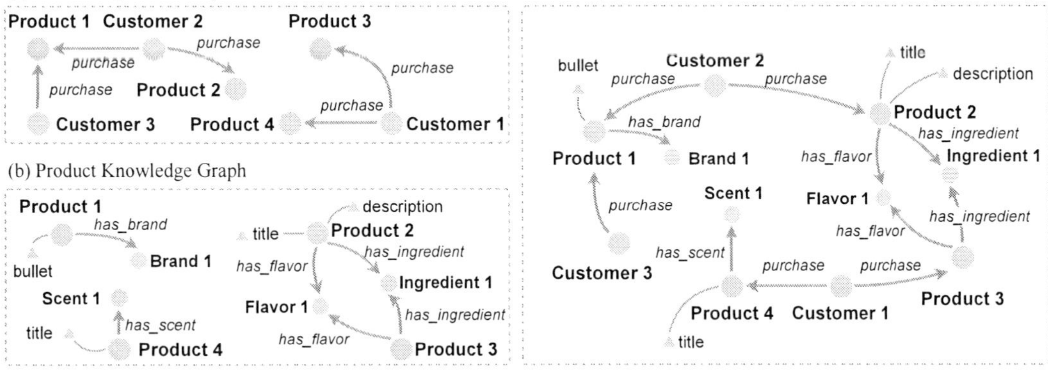

Figure 1: An illustration of the cross-source heterogeneous customer-product graph.

(e.g., "organic milk") instead of explicit names (e.g., "Horizon Organic Shelf-Stable 1% Lowfat Milk") which usually leads to a large number of candidates due to the ambiguity. However, with VAs' voice user interface (VUI), the number of products that can be presented to the customers is very limited, if not only one. In this work, we focus on the problem of *personalized entity resolution* in the shopping domain. Given a query and a list of retrieved candidates, we aim to return the product that is most likely to be purchased by a customer.

Beyond ambiguity. In the traditional news entity linking setting, each entity in the KB refers to a unique world object. In contrast, in e-commerce, the same product can have multiple variants. For example, a customer may like to stick to a toothpaste product of a certain brand and flavor, but choose different sizes (thus different entities) in each purchase. These entities in the target KB refer to the same product but have different properties (in this case, size). Therefore it is important to construct fine-grained knowledge graphs to profile products and capture the implicit connections between customers based on the properties of their purchased products.

We make three assumptions: (H1) customers tend to purchase products they have purchased in the past; (H2) customers tend to purchase products that share some properties; (H3) customers who purchased products with similar properties share similar interests. Based on these assumptions, we propose to represent customers and products as low-dimensional vectors learned from a graph of customers and products. Unlike social media networks with rich interactions among users, the customers of most shopping services are isolated, which prevents us from learning customer embeddings effectively. To address this issue, we propose to build a cross-source heterogeneous knowledge graph as Figure 1 depicts to indirectly establish rich connections among customers from a) users' purchase history (customer-product graph) and b) a product knowledge graph, and further jointly learn the representations of nodes in this graph using a Graph Neural Network (GNN)-based method. In Figure 1(c), for instance, we can build connections between Customer 1 and Customer 2 because their purchased products share the same ingredient attribute, and thus possibly recommend Product 2 to Customer 1 even though it does not appear in his/her purchase history. In addition to static customer embeddings, we further propose an attentive model to dynamically generate a history representation for each user based on the current query. Finally, the model predicts how likely a candidate will be purchased using entity, customer, and history representations.

Experiments on real purchase records collected from an online shopping service show that our method significantly improves the purchase rate of the top ranked products.

2 Methodology

Given a query q from a customer c, and a list of candidate products $\mathcal{P} = \{p_1, ..., p_L\}$, where L is the number of candidates, our goal is to predict the product that the customer will purchase based on their purchase history and the product knowledge graph. Specifically, we use purchase records $\{r_1, ..., r_H\}$ where H is the number of historical records. As Figure 2 illustrates, we jointly learn customer and product embeddings from a cross-source customer-product graph using GNN. To perform personalized ranking, we incorporate the learned customer embedding and history representation as additional features when calculating the confidence score of each candidate. We then rank all candidates by confidence score and return the top one.

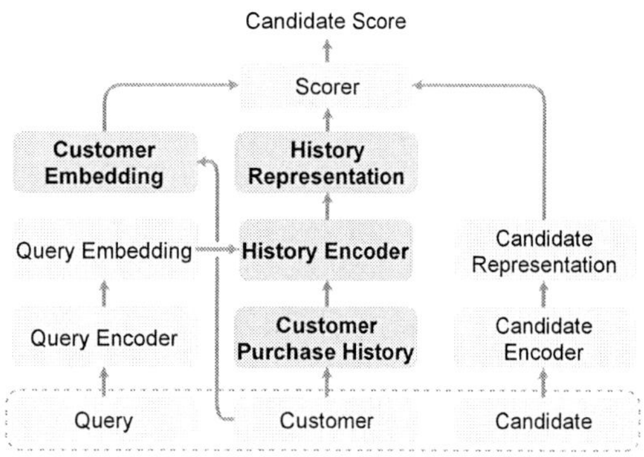

Figure 2: An illustration of our framework.

2.1 Candidate Retrieval

We first retrieve candidate products for each query using QUARTS (Nigam et al., 2019; Nguyen et al., 2020), which is an end-to-end neural model for product search. QUARTS has three major components: (1) an LSTM-based (long short-term memory) classifier adapted from the entailment model in (Rocktäschel et al., 2016) to predict whether a product-query pair is matched; (2) a variational encoder-decoder (VED) query generator that generates difficult negative examples to tackle the class imbalance issue in the training data as a search engine typically returns much more matched query-item examples than mismatched ones, and (3) a state combiner that switches between query representations computed by the classifier and generator. During training, the VED generator takes as input a matched product-query pair (I, Q) and generates a mismatched query Q_{gen} which is lexically similar to Q. The state combiner then merges $\boldsymbol{H}$, the representation computed by the classifier, and $\boldsymbol{H}_{\text{gen}}$, the representation computed by the generator, as $s\boldsymbol{H}_{\text{gen}} + (1-s)\boldsymbol{H}$, where s is a binary value that controls which query to use and whether the gradients are back-propagated to the classifier or generator.

2.2 Joint Customer and Product Embedding

The next step is to obtain the representations of customers and products. Customer embeddings are usually learned from user-generated texts (Preoţiuc-Pietro et al., 2015; Yu et al., 2016; Ribeiro et al., 2018) or social relations (Perozzi et al., 2014a; Grover and Leskovec, 2016; Zhang et al., 2018b), neither of which are available in the shopping dataset we use. Alternatively, we establish *indirect* connections among customers through their purchased products under hypothesis H3, and form a customer-product graph as shown in Figure 1(a). This graph only contains a single type of relation (i.e., `purchase`) and ignores product attributes. As a result, it tends to be sparse and less effective for customer representation learning.

In order to learn more informative embeddings, we propose to incorporate richer information from a product knowledge graph (Figure 1(b)) where products are not only connected to different attribute nodes (e.g., brands, flavors), but they may also be associated with textual features (e.g., `title`) and boolean features (e.g., `isOrganic`, encoded as a boolean vector).

By merging the product knowledge graph and the customer-product graph, we obtain a more comprehensive graph (Figure 1(c)) of higher connectivity. For example, in the original customer-product graph, `Customer 1` and `Customer 2` are disconnected because they do not share any purchase. In the new graph, they have an indirect connection through `Product 2` and `Product 3`, which share the same flavor and ingredient.

From this heterogeneous graph, we jointly learn customer and product representations using a two-layer Relational Graph Convolutional Network (Schlichtkrull et al., 2018). The embedding of each node is updated as:

$$\boldsymbol{h}_i^{l+1} = \text{ReLU}\Big(\boldsymbol{W}_0^l \boldsymbol{h}_i^l + \sum_{r \in R} \sum_{j \in N_i^r} \frac{1}{|N_i^r|} \boldsymbol{W}_r^l \boldsymbol{h}_j^l\Big),$$

where $\boldsymbol{h}_i^l$ is the representation of node i at the l-th layer, N_i^r is the set of neighbor indices of node i under relation $r \in R$, and $\boldsymbol{W}_0^l$ and $\boldsymbol{W}_r^l$ are learnable weight matrices.

In order to capture textual features (i.e., product titles, descriptions, and bullet[1]), we use a pretrained RoBERTa (Liu et al., 2019) encoder to generate a fix-sized representation for each product.

[1]Bullet points that outline the main features of a product.

Specifically, we concatenate textual features using a special separator token [SEP], obtain the RoBERTa representation for each token, and then use the averaged embedding to represent the whole sequence. To reduce the runtime, we calculate customer and product embeddings offline and cache the results.

2.3 Candidate Representation

In addition to the product embedding, we further incorporate the following features to enrich the representation of each candidate.

Rank: the order of the candidate returned by the product retrieval system.

Relative Price: how much a product's absolute price is higher or lower than the average price of all retrieved candidates as price is an important factor that affects purchasing decision.

Previously Purchased: a binary flag indicating whether a candidate has been purchased by the customer or not.

Textual Feature: we use RoBERTa to encode each candidate's textual features (i.e., title, bullet, description). This RoBERTa encoder is fine-tuned during training.

We concatenate these features with the product embedding and project the vector into a lower dimensional space using a feed forward network.

2.4 History Representation

Although customer embeddings can encode purchase history information, they are *static* and may not effectively provide the most relevant information for each specific query. For example, if the query is "bookshelf", the furniture-related purchase records are more likely to help the model predict the product that the customer will purchase, while if the query is "sulfate-free shampoo", the purchase records of beauty products are more relevant. To tackle this issue, we propose to generate a *query-aware* history representation $\boldsymbol{v}$ based on the current query $\boldsymbol{q}$ from all purchase record representations $\{\boldsymbol{v}_1, ..., \boldsymbol{v}_H\}$ of the customer.

We first represent each purchase record as the concatenation of the product embedding, product price, and purchase timestamp. The query-aware history representation is then calculated as a weighted sum of the customer's purchase record representations using an attention mechanism as follows.

$$e_i = \boldsymbol{v}^\top \tanh\left(\boldsymbol{W}_q \boldsymbol{q} + \boldsymbol{W}_v \boldsymbol{v}_i\right),$$

$$a_i = \text{Softmax}(e_i) = \frac{\exp(e_i)}{\sum_k^M \exp(e_k)},$$

$$\boldsymbol{v} = \sum_i^H a_i \boldsymbol{v}_i,$$

where $\boldsymbol{v}^\top$, $\boldsymbol{W}_q$, and $\boldsymbol{W}_v$ are learnable weights.

2.5 Candidate Ranking

We adopt a feed forward neural network that takes in the candidate, customer, and history representations, and returns a confidence score $\hat{y}_i$ which indicates how likely a candidate will be purchased. The confidence score is scaled to $(0, 1)$ using a Sigmoid function. During training, we optimize the model by minimizing the following binary cross entropy loss function.

$$\mathcal{L} = -\frac{1}{N}\sum_{i=1}^{N} y_i \log \hat{y}_i + (1 - y_i) \log(1 - \hat{y}_i),$$

where N denotes the total number of candidates, and $y_i \in \{0, 1\}$ is the true label. In the inference phase, we calculate confidence scores for all candidates for each session and return the one with the highest score.

3 Experiment

3.1 Data

Product Knowledge Graph. In our experiment, we use a knowledge graph of products in five categories (i.e., grocery, beauty, luxury beauty, baby, and health care), which contains 24,287,337 unique product entities. As Figure 1(b) depicts, the products in this knowledge graph are connected through attribute nodes, including brands, scents, flavors, and ingredients. This knowledge graph also provides rich attributes for each product node. We use two types of attributes in this work, textual features (i.e., title, description, and bullet) and binary features (e.g., isOrganic, isNatural).

Evalution Dataset. We randomly collect 1 million users' purchase sessions from November 2018 to October 2019 on an online shopping service. Each session contains a query, an obfuscated identifier, a timestamp, and a list of candidate products retrieved using QUARTS where only one product is purchased.

We split the sessions before and after September 1, 2019 into two subsets. The first subset only serves as the purchase history and is used to construct the customer-product graph. From the second subset, we randomly sample 22,000 customers with at least one purchase record in the first subset and take their last purchase sessions for training or evaluation. Specifically, we use 20,000 sessions for training, 1,000 for validation, and 1,000 for test. If a customer has multiple purchase sessions in the second subset, other sessions before the last one are also considered as purchase history when we generate history representations, while they are excluded from the customer-product graph, which is constructed from the first subset.

3.2 Experimental Setup

We optimize our model with AdamW (Loshchilov and Hutter, 2018) for 10 epochs with a learning rate of 1e-5 for the RoBERTa encoder, a learning rate of 1e-4 for other parameters, weight decay of 1e-3, a warmup rate of 10%, and a batch size of 100.

To encode textual features, we use the RoBERTa base model[2] with an output dropout rate of 0.5. To represent query words, we use 100-dimensional GloVe embeddings (Pennington et al., 2014) pre-trained on Wikipedia and Gigaword[3]. We set the size of pre-trained customer and product embeddings to 100 and freeze them during training.

We use separate fully connected layers to project candidate and history representations into 100-dimensional feature vectors before concatenating them for ranking. We use a two-layer feed forward neural network with a hidden layer size of 50 as the ranker and apply a dropout layer with a dropout rate of 0.5 to its input.

3.3 Quantitative Analysis

We compare our model to the state-of-the-art product search model QUARTS as the baseline. Because our target usage scenarios are VAs where only one result will be returned to the user, we use accuracy as our evaluation metric. We implement the following baseline ranking methods.

Purchased: We prioritize products previously purchased by the customer. If multiple candidates are previously purchased, we return the one ranked highest by QUARTS.

ComplEx: Customer and product embeddings are learned using ComplEx (Trouillon et al., 2016), a widely used knowledge embedding model that represents nodes in a knowledge graph as complex vectors and is able to capture antisymmetric relations using efficient dot product.

In Table 1, we show the relative gains compared to the baseline model QUARTS. With personalized features, our method effectively improves accuracy on both development and test sets.

We also conduct ablation studies by removing the following features and show results in Table 2.

Ranking: In this setting, our model ignores the original retrieval ranking returned by QUARTS.

Personalized Features: We remove personalized features (e.g., customer embedding, whether a product is previously purchased) in this setting.

Product Embedding: We remove pre-trained product embedding but still use textual features and binary features to represent products.

Joint Embedding: Customer and product embeddings are not jointly learned from the merged graph. Alternatively, customer embeddings are learned from the customer-product graph, and product embeddings are learned from the product knowledge graph.

In Table 2, from the results of Methods 6 and 7, we can see that removing either product or customer embedding degrades the performance of the model. The result of Method 8 shows that embeddings jointly learned from the merged cross-source graph achieve better performance on our downstream task. We also observe that the ranking returned by the product search system is still an important feature as Method 6 shows.

	Method	Dev Accuracy	Test Accuracy
1	QUARTS	0.0	0.0
2	Purchased	+10.5	+8.5
3	ComplEx	+25.7	+16.1
4	Our Model	**+32.9**	**+24.6**

Table 1: Relative gains compared to QUARTS. (%)

	Method	Dev Acc	Test Acc
4	Our Model	**+32.9**	**+24.6**
5	w/o Ranking	-17.1	-20.4
6	w/o Personalized Features	-10.5	-18.0
7	w/o Product Embedding	+25.2	+19.0
8	w/o Joint Embedding	+28.1	+20.4

Table 2: Ablation study. (%, relative gains compared to QUARTS.)

[2]https://huggingface.co/transformers/pretrained_models.html

[3]https://nlp.stanford.edu/projects/glove/

Query	Candidates	History
#1 vitamin c serum	* [3] instanatural vitamin c serum with hyaluronic acid & vit e - natural & organic anti wrinkle ...	* foundation makeup brush flat top kabuki for face - perfect for blending liquid, cream or flawless powder
	* [1] truskin vitamin c serum for face, topical facial serum with hyaluronic acid, vitamin e, 1 fl oz	* women's rogaine 5% minoxidil foam for hair thinning and loss, topical treatment for women's hair ...
	* [2] vitamin c serum for face - anti aging facial serum	* vita liberata advanced organics fabulous self-tanning gradual lotion with marula oil, 6.76 fl oz
	* [4] vitamin c serum plus 2% retinol, 3.5% niacinamide, 5% hyaluronic acid, 2% salicylic acid ...	* instanatural vitamin c serum with hyaluronic acid & vit e - natural & organic anti wrinkle reducer ...
	Our model promotes candidate 3 as this product was purchased by the customer.	
#2 toothpaste	* [2] crest 3d white whitening toothpaste, radiant mint, 3.5oz, twin pack	* crest 3d white toothpaste radiant mint (3 count of 4.1 oz tubes), 12.3 oz packaging may vary
	* [1] crest + scope complete whitening toothpaste, minty fresh, 5.4 oz, pack of 3	* skindinavia the makeup of control finishing spray, 8 fluid ounce
	* [3] pronamel gentle whitening enamel toothpaste for sensitive teeth, alpine breeze-4 ounces (pack of 3)	* crest 3d white toothpaste radiant mint (3 count of 4.1 oz tubes), 12.3 oz packaging may vary
	* [4] colgate cavity protection toothpaste with fluoride - 6 ounce (pack of 6)	* nivea shea daily mointure body lotion - 48 hour moisture for dry skin - 16.9 fl. oz. pump bottle, ...
	Although the previously purchased item is no longer available, with entity embedding learned from the cross-source graph, our model successfully promotes the most similar product.	
#3 sun dried tomatoes	* [3] 365 everyday value, **organic** sundried tomatoes in extra virgin olive oil, 8.5 oz	* #1 usda **organic** aloe vera gel - no preservatives, no alcohol - from freshly cut usa grown 100% pure ...
	* [1] 35 oz bella sun luci sun dried tomatoes julienne cut in olive oil (original version)	* **organic** aloe vera gel with 100% pure aloe from freshly cut aloe plant, not powder - no xanthan ...
	* [2] julienne sun-dried tomatoes - 16oz bag (kosher)	* wicked joe **organic** coffee wicked italian ground
	* [4] organic sun-dried tomatoes with sea salt, 8 ounces - salted, non-gmo, kosher, raw, vegan, ...	*thayers alcohol-free original witch hazel facial toner with aloe vera formula, clear, 12oz
	Our model promotes an organic product as the customer probably prefers organic products based on the shopping records.	

Table 3: Positive examples in the data set. Candidates are listed in the order returned by our method. The number before each candidate is the original ranking returned by QUARTS. In the candidate column, we highlight the purchased products . In the history column, we highlight related records .

3.4 Qualitative Analysis

In Table 3 and Table 4, we show some positive and negative examples in the data set. From Table 3 we can see that multiple sources of evidence in the constructed heterogeneous knowledge graphs are complimentary and the combination of them successfully promotes various entities which match customers' interests.

Table 4 shows examples where our model fails to return the correct item. In many cases, such as Example #4, the purchased product and the top ranked one only differ in packaging size. We also observe that sometimes customers may not repurchase a product even if it is in the candidate list.

To better understand the remaining errors, we randomly sample 100 examples where our model fails to predict the purchased items. As Figure 3 illustrates, we analyze these examples and classify the possible reasons into the following categories.

Different size. The predicted product and ground truth are the same product but differ in size. For example, while our model predicts "Lipton Herbal Tea Bags, Peach Mango, 20 ct", the customer purchases another item "Lipton Tea Herbal Peach Mango (pack of 2)", which is actually the same product in 2 pack.

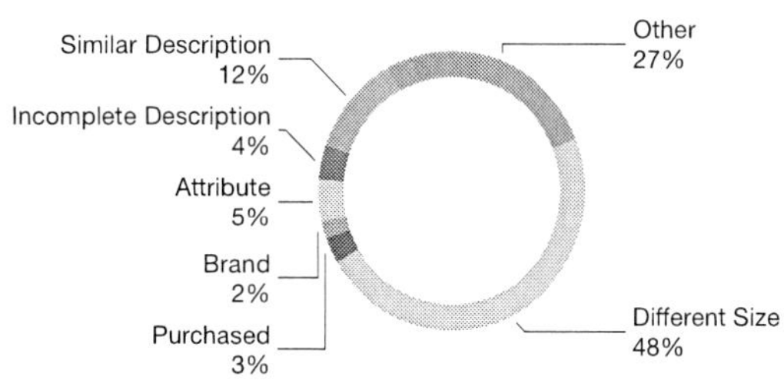

Figure 3: Distribution of remaining Errors.

Purchased. The customer purchased the predicted product before but decides not to repurchase it. This usually happens in categories (e.g., toothpaste) where customers are more willing to try new products. Additionally, customers may be less likely to repurchase a product in some categories such as books and electronics.

Uninformative title. The purchased product has

Query	Candidates	History
#4 wasabi almonds	* [8] blue diamond almonds, bold wasabi & soy sauce, 16 ounce (pack of 1)	* epsoak epsom salt 19 lb. bulk bag magnesium sulfate usp
	* [2] blue diamond almonds variety pack (1.5 ounce bags) (20 pack)	*** blue diamond almonds, bold wasabi & soy sauce, 16 ounce (pack of 1)**
	* [1] blue diamond almonds bold wasabi & soy sauce almonds, 25 ounce (pack of 1)	* signature trail mix, peanuts, m & m candies, raisins, almonds & cashews, 4 lb
	*** [6] blue diamond almonds, bold wasabi & soy, 1.5 ounce (pack of 12)**	* amazon brand - happy belly nuts, chocolate & dried fruit trail mix, 48 ounce
	Our model promotes candidate 8 which is previously purchased, whereas the customer selects another size.	
#5 cacao powder	* [5] anthony's organic cocoa powder, 2 lb, batch tested and verified gluten free & non gmo	*** anthony's organic cocoa powder, 2 lb, batch tested and verified gluten free & non gmo**
	* [1] viva naturals #1 best selling certified organic cacao powder from superior criollo beans, 1 lb bag	* vör all natural keto nut butter spread (10oz) | only two ingredients | no sugar, no salt | vegan ...
	* [2] navitas organics cacao powder, 16oz. bag - organic, non-gmo, fair trade, gluten-free	*** anthony's organic cocoa powder, 2 lb, batch tested and verified gluten free & non gmo**
	* [3] terrasoul superfoods raw organic cacao powder, 1 lb - raw | keto | vegan	* nutiva organic, neutral tasting, steam refined coconut oil from non-gmo, sustainably farmed coconuts ...
	*** [4] viva naturals certified organic cacao powder (2lb) for smoothie, coffee and drink mixes**	
	Our model promote "Anthony's Organic Cocoa Powder" as it has been purchased twice by the customer.	

Table 4: Negative examples in the data set.

an uninformative title and is therefore not promoted. For example, when the customer searches for "masaman curry paste maesri", our model promotes "Maesri Thai Masaman Curry - 4 oz (pack of 4)", while the customer purchases "6 Can (4oz. Each) of Thai Green Red Yellow Curry Pastes Set", which is also a Maesri product, but this key information is missing from its title.

Similar title. The title of the predicted product is similar to the titles of some purchased products in the customer's history in a less important aspect. For example, the model promotes a "moisturizing" shave gel because the customer has purchased a "moisturizing" body wash, whereas the customer decides to purchase a product for "sensitive skin".

Brand. The customer has purchased one or more products of the same brand.

Attribute. The customer has purchased one or more products with the same attribute (e.g., organic, keto, kosher).

Other. The model may fail to predict the purchased item in other uncategorized cases. For example, when a customer searches for "nail clippers" but has purchased only food in the past, the model is unlikely to utilize the history records to improve the ranking.

3.5 Remaining Challenges

Although our framework can improve the accuracy of predicting products that will be purchased, there are still some remaining challenges. We propose the following potential solutions for further improvement.

Incorporating more informative features. Some important features that affect purchase decisions are still missing in our framework, such as the average rating, customer review comments, and number of ratings. For example, we may promote the highest rated product for a customer who usually buys products with high ratings.

Building a more comprehensive cross-source customer-product graph. In this work, we merge the customer-product graph and product knowledge graph into a single graph, which has been proved to produce better embeddings for our target task. A natural extension is to include records from more sources, such as music or video playing history, and multimedia features such as product pictures.

Modeling the interactions among purchase behaviors. Our current attention-based method that generates history representations is "flat" and ignores the relationship among purchase behaviors. For example, for a customer who previously purchases a pod coffee maker, we should promote coffee capsules in the candidates over coffee beans or grounds.

Incorporating cohort features. When dealing with customers with limited or even no previous shopping records, a step forward is to cluster customers and produce cohort-based representations. In this way, customers can be better represented collectively through other similar customers, especially when we combine their interaction history from other domains and build a more comprehensive graph as suggested above.

To sum up, shopping is a complex behavior, the importance weights of various features may vary across types of products. For instance, customers may like to stick to the same brand for beauty products while changing the size, depending on their needs. In contrast, for clothing customers may care more about visual features rather than text descriptions, and for books customers rarely purchase the same book more than once. To tackle these remaining challenges, we aim to extend our framework to incorporate more multimedia features, extract knowledge from review comments, and present recommendation results in a more hierarchical way by clustering variants of the same product and presenting their different attributes.

4 Related Work

4.1 Neural Entity Linking

A variety of neural models (Gupta et al., 2017; Kolitsas et al., 2018; Cao et al., 2018; Sil et al., 2018; Gillick et al., 2019; Logeswaran et al., 2019; Wu et al., 2019; Agarwal and Bikel, 2020) have been applied to entity linking in recent years. Compared to traditional entity linking, our task is different in three aspects: (1) Our mentions are typically vague and occur in uninformative contexts, such as "add *toothpaste* to my cart" ; (2) A mention may be reasonably linked to multiple entities, while only one of them is considered "correct" (purchased by the customer); (3) The ground truth for the same mention can be different for different customers.

4.2 Personalized Recommendation

A recommender system is an information filtering system that aims to suggest a list of items in which a user may be interested. Content-based filtering (Billsus and Pazzani, 2000; Aciar et al., 2007; Wang et al., 2018) and collaborative filtering (Shardanand and Maes, 1995; Konstan et al., 1997; Linden et al., 2003; Zhao and Shang, 2010) are two common approaches used in recommender systems. In recent years, researchers have also applied neural methods to improve the quality of recommendations (Xue et al., 2017; He et al., 2017; Wang et al., 2019a,b). Recommender systems usually rank items based on the user's past behaviors (e.g., purchasing, browsing, rating) and current context (Linden et al., 2003; Smith and Linden, 2017), whereas the results are not constrained by queries. Instead, our task requires a specific query and only returns the product that is most likely to be purchased from a list of relevant candidates.

4.3 Graph Embedding

Various methods have been proposed to learn low-dimensional vectors for nodes in knowledge graphs. Knowledge graph embedding methods, such as TransE (Bordes et al., 2013), DistMult (Yang et al., 2014), ComplEx (Trouillon et al., 2016), and RotatE (Sun et al., 2018), typically represent the head entity, relation, and tail entity in each triplet in the knowledge graph as vectors and aim to rank true triplets higher than corresponding corrupted triplets. Matrix Factorization-based methods (He and Niyogi, 2004; Nickel et al., 2011; Qiu et al., 2018) represent the graph as a matrix and obtain node vectors by factorizing this matrix. Another category of frameworks (Perozzi et al., 2014b; Yang et al., 2015; Grover and Leskovec, 2016) use random walk to sample paths from the input graph and learn node embeddings from the sampled paths using neural models such as SkipGram and LSTM.

4.4 Heterogeneous Network

The earliest study of mining heterogeneous network dates back to (Sun et al., 2009), which coins the concept of Heterogeneous Information Network. After that, heterogeneous network has been applied to a range of tasks, including ranking (Ji et al., 2011), similarity search (Sun et al., 2011), link prediction (Dong et al., 2015), academic paper recommendation (Pan et al., 2015), and malicious account detection (Liu et al., 2018).

Recently, with the advent of graph neural network, many methods based on this new paradigm have been proposed to learn graph representations on heterogeneous graphs, such as Heterogeneous Graph Neural Network (HetGNN) (Zhang et al., 2019), Heterogeneous Graph Attention Network (HAN) (Wang et al., 2019c), and Heterogeneous Graph Transformer (HGT) (Hu et al., 2020).

5 Conclusion and Future Work

We propose a novel framework to jointly learn customer and product representations based on a cross-source heterogeneous graph constructed from customers' purchase history and the product knowledge graph to improve personalized entity resolution. Experiments show that our framework can effectively increase the purchase rate of the top ranked products. In the future, we plan to investigate better approaches to integrating personalized features and extend the framework to cross-lingual cross-media settings and generate conversations for more proactive and explainable entity recommendation and summarization.

References

Silvana Aciar, Debbie Zhang, Simeon Simoff, and John Debenham. 2007. Informed recommender: Basing recommendations on consumer product reviews. *IEEE Intelligent systems*, 22(3):39–47.

Oshin Agarwal and Daniel M Bikel. 2020. Entity linking via dual and cross-attention encoders. *arXiv preprint arXiv:2004.03555*.

Daniel Billsus and Michael J Pazzani. 2000. User modeling for adaptive news access. *User modeling and user-adapted interaction*, 10(2-3):147–180.

Antoine Bordes, Nicolas Usunier, Alberto Garcia-Duran, Jason Weston, and Oksana Yakhnenko. 2013. Translating embeddings for modeling multi-relational data. *Advances in neural information processing systems*, 26:2787–2795.

Yixin Cao, Lei Hou, Juanzi Li, and Zhiyuan Liu. 2018. Neural collective entity linking. In *Proceedings of the 27th International Conference on Computational Linguistics*, pages 675–686.

Yuxiao Dong, Jing Zhang, Jie Tang, Nitesh V Chawla, and Bai Wang. 2015. Coupledlp: Link prediction in coupled networks. In *Proceedings of the 21th ACM SIGKDD International Conference on Knowledge Discovery and Data Mining*, pages 199–208.

Dan Gillick, Sayali Kulkarni, Larry Lansing, Alessandro Presta, Jason Baldridge, Eugene Ie, and Diego Garcia-Olano. 2019. Learning dense representations for entity retrieval. In *Proceedings of the 23rd Conference on Computational Natural Language Learning (CoNLL)*, pages 528–537.

Aditya Grover and Jure Leskovec. 2016. node2vec: Scalable feature learning for networks. In *Proceedings of the 22nd ACM SIGKDD international conference on Knowledge discovery and data mining*, pages 855–864.

Nitish Gupta, Sameer Singh, and Dan Roth. 2017. Entity linking via joint encoding of types, descriptions, and context. In *Proceedings of the 2017 Conference on Empirical Methods in Natural Language Processing*, pages 2681–2690.

Xiangnan He, Lizi Liao, Hanwang Zhang, Liqiang Nie, Xia Hu, and Tat-Seng Chua. 2017. Neural collaborative filtering. In *Proceedings of the 26th international conference on world wide web*, pages 173–182.

Xiaofei He and Partha Niyogi. 2004. Locality preserving projections. In *Advances in neural information processing systems*, pages 153–160.

Ziniu Hu, Yuxiao Dong, Kuansan Wang, and Yizhou Sun. 2020. Heterogeneous graph transformer. In *Proceedings of The Web Conference 2020*, pages 2704–2710.

Heng Ji and Ralph Grishman. 2011. Knowledge base population: Successful approaches and challenges. In *Proc. ACL2011*.

Heng Ji, Joel Nothman, Ben Hachey, and Radu Florian. 2015. Overview of tac-kbp2015 tri-lingual entity discovery and linking. In *Proc. Text Analysis Conference (TAC2015)*.

Ming Ji, Jiawei Han, and Marina Danilevsky. 2011. Ranking-based classification of heterogeneous information networks. In *Proceedings of the 17th ACM SIGKDD international conference on Knowledge discovery and data mining*, pages 1298–1306.

Nikolaos Kolitsas, Octavian-Eugen Ganea, and Thomas Hofmann. 2018. End-to-end neural entity linking. In *Proceedings of the 22nd Conference on Computational Natural Language Learning*, pages 519–529.

Joseph A Konstan, Bradley N Miller, David Maltz, Jonathan L Herlocker, Lee R Gordon, and John Riedl. 1997. Grouplens: applying collaborative filtering to usenet news. *Communications of the ACM*, 40(3):77–87.

Greg Linden, Brent Smith, and Jeremy York. 2003. Amazon. com recommendations: Item-to-item collaborative filtering. *IEEE Internet computing*, 7(1):76–80.

Yinhan Liu, Myle Ott, Naman Goyal, Jingfei Du, Mandar Joshi, Danqi Chen, Omer Levy, Mike Lewis, Luke Zettlemoyer, and Veselin Stoyanov. 2019. Roberta: A robustly optimized bert pretraining approach. *arXiv preprint arXiv:1907.11692*.

Ziqi Liu, Chaochao Chen, Xinxing Yang, Jun Zhou, Xiaolong Li, and Le Song. 2018. Heterogeneous graph neural networks for malicious account detection. In *Proceedings of the 27th ACM International Conference on Information and Knowledge Management*, pages 2077–2085.

Lajanugen Logeswaran, Ming-Wei Chang, Kenton Lee, Kristina Toutanova, Jacob Devlin, and Honglak Lee. 2019. Zero-shot entity linking by reading entity descriptions. In *Proceedings of the 57th Annual Meeting of the Association for Computational Linguistics*, pages 3449–3460.

Ilya Loshchilov and Frank Hutter. 2018. Decoupled weight decay regularization. In *International Conference on Learning Representations*.

Thanh Nguyen, Nikhil Rao, and Karthik Subbian. 2020. Learning robust models for e-commerce product search. In *Proceedings of the 58th Annual Meeting of the Association for Computational Linguistics*, pages 6861–6869, Online. Association for Computational Linguistics.

Maximilian Nickel, Volker Tresp, and Hans-Peter Kriegel. 2011. A three-way model for collective learning on multi-relational data. In *Icml*, volume 11, pages 809–816.

Priyanka Nigam, Yiwei Song, Vijai Mohan, Vihan Lakshman, Weitian (Allen) Ding, Ankit Shingavi, Choon Hui Teo, Hao Gu, and Bing Yin. 2019. Semantic product search. In *Proceedings of the 25th ACM SIGKDD International Conference on Knowledge Discovery & Data Mining*, page 2876–2885, New York, NY, USA. Association for Computing Machinery.

Linlin Pan, Xinyu Dai, Shujian Huang, and Jiajun Chen. 2015. Academic paper recommendation based on heterogeneous graph. In *Chinese computational linguistics and natural language processing based on naturally annotated big data*, pages 381–392. Springer.

Xiaoman Pan, Boliang Zhang, Jonathan May, Joel Nothman, Kevin Knight, and Heng Ji. 2017. Cross-lingual name tagging and linking for 282 languages. In *Proc. the 55th Annual Meeting of the Association for Computational Linguistics (ACL2017)*.

Jeffrey Pennington, Richard Socher, and Christopher D. Manning. 2014. Glove: Global vectors for word representation. In *Empirical Methods in Natural Language Processing (EMNLP)*, pages 1532–1543.

Bryan Perozzi, Rami Al-Rfou, and S. Skiena. 2014a. Deepwalk: online learning of social representations. In *KDD '14*.

Bryan Perozzi, Rami Al-Rfou, and Steven Skiena. 2014b. Deepwalk: Online learning of social representations. In *Proceedings of the 20th ACM SIGKDD international conference on Knowledge discovery and data mining*, pages 701–710.

Daniel Preoţiuc-Pietro, Vasileios Lampos, and Nikolaos Aletras. 2015. An analysis of the user occupational class through twitter content. In *Proceedings of the 53rd Annual Meeting of the Association for Computational Linguistics and the 7th International Joint Conference on Natural Language Processing (Volume 1: Long Papers)*.

Jiezhong Qiu, Yuxiao Dong, Hao Ma, Jian Li, Kuansan Wang, and Jie Tang. 2018. Network embedding as matrix factorization: Unifying deepwalk, line, pte, and node2vec. In *Proceedings of the Eleventh ACM International Conference on Web Search and Data Mining*, pages 459–467.

M. H. Ribeiro, Pedro H. Calais, Yuri A. Santos, V. Almeida, and W. Meira. 2018. Characterizing and detecting hateful users on Twitter. In *Proceedings of the Twelfth International AAAI Conference on Web and Social Media (ICWSM 2018)*.

Tim Rocktäschel, Edward Grefenstette, K. Hermann, Tomás Kociský, and P. Blunsom. 2016. Reasoning about entailment with neural attention. *CoRR*, abs/1509.06664.

Michael Schlichtkrull, Thomas N Kipf, Peter Bloem, Rianne Van Den Berg, Ivan Titov, and Max Welling. 2018. Modeling relational data with graph convolutional networks. In *European Semantic Web Conference*, pages 593–607. Springer.

Upendra Shardanand and Pattie Maes. 1995. Social information filtering: algorithms for automating "word of mouth". In *Proceedings of the SIGCHI conference on Human factors in computing systems*, pages 210–217.

Avirup Sil, Gourab Kundu, Radu Florian, and Wael Hamza. 2018. Neural cross-lingual entity linking. In *Proceedings of the AAAI Conference on Artificial Intelligence*, volume 32.

Brent Smith and Greg Linden. 2017. Two decades of recommender systems at amazon.com. *Ieee internet computing*, 21(3):12–18.

Yizhou Sun, Jiawei Han, Xifeng Yan, Philip S Yu, and Tianyi Wu. 2011. Pathsim: Meta path-based top-k similarity search in heterogeneous information networks. *Proceedings of the VLDB Endowment*, 4(11):992–1003.

Yizhou Sun, Jiawei Han, Peixiang Zhao, Zhijun Yin, Hong Cheng, and Tianyi Wu. 2009. Rankclus: integrating clustering with ranking for heterogeneous information network analysis. In *Proceedings of the 12th International Conference on Extending Database Technology: Advances in Database Technology*, pages 565–576.

Zhiqing Sun, Zhi-Hong Deng, Jian-Yun Nie, and Jian Tang. 2018. RotatE: Knowledge graph embedding by relational rotation in complex space. In *International Conference on Learning Representations*.

Théo Trouillon, Johannes Welbl, Sebastian Riedel, Éric Gaussier, and Guillaume Bouchard. 2016. Complex embeddings for simple link prediction. International Conference on Machine Learning (ICML).

Donghui Wang, Yanchun Liang, Dong Xu, Xiaoyue Feng, and Renchu Guan. 2018. A content-based recommender system for computer science publications. *Knowledge-Based Systems*, 157:1–9.

Han Wang, Jin Guang Zheng, Xiaogang Ma, Peter Fox, and Heng Ji. 2015. Language and domain independent entity linking with quantified collective validation. In *Proceedings of the 2015 Conference on Empirical Methods in Natural Language Processing*, pages 695–704.

Hongwei Wang, Fuzheng Zhang, Mengdi Zhang, Jure Leskovec, Miao Zhao, Wenjie Li, and Zhongyuan Wang. 2019a. Knowledge-aware graph neural networks with label smoothness regularization for recommender systems. In *Proceedings of the 25th ACM SIGKDD International Conference on Knowledge Discovery & Data Mining*, KDD '19, page 968–977, New York, NY, USA. Association for Computing Machinery.

Hongwei Wang, Fuzheng Zhang, Miao Zhao, Wenjie Li, Xing Xie, and Minyi Guo. 2019b. Multi-task feature learning for knowledge graph enhanced recommendation. In *The World Wide Web Conference*, pages 2000–2010.

Xiao Wang, Houye Ji, Chuan Shi, Bai Wang, Yanfang Ye, Peng Cui, and Philip S Yu. 2019c. Heterogeneous graph attention network. In *The World Wide Web Conference*, pages 2022–2032.

Ledell Wu, Fabio Petroni, Martin Josifoski, Sebastian Riedel, and Luke Zettlemoyer. 2019. Scalable zero-shot entity linking with dense entity retrieval. *arXiv preprint arXiv:1911.03814*.

Hong-Jian Xue, Xinyu Dai, Jianbing Zhang, Shujian Huang, and Jiajun Chen. 2017. Deep matrix factorization models for recommender systems. In *IJCAI*, volume 17, pages 3203–3209. Melbourne, Australia.

Bishan Yang, Wen-tau Yih, Xiaodong He, Jianfeng Gao, and Li Deng. 2014. Embedding entities and relations for learning and inference in knowledge bases. *arXiv preprint arXiv:1412.6575*.

Zhilin Yang, Jie Tang, and William Cohen. 2015. Multi-modal bayesian embeddings for learning social knowledge graphs. *arXiv preprint arXiv:1508.00715*.

Yang Yu, Xiaojun Wan, and Xinjie Zhou. 2016. User embedding for scholarly microblog recommendation. In *Proceedings of the 54th Annual Meeting of the Association for Computational Linguistics (Volume 2: Short Papers)*.

Boliang Zhang, Ying Lin, Xiaoman Pan, Di Lu, Jonathan May, Kevin Knight, and Heng Ji. 2018a. ELISA-EDL: A cross-lingual entity extraction, linking and localization system. In *Proc. The 16th Annual Conference of the North American Chapter of the Association for Computational Linguistics: Human Language Technologies (NAACL-HLT2018)*.

Chuxu Zhang, Dongjin Song, Chao Huang, Ananthram Swami, and Nitesh V Chawla. 2019. Heterogeneous graph neural network. In *Proceedings of the 25th ACM SIGKDD International Conference on Knowledge Discovery & Data Mining*, pages 793–803.

Zhen Zhang, Hongxia Yang, Jiajun Bu, Sheng Zhou, Pinggang Yu, Jianwei Zhang, Martin Ester, and Can Wang. 2018b. Anrl: Attributed network representation learning via deep neural networks. In *IJCAI*, volume 18.

Zhi-Dan Zhao and Ming-Sheng Shang. 2010. User-based collaborative-filtering recommendation algorithms on hadoop. In *2010 Third International Conference on Knowledge Discovery and Data Mining*, pages 478–481. IEEE.

Jin Guang Zheng, Daniel Howsmon, Boliang Zhang, Juergen Hahn, Deborah McGuinness, James Hendler, and Heng Ji. 2014. Entity linking for biomedical literature. In *BMC Medical Informatics and Decision Making*.

A Semi-supervised Multi-task Learning Approach to Classify Customer Contact Intents

Li Dong
Amazon
ldonga@amazon.com

Matthew C. Spencer
Amazon
matsp@amazon.com

Amir Biagi
Amazon
biagiab@amazon.com

Abstract

In the area of customer support, understanding customers' intents is a crucial step. Machine learning plays a vital role in this type of intent classification. In reality, it is typical to collect confirmation from customer support representatives (CSRs) regarding the intent prediction, though it can unnecessarily incur prohibitive cost to ask CSRs to assign existing or new intents to the mis-classified cases. Apart from the confirmed cases with and without intent labels, there can be a number of cases with no human curation. This data composition (Positives + Unlabeled + multiclass Negatives) creates unique challenges for model development. In response to that, we propose a semi-supervised multi-task learning paradigm. In this manuscript, we share our experience in building text-based intent classification models for a customer support service on an E-commerce website. We improve the performance significantly by evolving the model from multiclass classification to semi-supervised multi-task learning by leveraging the negative cases, domain- and task-adaptively pretrained ALBERT on customer contact texts, and a number of un-curated data with no labels. In the evaluation, the final model boosts the average AUC ROC by almost 20 points compared to the baseline finetuned multiclass classification ALBERT model.

1 Introduction

As machine learning makes rapid advances in the area of natural language processing (NLP), it is becoming more common to aid customer support representatives (CSRs) with NLP models. This not only ensures timely and consistent replies to customers, but also reduces operational costs for organizations. We can see successful use cases from organizations such as Alibaba (Fu et al., 2020), Uber (Molino et al., 2018), Square (Fotso et al., 2018), AT&T (Gupta et al., 2010), IBM (Mani et al., 2018), Los Alamos National Laboratory (DeLucia and Moore, 2020), and US Navy (Powell et al., 2020). In general, identifying the intents of the coming contacts is the first step in customer support. Therefore, accurate intent classification is crucial.

Intent classification is a broad topic mostly falling under the umbrella of NLP. In this manuscript, we limit our discussion to intent classification in the area of customer support. In the past two decades, researchers have been trying to improve the efficiency of customer support by detecting customer intents with machine learning approaches (Molino et al., 2018; Powell et al., 2020; DeLucia and Moore, 2020; Hui and Jha, 2000; Gupta et al., 2010; Fotso et al., 2018; Mani et al., 2018; Sarikaya et al., 2011; Gupta et al., 2006; Xu and Sarikaya, 2013). We can loosely categorize these approaches into text classification (Molino et al., 2018; Powell et al., 2020; DeLucia and Moore, 2020; Hui and Jha, 2000; Gupta et al., 2010; Fotso et al., 2018), question-answer (QA) system (Mani et al., 2018) and automatic speech recognition (ASR) (Sarikaya et al., 2011; Gupta et al., 2006; Xu and Sarikaya, 2013). In this manuscript, we focus on using text classification methods to classify intents for customer support. To deal with unstructured text data, researchers use handcrafted features (Hui and Jha, 2000; Gupta et al., 2010), Bag-of-Words type of features (Powell et al., 2020), features from topic modeling (DeLucia and Moore, 2020) and vectorization type of features, such as word2vec (Fotso et al., 2018; Molino et al., 2018) and doc2vec (DeLucia and Moore, 2020). By consuming these features, classifiers determine the intent of a case and the case can be routed to specialists (Molino et al., 2018; Gupta et al., 2010; DeLucia and Moore, 2020; Powell et al., 2020) and/or a reply template from the "Answer Bank" can be provided (Molino et al., 2018; Fotso et al., 2018; Hui and Jha, 2000). A general intelligent

Proceedings of the 4th Workshop on e-Commerce and NLP (ECNLP 4), pages 49–57
August 5, 2021. ©2021 Association for Computational Linguistics

customer support loop can be seen in Figure 1.

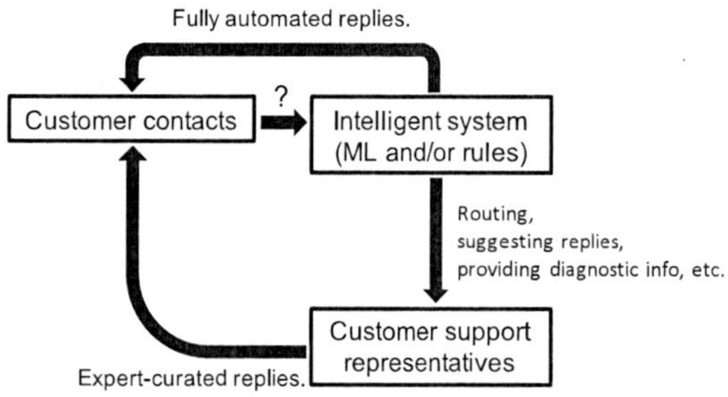

Figure 1: Intelligent customer support loop

To meet ever-changing business needs, the intent taxonomy is generally under active development (Molino et al., 2018; Fotso et al., 2018; DeLucia and Moore, 2020). It is not realistic to manually relabel all cases after each intent taxonomy update. This means that we have positive cases (P) with assigned intents and unlabeled cases (U) in data. Moreover, to maintain a high standard of customer satisfaction, intent classification is typically a human-in-the-loop process (Fu et al., 2020; Molino et al., 2018; Fotso et al., 2018; Gupta et al., 2010; Powell et al., 2020). Specifically, the CSRs are asked to confirm the intent predictions, a process we refer to as "curation" in this manuscript. The negative cases (N) identified by CSRs are indeed hard cases, since their prediction scores are above the preset confidence threshold yet they are mis-classified by the existing model. It is an active research area to create classifiers with only P and U (Elkan and Noto, 2008; Xu et al., 2017). Some research has explored models that also include N, but they have been only concerned with binary classifiers (Fei and Liu, 2015; Hsieh et al., 2019; Li et al., 2010).

In this manuscript, we adopt the semi-supervised paradigm and the multi-task approach to deal with the U and the multiclass N, respectively. Moreover, in contrast to the above-mentioned works about intent classification for customer support, we use the ALBERT pretrained language model (Lan et al., 2019) plus domain- and task-adaptive pretraining (Ramponi and Plank, 2020; Gururangan et al., 2020) to process texts. In the following sections, we describe how these techniques improve the model performance.

The paper outline is as follows. We start with Section 2 by elaborating the business background and how we pose it as a machine learning problem. Then we describe the details of the training data and models in Section 3, compare the models by conducting experiments with real data in Section 4, and discuss the results in Section 5. We conclude in Section 6.

2 Background

The E-commerce website of interest receives many support requests from customers in each second. There is a team of CSRs to actively address the requests via phone, online chat, and email channels. Identifying appropriate requests and grouping them into categories is not a trivial task. While a deep discussion of the taxonomy building process is out of the scope of this manuscript, it is sufficient to know that we have a taxonomy system that is similar to those described in (Molino et al., 2018; Fotso et al., 2018), where customized reply templates are pre-compiled for each customer contact intent. This study elaborates our journey building machine learning models to classify the intents.

3 Methodology

Since the inception of BERT (Devlin et al., 2019), an abundance of research in the area of NLP has demonstrated it to be an effective approach to transfer knowledge from pretrained language models to downstream tasks (Xia et al., 2020; Wang et al., 2018, 2019a; Rajpurkar et al., 2016; Lai et al., 2017). Following BERT's architecture, there is a stream of research that achieve comparable or better performance, to name a few (Lan et al., 2019; Liu et al., 2019; Wang et al., 2019b; Clark et al., 2020; Yang et al., 2019; Sanh et al., 2019). Among these BERT variants, ALBERT aims to strike a balance between model performance and model size (Lan et al., 2019). Therefore, we use albert-base-v2 as the backbone encoder and perform further pretraining and finetuning. The implementation is based on Transformers from Huggingface (Wolf et al., 2019).

3.1 Training Data

3.1.1 Features

The input to the model is a collection of emailed support requests in text format. The texts are minimally preprocessed, including removing invalid characters, lowercasing letters and replacing some obvious entities with consistent words, such as replacing urls and emails to url_id and email_id.

3.1.2 Targets

In industrial machine learning applications, it is typical to construct a feedback loop to collect training data. In most cases, it is straightforward to obtain a simple "yes" or "no" from human labelers with respect to the predictions. That means the human labelers only need to accept or dismiss the recommendations. Those "yes" cases are confirmed positive ones with explicit labels. However, in a common multiclass classification setting, the "no" cases can have any other label, so the labels are effectively unknown. In some scenarios, such as object detection in computer vision, it is not hard to ask human labelers to assign a label to those negative cases. However, it is highly non-trivial to ask for a valid label in many NLP applications, owing to the size of the taxonomy and the necessary domain-expertise, as is the case for the intent classification in this manuscript. Therefore, in our training data, we only have "yes" or "no" feedback to each case in each intent class.

Since the scope of the intent taxonomy is not trying to cover all customer support requests, there are many requests falling out of the scope of the taxonomy but still scored by the model. The negative cases are either out-of-scope requests or in-scope requests falling in the wrong bucket. The former one is more probable, since the requests are false positives for existing classes with high confidence scores above the preset thresholds. In this manuscript, we tried two ways to deal with this situation.

1. We can simply exclude the negative cases from training data, since they do not come with labels. In this scenario, it is a multiclass classification model trained on positive cases, i.e. confirmed intents. However, we lose valuable signals by excluding the negative cases.

2. Since the negative cases are indeed hard negatives and contain valuable signals, we can use the multi-task learning paradigm to elegantly treat the negatives for each intent class as the negative samples for a binary classification task. In this scenario, we have a binary classification task for each class plus a multiclass classification task for all classes. It is also not necessary to examine the negative cases and assign them to appropriate new or existing classes, especially when the labeling efforts outweigh the benefits it could bring to model development. With this approach, we make full use of the signals in the training data.

Apart from the multiclass positive (P) and negative (N) cases mentioned above, we also have the un-curated cases that do not come with labels, i.e. the U cases. We adopt an iterative semi-supervised approach to deal with them. The approach is described in Section 3.2.2.

3.2 Models

3.2.1 ALBERT

Following the pretraining-finetuning framework for language models, we start with a finetuned ALBERT. We simply remove the masked language model (MLM) head and the sentence order prediction (SOP) head from ALBERT and add a sequence classification head. Following the convention from (Devlin et al., 2019), the final hidden vector corresponding to the first input token [CLS] is used for classification. We denote this vector as the classification vector in the rest of the manuscript. We note that this ALBERT model is trained as a multiclass classification with only *positive* cases.

3.2.2 SS MT D/TAPT ALBERT

The pretrained language models are mostly trained on well-known corpora, such as Wikipedia, Common Crawl, BookCorpus, Reddit, etc. However, in many cases, we need to apply the language models to very different domains, like BioMed, scientific publication, or product reviews. For these types of problems, researchers have found that, in addition to finetuning on specific downstream tasks, it is beneficial to adapt the language models to the domain- and task-specific corpus, i.e. domain-adaptive pretraining (DAPT) and task-adaptive pretraining (TAPT) (Gururangan et al., 2020). This is achieved by further training the language modeling tasks, such as MLM, with the corpus of the domain and the task. We note that it can be difficult to rigorously define *domain* in NLP. For the DAPT training in this manuscript, we simply use customer contacts in the past few months as the domain corpus and follow the training recommendations from (Gururangan et al., 2020).

To make full use of the feedback from CSRs, we include the negatively confirmed cases and treat each class as a separate binary classification task in addition to the multiclass classification task. We accomplish the modeling with the multi-task (MT) learning paradigm (Liu et al., 2019). In this case, we have $n+1$ tasks, i.e. n binary classification tasks and 1 multiclass classification task. As illustrated on the left of Figure 2, we train the model in an end-to-end fashion. This means the $n+1$ tasks are finetuned jointly sharing the same encoder. We note that every positive sample belongs to two tasks (the multiclass classification task and one binary task) and each negative sample only belongs to the corresponding binary classification task. In inferencing time, as illustrated on the right of Figure 2, the model first processes the case text through the encoder to get the classification vector. Then the multiclass classification task consumes the vector and predicts the class. In the end, the same vector is routed to the binary task corresponding to that class, predicting the probability of the intent class accepted by the CSRs.

To make it more concrete, we can see the training loss implementation in Equation (1). y^b is the binary label, i.e. 1 means it is a positive sample and its intent class is confirmed by CSRs with "yes". l^m is the multiclass task loss. $\boldsymbol{y}^m$ is the one-hot encoded n-dimensional multiclass label vector. $\boldsymbol{l}^b$ is the loss function vector for n binary tasks. N is the number of samples. Typical cross-entropy loss is used for all tasks here.

$$\mathcal{L} = \frac{1}{N}\sum_{i=1}^{N}(y_i^b \cdot l_i^m + \boldsymbol{y}_i^m \cdot \boldsymbol{l}_i^b) \tag{1}$$

For the inferencing process, we refer to Equations (2)-(5). $\boldsymbol{x}$ is the tokenized sequence vector. $\boldsymbol{u}$ is the classification vector, i.e. the embedding vector for the CLS token. f^m is the multiclass classifier. f_k^b is the binary classifier for intent class k.

$$\boldsymbol{u} = Encoder(\boldsymbol{x}) \tag{2}$$

$$\hat{\boldsymbol{y}}^m = f^m(\boldsymbol{u}) \tag{3}$$

$$k = \arg\max_i \hat{\boldsymbol{y}}^m(i), i \in [0...n-1] \tag{4}$$

$$\hat{y}^b = f_k^b(\boldsymbol{u}) \tag{5}$$

Moreover, we add the semi-supervised (SS) strategy to take advantage of the un-curated data. While a large volume of model predictions are reviewed by the CSRs each second, we believe there are still a number of qualified cases that we miss. Therefore, we can train the model, make prediction on the un-curated cases, choose the high-confidence ones, and re-train the model with the labeled data plus the high-confidence cases. We follow this in an iterative manner until the improvement diminishes such that it cannot justify the training cost. We note that we only augment the data of the multiclass classification task and the data for the binary classification tasks remain unchanged throughout the iterative process. The same strategy is recently used by (Schick and Schütze, 2020) to create small language models that have similar performance to BERT and (Xie et al., 2020) to achieve state-of-the-art performance on Imagenet in computer vision.

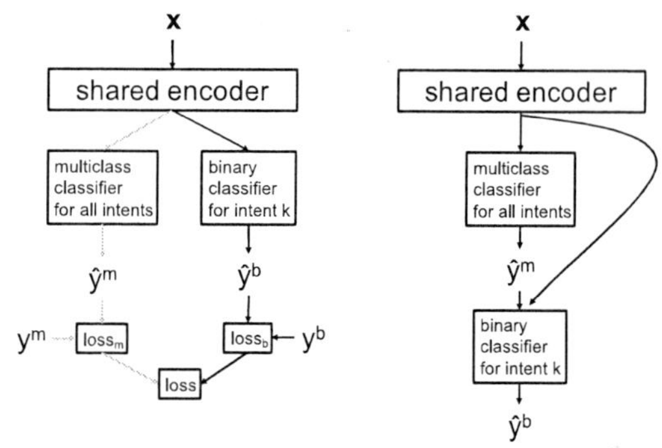

Figure 2: Training (left) and inferencing (right) for the multi-task learning strategy, where $k \in [0...n-1]$, and n is the number of intent classes. In training time, the green path is only executed when **x** is a positive sample.

Adding up the techniques described above, we denote this model as SS MT D/TAPT ALBERT.

4 Experiments and Results

4.1 Data and Experimental Setup

For confidentiality reasons, we can only share directional numbers about the training data. In this study, we consider 9 customer intent classes. The curated data is unbalanced among classes, ranging from a few thousand to tens of thousands of records per class. The class with the most samples is roughly 40 times as much as the class with the least samples. For each class, the ratio of positive-to-negative cases in the curated data is about 4. The un-curated data is roughly 20 times of the curated data. We use both the curated and un-curated data for DAPT and only curated data for TAPT. In the semi-supervision process, for each class, we select high-confidence samples from the un-curated data in each iteration to be roughly two to three times of the volume of the labeled samples in the curated data. Table 1 shows a few sample training data with dummy features and intents. The last column

Table 1: Sample training data and how different training strategies incorporate them.

Curation	Composition	Features	Targets		Training data for				
		Messages	Intents	CSR responses	Multiclass task	Binary tasks	DAPT	TAPT	SS
Curated	Positives	Could you help me?	General inquiry	Yes	Yes	Yes (+)	Yes	Yes	Yes
		How to setup account?	Account issue	Yes	Yes	Yes (+)	Yes	Yes	Yes
	Negatives	How much is this?	Account issue	No	No	Yes (-)	Yes	Yes	Yes
		Can you fix this issue?	General inquiry	No	No	Yes (-)	Yes	Yes	Yes
Un-curated	Unlabeled	What's this?	General inquiry	N/A	No	No	Yes	No	Yes
		Please help.	N/A	N/A	No	No	Yes	No	Yes

shows how different strategies incorporate them in training.

After being processed with the ALBERT tokenizer, the total data amounts to about 800 million tokens with an average of about 80 per sample. We performed all experiments on Sagemaker on AWS. We used 2 ml.p3.16xlarge instances with distributed data parallelism for DAPT and TAPT, 1 ml.p3.8xlarge instance for finetuning language models, and 1 ml.p3.8xlarge instance for batch inferencing testing data.

We hold out a portion of the data as development data to tune hyperparameters. We follow the suggestions from (Gururangan et al., 2020; Liu et al., 2019) for DAPT and TAPT and (Devlin et al., 2019) for finetuning. For the end-to-end multi-task learning process, we kept a unit weight for each task and did not explore different weight combinations. More research about tuning task weights in multi-task learning can be found in (Cipolla et al., 2018).

4.2 Evaluation

4.2.1 Pretrained models

In this section, we evaluate the performance of the pretrained language models, the out-of-the-box ALBERT and the D/TAPT ALBERT. We note that the pretrained language models are evaluated before any finetuning happens.

To visually demonstrate how the adaptive pretraining improves the clustering performance of the classification vector, we sample a couple thousand cases per class and apply t-SNE (Van Der Maaten and Hinton, 2008) to the reduced classification vector for each case. We reduce the dimension of the classification vectors from 768 to 50 with PCA to keep the computational cost of t-SNE in check. In Figure 3, we can see how clustering improves from the vanilla ALBERT on the left to D/TAPT ALBERT on the right.

To more quantitatively assess the performance of the off-the-shelf pretrained ALBERT and the D/TAPT ALBERT, we sample a couple thousand

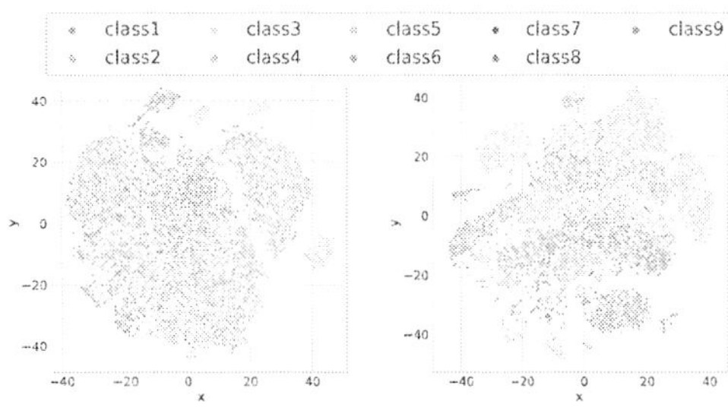

Figure 3: t-SNE plots using the dimension-reduced classification vectors from the off-the-shelf pretrained ALBERT (left) and the D/TAPT ALBERT (right).

Table 2: Average kNN prediction accuracy using the classification vectors from the pretrained models

ALBERT	D/TAPT ALBERT
0%	+33%

cases per class and use k-nearest-neighbor classifiers (kNN) to predict each sample's class based on its k neighbors. We use the Euclidean distance between the classification vector for each case as the similarity metric for kNN. We compute the average accuracy by varying k from 3 to 99 in interval of 2 and report it in Table 2. As a result, D/TAPT lifts the accuracy by more than 30 points compared to the vanilla ALBERT. Similar performance lift is also observed in (Reimers and Gurevych, 2019). This illustrates that D/TAPT can improve the clustering performance of the classification vector when the clustering rules are closely related to the domain corpus. The absolute accuracy values are not reported here for confidentiality reasons.

4.2.2 Finetuned models

In practice, for each class, we expect to route more positive cases and less negative cases to our CSRs with machine learning models. That means we expect our models to better differentiate positives from negatives for each class. Area Under the Curve - Receiver Operating Characteristics (AUC

Table 3: The average and sample-weighted average AUC ROC for different experiment settings

Model	avg AUC ROC	wavg AUC ROC
ALBERT	+0%	+0%
+ MT	+17.8%	+14.3%
+ MT DAPT	+18.4%	+ 15.8%
+ MT D/TAPT	+19.0%	+16.1%
+ SS MT D/TAPT	+19.9%	+17.0%

ROC) is a natural metric for such binary classification problem. We note that the commonly-used *accuracy* metric is not appropriate in this context since the negatives do not have ground truth labels in our data. The evaluation data is from recent few weeks. For confidentiality reasons, we hide the axis for AUC ROC and make the values relative to the baseline finetuned ALBERT model for each class.

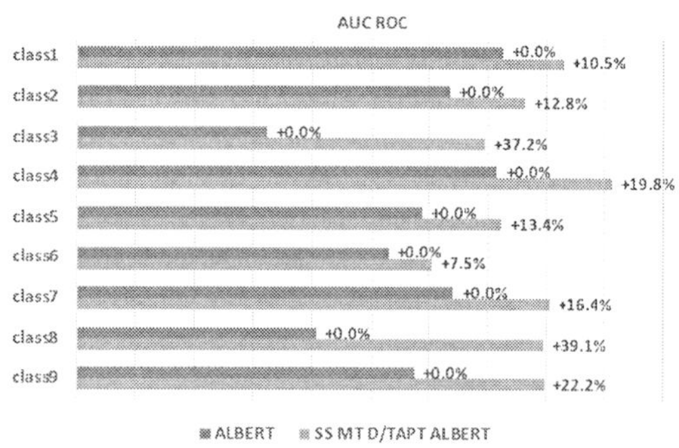

Figure 4: The AUC ROC of each class for finetuned ALBERT and SS MT D/TAPT ALBERT

In Figure 4, for each class, we can observe consistent improvement of SS MT D/TAPT ALBERT over finetuned ALBERT in terms of AUC ROC. Overall, the SS MT D/TAPT ALBERT model brings 19.9 points increase in average AUC ROC and 17 points increase in sample-weighted average AUC ROC, compared to the finetuned ALBERT model.

Furthermore, it is interesting to see how each strategy in the SS MT D/TAPT ALBERT model contributes to the performance improvement. In Table 3, we show the average and sample-weighted average AUC ROC improvement by incrementally adding one strategy at a time. We can see that the MT strategy boosts the average AUC ROC by 17.8 points and the sample-weighted average AUC ROC by 14.3 points, compared to the finetuned ALBERT. This demonstrates the effectiveness of including negative signals with MT strategy. On top of MT, we apply DAPT, D/TAPT and SS incrementally. Each strategy pushes up the average and sample-weighted average AUC ROC by roughly 1 point.

5 Discussion

Apart from processing the dismissed recommendations with this multi-task setting, there is another heuristic approach that is commonly adopted under this circumstance. We can group all the dismissed recommendations into an extra bucket *Others* (Fotso et al., 2018). The advantage of this approach is that we can pose the problem as a straightforward multiclass classification. The disadvantage is that the dismissed recommendations can either be mis-classified and belong to other existing classes, or belong to unknown classes that might be included in the future taxonomy. In the former scenario, the dismissed recommendations create noise for their true class and the *Others* class; In the latter scenario, the dismissed recommendations can seemingly improve performance for current taxonomy, while they can pollute the future training when the unknown classes are launched in the updated taxonomy. In both scenarios, grouping the dismissed recommendations into *Others* can negatively impact the training.

In terms of computational cost, both adaptive pretraining and semi-supervision consume a considerable amount of power, since the former is typically trained on the MLM task through a large corpus and the latter is a iterative finetuning and inferencing process where the data for inferencing are often in large volume. In the meantime, the MT strategy is a cost-effective way to improve model performance by considering negative samples. By examining Table 3, compared to the baseline finetuned ALBERT, we can see the MT strategy increases the average AUC ROC by 17.8 points while D/TAPT and SS add 2.1 points on top of that. The additional cost for the MT strategy, compared to the typical multiclass classification strategy, is simply a binary classifier for each class. It is negligible in both training and inferencing.

For the sake of easy implementation of the end-to-end multi-task training, we only feed the training data related to one task in each batch. In this way, we can keep the loss function for each task separate. It is possible that including data for various tasks in each batch can bring benefits to training. This assumption can be explored in future studies.

This study is only concerned with corpus in English. Similar modeling strategies can be followed for other high-resource languages which we have ample training data. However, as in the customer service departments of most global organizations, it is common to receive customer contacts in various low-resource languages, in which case the training data is scarce. Recent advances in cross-lingual language models, such as mBERT (Devlin et al., 2019), XLM (Conneau and Lample, 2019), Unicoder (Huang et al., 2019) and FILTER (Fang et al., 2020), can shed light on this situation and we plan to investigate it in the future.

In the area of customer support, both (Molino et al., 2018) and (Fotso et al., 2018) propose neural networks that combine unstructured text features from customers' messages and structured features describing customers' interaction with the platforms. They empirically demonstrated benefits of including the latter feature group. The next step for our study is to evaluate the influence of the customer-website interaction features, when combining with advanced language models.

For the model candidates with multi-task strategy in this manuscript, we train all tasks jointly with an end-to-end multi-task deep learning approach, as described in the left plot of Figure 2. We want to point out the isolating effect of the end-to-end training approach. In one experiment, we trained the tasks independently, i.e. we first trained the multiclass classification task with the off-the-shelf ALBERT, and then, for the binary tasks, we trained n logistic regression binary classifiers with the classification vector from the multiclass classification task. We still achieved 12.2 and 8.2 points above the baseline in terms of average AUC ROC and sample-weighted average AUC ROC. On one hand, this shows that even training simpler models independently can still bring performance lifts, thus emphasizing the powerful signal brought by the negative cases; On the other hand, if compared to the ALBERT + MT model in Table 3, it also shows the benefits of end-to-end training.

As in most machine learning applications, the actual model performance is determined by the choice of the operational point for each intent class and the operational point is determined from the precision-recall (PR) curve. For the sake of brevity, we ignore the PR plots because, for each class, the PR curve of the baseline ALBERT model is well under the envelop of the PR curve of the SS MT D/TAPT ALBERT model. This is expected due to the large boost presented in Figure 4. We note that the AUC ROC can be a decent indication of AUC PR when the data is not so skewed (Davis and Goadrich, 2006). Therefore, the SS MT D/TAPT ALBERT indeed outperforms the baseline for every choice of operational point.

6 Conclusion

In this manuscript, we demonstrated and discussed the model performance improvement brought by multi-task learning, adaptive pretraining for ALBERT, and semi-supervised learning in the application of customer support on an e-commerce website. We observe $\sim$20 points performance increase in average AUC ROC when comparing the final model to the baseline multiclass classification model. This paradigm can be particularly helpful when there is a feedback system collecting confirmation from labelers. Future studies can extend this paradigm to more complex situations, such as when the intent taxonomy is deeply hierarchical or considering more feedback information than simple "yes" or "no".

Acknowledgments

The authors wish to thank Harsha Aduri and Jieyi Jiang for providing support in data preparation, Jasmine Qi and Ilknur Egilmez for providing comments for the manuscript. We also thank the anonymous reviewers for their valuable suggestions.

References

Roberto Cipolla, Yarin Gal, and Alex Kendall. 2018. Multi-task Learning Using Uncertainty to Weigh Losses for Scene Geometry and Semantics. In *2018 IEEE/CVF Conference on Computer Vision and Pattern Recognition*, pages 7482–7491, Salt Lake City, UT, USA.

Kevin Clark, Minh-Thang Luong, Quoc V. Le, and Christopher D. Manning. 2020. ELECTRA: Pre-training Text Encoders as Discriminators Rather Than Generators. *arXiv preprint*.

Alexis Conneau and Guillaume Lample. 2019. Cross-lingual Language Model Pretraining. In *Advances in Neural Information Processing Systems*, volume 32, pages 7059–7069. Curran Associates, Inc.

Jesse Davis and Mark Goadrich. 2006. The relationship between precision-recall and ROC curves. In *ACM International Conference Proceeding Series*, volume 148, pages 233–240.

Alexandra DeLucia and Elisabeth Moore. 2020. Analyzing HPC Support Tickets: Experience and Recommendations. *arXiv preprint*.

Jacob Devlin, Ming-Wei Chang, Kenton Lee, and Kristina Toutanova. 2019. BERT: Pre-training of Deep Bidirectional Transformers for Language Understanding. In *Proceedings of the 2019 Conference of the North American Chapter of the Association for Computational Linguistics: Human Language Technologies, Volume 1 (Long and Short Papers)*, pages 4171–4186, Minneapolis, Minnesota. Association for Computational Linguistics.

Charles Elkan and Keith Noto. 2008. Learning Classifiers from Only Positive and Unlabeled Data. In *Proceedings of the 14th ACM SIGKDD International Conference on Knowledge Discovery and Data Mining*, KDD '08, pages 213–220, New York, NY, USA. Association for Computing Machinery.

Yuwei Fang, Shuohang Wang, Zhe Gan, Siqi Sun, and Jingjing Liu. 2020. FILTER: An Enhanced Fusion Method for Cross-lingual Language Understanding. *arXiv preprint*.

Geli Fei and Bing Liu. 2015. Social Media Text Classification under Negative Covariate Shift. In *Proceedings of the 2015 Conference on Empirical Methods in Natural Language Processing*, pages 2347–2356, Lisbon, Portugal. Association for Computational Linguistics.

Stephane Fotso, Philip Spanoudes, Benjamin C. Ponedel, Brian Reynoso, and Janet Ko. 2018. Attention fusion networks: Combining behavior and E-mail content to improve customer support. *arXiv preprint*.

Zhenxin Fu, Shaobo Cui, Mingyue Shang, Feng Ji, Dongyan Zhao, Haiqing Chen, and Rui Yan. 2020. Context-to-Session Matching: Utilizing Whole Session for Response Selection in Information-Seeking Dialogue Systems. In *Proceedings of the ACM SIGKDD International Conference on Knowledge Discovery and Data Mining*, volume 20, pages 1605–1613.

Narendra Gupta, Mazin Gilbert, and Giuseppe Di Fabbrizio. 2010. Emotion Detection in Email Customer Care. In *Proceedings of the NAACL HLT 2010 Workshop on Computational Approaches to Analysis and Generation of Emotion in Text*, pages 10–16, Los Angeles, CA. Association for Computational Linguistics.

Narendra Gupta, Gokhan Tur, Dilek Hakkani-Tur, Srinivas Bangalore, Giuseppe Riccardi, and Mazin Gilbert. 2006. The AT&T spoken language understanding system. *IEEE Transactions on Audio, Speech, and Language Processing*, 14(1):213–222.

Suchin Gururangan, Ana Marasović, Swabha Swayamdipta, Kyle Lo, Iz Beltagy, Doug Downey, and Noah A Smith. 2020. Don't Stop Pretraining: Adapt Language Models to Domains and Tasks. In *Proceedings of the 58th Annual Meeting of the Association for Computational Linguistics*, pages 8342–8360, Online. Association for Computational Linguistics.

Yu-Guan Hsieh, Gang Niu, and Masashi Sugiyama. 2019. Classification from Positive, Unlabeled and Biased Negative Data. In *Proceedings of the 36th International Conference on Machine Learning*, volume 97 of *Proceedings of Machine Learning Research*, pages 2820–2829, Long Beach, CA, USA. PMLR.

Haoyang Huang, Yaobo Liang, Nan Duan, Ming Gong, Linjun Shou, Daxin Jiang, and Ming Zhou. 2019. Unicoder: A Universal Language Encoder by Pretraining with Multiple Cross-lingual Tasks. In *Proceedings of the 2019 Conference on Empirical Methods in Natural Language Processing and the 9th International Joint Conference on Natural Language Processing (EMNLP-IJCNLP)*, pages 2485–2494, Hong Kong, China. Association for Computational Linguistics.

Schubert Cheung Hui and G. Jha. 2000. Data mining for customer service support. *Information and Management*, 38(1):1–13.

Guokun Lai, Qizhe Xie, Hanxiao Liu, Yiming Yang, and Eduard Hovy. 2017. RACE: Large-scale ReAding comprehension dataset from examinations. In *Proceedings of the 2017 Conference on Empirical Methods in Natural Language Processing*, pages 785–794, Copenhagen, Denmark. Association for Computational Linguistics.

Zhenzhong Lan, Mingda Chen, Sebastian Goodman, Kevin Gimpel, Piyush Sharma, and Radu Soricut. 2019. Albert: A lite bert for self-supervised learning of language representations. *arXiv preprint*.

Xiao-Li Li, Bing Liu, and See-Kiong Ng. 2010. Negative Training Data Can be Harmful to Text Classification. In *Proceedings of the 2010 Conference on Empirical Methods in Natural Language Processing*, 11, pages 218–228, Cambridge, MA, USA. Association for Computational Linguistics.

Xiaodong Liu, Pengcheng He, Weizhu Chen, and Jianfeng Gao. 2019. Multi-Task Deep Neural Networks for Natural Language Understanding. In *Proceedings of the 57th Annual Meeting of the Association for Computational Linguistics*, pages 4487–4496, Florence, Italy. Association for Computational Linguistics.

Senthil Mani, Neelamadhav Gantayat, Rahul Aralikatte, Monika Gupta, Sampath Dechu, Anush Sankaran, Shreya Khare, Barry Mitchell, Hemamalini Subramanian, and Hema Venkatarangan. 2018. Hi, How Can I Help You?: Automating Enterprise IT Support Help Desks. In *Proceedings of the Thirty-Second AAAI Conference on Artificial Intelligence, (AAAI-18), the 30th innovative Applications of Artificial Intelligence (IAAI-18), and the 8th AAAI Symposium on Educational Advances in Artificial Intelligence (EAAI-18)*, pages 7688–7695, New Orleans, Louisiana, USA, February 2-7, 2018. AAAI Press.

Piero Molino, Huaixiu Zheng, and Yi Chia Wang. 2018. COTA: Improving the speed and accuracy of customer support through ranking and deep networks. *Proceedings of the ACM SIGKDD International Conference on Knowledge Discovery and Data Mining*, 4:586–595.

Michael Powell, Jamison A Rotz, and Kevin D O'Malley. 2020. How Machine Learning Is Improving U.S. Navy Customer Support. In *Proceedings of the AAAI Conference on Artificial Intelligence*, volume 34, pages 13188–13195.

Pranav Rajpurkar, Jian Zhang, Konstantin Lopyrev, and Percy Liang. 2016. SQuad: 100,000+ questions for machine comprehension of text. In *Proceedings of the 2016 Conference on Empirical Methods in Natural Language Processing*, pages 2383–2392, Austin, Texas. Association for Computational Linguistics.

Alan Ramponi and Barbara Plank. 2020. Neural Unsupervised Domain Adaptation in NLP—A Survey. *arXiv preprint*.

Nils Reimers and Iryna Gurevych. 2019. Sentence-BERT: Sentence Embeddings using Siamese BERT-Networks. In *Proceedings of the 2019 Conference on Empirical Methods in Natural Language Processing and the 9th International Joint Conference on Natural Language Processing (EMNLP-IJCNLP)*, pages 3982–3992, Hong Kong, China. Association for Computational Linguistics.

Victor Sanh, Lysandre Debut, Julien Chaumond, and Thomas Wolf. 2019. DistilBERT, a distilled version of BERT: smaller, faster, cheaper and lighter. *arXiv preprint*.

Ruhi Sarikaya, Geoffrey E Hinton, and Bhuvana Ramabhadran. 2011. Deep belief nets for natural language call-routing. In *2011 IEEE International Conference on Acoustics, Speech and Signal Processing (ICASSP)*, pages 5680–5683, Prague, Czech Republic. IEEE.

Timo Schick and Hinrich Schütze. 2020. It's Not Just Size That Matters: Small Language Models Are Also Few-Shot Learners. *arXiv preprint*.

Laurens Van Der Maaten and Geoffrey Hinton. 2008. Visualizing data using t-SNE. *Journal of Machine Learning Research*, 9:2579–2625.

Alex Wang, Yada Pruksachatkun, Nikita Nangia, Amanpreet Singh, Julian Michael, Felix Hill, Omer Levy, and Samuel Bowman. 2019a. SuperGLUE: A Stickier Benchmark for General-Purpose Language Understanding Systems. In *Advances in Neural Information Processing Systems*, volume 32, pages 3266–3280. Curran Associates, Inc.

Alex Wang, Amanpreet Singh, Julian Michael, Felix Hill, Omer Levy, and Samuel Bowman. 2018. GLUE: A multi-task benchmark and analysis platform for natural language understanding. In *Proceedings of the 2018 EMNLP Workshop BlackboxNLP: Analyzing and Interpreting Neural Networks for NLP*, pages 353–355, Brussels, Belgium. Association for Computational Linguistics.

Wei Wang, Bin Bi, Ming Yan, Chen Wu, Zuyi Bao, Jiangnan Xia, Liwei Peng, and Luo Si. 2019b. StructBERT: Incorporating Language Structures into Pre-training for Deep Language Understanding. *arXiv preprint*.

Thomas Wolf, Lysandre Debut, Victor Sanh, Julien Chaumond, Clement Delangue, Anthony Moi, Pierric Cistac, Tim Rault, Rémi Louf, Morgan Funtowicz, and Jamie Brew. 2019. Transformers: State-of-the-art natural language processing. *arXiv preprint*.

Patrick Xia, Shijie Wu, and Benjamin Van Durme. 2020. Which *BERT? A Survey Organizing Contextualized Encoders. *arXiv preprint*.

Qizhe Xie, Minh-Thang Luong, Eduard Hovy, and Quoc V. Le. 2020. Self-Training With Noisy Student Improves ImageNet Classification. In *2020 IEEE/CVF Conference on Computer Vision and Pattern Recognition (CVPR)*, pages 10684–10695, Seattle, WA, USA.

Puyang Xu and Ruhi Sarikaya. 2013. Convolutional neural network based triangular CRF for joint intent detection and slot filling. In *2013 IEEE Workshop on Automatic Speech Recognition and Understanding*, pages 78–83, Olomouc, Czech Republic. IEEE.

Yixing Xu, Chang Xu, Chao Xu, and Dacheng Tao. 2017. Multi-Positive and Unlabeled Learning. In *Proceedings of the Twenty-Sixth International Joint Conference on Artificial Intelligence, (IJCAI-17)*, pages 3182–3188, Melbourne, Australia.

Zhilin Yang, Zihang Dai, Yiming Yang, Jaime Carbonell, Ruslan Russ R Salakhutdinov, and Quoc V Le. 2019. XLNet: Generalized Autoregressive Pretraining for Language Understanding. In *Advances in Neural Information Processing Systems*, volume 32, pages 5753–5763, Vancouver, Canada. Curran Associates, Inc.

"Are you calling for the vaporizer you ordered?" Combining Search and Prediction to Identify Orders in Contact Centers

Abinaya K
Flipkart Data Science
Bangalore, India
abinaya.k@flipkart.com

Shourya Roy
Flipkart Data Science
Bangalore, India
shourya.roy@flipkart.com

Abstract

With the growing footprint of ecommerce worldwide, the role of contact center is becoming increasingly crucial for customer satisfaction. To effectively handle scale and manage operational cost, automation through chatbots and voice-bots are getting rapidly adopted. With customers having multiple, often long list of active orders - the first task of a voice-bot is to identify which one they are calling about. Towards solving this problem which we refer to as *order identification*, we propose a two-staged real-time technique by combining search and prediction in a sequential manner. In the first stage, analogous to retrieval-based question-answering, a fuzzy search technique uses customized lexical and phonetic similarity measures on noisy transcripts of calls to retrieve the order of interest. The coverage of fuzzy search is limited by no or limited response from customers to voice prompts. Hence, in the second stage, a predictive solution that predicts the most likely order a customer is calling about based on certain features of orders is introduced. We compare with multiple relevant techniques based on word embeddings as well as ecommerce product search to show that the proposed approach provides the best performance with 64% coverage and 87% accuracy on a large real-life data-set. A system based on the proposed technique is also deployed in production for a fraction of calls landing in the contact center of a large ecommerce provider; providing real evidence of operational benefits as well as increased customer delight.

1 Introduction

With increasing penetration of ecommerce, reliance on and importance of contact centers is increasing. While emails and automated chat-bots are gaining popularity, voice continues to be the overwhelming preferred communication medium leading to millions of phone calls landing at contact centers. Handling such high volume of calls by human agents leads to hiring and maintaining a large employee base. Additionally, managing periodic peaks (owing to sale periods, festive seasons etc.) as well as hiring, training, monitoring make the entire process a demanding operation. To address these challenges as well as piggybacking on recent progress of NLP and Dialog Systems research, voice-bots are gaining popularity. Voice-bot is a common name of automated dialog systems built to conduct task-oriented conversations with callers. They are placed as the first line of response to address customer concerns and only on failure, the calls are transferred to human agents. Goodness of voice-bots, measured by automation rate, is proportional to the fraction of calls it can handle successfully end-to-end.

Customers' contacts in ecommerce domain are broadly about two types viz. for general enquiry about products before making a purchase and post purchase issue resolution; with overwhelming majority of contacts are of the latter type. For post purchase contacts, one of the first information that a voice-bot needs to gather is which product the customer is calling about. The most common practice has been to enumerate all products she has purchased, say in a reverse chronological order, and asking her to respond with her choice by pressing a numeric key. This is limiting in two important ways. Firstly, it limits the scope to a maximum of ten products which is insufficient in a large fraction of cases. Secondly and more importantly, listening to a long announcement of product titles to select one is a time-consuming and tedious customer experience.

In this paper, we introduce the problem of *order identification* and propose a technique to identify or predict the product of interest for which a cus-

Proceedings of the 4th Workshop on e-Commerce and NLP (ECNLP 4), pages 58–69
August 5, 2021.

Fuzzy Search		Predictive Model	
Customer Utterance	**Product titles of active orders with fuzzy search match**	**Product titles of active orders with top-1 match from predictive model**	**Top-k features for the prediction**
`maine order kiya tha to toner 25 ke dikha to uska`	[Aiwa Professional 102 //00 High Quality 40 PCS Socket Set, Hidelink Men Brown Genuine Leather Wallet, CEDO XPRO Edge To Edge Tempered Glass for Realme XT, Realme X2, **Protoner 25 kg PVC weight with 4 rods and Flat bench Home Gym Combo**]	[Sonata 77085PP02 Volt Analog Watch - For Men, Oxhox HBS-730 Wireless compatible with 4G redmi Headset with Mic Bluetooth Headset, **MyTech With Charger M3 Smart Band Fitness Band**]	*number of days since return initiation, Selling Price, is incident created in last 2 days?*
`i can 2000 green color mobile phone`	[Surat Dream Portable Mini Sewing Machine Handheld Handy Stitch Machine Manual Cordless Electric Stitching Machine Electric Sewing Machine, **I Kall K1000 (Green, 64 GB)**, I Kall K1000 (Blue, 64 GB)]	[**Whirlpool 7.5 kg 5 Star, Hard Water wash Fully Automatic Top Load Grey**, Asian Running Shoes For Women]	*days since incident creation, days since last chat, rank wrt selling price*
`blue 2 dead phone ke liye`	[Hardys Full Sleeve Solid Men Jacket, Brawo Party Wear Party Wear For Men, **T GOOD Lite SH12 Bluetooth Headset, T GOOD Lite SH12 Bluetooth Headset,** SPINOZA Pink diamond studded attractive butterfly stylish women Analog Watch - For Girls]	[Ncert Chemistry Class 12 (Part 1 And 2) Combo 2 Book (K.C.G), **STROM COLLECTION Men Formal Black Genuine Leather Belt**, OPPO F15 (Blazing Blue, 128 GB)]	*is cancelled?, is incident created in last 2 days?, number of days since return initiation*

Table 1: Examples of top matches from fuzzy search and predictive model. The first column shows transcribed customer utterances and the second column shows all active orders at the time of the call with the top match from fuzzy search emphasized. The examples under Predictive Model shows the most likely order at the time of the call along with top-k features leading to the prediction.

tomer has contacted the contact center[1]. We do it in a natural and efficient manner based on minimal or no explicit additional input from the customer through a novel combination of two complementary approaches viz. **search** and **prediction**. The system is not restricted by the number of products purchased even over a long time period. It has been shown to be highly accurate with 87% accuracy and over 65% coverage in a real-life and noisy environment.

After customer verification, a question was introduced in the voice-bot flow "`Which product you are calling about?`". Her response was recorded and transcribed by an automatic speech recognition (ASR) system to text in real-time. We modeled the **search** problem as a task to retrieve the most matching product considering this response as a query over the search space of all active products represented as a set of product attributes e.g. title, description, brand, color, author etc. While simple in formulation, the task offers a few practical challenges. Customers do not describe their products in a standard manner or as it is described in the product catalog. For example, to describe a *"SAMSUNG Galaxy F41 (Fusion Blue, 128 GB) (6 GB RAM)"* phone, they may say *F41*, *Galaxy F41*, *mobile*, *phone*, *mobile phone*, *cellphone*, *Samsung mobile*, etc. (more examples can be seen in Table1). Secondly, the responses from customers varied widely from being heavily code-mixed to having only fillers (*ummms*, *aahs*, *whats* etc.) to blank responses. This is complemented owing to the background noise as well as imperfections in ASR systems. Finally, in a not so uncommon scenario, often customers' active orders include multiple instances of the same product, minor variations thereof (e.g. in color), or related products which share many attributes (e.g. *charger* for *"SAMSUNG Galaxy F41 (Fusion Blue, 128 GB) (6 GB RAM)"*) which are indistinguishable from their response to the prompt.

We propose an unsupervised n-gram based *fuzzy search* based on a round of pre-processing followed by custom lexical and phonetic similarity metrics.

[1] We use the terms order and product interchangably to mean different things customers have purchased.

In spite of its simplicity, this solution achieves 32% coverage with an accuracy of 87%, leveraging the relatively small search space. The custom nature of this solution achieves much higher accuracy compared to more sophisticated general purpose product search available on ecommerce mobile apps and websites. This simple technique also does not require additional steps such as named entity recognition (NER) which has been used for product identification related work in literature (Wen et al., 2019). Additionally, NER systems' performance are comparatively poor on ASR transcripts owing to high degree of recognition and lexical noise (e.g. missing capitalization etc) (Yadav et al., 2020).

While fuzzy search works with high accuracy, its coverage is limited owing to various mentioned noise in the data. We observed that about 25% of callers did not answer when asked to identify the product they were calling about. To overcome this challenge, we introduced a complementary solution based on *predictive modeling* which does not require explicit utterances from customers. In simple words, the model creates a ranking of active orders on the basis of likelihood of a customer calling about them. This is based on the intuition that certain characteristics of orders make them more likely to call about e.g. a return, an orders which was supposed to be delivered on the day of calling etc. Based on such features of orders and customer profile, a random forest model gives prediction accuracy of 72%, 88% and 94% at top-1, 2, and 3. For high confidence predictions, the voice-bot's prompt is changed to "`Are you calling for the <PRODUCT-NAME> you ordered?`" For right predictions, not only it reduces the duration of the call, also increases customer delight by the personalized experience. In combination, fuzzy search and predictive model cover 64.70% of all voice-bot calls with an accuracy of 87.18%.

Organization of the paper: The rest of the paper is organized as follows. Section 2 narrates the background of order identification for voice-bot, sections 3 discusses the proposed approach and sections 4 and 5 discuss the datasets used in our study and experiments respectively. Section 6 briefs some of the literature related to our work before concluding in section 7.

2 Background

A typical call flow of the voice-bot would start with greeting followed by identity verification, order identification and confirmation to issue identi-

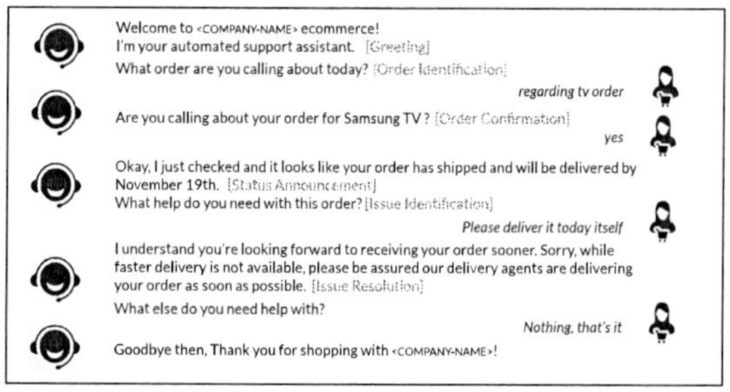

Figure 1: Sample conversation between voice-bot and the customer.

fication and finally issue resolution or transfer to human agent if needed. Figure 1 shows a sample conversation between a bot and a customer with multiple active orders, where the customer is asked to identify the order she called for.

Customers' responses to this question are transcribed to text in real-time using an ASR model. There were some practical difficulties in identifying the corresponding order from the transcribed customer utterances. When asked to identify the order, customers were not sure what they had to talk about, resulting in generic responses like *'hello'*, *'hai'*, *'okay'*, etc. in around 23% of the calls. Some customers straightaway mentioned about the issue instead of describing the product - for eg., *'refund order'*, *'order return karne ke liye call kiya hai'*, *'mix match pick up cancel'*, etc. We also noticed a prevalence of blank transcripts in around 22% of the calls, mostly from customers who have interacted with the voice-bot in the past. We believe this is due to the change in the call flow of voice-bot from what they have experienced in the past. Another major challenge comes from the ASR errors especially in the context of code-mixed utterances. The transcription noise especially on product tokens (*'mam record'* for *'memory card'*, *'both tropage'* for *'boAt Rockerz'*) made it more difficult to identify the right order. Also by nature of ASR, various lexical signals like capitalization, punctuation are absent in the ASR transcribed text, thereby making the task of order search more challenging.

After the order is identified or predicted, the customer is asked to confirm the chosen order. The customer can confirm positively and continue the conversation with the voice-bot or respond negatively and fallback to human agents. The ideal expectation from order search is to return a single matching order but in cases where multiple similar products exist, the voice-bot may prompt again to help disambiguate.

3 Proposed Approach

We propose to solve the problem of order identification through two steps. In the first phase (fuzzy search), we model the problem as a retrieval-based question-answering task where customer utterance is the query and the set of active orders of the customer is the search space. Towards solving this, we employ a sequence of matching techniques leveraging lexical and phonetic similarities. In the second phase (order prediction), we build a supervised learning model to predict the likelihood of the customer calling regarding different active orders. This later phase does not depend on customer utterances and hence does not get affected by transcription inaccuracies. Both of these approaches are discussed in detail in this section.

3.1 Fuzzy Search

Given the customer utterance and the product attributes of the active orders, fuzzy search proceeds in multiple rounds of textual similarity measures like direct, partial and phonetic match to retrieve the corresponding order, customer called for. These stages are invoked sequentially until a matching order is found. Sequentiality is introduced in fuzzy search in order to maximize the coverage while keeping the false positives low. Various stages involved in fuzzy search is shown in appendix A. Various stages in fuzzy search are detailed below. We use the terms {*token* and *word*} and {*utterance* and *query*} interchangeably.

3.1.1 Pre-processing

We observed prevalence of generic texts like *hello, haan, ok* in the customer utterances, which are of no use in retrieving the order. Hence, such commonly used tokens are to be removed from the query. Also, by nature of ASR, acronyms are transcribed as single letter split words for eg., *a c* for *AC*, *t v* for *TV*, etc. We followed the pre-processing steps as below.

- Removal of generic tokens: The commonly used tokens are identified by taking top 5% of frequently spoken tokens and are manually examined to ensure no product specific terms are removed.

- Handle split words: The split words are handled by joining continuous single letter words.

After these pre-processing steps, some of the customer utterances containing only the generic tokens would become blank, such cases are considered to have no match from the active orders. For non blank processed queries, we use the following similarity measures to identify the matching order(s).

Let q denote the pre-processed customer query composed of query tokens. Let $\{p_i\}_{i=1}^{P}$ denotes list of active orders where p_i denote the product title corresponding to i^{th} order. Product titles are typically concatenation of brand, model name, color, etc- *'Redmi Note 9 Pro (Aurora Blue, 128 GB) (4 GB RAM)'*, *'Lakme Eyeconic Kajal (Royal Blue, 0.35 g)'* are some sample product titles.

3.1.2 Direct Match

The objective of direct match is to handle relatively easier queries, where customer utterance contains product information and is transcribed without any noise. Direct Match looks for exact text matches between query tokens and the tokens of product title. Each product is assigned a score basis the fraction of query tokens that matches with tokens from the corresponding product title. Score for the ith product is obtained as

$$s_i = \frac{1}{|q|} \sum_{x:q} \mathbb{1}_{\{y:y \in p_i, y==x\}!=\phi}$$

where $\mathbb{1}_x$ indicates the indicator function which is 1 if x is true else 0. Product(s) with the maximum score are considered the possible candidate products for a direct match. Direct match between the query and any of the products is said to occur in the following cases.

- Score of 1 would indicate that the product title includes all query tokens. Hence if the maximum score is 1, all product(s) with the score of 1 are returned by direct match.
- If the max score is less than 1, direct match is limited to single candidate retrieval so as to avoid false positive due to similar products in the active orders.

3.1.3 Partial Match

In order to handle partial utterances of product names by the customers and to account for ASR errors in product specific terms of customer utterances, partial match is introduced. For example, partial product utterances like *'fridge'* for *'refrigerator"*, *'watch'* for *'smart watch'* and ASR misspelled utterances like *'sandel'* for *'sandal'*, would be handled by partial match. Algorithm 1 elucidates various steps in partial matching. It uses partial similarity (Sim) between the n-grams from query and the product titles. We start with individual tokens and then move to bigram, trigram, etc till 4-gram. Match at a higher n is clearly more promising than a lower n. For eg, a customer could ask for 'JBL wired headset' and the active orders could include *'boAt Wired Headset'* and a *'JBL Wired Headset'*. In such cases, token similarity or bigram similarity might treat both of these headsets as matching orders, however trigram similarity would result in a correct match. i.e., for cases with similar products in the active orders, going for a higher n would help reduce the false positives if customer had specified additional details to narrow the order.

Algorithm 1: n-gram based partial match

Result: R

$R = \phi, Q_0^{'} = q$

for $n = \{1,2,3,4\}$ **do**

  $Q_n = ngrams^{'}(q, n, Q_{n-1}^{'})$

  $Q_n^{'} = \phi$

  for $i=1:P$ **do**

    $P_{in} = ngrams(p_i, n)$

    $s_i = \frac{1}{|Q_n|} \sum_{x:Q_n} \mathbb{1}_{\{y:y \in P_{in}, Sim(x,y)>\theta\}!=\phi}$

    $Q_n^{'} = Q_n^{'} \cup \{x \in Q_n : \{y \in P_{in} : Sim(x,y) > \theta\}! = \phi\}$

  $\hat{p} = \{p_i : s_i == max(s_i), max(s_i)! = 0\}$

  if $|\hat{p}| == 1$ *or* $max(s_i) == 1$ **then**

    $R = \hat{p}$

Let $Q_n^{'}$ refer to the n-grams in query string that had a match with any of the product n-grams, $ngrams$ represent a function to return all possible n-grams of input string and $ngrams^{'}$ return the surrounding n-grams of $Q_{n-1}^{'}$. For $n \geq 2$, Q_n would only contain n-grams with one or more product tokens. At a particular n, we obtain a similarity score s_i for each active order, based on the proportion of n-grams in Q_n, that finds a match with n-grams in corresponding product titles and the orders with maximum score are considered candidate orders $(\hat{p})$ for successful match. At any n, matching order(s) is said to have found if n-grams from any order finds a match with all n-grams included in Q_n i.e., $max(s_i) == 1$ or when there is only one candidate product i.e., $|\hat{p}| == 1$.

If none of the products finds a match at higher n, the matched products as of level $n-1$ is considered. A threshold on the similarity measure is imposed to indicate whether two n-grams match.

3.1.4 Phonetic Match

ASR errors on product specific tokens imposes additional challenges in identifying the corresponding order. For example, *'in clinics hot 94'* for *'Infinix Hot 9 Pro'*, *'mam record'* for *'memory card'*, *'double back'* for *duffel bag*, etc. To handle such queries, we consider similarity between phonetic representations of n-grams of product title with that of customer utterance. Algorithmically, phonetic match works similar to fuzzy match (as in algorithm 1), with the important difference the similarity score (Sim) is on phonetic representation of n-grams. With this, strings like *'mam record'*, *'memory card'*, *'double back'*, *duffel bag* are mapped to *'MANRACAD'*, *'MANARACAD'*, *'DABLABAC'* and *'DAFALBAG'* respectively. Clearly, the noisy transcribed tokens are much closer to the original product tokens in the phonetic space.

3.2 Order Prediction

The objective of this step is to build a predictive model for ranking of active orders based on the likelihood of why a customer is calling. We formulate it as a classification problem on active orders and learn a binary classifier to predict the likelihood of customer calling for each order.

3.2.1 Feature Engineering:

The features used in the model are broadly categorized into 4 categories, i.e., order specific, transaction specific, product specific and self serve related features.

- **Order-specific** features includes *order status, is delivery due today?, is pickup pending?, Is Refund issued?* , etc. These features are specific to the time when customer calls.
- **Transaction-specific** features include *price of the product, shipping charges, order payment type*, etc
- **Product-specific** features include product attributes like *brand, vertical, is this a large item?* , etc. These features are not dependent on the time of the customer call.
- **Self-serve** features like *number of days since last chat conversation, number of days since last incident creation*, etc.

It is important to note that the likelihood of a customer calling for an order is highly related to the features of other active orders of the customer. For example, the chances of customer calling for an order that just got shipped are less when there is another order whose refund is pending for a long time. The formulation by default doesn't consider the relationship among features of other active orders. Hence this is overcome by creating derived features that brings in the relative ordering between features of active orders of a customer. Some of derived features include rank of the order with respect to ordered date (customers are more likely to call for a recent order than older ones), if refund is pending for any other order, if there are existing complaints for other orders etc.

Preprocessing: Together with these derived features, we have a total of 42 features mix of categorical and numerical. Low cardinality features like order status are one hot encoded, high cardinality features like brand, category, etc are label encoded and the numerical features are standard normalized. The labels available in our dataset is at a call level. Since the classification is at an order level, the label is assigned 1 or 0 depending on whether it's the order the customer called for.

3.2.2 Model Details

In order to learn a binary classifier for order prediction, we experiment with various standard machine learning models like Logistic regression, tree based ensemble model like Random Forest and deep learning models like Deep Neural Network (DNN). As a baseline, we compare with the reverse chronological ranking of orders with respect to date of order. Various hyper parameters involved in these models are tuned using grid search. More details on the range of hyper parameters considered and the chosen best hyper parameter is available in appendix B.

4 Dataset

This section discusses details of the datasets used for order search and order prediction experiments.

Search Dataset: In order to collect data for order search experimentation, customers with multiple active orders were asked to describe the product they are calling for. The transcribed customer utterances along with the product attributes of the orders like product title, brand, etc constitute our dataset. We had a small development dataset of about $2.5K$ calls and a large test set of about $95K$ calls. The development set was used to build and tune the *fuzzy search* technique. The performance on both datasets are reported in section 5.1.

Prediction Dataset: The dataset for predictive modeling is collected from the live customer calls. The dataset contains features of active orders and the customer chosen order, which would serve as ground truth. We came up with a variety of features from order, product related ones to self serve related ones and are collected online or offline depending whether the feature is dependent on the time when customer calls. The features for the active orders and the customer chosen order for $150K$ customer calls constitute our prediction dataset. The experiments and results on this dataset is given in section 5.2.

5 Experiments and Results

The performance of an order search algorithm is evaluated using *Coverage* and *Accuracy*. Coverage refers to the fraction of calls, where proposed technique gave a match. Among the cases where match is found, accuracy refers to the fraction of correct matches. The rest of this section discusses the experiments and results on the development and test sets of the search dataset followed by order prediction experiments and finally the performance combining search and prediction for order identification.

5.1 Order Search Results

We compare our approach fuzzy search with the following two approaches viz. manual baseline and ecommerce search. In manual baseline, customer utterances were tagged for product entities by human agents handling those calls to get a baseline on the coverage. Ecommerce search refers to the general purpose product search used by consumers on ecommerce websites and mobile apps. This latter approach relies on NER for detecting product entities, which we had done through a NER model based on conditional random fields (CRF) (Lafferty et al., 2001).

Figure 2 shows the coverage of fuzzy search vs these two approaches on the **development** set of search dataset. As shown, we had a total of 2515 customer utterances, of which human annotators could spot product entities only in 34% of them demonstrating the difficulty of the task. Fuzzy search and ecommerce search had a coverage of 32.1% and 17.2% respectively. Both fuzzy and ecommerce search have an overlap with the remaining 66% data that manual annotations couldn't cover, showing that product entity malformations due to transcription noise is overcome by these models significantly. The coverage of ecommerce search is affected by poor NER performance on noisy ASR transcripts. At this point, an attentive reader may refer back to Table 1 to see some of the sample matches returned by fuzzy search. Some more qualitative results are shown in Appendix-C to understand the gap between fuzzy and ecommerce search further. Clearly, our customized ap-

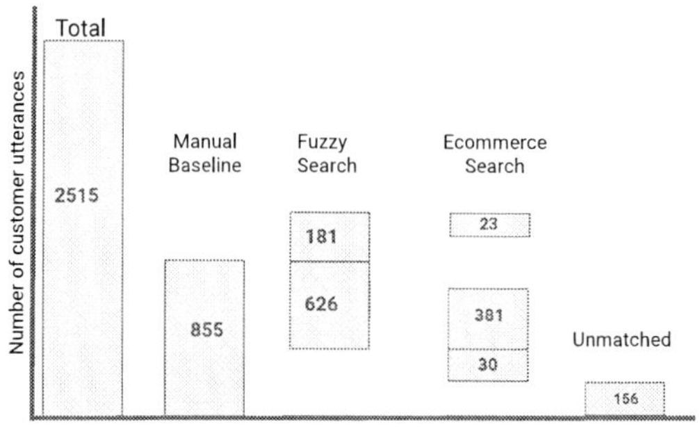

Figure 2: Comparison of coverage of fuzzy search against manual baseline and ecommerce search on development set. Vertical placements are indicative of overlaps between different sets.

proach fuzzy search performs better than ecommerce search.

As a second experiment, we compare fuzzy search against text embedding based approaches - *fasttext based similarity modelling* and *fuzzy search on fasttext*. The former obtains the relevance of a customer utterance to a product by taking cosine similarity between their corresponding sentence embeddings and the most relevant orders(s) with similarity over a threshold is considered. Sentence embeddings are obtained by averaging the word embeddings obtained from a Fasttext model(Bojanowski et al., 2017) trained on customer utterances and product titles. *Fuzzy search on fasttext* combines the benefits of customisations in fuzzy search and the semantics from fasttext, where fuzzy search is done on text embeddings, with textual similarity replaced by cosine similarity over fasttext embeddings of n-grams.

Table 2 shows the coverage and accuracy of single and multiple matches retrieved by various order search approaches on live contact center calls, that constitute the **test** set of search dataset. Fuzzy search is found to perform better with 18.02% single order matches with an accuracy of 86.33%. Similarity modelling on fasttext is found to have lesser coverage and accuracy than fuzzy search. Decrease in accuracy is attributed to calls with multiple similar orders and the retrieval fetches one of them as a match but customer chose a different order during the call. Fuzzy search on fasttext performs on par with fuzzy search on text, showing that semantics captured by word embeddings does not add incremental value. This, we believe, is owing to the lexical nature of product titles and unambiguous context of customer utterances. Fuzzy search despite being unsupervised, experimented on development data, the coverage and accuracy hold good on real life calls as well.

Upon deep diving into the multiple order matches from fuzzy search, we found around 38% of such multiple matches had exact same product (same make and model), 49% of them were same product type - can be different model, color etc (e.g., multiple t-shirts), some of them being similar products (e.g., shampoo, hair conditioner, hair serum of the same brand). Multiple matches, though not acted upon by voice-bot, are still valid matches.

5.2 Order Prediction Results

The performance of order prediction is measured by top-k accuracy(A_k) given by the fraction of calls where the model predicted the ground truth order in top-k predictions. We use Prediction dataset with train/val/test split of 70/10/20 respectively for training order prediction models. Table 3 shows the top-k accuracy of various prediction models. Random Forest, a decision tree based ensemble model is found to perform better at both top-1 and top-2 accuracy of 72.52% and 88.71% respectively and marginally under performing than Deep Neural Network (DNN) at top-3 thereby showing the characteristics of the orders indeed decide the order, customer calls for.

The reader may again refer to Table 1 where the rightmost two columns show some of the sample top-1 predictions and the features that led to such predictions by the Random Forest model. In the first example shown in table 1, among many orders, model predicted *fitness band*, which the customer has already initiated return process and have an existing complaint lodged. Upon looking into the top features that govern the model's predictions, we found self serve features like *chat before call*, *existing complaints before call*, etc. in addition to the *rank wrt ordered date and selling price* to be on top, showing that the customers explore self serve before calling. We show the Shapley Values plot of the feature importance in figure 3. We introduce a threshold on the likelihood of top ranked prediction to improve the accuracy while marginally compromising on coverage. With a threshold of 0.6, top-1 predictions from Random Forest had a coverage and accuracy of 62.5% and 84% respectively.

Both order search and order prediction is also evaluated on an out-of-time data, consisting of $13K$ customer calls. Table 4 shows the coverage and accuracy of order search and order prediction indi-

Approach	Coverage (in %)		Accuracy (in %)	
	Single	Multiple	Single	Multiple
Fuzzy Search	**18.02**	9.62	**86.33**	70.19
Fasttext based Similarity modelling	17.93	4.28	71.03	63.34
Fuzzy Search on fasttext	17.09	**10.47**	85.36	**71.22**

Table 2: Coverage and accuracy of single and multiple matches from order search approaches on the test set

Model	A_1	A_2	A_3
Rev. Chronological	40.09	75.17	87.74
Logistic Regression	71.00	88.00	93.70
Random Forest	**72.52**	**88.71**	94.09
DNN	70.34	88.33	**94.34**

Table 3: Top-k accuracies(%) of order prediction models

Approach	Coverage	Accuracy
Fuzzy Search	20.32	86.83
Order Prediction	58.1	84.46
Search + Prediction	64.7	87.18

Table 4: Performance of Search and Prediction

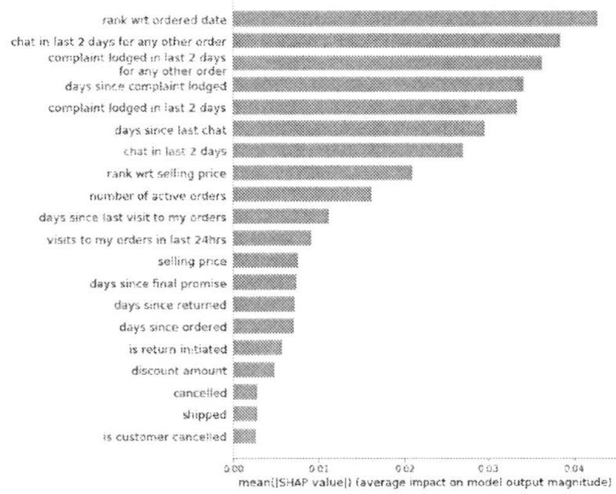

Figure 3: Feature importance of top 20 features for Random Forest model. Features with prefix *'rank'* or suffix *'for any other order'* are derived features introduced to bring relation with other active orders.

vidually and the overall coverage by having both search and prediction in place. Order prediction resulted in an incremental coverage of 44% while maintaining same accuracy.

6 Related work

Order identification has not been much explored in the literature. Most related problem is on NER to identify product entities (Putthividhya and Hu, 2011; Joshi et al., 2015; More, 2016). In the literature, there are many studies focused on NER for product entity extraction ranging from classical techniques (Brody and Elhadad, 2010) to recent deep learning approaches that make use of word embeddings (Majumder et al., 2018; Jiang et al., 2019). While entity extraction from text is well researched in the literature, NER on speech is less studied. Most initial works on speech had a two staged approach - ASR followed by NER (Cohn et al., 2019), recent works directly extract entities from speech (Ghannay et al., 2018; Yadav et al., 2020). While NER helps in ecommerce search on websites and apps, the specific nature of order identification problem and the limited search space of active orders make NER unnecessary.

Another related line of works is on sentence similarity tasks. Owing to the success of word embeddings (Mikolov et al., 2013; Bojanowski et al., 2017), there is a lot of literature on textual similarity related tasks, that make use of word embeddings in a supervised (Yao et al., 2018; Reimers and Gurevych, 2019; Shen et al., 2017) and unsupervised fashion (Arora et al., 2016). (Wieting et al., 2015) showed that simple averaging of word embeddings followed by cosine similarity could provide competitive performance on sentence similarity tasks. We have compared word embeddings based approaches to show that additional semantics does not help in order identification problem.

7 Conclusion

In this paper, we present one of the first studies exploring order identification for ecommerce contact centers. The proposed two-staged fuzzy search and order prediction technique provide 64% coverage at 87% accuracy on a large real-life dataset which are significantly better than manual baseline and relevant comparable techniques. Order prediction though developed for voice-bot, could also be used in other places like chat bot or non bot calls, where we can ask proactively if this is the order customer is looking for help. Finally, going beyond the scientific impact of this work, the proposed solution is also deployed in production for a fraction of calls landing in the contact center of a large ecommerce provider leading to real-life impact.

References

Sanjeev Arora, Yingyu Liang, and Tengyu Ma. 2016. A simple but tough-to-beat baseline for sentence embeddings.

Piotr Bojanowski, Edouard Grave, Armand Joulin, and Tomas Mikolov. 2017. Enriching word vectors with subword information. *Transactions of the Association for Computational Linguistics*, 5:135–146.

Samuel Brody and Noemie Elhadad. 2010. An unsupervised aspect-sentiment model for online reviews. In *Human language technologies: The 2010 annual conference of the North American chapter of the association for computational linguistics*, pages 804–812.

Ido Cohn, Itay Laish, Genady Beryozkin, Gang Li, Izhak Shafran, Idan Szpektor, Tzvika Hartman, Avinatan Hassidim, and Yossi Matias. 2019. Audio de-identification-a new entity recognition task. In *Proceedings of the 2019 Conference of the North American Chapter of the Association for Computational Linguistics: Human Language Technologies, Volume 2 (Industry Papers)*, pages 197–204.

Sahar Ghannay, Antoine Caubriere, Yannick Esteve, Antoine Laurent, and Emmanuel Morin. 2018. End-to-end named entity extraction from speech. *arXiv preprint arXiv:1805.12045*.

Yufan Jiang, Chi Hu, Tong Xiao, Chunliang Zhang, and Jingbo Zhu. 2019. Improved differentiable architecture search for language modeling and named entity recognition. In *Proceedings of the 2019 Conference on Empirical Methods in Natural Language Processing and the 9th International Joint Conference on Natural Language Processing (EMNLP-IJCNLP)*, pages 3576–3581.

Mahesh Joshi, Ethan Hart, Mirko Vogel, and Jean David Ruvini. 2015. Distributed word representations improve ner for e-commerce. In *Proceedings of the 1st Workshop on Vector Space Modeling for Natural Language Processing*, pages 160–167.

John Lafferty, Andrew McCallum, and Fernando CN Pereira. 2001. Conditional random fields: Probabilistic models for segmenting and labeling sequence data.

Bodhisattwa Prasad Majumder, Aditya Subramanian, Abhinandan Krishnan, Shreyansh Gandhi, and Ajinkya More. 2018. Deep recurrent neural networks for product attribute extraction in ecommerce. *arXiv preprint arXiv:1803.11284*.

Tomas Mikolov, Kai Chen, Greg Corrado, and Jeffrey Dean. 2013. Efficient estimation of word representations in vector space. *arXiv preprint arXiv:1301.3781*.

Ajinkya More. 2016. Attribute extraction from product titles in ecommerce. *arXiv preprint arXiv:1608.04670*.

Duangmanee Putthividhya and Junling Hu. 2011. Bootstrapped named entity recognition for product attribute extraction. In *Proceedings of the 2011 Conference on Empirical Methods in Natural Language Processing*, pages 1557–1567.

Nils Reimers and Iryna Gurevych. 2019. Sentence-bert: Sentence embeddings using siamese bert-networks. *arXiv preprint arXiv:1908.10084*.

Yikang Shen, Wenge Rong, Nan Jiang, Baolin Peng, Jie Tang, and Zhang Xiong. 2017. Word embedding based correlation model for question/answer matching. In *Proceedings of the AAAI Conference on Artificial Intelligence*, volume 31.

Musen Wen, Deepak Kumar Vasthimal, Alan Lu, Tian Wang, and Aimin Guo. 2019. Building large-scale deep learning system for entity recognition in e-commerce search. In *Proceedings of the 6th IEEE/ACM International Conference on Big Data Computing, Applications and Technologies*, pages 149–154.

John Wieting, Mohit Bansal, Kevin Gimpel, and Karen Livescu. 2015. Towards universal paraphrastic sentence embeddings. *arXiv preprint arXiv:1511.08198*.

Hemant Yadav, Sreyan Ghosh, Yi Yu, and Rajiv Ratn Shah. 2020. End-to-end named entity recognition from english speech. *arXiv preprint arXiv:2005.11184*.

Haipeng Yao, Huiwen Liu, and Peiying Zhang. 2018. A novel sentence similarity model with word embedding based on convolutional neural network. *Concurrency and Computation: Practice and Experience*, 30(23):e4415.

A Flow of Fuzzy Search

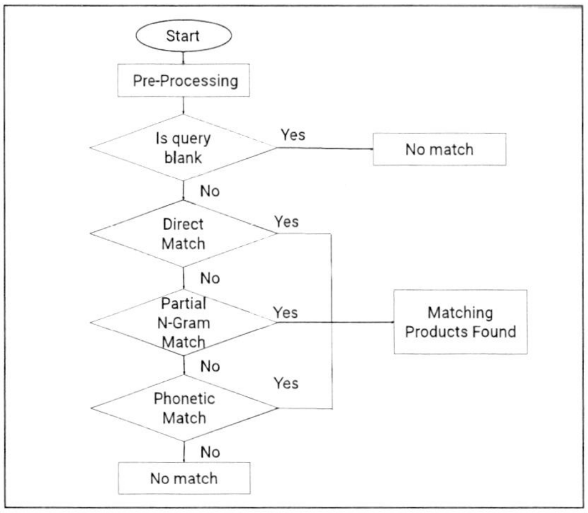

Figure 4: Flow Chart showing the stages involved in fuzzy search

B Hyper-parameter tuning for Order Prediction

Model	Hyper-parameter	Range of values	Best hyper-parameter
Logistic Regression	penalty	l1, l2, elasticnet,none	l2
	tol	[1e-2,1e-6]	1e-5
	C	[1e2, 1e-2]	1
Random forest	n_estimators	[10,1000]	50
	criterion	gini,entropy	gini
	max_depth	10, 20, 50, 100	20
	min_samples_leaf	2,10,50,100	10
	bootstrap	False, True	True
DNN	number of hidden layers	2,3	2
	number of neurons	50,100,200	100
	lr	[1e-2,1e-4]	1e-3
	activation	relu, sigmoid, leaky relu, tanh	leaky relu

Table 5: Range of values for various hyper-parameters and the chosen hyper-parameter with best top-1 accuracy on validation set for various order prediction models

C Sample predictions from fuzzy search & ecommerce search

Customer Utterance	Product titles of active orders	Comments
mi tv ke baare mein	[STAMEN 153 cm (5 ft) Polyester Window Curtain (Pack Of 4), Sauran 26-55 inch Heavy TV Wall Mount for all types of Fixed TV Mount Fixed TV Mount, **Mi 4A 100 cm (40) Full HD LED Smart Android TV**, Leemara Virus Protection, Anti Pollution, Face Mask, Reusable-Washable Outdoor Protection Cotton Safety Mask]	✓Fuzzy Search ✓Ecommerce Search
cover ke baare mein **mobile cover** ke baare mein	[**Aspir Back Cover for Vivo V15, Mobi Elite Back Cover for Vivo V15**, RUNEECH Back Camera Lens Glass Protector for VIVO V 20, Shoes Kingdom Shoes Kingdom _LB791 Mocassins Casual Loafers For Men (Brown) Loafers For Men, **Aspir Back Cover for Vivo V20**, CatBull In-ear Bluetooth Headset]	✓Fuzzy Search ✗Ecommerce Search
datacable ke liye	[Easy Way Fashion Doll with Dresses Makeup and Doll Accessories, **Vrilliance Traders Type C Compatible Fast Data Cable Charging Cable for Type C Android Devices (1.2 M,Black) 1.2 m USB Type C Cable**]	✓Fuzzy Search ✗Ecommerce Search
in clinics hot 94	[JOKIN A1 MULTI FUNCTIONAL SMARTWATCH Smartwatch, **Infinix Hot 9 Pro (Violet, 64 GB)**, Vivo Z1Pro (Sonic Blue, 64 GB), Vivo Z1Pro (Sonic Blue, 64 GB), Vivo Z1Pro (Sonic Blue, 64 GB), Tech Unboxing Led Rechargeable Fan With Torch 120 mm 3 Blade Exhaust Fan]	✓Fuzzy Search ✗Ecommerce Search
chappal ke liye paanch sau saat sattar pe ka product tha mera	[Highlander Full Sleeve Washed Men Jacket, **Oricum Slides**, BOLAX Black Slouchy woolen Long Beanie Cap for Winter skull head Unisex Cap, **Oricum Slides**, BOLAX Black Slouchy woolen Long Beanie Cap for Winter skull head Unisex Cap]	✗Fuzzy Search ✓Ecommerce Search

Table 6: Examples of predictions from fuzzy search and ecommerce search. First column shows the customer utterances along with the NER predictions emphasized. Second column shows all active orders at the time of call, with matching orders emphasized. Last column shows the correctness of order search approaches.

Identifying Hijacked Reviews

Monika Daryani
Texas A&M University
College Station, TX 77843
monikadaryani@tamu.edu

James Caverlee
Texas A&M University
College Station, TX 77843
caverlee@tamu.edu

Abstract

Fake reviews and review manipulation are growing problems on online marketplaces globally. *Review Hijacking* is a new review manipulation tactic in which unethical sellers "hijack" an existing product page (usually one with many positive reviews), then update the product details like title, photo, and description with those of an entirely different product. With the earlier reviews still attached, the new item appears well-reviewed. However, there are no public datasets of review hijacking and little is known in the literature about this tactic. Hence, this paper proposes a three-part study: (i) we propose a framework to generate synthetically labeled data for review hijacking by swapping products and reviews; (ii) then, we evaluate the potential of both a Twin LSTM network and BERT sequence pair classifier to distinguish legitimate reviews from hijacked ones using this data; and (iii) we then deploy the best performing model on a collection of 31K products (with 6.5 M reviews) in the original data, where we find 100s of previously unknown examples of review hijacking.

1 Introduction

Reviews are an essential component of many online marketplaces, helping new consumers assess product quality, legitimacy, and reliability. Recent surveys indicate that an overwhelming majority of people read reviews (Murphy, 2020). Indeed, 79% of people overall and 91% of people ages 18-34 trust online reviews as much as personal recommendations (Kaemingk, 2020). Naturally, reviews have become a target of manipulation, misuse, and abuse (Mukherjee et al., 2012).

In this paper, we focus on the problem of *review hijacking*, a relatively new attack vector and one that has received little, if any, research attention. Review hijacking is a fraud technique wherein a blackhat seller "hijacks" a product page that typically has already accumulated many positive reviews and then replaces the hijacked product with a different product (typically one without any positive reviews). The sellers then reap the ratings "halo" from consumers who assume the new product is highly rated. This review hijacking (also referred to as *review reuse* or *bait-and-switch reviews*) provides the sellers with a shortcut to many undeserved positive reviews.

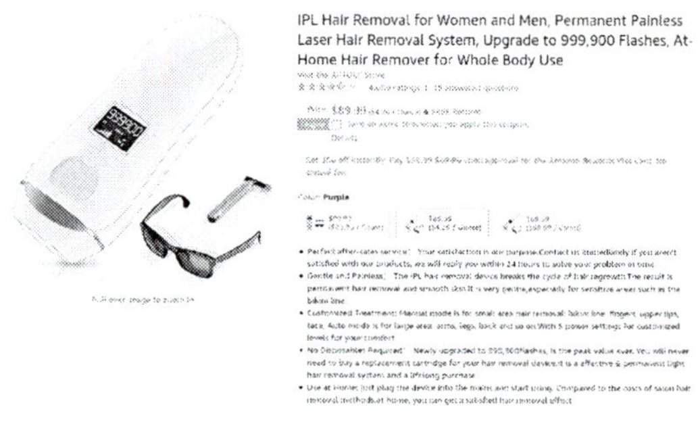

Figure 1: An example of review hijacking on Amazon (May 7, 2021)

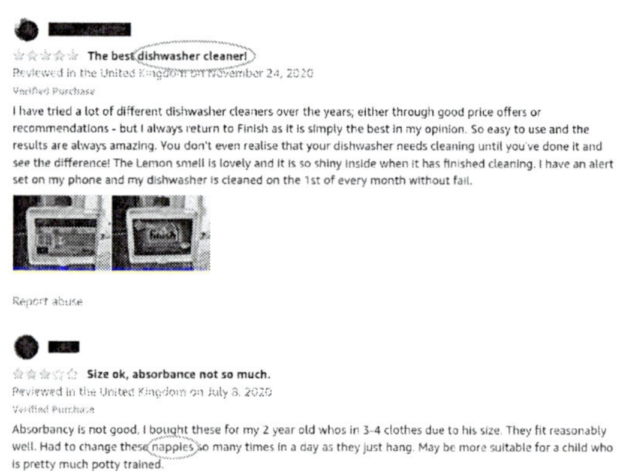

Figure 2: Hijacked reviews associated with the hair removal product in Figure 1

Proceedings of the 4th Workshop on e-Commerce and NLP (ECNLP 4), pages 70–78
August 5, 2021.

An example is shown in Figure 1 which we discovered in the first week of May 2021. This hair removal product has 4,069 reviews with an average rating of close to five stars. On inspection of the reviews (see Figure 2), we find many that refer to other products like dishwasher cleaners and diapers. Also, these reviews are for verified purchases which can provide added weight to the ostensible veracity of the reviews.

We have identified at least three different methods that blackhat sellers adopt to conduct review hijacking depending on the particular e-commerce platform. A seller can incrementally change aspects of their own product (like the title, photo, description), resulting in an entirely new product, though still associated with the original reviews. Alternatively, a seller can add his product as a product variation of some other product to aggregate reviews from the former product. One can also merge reviews from some other products to their own by changing country or using some other platform-specific loopholes.

While review hijacking has been recognized in the press and social media as a growing problem, e.g., (Swearingen, 2019; Walsh, 2020; Sterling, 2019; Dascalescu, 2019; Nguyen, 2018; Dzieza, 2019), there has been no structured research to date on identifying review hijacking. We attribute this to several key challenges:

- First, there are no standard datasets of review hijacking, nor are there gold labels of known examples. Hence, it is challenging to validate models that aim to uncover review hijacking.
- Second, review hijacking is a targeted attack vector with a skewed distribution, and so there are no simple approaches to find examples. In a preliminary investigation, we manually labeled hundreds of reviews and found fewer than 0.01% reviews that could be considered part of a review hijacking attack.
- Third, many reviews cannot easily be labeled as hijacked or not. For example, reviews like "Great product! Five stars!" are generic and could potentially be associated with any product.
- Finally, hijackers may adopt sophisticated techniques to avoid detection. For example, some products may have a mix of legitimate reviews to camouflage the hijacked ones (e.g., by incentivizing reviewers to contribute a review about the hair removal product).

Hence, this paper proposes an initial investigation into the potential of identifying review hijacking. We conduct a three-part study. Due to the challenges of finding high-quality examples of review hijacking, we first propose a framework to generate synthetic examples of review hijacking by swapping products and reviews. We do so both at the inter-category level (where presumably it should be easier to determine if a review is associated with a product) and at the intra-category level (where product similarity within the category may make this more challenging). Over this synthetic dataset, we evaluate the potential of both a Twin LSTM network and BERT sequence pair classifier to distinguish legitimate reviews from hijacked ones. Based on the encouraging results from this experiment, we then deploy the BERT sequence pair classifier algorithm on a real collection of 31K products (with 6.5 M reviews). By averaging the review scores from the classifier for each product, we find that products with an average review score (or *suspiciousness* score) > 0.5 have 99.95% of the listings containing unrelated or hijacked reviews. These findings suggest the promise of large-scale detection of review hijacking in the wild.

2 Related Work

The manipulation of reviews and review platforms has been widely studied, e.g., (Gössling et al., 2018; Jindal and Liu, 2007; Kaghazgaran et al., 2017; Mukherjee et al., 2012, 2013), though there is little research literature on the problem of review hijacking. Here, we highlight several efforts related to the methods proposed in this paper. Higgins et al. developed models for an essay rating system to detect bad-faith essays by comparing the essay titles to the essay text to determine whether the title and text were in agreement through the use of word similarity (Higgins et al., 2006). A similar idea motivates our approach that compares product titles/descriptions with review text. Louis and Higgins continued this line of research to determine whether a particular essay was related to the essay prompt or question by expanding short prompts and spell correcting the texts (Louis and Higgins, 2010). Rei and Cummins extended this work and combined various sentence similarity measures like TF-IDF and Word2Vec embeddings with moderate improvement over Higgins' work (Rei and Cummins,

2016). Apart from the essay space, Ryu et al. investigated the detection of out-of-domain sentences (Ryu et al., 2017). They proposed a neural sentence embedding method representing sentences in a low-dimensional continuous vector space that emphasizes aspects in-domain and out-of-domain for a given scenario. In another direction, fake news detection and clickbait detection can be viewed as related tasks. For example, Hanselowski et al.used a BiLSTM model with attention to determine if the headline of a news article agrees, disagrees, or is unrelated to the text as part of a Fake News Challenge (Hanselowski et al., 2018).

3 Generating Synthetic Examples of Review Hijacking

In our preliminary investigation, we examined hundreds of reviews from the Amazon dataset provided by McAuley (Ni et al., 2019). The dataset contains 233.1 million reviews from May 1996 to October 2018, with reviews and product information including title, description, etc. However, we find very few examples of review hijacking. Hence, we concluded that hiring crowd labelers or subject matter experts to label product-review pairs as hijacked or not hijacked might not be fruitful. Instead, we propose a method to generate synthetic examples for studying the potential of models to identify hijacked reviews.

3.1 Preliminaries

As a first step, we prepared the Amazon dataset. For each product i, we combined the description (product text provided by the seller), title (the name of the product), the brand of the product, and features (product features like color or size) into a single *product text* P_i. We also removed products with fewer than five reviews.

For each review j, we combined the reviewText (the text in the review body), the style (which contains some optional product features like color or size), and summary (which is the headline of the review) into a single *review text* R_j.

Hence, our goal is to determine if each review j associated with the product i, is actually related to the product or not. If the review is unrelated, we can conclude that there is potential evidence of review hijacking for the product. Of course, there could be other reasons for a review for being unrelated to a product, like an error by the reviewer. We leave this fine-grained determination as future work.

3.2 Swapping Reviews

Given these products and reviews, we propose to randomly swap reviews between a pair of distinct products, yielding a collection of unrelated product-review pairs. As a first step, we assume that all reviews are actually related to the associated product. Hence, we have a large set of product-review pairs with the label **related** (= 0). Of course, we know that our data has some hijacked reviews (on the order of $< 0.01\%$), so we will tolerate some errors in these labels.

By randomly swapping product-review pairs, we get a set of product-review pairs with the label **unrelated** (= 1). For example, Figure 3 shows a simple example of a basketball and a phone, each with an associated review. We swap reviews among the products to generate **unrelated** (= 1) labels in addition to the original **related** (= 0) labels.

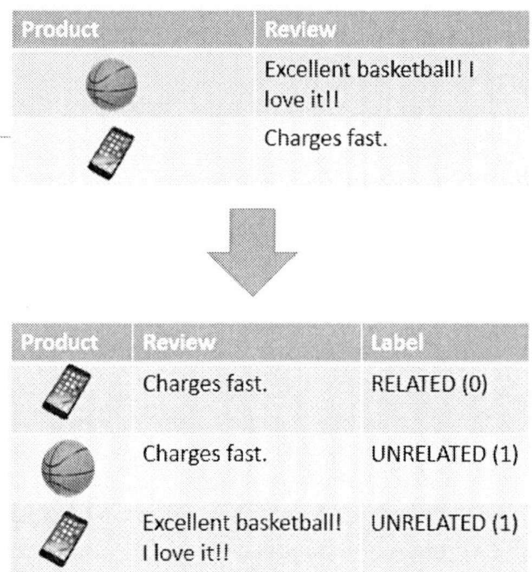

Figure 3: Generation of Synthetic Label and Data by Swapping Reviews among Dissimilar Products

But, how do we select which products to select for randomly swapping reviews? Randomly selecting products may lead to such a clear mismatch between the review text and the product text that detection would be trivial. On the other hand, selecting closely related products (e.g., by selecting Samsung mobile covers from two different brands) may yield reviews that are essentially undetectable as possible hijacking. Hence, we propose two methods for finding pairs of dissimilar products for review swapping.

Inter-Category Swapping. The first approach takes a product text P_i composed of the title, features, and description from one category (e.g., Beauty, Clothing, Electronics) and the review texts R_j of a product in another category for **unrelated** reviews. For **related** reviews, we take the original product-review pairs. We obtained a set of $\approx 59k$ reviews with $\approx 25k$ unrelated reviews and $\approx 34k$ related reviews.

Intra-category Swapping. The first approach handles hijacking across categories. For hijacking occurring within a product category, we use Jaccard distance. We converted product titles for each product into TF-IDF feature matrices, found pairwise Jaccard distances between them, and we formed product pairs (A_1, A_2) with Jaccard distance 0. Then, we took the product text P_i of one product A_1, and the review text R_j of another product A_2 and labeled this as **unrelated**. Similarly, we took the product text of A_2 and a review of A_1 as **unrelated**. For **related** labels, we took the product text, and the review text of A_1, and likewise for A_2 to get another set of related data. We obtained a set of $\approx 56k$ reviews with $\approx 22k$ unrelated reviews and $\approx 34k$ related reviews.

4 Identifying Synthetic Examples

Given these synthetic datasets of hijacked reviews, can we detect them? In this section, we report on experiments with two approaches: one based on a Twin LSTM and one based on BERT Sentence Pair Classification.

We shuffled the product-review pairs and split them into training, validation and test set in ratio 70:10:20 for both of the datasets. The actual number of reviews in each set depends on the swapping categories and is discussed in Section 3.2 We train on the train set, tune models on the validation set, and have reported results on the test set.

4.1 Twin LSTM Network

The first approach adopts a Twin neural network which has shown success in comparing images and text. This network uses the same weights in parallel in tandem on two inputs to return output based on the relation or distance between them (Chicco, 2021). Concretely, we compare sentence pairs and determine if they are similar or not. We tokenized our inputs and converted them into sequences. Then we used 300-dimensional GloVe (Pennington et al., 2014) embeddings and formed an embedding matrix for our tokens. We get two embedding matrices for both inputs, which we feed into the LSTM network illustrated in Figure 4. We use twin LSTM networks with two layers of 64 nodes each, with a dropout of 0.01. We calculate the cosine similarity between the two input embeddings and evaluate the performance by computing cross-entropy loss using accuracy and AUC (Area Under Curve). It takes 13 epochs with Adam optimizer and learning rate of 0.00001 to get the result.

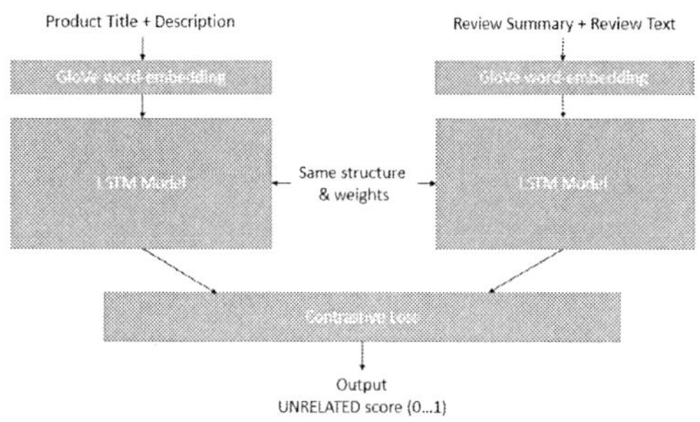

Figure 4: Twin LSTM Network

4.2 BERT Sequence Pair Classifier

The second approach adopts the popular BERT pre-trained language model (Devlin et al., 2019). Since BERT provides a deep bidirectional representation, conditioned on text in both directions, we expect this method to perform better than the twin neural network, which uses GLOVE embeddings. Our model is prepared from the BERT BASE model (bert_12_768_12) from GluonNLP. We add a layer on top for classification, as shown in Figure 5. We use Adam optimizer for optimizing this classification layer and get results with only 3 epochs.

Now we form the sentence pairs for classification. Like the previous method, the first sentence is the product text P_i (a concatenation of product title, features, and description). The second sentence is the review text R_j (a concatenation of the review summary and review text). We then tokenize the sentences, insert [CLS] at the start, insert [SEP] at the end and between both the sentences, and generate segment ids to specify if a token belongs to the first sentence or the second one. We now run the BERT fine-tuning with these sequences as inputs. We get the output as an *unrelated score* $u(i, j)$ between 0 and 1. For texts longer than 512 tokens, we truncate and take the first 512 tokens for our model. As 99% of the review texts have fewer than

512 tokens, this choice impacts very few reviews.

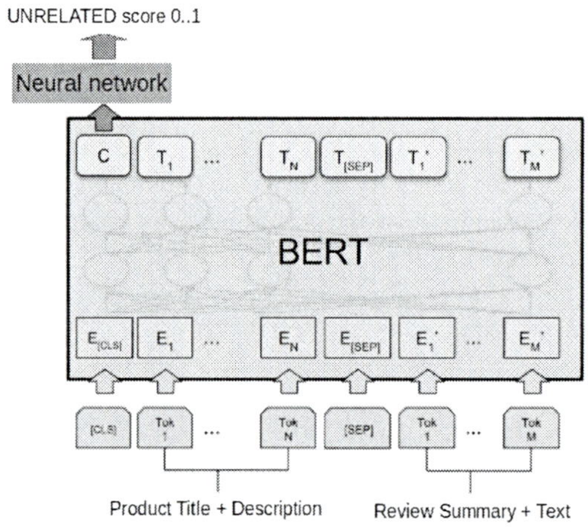

Figure 5: BERT Sequence Pair Classifier

4.3 Results

Table 1 shows the results reported on test data using these two approaches. We see that the Twin LSTM Network provides more than 80% accuracy and high ROC result on both inter-category and intra-category datasets. The BERT-based classifier has more than 90% accuracy and ROC result for both datasets. We see that both methods perform better on the inter-category dataset than the intra-category one. In the inter-category dataset, we obtain unrelated reviews by taking products from one category and review texts from another. Hence, models trained on this dataset can learn product features of one category at a time and develop expertise in that category. The intra-category dataset is more challenging for both approaches. Since products are drawn from the same category, there can be less clarity in distinguishing features of the reviews.

Paired with this summary table (Table 1), we show in Figures 6, 7, 8 and 9 the ROC curve for the BERT-based model and Twin LSTM network. We can clearly see that BERT-based model performs better than LSTM. We can also see how both models perform better on the inter-category dataset rather than the intra-category one.

5 Detecting Hijacked Reviews In-the-Wild

Even though encouraging, these results are on synthetic data, and the data itself may contain noisy labels. Hence, we next turn to the task of uncov-

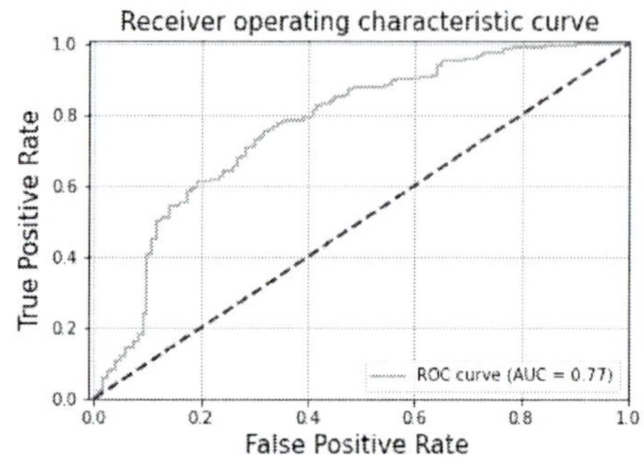

Figure 6: ROC curve for Twin LSTM network run on Intra-category data (Jaccard distance)

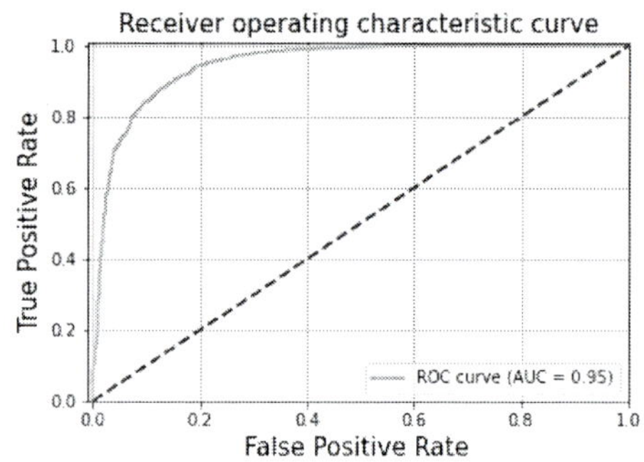

Figure 7: ROC curve for BERT seq. pair classifier run on Intra-category data (Jaccard distance)

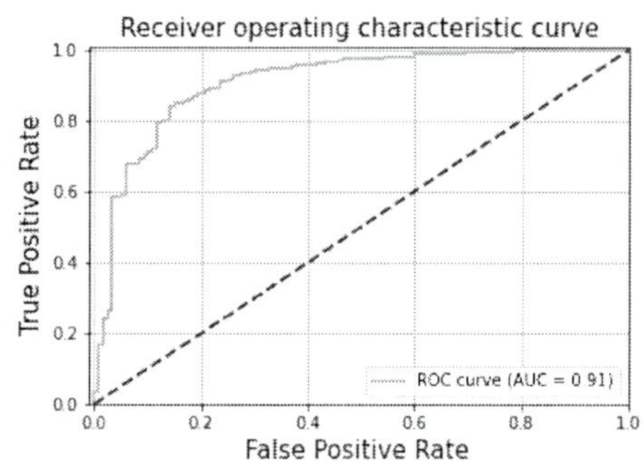

Figure 8: ROC curve for Twin LSTM network run on Inter-category data

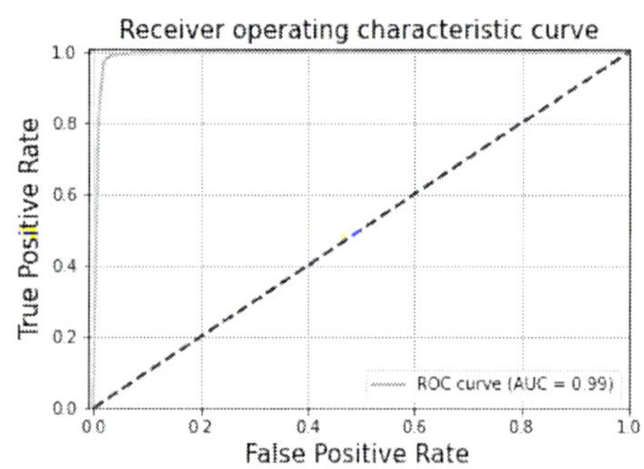

Figure 9: ROC curve for BERT seq. pair classifier run on Inter-category data

Model	Synthetic Data	Accuracy	ROC result
Twin LSTM Network	Intra-category	0.823	0.770
	Inter-category	0.885	0.910
BERT Sequence Pair Classifier	Intra-category	0.916	0.948
	Inter-category	0.965	0.993

Table 1: Hijacked review detection accuracy reported on the test set

ering hijacked reviews in-the-wild. Can a model trained over synthetic data identify actual hijacked reviews?

5.1 Approach and Results

For this experiment, we used the BERT sequence pair classifier and applied it to a dataset of 31K products (with 6.5 M reviews) with the original product-review pairs intact. These 31K products were held out and not used during the training.

For each product-review pair, we take the unrelated score output from the trained BERT-based model as $u(i, j)$. For a product i with n reviews, we calculate an average suspiciousness review score as follows:

$$score_i = \frac{\sum_{j=1}^{n} u(i, j)}{n}$$

Based on this suspiciousness score, we plot the distribution of all 31K products in Figure 10. Unsurprisingly, the vast majority of products have a very low suspiciousness score. About 99% of products have scored < 0.3, reinforcing our initial assumption about a skewed class distribution. In other words, the vast majority of the reviews on listings seem to be related to the product itself. However, we find many cases of potential review hijacking (see the right side of Figure 10), indicating that this targeted attack is indeed a threat to review platforms.

We manually checked a sample of 200+ products with a suspiciousness score of > 0.5. We found that all but one of the products contained reviews referring to a different product. While there is uncertainty as to the mechanism leading to an unrelated review, we hypothesize that these are indeed previously unknown cases of review hijacking. And in an encouraging direction, these results indicate the promise of training models over synthetic hijacked reviews for uncovering actual instances.

5.2 Case Study

In this section, we discuss three sample products three sample products and their distribution of unrelated scores $u(i, j)$ that are assigned by the BERT-based model. These three products are from the Cellphone & Accessories category.

Figure 11 shows the unrelated score distribution for all of the reviews of product-1. Product-1 has an average unrelated review score of 0.9 to 1.0. We can see from the distribution that most reviews have a high unrelated score (> 0.9). We manually inspect these reviews and observe that these reviews are indeed unrelated. Hence, we conclude that this product is an example of review hijacking.

Figure 12 shows the unrelated score distribution for product-2. Product-2 has an average review score of 0.0 to 0.1, meaning most of the reviews seem appropriate. We can see from the distribution that most reviews have a low unrelated score (< 0.1), and a few have a high score (> 0.9). We manually inspect the reviews with high unrelated scores (> 0.9) and observe that these reviews are either misclassified by our BERT-based model or do not have enough information to determine the label (e.g., reviews like "Great Product!"). Thus, we conclude that this product is not an example of review hijacking.

Finally, Figure 13 shows the unrelated review score distribution for product-3. Product-3 has an average review score of 0.5 to 0.6. We can see from the distribution that about 55% of the reviews have a high unrelated score, while 35% reviews have a low unrelated score. We manually inspect reviews with high unrelated scores (> 0.9) and observe that these reviews are indeed unrelated to the product. We also inspect the reviews with low unrelated scores (< 0.1 and < 0.2) and observe that most are related to the product. As this product has a mix of related and unrelated reviews, we hypothesize that it is also an example of review hijacking containing some related reviews.

6 Conclusion, Limitations and Next Steps

This paper has examined the challenge of identifying hijacked reviews. Since we know little about

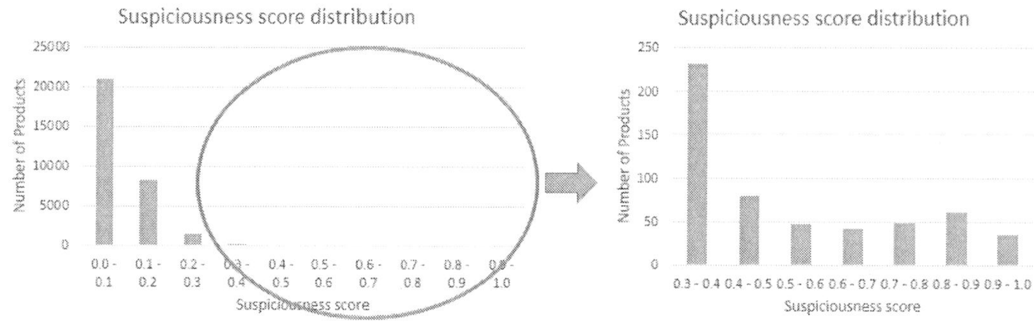

Figure 10: Average Review Score vs. Number of Products

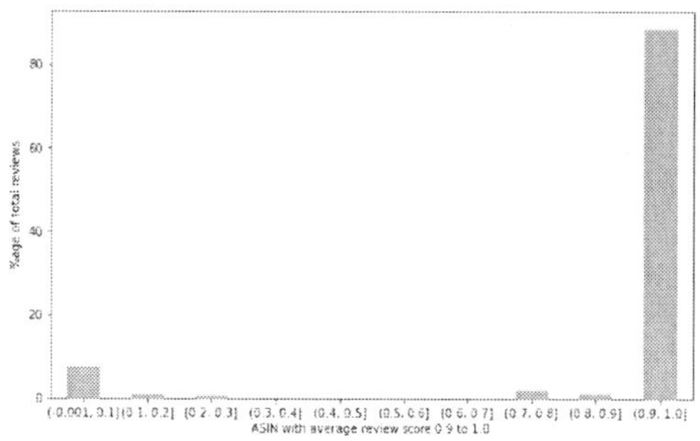

Figure 11: Unrelated Review Score Distribution for Product-1 showing predominantly unrelated reviews

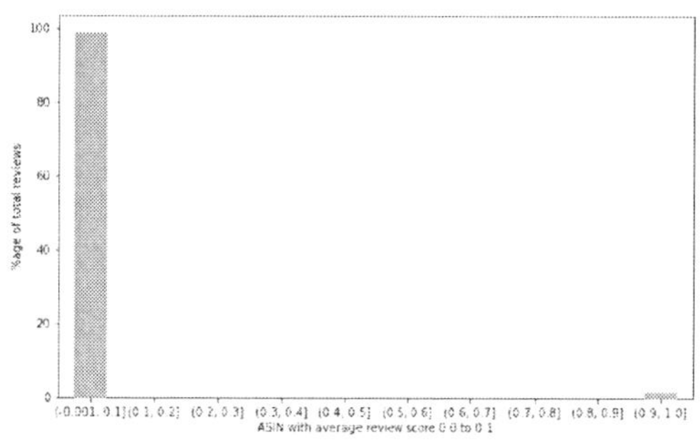

Figure 12: Unrelated Review Score Distribution for Product-2 showing predominantly related reviews

these hijacked reviews, we first proposed to generate synthetic examples by swapping the reviews of a product with reviews on an unrelated product. We then tested the viability of a Twin LSTM network and BERT sentence pair classifier to uncover these unrelated reviews. Both approaches provided excellent results on synthetic data, but do they actually identify hijacked reviews in the wild? Our preliminary investigation showed that a model trained over synthetic data could detect many examples of previously unknown cases of review hijacking.

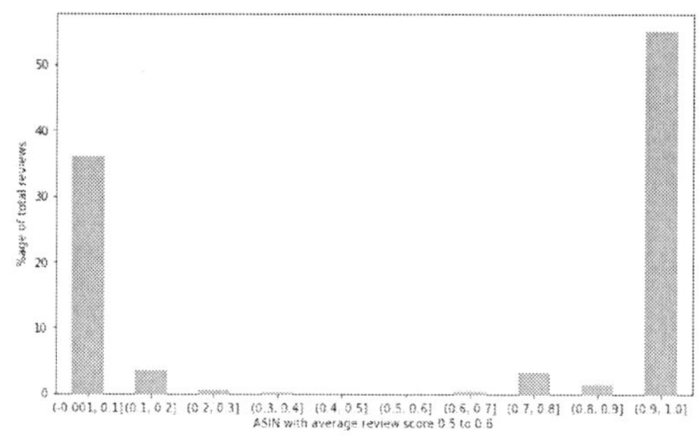

Figure 13: Unrelated Review Score Distribution for Product-3 showing a roughly equal mix of related and unrelated reviews

Our method also has some limitations. First, the major drawback occurs because the data is labeled synthetically. Hence, there is no way to find the actual recall for our approach. Calculating recall requires manual labeling of all product-review pairs, which is an expensive process. Second, our method is dependent on the accuracy of labeling methods. For the intra-category case, our method cannot detect products hijacked with similar wording in the same category since their Jaccard distance is low. For example, if there are two products, "iPhone X" and "iPhone 5C cover", the products will have a low Jaccard distance, and the reviews hijacked among them cannot be labeled correctly. Therefore, our ML model can also not learn this kind of review hijacking. Third, generic reviews like "Good product!" and "Product shipped fast" were labeled hijacked and not hijacked depending on what product they belonged to. Ideally, we would want to label all of them as not hijacked. This random labeling adds to the noise in the labels.

In our continuing work, we are interested in two main directions: data and methods. From a data perspective, we are investigating more refined methods to generate synthetic labels. Can we couple crowd labelers with our swapping approach to construct better product-review pairs? We are also interested in updating the data itself. Our dataset covers reviews up to 2018, though many media reports of review hijacking were not until 2019. There could have been a rise in review hijacking that is not as prominent in our data. From a methods perspective, we have focused purely on text-based signals. Incorporating image-based features like from the product itself and user-submitted images could help identify examples of review hijacking. We are also interested in adopting recent advances in pre-trained language models like T5, DeBERTa, and RoBERTa. We are also focusing on using e-commerce specific text (like product catalog data) to instill domain-specific knowledge during the pre-training of language models versus BooksCorpus and English Wikipedia used in BERT.

References

Davide Chicco. 2021. *Siamese Neural Networks: An Overview*, pages 73–94. Springer US, New York, NY.

Dan Dascalescu. 2019. Swapped product listings on amazon - web applications stack exchange. Webapps Stackexchange.

Jacob Devlin, Ming-Wei Chang, Kenton Lee, and Kristina Toutanova. 2019. BERT: Pre-training of deep bidirectional transformers for language understanding. In *Proceedings of the 2019 Conference of the North American Chapter of the Association for Computational Linguistics: Human Language Technologies, Volume 1 (Long and Short Papers)*, pages 4171–4186, Minneapolis, Minnesota. Association for Computational Linguistics.

Josh Dzieza. 2019. Even amazon's own products are getting hijacked by imposter sellers. The Verge.

Stefan Gössling, C Michael Hall, and Ann-Christin Andersson. 2018. The manager's dilemma: a conceptualization of online review manipulation strategies. *Current Issues in Tourism*, 21(5):484–503.

Andreas Hanselowski, Avinesh PVS, Benjamin Schiller, Felix Caspelherr, Debanjan Chaudhuri, Christian M. Meyer, and Iryna Gurevych. 2018. A retrospective analysis of the fake news challenge stance-detection task. In *Proceedings of the 27th International Conference on Computational Linguistics*, pages 1859–1874, Santa Fe, New Mexico, USA. Association for Computational Linguistics.

Derrick Higgins, Jill Burstein, and Yigal Attali. 2006. Identifying off-topic student essays without topic-specific training data. *Natural Language Engineering*, 12(2):145.

Nitin Jindal and Bing Liu. 2007. Review spam detection. In *Proceedings of the 16th International Conference on World Wide Web*, WWW '07, page 1189–1190, New York, NY, USA. Association for Computing Machinery.

Diana Kaemingk. 2020. Online reviews statistics to know in 2021. Qualtrics.

Parisa Kaghazgaran, James Caverlee, and Majid Alfifi. 2017. Behavioral analysis of review fraud: Linking malicious crowdsourcing to amazon and beyond. In *Proceedings of the International AAAI Conference on Web and Social Media*, volume 11.

Annie Louis and Derrick Higgins. 2010. Off-topic essay detection using short prompt texts. In *Proceedings of the NAACL HLT 2010 Fifth Workshop on Innovative Use of NLP for Building Educational Applications*, IUNLPBEA '10, page 92–95, USA. Association for Computational Linguistics.

Arjun Mukherjee, Bing Liu, and Natalie Glance. 2012. Spotting fake reviewer groups in consumer reviews. In *Proceedings of the 21st international conference on World Wide Web*, pages 191–200.

Arjun Mukherjee, Vivek Venkataraman, Bing Liu, Natalie Glance, et al. 2013. Fake review detection: Classification and analysis of real and pseudo reviews. *UIC-CS-03-2013. Technical Report*.

Rosie Murphy. 2020. Local consumer review survey 2020. Bright Local.

Nicole Nguyen. 2018. Here's another kind of review fraud happening on amazon. BuzzFeed News.

Jianmo Ni, Jiacheng Li, and Julian McAuley. 2019. Justifying recommendations using distantly-labeled reviews and fine-grained aspects. In *Proceedings of the 2019 Conference on Empirical Methods in Natural Language Processing and the 9th International Joint Conference on Natural Language Processing (EMNLP-IJCNLP)*, pages 188–197.

Jeffrey Pennington, Richard Socher, and Christopher D Manning. 2014. Glove: Global vectors for word representation. In *Proceedings of the 2014 conference on empirical methods in natural language processing (EMNLP)*, pages 1532–1543.

Marek Rei and Ronan Cummins. 2016. Sentence similarity measures for fine-grained estimation of topical relevance in learner essays. In *Proceedings of the 11th Workshop on Innovative Use of NLP for Building Educational Applications*, pages 283–288, San Diego, CA. Association for Computational Linguistics.

Seonghan Ryu, Seokhwan Kim, Junhwi Choi, Hwanjo Yu, and Gary Geunbae Lee. 2017. Neural sentence embedding using only in-domain sentences for out-of-domain sentence detection in dialog systems. *Pattern Recognition Letters*, 88:26–32.

Greg Sterling. 2019. Review fraud: Hijacked amazon reviews a big problem says consumer reports. Search Engine Land.

Jake Swearingen. 2019. Hijacked reviews on amazon can trick shoppers. Consumer Reports.

Hannah Walsh. 2020. How ebay's review system is promoting fake, counterfeit and even dangerous products. Which.

Learning Cross-Task Attribute - Attribute Similarity for Multi-task Attribute-Value Extraction

Mayank Jain [*], Sourangshu Bhattacharya[*], Harshit Jain[**], Karimulla Shaik[**], and Muthusamy Chelliah[**]

[*]Computer Science & Engineering, IIT Kharagpur, India.
jmayank@gmail.com, sourangshu@iitkgp.ac.in
[**]Flipkart India Pvt. Ltd., Bengaluru, India.
{ harshit.jain,karimulla.shaik,muthusamy.c}@flipkart.com,

Abstract

Automatic extraction of product attribute-value pairs from unstructured text like product descriptions is an important problem for e-commerce companies. The attribute schema typically varies from one category of products (which will be referred as vertical) to another. This leads to extreme annotation efforts for training of supervised deep sequence labeling models such as LSTM-CRF, and consequently not enough labeled data for some vertical-attribute pairs. In this work, we propose a technique for alleviating this problem by using annotated data from related verticals in a multi-task learning framework. Our approach relies on availability of similar attributes (labels) in another related vertical. Our model jointly learns the similarity between attributes of the two verticals along with the model parameters for the sequence tagging model. The main advantage of our approach is that it does not need any prior annotation of attribute similarity. Our system has been tested with datasets of size more than 10000 from a large e-commerce company in India. We perform detailed experiments to show that our method indeed increases the macro-F1 scores for attribute value extraction in general, and for labels with low training data in particular. We also report top labels from other verticals that contribute towards learning of particular labels.

1 Introduction

Online e-commerce marketplaces (e.g., Flipkart) operate by efficiently matching customer queries and browsing habits to appropriate seller inventory. Inventory is stored in a catalog which consists of images, structured attributes (key-value pairs) and unstructured textual description as shown in figure 1. Products of same kind (e.g., digital camera) are thus described using a unique set of attributes (e.g., zoom, resolution) – helping

Figure 1: **A snapshot of structured attributes and product description - underlined words wherein is important, additional information not provided by seller in attributes.**

faceted navigation, merchandizing, search ranking and comparative summary.

Onboarding products in a catalog requires populating the structured as well as unstructured parts. The time a seller has to spend on a product addition request is proportional to the quantum of information that he/she has to provide. On the other hand, correctness and completeness of catalog results in better product discovery, leading to a trade-off with its onboarding time. A good amount of attributes information is present in product description as well. This motivates us to extract the information from unstructured text instead of explicitly asking sellers for attributes. Additional information in description (e.g., precise features, relation between products) as shown in figure 1 helps to enrich the catalog as well. The extracted attributes can be used to check consistency between unstructured and structured data provided by seller and thus quality control of addition request.

Proceedings of the 4th Workshop on e-Commerce and NLP (ECNLP 4), pages 79–87
August 5, 2021.

We design supervised deep learning techniques for the problem of attribute value extraction. Figure 2, shows a typical input sentence and the corresponding `B, I, O` tags. The task of our model is to predict the tags given an input sentence. This problem is related supervised sequence labelling problem (Zheng et al., 2018; Lample et al., 2016). However, this technique needs a lot of training data points (sentence - label pairs) to perform effectively, which in turn requires massive annotation efforts on the part of e-commerce companies - reduction of which is an ongoing challenge; OpenTag (Zheng et al., 2018) uses active learning to annotate only most informative examples.

E-commerce companies however have the products categorized as different verticals, e.g. *dress*, *jeans*, etc. Each of these verticals have a different set of attributes, and hence needs to annotated using different models. A lot of the attributes among these verticals are common, or related though. Hence, it should be possible to borrow information from annotations given in different verticals, to improve the prediction performance of a given vertical. The only challenge is that correspondences between similar labels of different verticals is not available readily.

Our main contribution here is thus to develop a multi-task learning (MTL) model (Ruder, 2017) which can simultaneously learn attribute extraction and attribute-attribute similarity for multiple verticals (here we report with only two verticals at a time). We do so by using a soft coupling loss function across pairs of similar (context,label) combinations between the two tasks, where similarity is learned using attention mechanism. The naive version of such an objective will be prohibitively large to optimize. We propose to use a cosine similarity based shortlist, which makes the solution feasible.

We validate our method using a large corpus (more than 10000 product descriptions, across 6 verticals) collected from the e-commerce company - Flipkart. Extensive experimentation shows that our method improves performance of prediction on almost all the verticals, and especially shows upto 50% improvement for many labels which have low number of training examples. This is especially interesting since we find that number of instances with an attribute is highly skewed across the attributes. Detailed analysis also confirms that the attention mechanism indeed discovers similar attributes from other verticals to borrow information from.

Words	Black	levis	jeans	for	mens	with	cotton	blend	fabric
Attributes	B color	B brand	O	O	B Ideal_for	O	B Fabric	I Fabric	O

Figure 2: Sample tagged data from Jean Vertical.

2 Related Work

Attribute extraction: Various tokens (e.g., Apple) in an offer title are classified into attribute names (e.g., brand) relevant to the product (e.g., smartphone) (Joshi et al., 2015). For recognizing attributes (e.g., product family) in a short text segment, missing KB entries are leveraged through word embeddings learned on an unlabeled corpus (Kozareva et al., 2016). (Joshi et al., 2015) investigates whether distributed word vectors benefit NER in the e-commerce domain where entities are item properties (e.g., brand name, color, material, clothing size). (Xu et al., 2019) regards each attribute as a query and adopts only one global set of BIO tags for any attribute to reduce the burden of attribute tag or model explosion. OpenTag (Zheng et al., 2018) uses active learning along with a deep tagging model to update a product catalog with missing values for many attributes of interest from seller-provided title/description. To create the initial labeled data set, (Rezk et al., 2019) proposes bootstraping of seed data by extracting new values from unstructured text in a domain/language-independent fashion. Through category conditional self-attention and multi-task learning, a knowledge extraction model Attribute prediction and value extraction tasks are jointly modelled (Zhu et al., 2020) from multiple aspects towards interactions between attributes and values. Contrastive entity linkage (Embar et al., 2020) helps identify grocery product attribute pairs that share same value (e.g., brand, manufacturer, product line) and differ from each other (e.g., package size, color). Retailers do not always provide clean data as textual descriptions in product catalog (e.g., non-distinctive names (cotton, black t-shirt), blurred distinction (Amazon is a product/vs. brand), homonyms (Apple)). (Alonso et al., 2019) discovers such attribute relationships towards a brand-product knowledge graph from diverse input data sources.

Multi-task Learning (MTL): Significant theoretical interest exists in MTL since it offers excellent generalization performance in domains where training data is scarce (Maurer et al., 2016). In NLP, (Collobert and Weston, 2008) proposed a unified deep learning architecture for many common tasks e.g. POS tagging, chunking, etc. (Yang and Hospedales, 2017) presented a new representation MTL framework that learns cross-task sharing structure at every layer in a deep network. (Rijula Kar, 2018) proposed a task-sensitive representation learning framework that learns mention-dependent representations for NED, and violates norm to share parameters in the final layer.

(Wang et al., 2020) treats each attribute as a question finding the best answer span corresponding to its value in product context - modelled by a BERT encoder shared across all attributes for scalability. A distilled masked language model improving generalizability is then integrated with the encoder into a unified MTL framework. (Karamanolakis et al., 2020) applies to thousands of product categories organized in a hierarchical taxonomy. However, existing methods do not automatically discover attribute-attribute similarity from data, without taking attribute hierarchy as input.

3 Methods

In this section, we describe a novel multi-task approach to improving the accuracy of a supervised attribute value extraction system. We start with the attribute-value extraction system, based on deep bidirectional LSTM model, described in OpenTag (Zheng et al., 2018). Our main idea here is to leverage the information contained in instances of related tasks, e.g. in our case related domains / verticals of products. The key challenge in our case is that the set of labels across verticals need not be same, or even *aligned*. For example, the label `PROCESSOR_TYPE` is a valid label for `LAPTOP` vertical but does not make sense for `DRESS` vertical. On the other hand, the set of values for the common label `BRAND` will be very different for the vertical `DRESS` compared to the vertical `LAPTOP`. Hence, our core challenge here is to determine the similarities between labels automatically in the context of each vertical in order to leverage the information from a related vertical. The proposed architecture is described in figure 3.

3.1 Problem setup

Each instance of the (single-task) attribute-value extraction problem comes with an input sentence denoted by a sequence of words $\mathbf{w} = \{w_1, \dots, w_n\}$ and a corresponding set of labels $\mathbf{y} = \{y_1, \dots, y_n\}$. The task is to design a supervised ML algorithm which given the input sentence $\mathbf{w}$, predicts the output labels $\mathbf{y}$. Here, the labels correspond to the attributes, e.g. `COLOR`, and words correspond to the predicted values. Following common practice, we use 3 types of labels (also called tags): `B, I, O`. Here `B` and `I` are prepended to the label to indicate begining and end of a multi-word tag, respectively, while `O` refers to no tag for the word. For example, the multi-word color "light green" may be tagged as `B_COLOR` and `I_COLOR`.

This is an instance of sequence labeling problem (Lample et al., 2016), and the LSTM-CRF model proposed by Lample et al. (Lample et al., 2016) is the a state of the art model for this task. For each word w_i, we obtain the corresponding word embedding x_i using a concatenation of its glove embedding (Pennington et al., 2014) and it's character based embedding. The word embeddings of a sentence $\mathbf{x} = \{x_1, \dots, x_n\}$ is passed through a Bidirectional LSTM (BiLSTM) layer to produce the context sensitive word embedding $\mathbf{h}$:

$$\mathbf{h} = \text{BiLSTM}(\mathbf{x}) \quad (1)$$

We call this the the embedding layer for our input which is common to both single and multi-task models. Figure 3(a) describes the architecture in detail.

For the multi-task attribute-value extraction problem, the input is a sentence $w_j^t j = 1, \dots, n$, and the output of model is a sequence of labels $y_j^t, j = 1, \dots, n$, where $t = 1, \dots, T$. In this paper we only consider the setting of $T = 2$, i.e. we learn from 2 tasks at a time, due to scalability reasons. However, in theory our method can be extended to learning from more than 2 tasks. We compute the word embeddings $\mathbf{x}$ and context dependent word embeddings $\mathbf{h}$ in a similar manner as described above.

3.2 Single-task attribute-value extraction

We use the LSTM-CRF model with character embeddings (Lample et al., 2016; Zheng et al., 2018) as our baseline single task model. For a given input sentence the word embeddings $\mathbf{x}$ and the con-

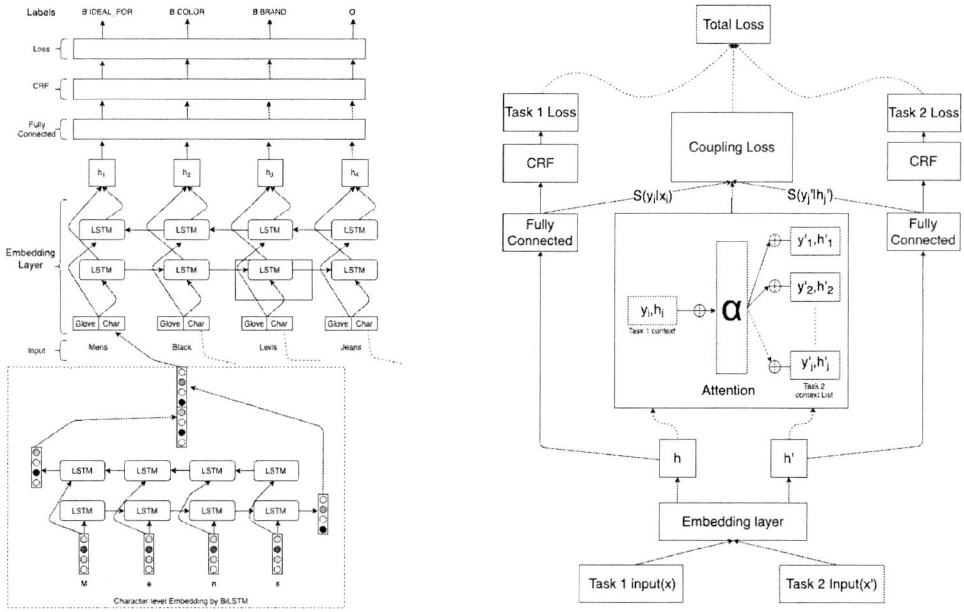

(a) (b)

Figure 3: (a) Architecture of single task model showing the sentence embedding layers (b) High-level architecture of the multi-task attribute-value extraction model

text sensitive word embeddings $\mathbf{h}$ are computed as described above. The context sensitive word embeddings $h_i, i = 1, \ldots, n$ is then passed through a fully connected layer to produce the score $s(y)$ for every possible label y. This is parameterized by the matrix $W \in R^{d \times k}$ and $b \in R^k$ where d is the dimension of h_i and k is the total number of possible labels. Hence the score vector for every label is computed as:

$$s_i(.|\mathbf{x}) = W \times h_i + b \forall i = 1, \ldots, n$$

where n is the length of sentence. We can interpret the kth component of s_i, denoted as $s_i(y = k|h_i)$, as the score of class k for word w_i . Now, given a sequence of words vectors $\mathbf{x}$, a sequence of score vectors $\{s_1(y|\mathbf{x}), \ldots, s_n(y|\mathbf{x})\}$, and a sequence of keys $\mathbf{y}$, a linear-chain CRF defines a global score $C \in R$ as,

$$C(\mathbf{x}, \mathbf{y}) = \sum_{i=1}^{n} s_i(y_i|\mathbf{x}) + \sum_{i=1}^{n-1} T(y_i, y_{i+1}|\mathbf{x})$$

Here, $s(y|\mathbf{x})$ is the yth component of the s vector and $T(y, y')$ is the transition score from label y to y', which is used to capture label dependency.

A softmax over all possible tag sequences yields a probability for the sequence $\mathbf{y}$. $P(\mathbf{y}|\mathbf{x}) = \frac{e^{C(\mathbf{x},\mathbf{y})}}{\sum_{\mathbf{y}' \in \mathcal{Y}} e^{C(\mathbf{x},\mathbf{y}')}}$ During training, we maximize the log-probability of the correct key sequence: $log(P(\mathbf{y}|\mathbf{x})) = C(\mathbf{x}, \mathbf{y}) - log(\sum_{\mathbf{y}' \in \mathcal{Y}} e^{C(\mathbf{x},\mathbf{y}')})$ Here $\mathcal{Y}$ is the set of all possible labellings for sequence $\mathbf{x}$. Given a dataset of sequences and labels $\mathcal{D} = \{(\mathbf{x}_j, \mathbf{y}_j), j = 1, \ldots, m$, we can define the CRF loss as the negative log-likelihood:

$$L_{CRF}(W, b) = \sum_{j=1}^{m} -log(P(\mathbf{y}_j|\mathbf{x}_j))$$

(Lample et al., 2016) describes a method for learning the model parameters and inferring the partition function and scores by minimizing the above objective w.r.t. W and b.

3.3 Multi-task attribute-value extraction

As mentioned above, for multi-task attribute-value extraction, we have sequence and label combinations $(\mathbf{x}^t, \mathbf{y}^t)$ for two tasks, $t \in \{1, 2\}$. We also note that we have a common set of embedding layers (both word representation and BiLSTM) for the two tasks. However, the feedforward layer used for scoring the labels are specific to the tasks. Hence:

$$s_i^t(.|\mathbf{x}) = W^t \times h_i + b^t, \forall i = 1, \ldots, n; \forall t = \{1, 2\}$$

The score and loss functions can be defined analogously to the single task model as: $C^t(\mathbf{x},\mathbf{y}) = \sum_{i=1}^{n} s_i^t(y_i|\mathbf{x}) + \sum_{i=1}^{n-1} T^t(y_i, y_{i+1}|\mathbf{x})$, and $log(P^t(\mathbf{y}|\mathbf{x})) = C^t(\mathbf{x},\mathbf{y}) - log(\sum_{\mathbf{y}'\in\mathcal{Y}} e^{C^t(\mathbf{x},\mathbf{y}')})$. Given the multi-task dataset $\mathcal{D}^t = \{(\mathbf{x}_j^t, \mathbf{y}_j^t), j = 1,\ldots,m^t, t = \{1,2\}$, our loss function can be written as:

$$L_{CRF}(W,b) = \sum_{t=1}^{2}\sum_{j=1}^{m^t} -log(P^t(\mathbf{y}_j^t|\mathbf{x}_j^t))$$

Hence, only parameters of the embedding layers get affected by the multi-task paradigm here, since those are the only shared layers between the tasks. However, these parameters are independent of the labels and are thus relatively robustly learned by just using a reasonably large corpus of input sentences. Another mechanism for borrowing information between tasks is through "soft coupling" (Ruder, 2017) of various scores or parameters which are not explicitly shared. In the next section, we devise a soft coupling loss between instances of the two tasks which achieve transfer of information at the granularity of labels.

3.4 Coupling loss

The principle we use for coupling of scores $s_i^t(y|x)$ is: *similar labels in similar contexts should have similar scores*. Recall that the dataset for multi-task attribute value extraction consists of two sets of instances $\mathcal{D}^1$ and $\mathcal{D}^2$, for each of the two tasks. Since we are attempting to compare the model predictions for the two tasks, the coupling loss depends on two *contexts*, one from each task: $(\mathbf{x}_j, \mathbf{y}_j, i)$ and $(\mathbf{x}_{j'}, \mathbf{y}_{j'}, i')$. Here, j and j' denotes indices of instances for the two tasks, and i and i' indices within the each sentence instance to the two tasks. We note that since the are ~ 1000 instances for each task, and ~ 10 length sentences for each instance, the total number of terms for this loss will be $\sim 10^8$ $((10 \times 1000)^2)$. This is prohibitively large for our training purpose, and also is wasteful, since not all *contexts* (combination of instance j and position i) are related to each other.

Hence, as a first step we create a shortlist of pairs of contexts $((i,j),(i',j'))$ which can borrow informations from each other, by thresholding on the cosine similarity between the a windows around the contexts $u_{i,j}$ and $u'_{i',j'}$:

$$L = \{((i,j),(i',j')) \mid \text{cosine\_sim}(u_{i,j}, u'_{i',j'}) > \text{thresh}\}$$

Here, note that $u(i,j)$ is the word embedding of a window around the context (i,j).

Context coupling error: Our next challenge is to design a mechanism to figure out similar contexts and similar labels. We use the softmax attention mechanism to automatically learn the similar label-context combinations, simultaneously as we also learn the scoring function. For efficiency of parameters, we use the Luong attention. Hence the attention score for context (i,j) from task 1 over context (i',j') from task 2 is given by:

$$A(j,i,j',i') = \frac{e^{\alpha(j,i,j',i')}}{\sum_{(\hat{j},\hat{i})\in L(j,i)} e^{\alpha(j,i,\hat{j},\hat{i})}}$$
$$\alpha(j,i,j',i') = u(i,j)^T \text{diag}(\mathbf{a}) u(i',j')$$

Here, $\mathbf{a} = (a_1, ..., a_d)$ are learnable parameters of same dimension as the word embeddings, and $L(j,i) = \{(j',i') | ((i,j),(i',j')) \in L\}$. The *context-coupling error* is defined as:

$$CCE(L,\mathbf{a}) = \sum_{((j,i),(j',i'))\in L} A(j,i,j',i') \times |(s_i(y_{ji}|\mathbf{x}_j) - s'_{j'}(y'_{j',i'}|\mathbf{x}_{j'})|$$

We note that this score is selecting the similar contexts from second task since it normalizes the attention score over the contexts of the second task. Symmetrically, we can define the attention score of context (i',j') from task 2 over (i,j) from task 1 as:

$$A'(j,i,j',i') = \frac{e^{\alpha'(j,i,j',i')}}{\sum_{(\hat{j},\hat{i})\in L(j',i')} e^{\alpha(\hat{j},\hat{i},j',i')}}$$
$$\alpha'(j,i,j',i') = u(i,j)^T \text{diag}(\mathbf{a}') u(i',j')$$

Hence the context coupling error in reverse direction is given by:

$$CCE'(L,\mathbf{a}') = \sum_{((j,i),(j',i'))\in L} A'(j,i,j',i') \times |(s_i(y_{ji}|\mathbf{x}_j) - s'_{j'}(y'_{j',i'}|\mathbf{x}_{j'})|$$

Label coupling error In addition to the context coupling error defined above, we also take into account the explicit similarity between only labels, using a character k-gram based embedding of the labels in the context (i,j) as: $v_{i,j}$. Hence, the label coupling error is given as:

$$LCE((i,j),(i',j')) = \text{SoftMax}(v_{i,j} \cdot v'_{i',j'}) \times |(s_i(y_{ji}|\mathbf{x}_j) - s'_{j'}(y'_{j',i'}|\mathbf{x}_{j'})|$$

LCE' is defined analogously. The label embeddings, $v_{i,j}$, are learned jointly with the model. The *total coupling error* between contexts (i,j) and (i',j') from the two tasks respectively, is the sum of context coupling error and the label coupling error:

$$TCE(L, \mathbf{a}, \mathbf{a}', \mathbf{v}) = \sum_{((i,j),(i',j')) \in L} [CCE((i,j),(i',j')) + CCE'((i,j),(i',j')) + LCE((i,j),(i',j')) + LCE'((i,j),(i',j'))]$$

We optimize the sum total of all the CRF losses and total coupling error in order to obtain model parameters. We use stochatic gradient descent, where minibatches are constructed from three lists: $\mathcal{D}^1$, $\mathcal{D}^2$, and L. Samples from the first two lists are used to calculate the CRF losses, while samples from L are used to calculate total coupling error, and the corresponding updates.

4 Experimental Results

In this section, we report results from our proposed method for multi-task attribute extraction, against single task attribute extraction. We implemented our model using tensorflow on a 8-core Centos machine. We used 300 dimensional pre-trained Glove vectors. We have also experimented with other customized word embeddings e.g. fasttext, but did not achieve significantly better results. For this work, we use single layer BiLSTM as the embedding layer. The hidden layer size for BiLSTM layer was set to 700. We have experimented with other embedding layer architectures, e.g. hidden layer sizes ranging from 300 to 900, and also two layer BiLSTMs with hidden layer sizes (500,700). However, the performance of single layer LSTM with hidden layer size 700 was found to be similar or better than others. For training, the batch size was chosen to be 30 for both the CRF loss batches and for coupling loss batches sampled from the shortlist L. ADAM was used as optimizer and we trained for maximum of 30 epochs. We trained the model for 30 epochs.

Table 1: Dataset Characterstics.

Vertical	# labels	# Examples (Train, Test)	# Exmpl. / label (max , min)
Jean	37	2206 , 948	1387,1
Trouser	38	1993, 856	1350, 1
Dress	30	4088, 1753	2241, 1
Mangalsutra	38	363, 157	333, 1
Chain	76	2068, 888	1195, 1
Jewellery	68	4863, 2085	4518, 1

Table 2: Similar Task Pairs for MTL

(Dress, Jean), (Mangalsutra, Jewellary)
(Trouser , Jean), (Chain, Jewellary),
(Mangalsutra, Chain)

Evaluation Metric As reported below, the datasets for this problem show extreme skew in terms of occurrence of labels. Hence, we use the standard metrics of *macro precision*, *macro recall*, and *macro F1 score*. We also report the micro-accuracy. While computing the macro-metrics (precision, recall and F1), we ignore the 'O' label. It is clear that macro-F1 score without the 'O' label, is the most representative metric here, from an application point of view.

4.1 Datasets

The dataset used here are taken from actual systems for product delivery used in Flipkart. We performed our experiments using data (both product descriptions, and ground truth annotations) from six verticals: `Dress`, `Jean`, `Mangalsutra`[1], `Chain`, `Trouser` and `Jewellery` available on Flipkart. These verticals are chosen based on three factors (1) GMV (Gross Merchandise Value), (2) Volume of data available and (3) Verticals with rich product descriptions. Number of labels in each vertical and number of tagged description in train and test data for each vertical is shown in table 1. The words in product descriptions for each vertical are tagged using `B`, `I`, `O` (short for beginning, inside, and outside) format where the B prefix before a tag indicates that the token is the beginning of a tag, and an I prefix before a tag indicates that the token is inside a tag and An O tag indicates that a token belongs to no tag.

Table 2 shows the pairs of similar tasks (verticals) which were trained togather for MTL. The pairs were chosen manually based on probability

[1]A type of Necklace

of occurrence similar labels in these tasks. The results for the each of the verticals is the best achieved for these pairs of tasks. Note that, while we have to manually provide a similar pair of tasks, the similarity between labels is automatically deciphered.

4.2 Performance Comparison

Table 3: Comparison of macro-F1 scores between single-task and multi-task models for various verticals

Vertical	Prec.	Recall	Acc.	F1
Single-task				
Dress	91.28	84.85	98.44	87.95
Jean	80.18	74.78	97.49	77.39
Mangalstr.	87.41	83.58	98.27	85.45
Trouser	78.52	71.91	98.83	75.07
Jewellery	71.06	72.13	97.94	**71.59**
Chain	58.61	49.63	96.59	53.75
Multi-task				
Dress	91.14	85.70	98.48	**88.23**
Jean	84.66	76.41	98.94	**80.32**
Mangalstr.	90.06	84.71	98.45	**87.30**
Trouser	78.94	75.32	98.90	**77.08**
Jewellery	70.94	69.60	97.83	70.26
Chain	64.51	55.90	96.75	**59.90**

In this section, we illustrate the effectiveness of our multi-task learning method. Table 3, reports the best performances of single and multi-task models for all the six verticals studied here. We can see that except for jewellery, multi-task model improve performance in terms of F1 score for all other verticals. For some verticals, e.g. chain, the improvement is more than 5 percent, while for other verticals the improvement lies in the 2 percent range. We note that the improvement depends on two main factors: whether we can find a close enough vertical to borrow from, and the number of examples already present in the current vertical. For example we can see that the vertical "Jewellery" has about 5000 examples, and also does not have a very close other vertical to borrow information from. Hence in it's case MTL is not able to improve the performance.

In table 4, we report the fine-grained improvements of top 5 labels for the verticals: Trouser, Jean, Mangalsutra, and Chain. We note that the top improvements for these verticals are in the range of 51%, 46%, 29% and 22% respectively. We also note that number of examples for these labels in the training dataset (#ex column) are respectively 6, 15, 6, and 7. Hence this table further corroborates our claim that MTL improves the performance for labels with lower amount of information in the single task training set.

Table 4: Attribute-wise percentage improvement on various tasks

Attribute	#Ex.	Task	Prec.	Recall	F1-Sc.	%Imp.
Trouser						
I_occas.	6	single	1.0	0.17	0.29	0.51
		multi	1.0	0.67	0.8	
I_suitab.	3	single	1.0	0.33	0.5	0.3
		multi	1.0	0.67	0.8	
B_suitab.	6	single	0.4	0.33	0.36	0.1
		multi	0.43	0.5	0.46	
I_brand	283	single	0.91	0.88	0.89	0.03
		multi	0.92	0.92	0.92	
B_pattern	308	single	0.88	0.9	0.89	0.03
		multi	0.88	0.95	0.92	
Jean						
I_pattern	15	single	0.33	0.07	0.11	0.46
		multi	1.0	0.4	0.57	
I_suitab.	2	single	0.5	0.5	0.5	0.17
		multi	1.0	0.5	0.67	
B_suitab.	5	single	0.5	0.4	0.44	0.13
		multi	1.0	0.4	0.57	
I_ref._fit	14	single	1.0	0.57	0.73	0.05
		multi	1.0	0.64	0.78	
B_pattern	206	single	0.9	0.89	0.89	0.02
		multi	0.92	0.91	0.91	
Mangalsutra						
I_diamnd	6	single	0.0	0.0	0.0	0.29
		multi	1.0	0.17	0.29	
B_diamnd	19	single	0.82	0.47	0.6	0.09
		multi	0.85	0.58	0.69	
B_chain	19	single	0.94	0.84	0.89	0.03
		multi	0.94	0.89	0.92	
B_brand	112	single	0.97	0.92	0.94	0.03
		multi	0.97	0.97	0.97	
I_gemst.	37	single	1.0	0.89	0.94	0.02
		multi	1.0	0.92	0.96	
Chain						
I_warr.	7	single	0.64	1.0	0.78	0.22
		multi	1.0	1.0	1.0	
I_weight	51	single	0.68	0.8	0.74	0.08
		multi	0.76	0.88	0.82	
I_width	18	single	0.68	0.83	0.75	0.04
		multi	0.75	0.83	0.79	
B_weight	26	single	0.76	0.85	0.8	0.04
		multi	0.79	0.88	0.84	
I_color	92	single	0.93	0.59	0.72	0.04
		multi	0.86	0.67	0.76	

4.3 Validation of Attribute Similarity

In this section, we validate the learned attribute-attribute similarity, by studying the attribute-wise F1-scores for the similar attribute pairs. Figure 4-(a) shows the full attention heatmap for all labels between the pair of tasks: Mangasutra - Chain. Here the attention is normalised over the attributes of y-axis (task chain). It is clear from the heatmap

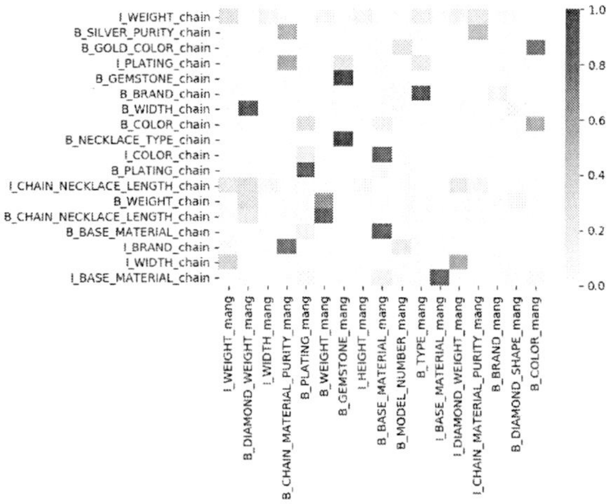

(a)

Borrower-Chain	Lender-Mangalstr.(Att.[2])
B_base_mat.	B_base_mat. (0.86)
I_weight	I_weight (0.28)
B_necklace_type	B_gemstone (1.0)
B_color	B_color (0.56)
B_gemstone	B_gemstone (1.0)
I_brand	B_mat._purity (0.79)
B_plating	B_plating (0.9)
B_brand	B_type (0.9)
I_base_mat.	I_base_mat. (0.83)
B_weight	B_weight (0.67)

(b)

Figure 4: (a) Attention Heatmap between labels of Chain (task 1) and Mangalsutra (task 2). (b) Attribute pairs with highest attention values, and the corresponding attention score.

that attention mechanism is indeed choosing the similar labels between the pairs of tasks, irrespective of whether there is an improvement in accuracy for the pair of labels.

In figure 4-(b), we report the topmost pairs of labels with the highest attention scores, along with the corresponding increase in accuracy. The left column borrower labels(Chain) and right column shows Lender labels(Mangalsutra) which got the highest average attention weights across all contexts-pairs in the list L. The value in brackets shows the attention value. The bold entries appear in top-5 attributes, with highest F1-scores in table 4. One can also see non-obvious correspondences, e.g. `Necklace_type` from chain can borrow all the information from `Gemstone` from lender vertical Mangalsutra. We can also see that in most of the cases, the labels from task 1 borrow information from corresponding labels of task 2, even though this information was not explicitly furnished. This observation provides us further confidence that the attention mechanism used for discovery of similar labels and similar contexts, indeed works effectively.

This observation further validates the effectiveness of our attention model in extracting similar pairs of labels between two tasks using the coupling loss. We believe this mechanism can be applied in many more situations to shortlist important and similar attributes in other contexts, while jointly learning a prediction model.

5 Conclusion

In this paper, we study attribute-value extraction from production description in the e-commerce domain. Many of the attributes occur in very few descriptions. Hence the amount of supervised training data available for these attributes is very low, which leads to low prediction performance We thus propose a novel multi-task learning based algorithm which borrows information from related domains (i.e., category/vertical) in order to improve prediction performance of infrequently occurring attributes. We validate the proposed method with extensive experimental evaluation on a large dataset of six verticals from a prominent, e-commerce company. The proposed technique not only achieves higher accuracy on verticals with similar labels, but also can be used for discovering attribute similarities across verticals.

References

Omar Alonso, Vasileios Kandylas, and Rukmini Iyer. 2019. Unsupervised Construction of a Product Knowledge Graph. In *Proceedings of the SIGIR 2019 Workshop on eCommerce, co-located with the 42st International ACM SIGIR Conference on Research and Development in Information Retrieval, eCom@SIGIR 2019, Paris, France, July 25, 2019 (CEUR Workshop Proceedings)*, Jon Degenhardt, Surya Kallumadi, Utkarsh Porwal, and Andrew Trotman (Eds.), Vol. 2410. CEUR-WS.org. http://ceur-ws.org/Vol-2410/paper23.pdf

Ronan Collobert and Jason Weston. 2008. A unified architecture for natural language processing: deep neural networks with multitask learning. In *ICML '08*.

Varun Embar, Bunyamin Sisman, Hao Wei, Xin Luna Dong, Christos Faloutsos, and Lise Getoor. 2020. Contrastive Entity Linkage: Mining Variational Attributes from Large Catalogs for Entity Linkage. In *Automated Knowledge Base Construction*. https://openreview.net/forum?id=fR44nF03Rb

Mahesh Joshi, Ethan Hart, Mirko Vogel, and Jean-David Ruvini. 2015. Distributed Word Representations Improve NER for e-Commerce. In *Proceedings of the 1st Workshop on Vector Space Modeling for Natural Language Processing*. Association for Computational Linguistics, Denver, Colorado, 160–167. https://doi.org/10.3115/v1/W15-1522

Giannis Karamanolakis, Jun Ma, and Xin Dong. 2020. TXtract: Taxonomy-Aware Knowledge Extraction for Thousands of Product Categories. *ArXiv* abs/2004.13852 (2020).

Zornitsa Kozareva, Qi Li, Ke Zhai, and Weiwei Guo. 2016. Recognizing Salient Entities in Shopping Queries. In *Proceedings of the 54th Annual Meeting of the Association for Computational Linguistics (Volume 2: Short Papers)*. Association for Computational Linguistics, Berlin, Germany, 107–111. https://doi.org/10.18653/v1/P16-2018

Guillaume Lample, Miguel Ballesteros, Sandeep Subramanian, Kazuya Kawakami, and Chris Dyer. 2016. Neural Architectures for Named Entity Recognition. In *Proceedings of the 2016 Conference of the North American Chapter of the Association for Computational Linguistics: Human Language Technologies*. Association for Computational Linguistics, San Diego, California, 260–270. https://doi.org/10.18653/v1/N16-1030

Andreas Maurer, Massimiliano Pontil, and Bernardino Romera-Paredes. 2016. The Benefit of Multitask Representation Learning. *Journal of Machine Learning Research* 17, 81 (2016), 1–32. http://jmlr.org/papers/v17/15-242.html

Jeffrey Pennington, Richard Socher, and Christopher D Manning. 2014. Glove: Global vectors for word representation. In *Proceedings of the 2014 conference on empirical methods in natural language processing (EMNLP)*. 1532–1543.

Martín Rezk, Laura Alonso Alemany, Lasguido Nio, and Ted Zhang. 2019. Accurate Product Attribute Extraction on the Field. *2019 IEEE 35th International Conference on Data Engineering (ICDE)* (2019), 1862–1873.

Sourangshu Bhattacharya Anirban Dasgupta Soumen Chakrabarti Rijula Kar, Susmija Reddy. 2018. Task-Specific Representation Learning for Web-scale Entity Disambiguation. In *Association for the Advancement of Artificial Intelligence (AAAI)*.

Sebastian Ruder. 2017. An Overview of Multi-Task Learning in Deep Neural Networks. *ArXiv* abs/1706.05098 (2017).

Qifan Wang, Li Yang, Bhargav Kanagal, Sumit Sanghai, D Sivakumar, Bin Shu, Zac Yu, and Jon Elsas. 2020. Learning to Extract Attribute Value from Product via Question Answering: A Multi-task Approach. In *Proceedings of the 26th ACM SIGKDD International Conference on Knowledge Discovery & Data Mining*. 47–55.

Huimin Xu, Wenting Wang, Xin Mao, Xinyu Jiang, and Man Lan. 2019. Scaling up Open Tagging from Tens to Thousands: Comprehension Empowered Attribute Value Extraction from Product Title. In *Proceedings of the 57th Annual Meeting of the Association for Computational Linguistics*. Association for Computational Linguistics, Florence, Italy, 5214–5223. https://doi.org/10.18653/v1/P19-1514

Yongxin Yang and Timothy M. Hospedales. 2017. Deep Multi-task Representation Learning: A Tensor Factorisation Approach. *ArXiv* abs/1605.06391 (2017).

Guineng Zheng, Subhabrata Mukherjee, Xin Luna Dong, and Feifei Li. 2018. OpenTag: Open Attribute Value Extraction from Product Profiles. In *Proceedings of the 24th ACM SIGKDD International Conference on Knowledge Discovery and Data Mining* (London, United Kingdom) *(KDD '18)*. Association for Computing Machinery, New York, NY, USA, 1049–1058. https://doi.org/10.1145/3219819.3219839

Tiangang Zhu, Yue Wang, Haoran Li, Youzheng Wu, Xiaodong He, and Bowen Zhou. 2020. Multimodal Joint Attribute Prediction and Value Extraction for E-commerce Product. *arXiv preprint arXiv:2009.07162* (2020).

Unsupervised Class-Specific Abstractive Summarization of Customer Reviews

Thi Nhat Anh Nguyen, Mingwei Shen, Karen Hovsepian
PARS *, Amazon.com, Seattle
{tnguynr, mingweis, khhovsep}@amazon.com

Abstract

Large-scale unsupervised abstractive summarization is sorely needed to automatically scan millions of customer reviews in today's fast-paced e-commerce landscape. We address a key challenge in unsupervised abstractive summarization – reducing generic and uninformative content and producing useful information that relates to specific product aspects. To do so, we propose to model reviews in the context of some topical classes of interest. In particular, for any arbitrary set of topical classes of interest, the proposed model can learn to generate a set of class-specific summaries from multiple reviews of each product without ground-truth summaries, and the only required signal is class probabilities or class label for each review. The model combines a generative variational autoencoder, with an integrated class-correlation gating mechanism and a hierarchical structure capturing dependence among products, reviews and classes. Human evaluation shows that generated summaries are highly relevant, fluent, and representative. Evaluation using a reference dataset shows that our model outperforms state-of-the-art abstractive and extractive baselines.

1 Introduction

As volume and scope of online customer reviews continue to explode, so does the need for online sellers to digest and draw insights to improve products. Today, both sellers and customers manually sift through hundreds of reviews across competing products to decipher systemic or trending concerns from isolated or irrelevant issues. Opinion summarization technology run across millions of reviews has drawn much attention due to its potential for streamline defect discovery, trend analysis, product development, provided that summaries are informative and fluent.

This work concerns abstractive summarization of product reviews. Abstractive summaries which contain new phrases and words not found in original documents are often more fluent, more concise and more informative given the same length than extractive ones which only contain words, phrases and sentences from the original documents.

Current state-of-the-art methods for abstractive summarization are based on supervised deep-learning language models (Sutskever et al., 2014; Nallapati et al., 2016; Gu et al., 2016; See et al., 2017), and rely on large amount of human-written ground-truth summaries. Because text summarization systems are domain-sensitive (Isonuma et al., 2017) and ground-truth opinion summaries are expensive to obtain, unsupervised opinion summarization has recently garnered significant attention with noteworthy efforts (Ma et al., 2018; Wang and Ren, 2018; Bražinskas et al., 2020b). Unfortunately, summaries generated by unsupervised models are often generic and uninformative, and do not provide useful information about different aspects of the product.

To make review summaries more useful to users, we propose a class-specific unsupervised abstractive summarization model, which can generate class-specific summaries from multiple reviews of each product, according to any predefined set of topical classes of interest for the users. The model can be trained without using any ground-truth summaries. The only additional signal required for the model is the class probabilities or class label for each review generated by an independent black-box classifier, or provided by annotators. An example set of such topical classes is the set of major issue classes that products might be subjected to, including misleading product description, poor quality, sizing/fit/style issues, etc. See Table 1 for example class-specific summaries generated from reviews of a product according those topical classes.

To generate class-specific summaries for arbi-

* Product Assurance, Risk, and Security https://www.amazon.jobs/en/teams/product-assurance-risk-security

Proceedings of the 4th Workshop on e-Commerce and NLP (ECNLP 4), pages 88–100
August 5, 2021.

trary classes, existing opinion summarization models require either i) a large training set of ground-truth summaries per class, or ii) a complicated and costly training set comprising multiple types of manual annotations such as token tags, aspect-opinion phrase pairs, and phrase labels (Suhara et al., 2020). In contrast, our model only needs review-class label pairs.

The proposed model Class-CopyCat combines a generative variational autoencoder (VAE) model with a hierarchical structure that captures dependence among products, reviews and classes, allowing the representation of class-specific information through class latent variables. We also propose an integrated two-layer filter mechanism consisting of a class-correlation gate and a set of class-specific importance coefficients which focus on class-related words, and thus reduce irrelevant or generic information and increase informativeness with respect to (w.r.t.) each class of interest.

Our contributions can be summarized as follows:

- We solve a new, practical problem that has not been addressed before: to train a model to generate class-specific summaries from multiple reviews of each product using only class probabilities or class label for each review.
- We propose a novel hierarchical latent variable generative model to capture dependence among group/class/review latent variables and reviews. This allows us to generate class-specific summaries from the variational distributions of respective class latent variables.
- We propose a two-layer filter mechanism to extract class-specific information and key words, and reduce irrelevant information in the summaries, as detailed in Sec. 3.2.3.
- Our human evaluation and experiments with a reference dataset show that the proposed model outperforms state-of-the-art baselines in a wide range of evaluation metrics.

<table>
<tr><td>Summ. for chosen classes of interest</td><td>Class 1. Misleading Product Description:
These tights are not pink. The color is very much nude.
Class 2. Poor Quality:
The tights ripped after one wash. I would not buy these.
Class 3. Sizing/fit/style issue:
The sizing was way off.</td></tr>
<tr><td>Reviews</td><td>... the "pink" color these come in is not the pink ... || It lasted through one wear and one wash. After that the threads started streaking. Not worth the buy... || ... The sizing for these tights was not clear, ... way too big. || ... These tights ripped the first time my daughter wore them. Take a pass on these. || ... these tights are not pink... || ... They all have holes after first time wear... || The color says pink, but these are not pink. They are nude... || These tights are incredibly small compared to other brands and the pink color is more in line with nude...</td></tr>
</table>

Table 1: Summaries generated by our model for chosen classes; colors encode their alignment to input reviews. The reviews are truncated, and delimited with '||'.

2 Prior Work

2.1 Abstractive Summarization

Prior to deep-learning language models, abstractive summarization is considered a very hard problem, with limited success using graph mining (Ganesan et al., 2010; Filippova, 2010; Yang and Fang). More recent approaches view abstractive summarization as a text to text generation problem using sequence to sequence (Seq2Seq) neural models (Sutskever et al., 2014). These models usually employ an encoder-decoder structure. The encoder encodes documents into feature space, from which the decoder generates summaries. Such models tend to be "over creative" and may generate completely new outputs, which is not desirable. The prominent strategy to mitigate this problem is to use pointer networks as used in (Nallapati et al., 2016; Gu et al., 2016). Pointer networks (Vinyals et al., 2015) are an extension of attentive recurrent neural networks (RNN); they use attention as a pointer to select which tokens of the input sequence should be copied to the output. More recently, pointer-generator networks (See et al., 2017) add a switching mechanism to select between copying and generating new words. These supervised deep models require a large amount of text and human-written summary pairs for training (Hermann et al., 2015; Sandhaus, 2008; Narayan et al., 2018). Recent works on unsupervised abstractive summarization include SummaryLoop (Laban et al., 2020) for single document summarization, and MeanSum (Chu and Liu, 2019) and CopyCat (Bražinskas et al., 2020b) for multi-document summarization.

2.2 Context-aware document summarization

Our class-specific summarization problem is also related to context-aware summarization. In (Ma et al., 2018) and (Wang and Ren, 2018), the sentiment class of a product review is used as contextual information for summarization. In (Khatri et al., 2018), a contextual text summarization model based on Seq2Seq architecture is proposed for product description summarization. It includes three different components as contextual information: metadata provided by sellers (e.g. product title, tags and category), search query, and document titles used to discover the document (e.g. via recommendation). In (Narayan et al., 2018) and (Wang et al., 2018), document topics are pre-learned by a Latent Dirichlet Allocation topic model, and used as contextual information for text summarization. These context-aware models are useful for generating more document centric summaries, overcoming the problem of generic summaries. However, these models only target single-document summarization, and they must be trained via supervised-learning using a large set of human-written ground-truth summaries.

OpinionDigest is an opinion summarization framework that does not rely on gold summaries for training (Suhara et al., 2020). However, to generate summaries specific to an arbitrary topic or class, OpinionDigest has to use an Opinion Extraction model (Miao et al., 2020) pretrained for that topic using a training set produced with significant human annotation effort for each review, including token tagging, aspect-opinion phrase pairing, and labelling selected phrases per topic. The high cost of obtaining such training sets motivated our proposed solution.

3 Proposed Abstractive Class-Specific Multi-Review Summarization

We start with a high level description of the proposed model (Sec. 3.1), before presenting in greater detail the encoder and decoder subnets (Sec. 3.2, 3.3). Later, we introduce the loyalty term that discourages summaries containing false information (Sec. 3.4), and describe how the trained model generates class-specific summaries (Sec. 3.5).

3.1 Overview of the proposed model

Given a predefined set of T topical classes, our model generates multiple summaries, one for each class that may be present in a group of reviews; each group corresponds to a product. The model makes use of an independent classifier $\beta(.)$, which probabilistically assign each review to these classes; $\beta(r_i)_j$ denotes the probability that review r_i belongs to a class j for $j = 1, ..., T$. We propose a hierarchical latent variable structure to capture relation among products, reviews and classes as shown in Figure 1.

The model defines three sets of latent variables to represent products, classes, and individual re-

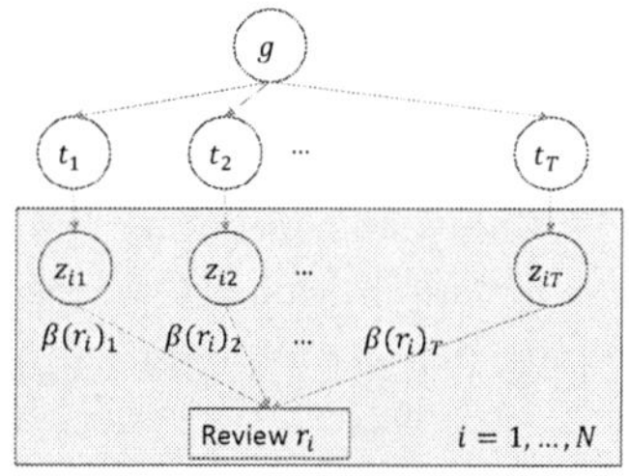

Figure 1: Graphical representation of the model

views. Each product (or group) is associated with a group variable g, which captures the group's overall semantics. Within each product, each class j is associated with a class variable t_j ($j = 1, ..., T$). Each class latent variable conditions on g, but focuses more on class-related words and information; and hence, it captures common themes and opinions about the product for that class. Finally, each review r_i ($i = 1, ..., N$) is associated with a review latent code $\mathbf{z}_i = [z_{ij}]_{j=1}^T$, which conditions on the class representation and captures content of individual reviews; z_{ij} denotes the review code for r_i given a class j. The class distribution $\beta(r_i)$ is used to soft-gate $\mathbf{z}_i$ in review reconstruction.

Our model's posterior inference is based on the VAE model (Kingma and Welling, 2013), also used in the CopyCat summarization model (Bražinskas et al., 2020b), with the latter serving as the inspiration for our model. As is standard with VAEs, our encoder, parameterized with ϕ, produces the variational posterior distributions of the latent variables $g \sim q_\phi(g|r_{1:N})$, $t_j \sim q_\phi(t_j|r_{1:N}, [\beta(r_i)]_{i=1}^N, g)$, and $z_{ij} \sim q_\phi(z_{ij}|r_i, t_j)$. As shown in Sec. 3.2, the variational posterior of t_j is designed to depend on class distributions of all reviews in the group $[\beta(r_i)]_{i=1}^N$, and that class-related information represented by t_j is computed using a two-layer filter mechanism. We also note that we choose to represent each review r_i using a collection of review variables $[z_{ij}]_{j=1}^T$, each corresponding to a class, instead of using a single review encoding as in CopyCat and typical VAE models, for better representation of class-related information. Encoder design is discussed in details in Sec. 3.2.

The decoder, parameterized by θ, reconstructs the review r_i from the posterior samples $\mathbf{z}_i$, $\beta(r_i)$ and all other reviews in the group r_{-i}. The reconstruction probability is hence defined as $p_\theta(r_i|\beta(r_i), \mathbf{z}_i, r_{-i})$. Here, we follow CopyCat's recommendation and let the decoder to directly access other reviews in the group to allows the reconstruction of fine-grain common group details, such

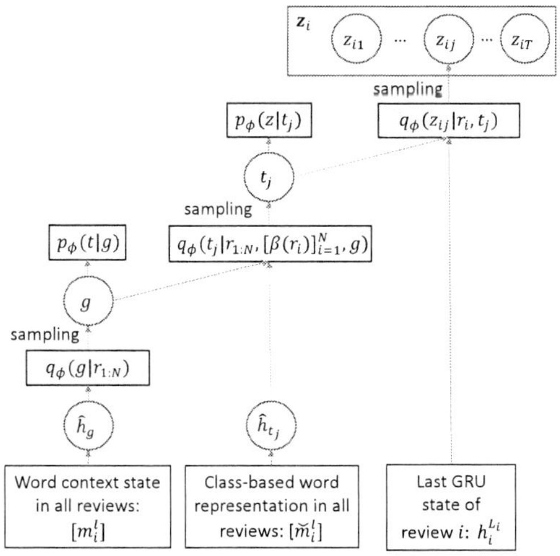

Figure 2: Generation of the latent code $\mathbf{z}_i$ for a review r_i by the encoder. Yellow boxes represent the neural networks that compute the prior and variational posterior distributions of latent codes.

as product names, product-specific attributes and characteristics. As we detail in Sec. 3.5, the trained model can generate a summary for a group of reviews for a given class j by decoding the mean of the class-dependent and review-agnostic z_{*j} prior.

The variational loss objective for our model is

$$\mathcal{L}_{VAE}(\theta, \phi, r_{1:N}) = \mathop{\mathbb{E}}_{g \sim q_\phi(g|r_{1:N})} \Bigg[\mathop{\mathbb{E}}_{\mathbf{t} \sim q_\phi(\mathbf{t}|r_{1:N}, [\beta(r_i)]_{i=1}^N, g)} \Bigg(\sum_{i=1}^{N} \mathop{\mathbb{E}}_{\mathbf{z}_i \sim q_\phi(\mathbf{z}_i|r_i, \mathbf{t})} [-\log p_\theta(r_i|\mathbf{z}_i, \beta(r_i), r_{-i})] + \sum_{i=1}^{N} D_{KL}[q_\phi(\mathbf{z}_i|r_i, \mathbf{t}) || p_\phi(\mathbf{z}_i|\mathbf{t})] \Bigg) + D_{KL}[q_\phi(\mathbf{t}|r_{1:N}, [\beta(r_i)]_{i=1}^N, g) || p_\phi(\mathbf{t}|g)] \Bigg] + D_{KL}[q_\phi(g|r_{1:N}) || p_\phi(g)], \quad (1)$$

where $p_\phi(.)$ denotes a prior distribution, and D_{KL} denotes Kullback Leibler divergence between the variational posterior and prior distributions of a latent variable. Later, in Sec. 3.4, we will improve this loss with an additional loyalty term.

3.2 The Encoder

Fig. 2 shows how the encoder produces latent codes g, $\mathbf{t}$, and $\mathbf{z}_i$. As with standard VAE, we use Gaussian distributions with diagonal covariances for the prior and variational distributions.

3.2.1 Text representation component

The encoder starts with a text representation component which includes a word embedding unit, a GRU encoder (Cho et al., 2014), and a class-correlation gate, as shown in Fig. 3.

Words in reviews are embedded into word embeddings, and then transformed by a GRU encoder to obtain hidden states. Let L_i denote the length of review r_i; w_i^l and h_i^l denote the word embedding and GRU hidden state for the l-th word in review r_i, for $l = 1, ..., L_i$. Word embeddings and GRU hidden states are concatenated into word context states: $m_i^l = [w_i^l \circ h_i^l]$. They are later used to compute group latent codes g (Sec. 3.2.2).

Word context states are also fed to a class-correlation gate to generate class-based word representation, which pays more attention to words related to the class of the review. First, the concatenation of each word context state and the class vector $\beta(r_i)$ of the review is fed to a feed-forward neural network (FFNN) with tanh non-linearity to give a class influence vector for each word:

$$c_i^l = \tanh(W[m_i^l \circ \beta(r_i)] + b),$$

where c_i^l has the same dimension as m_i. The class-based word representation is then computed as

$$\check{m}_i^l = m_i^l \odot c_i^l,$$

where $\odot$ is the element-wise multiplication operation. The class-based word representations later contribute to the class latent codes (Sec. 3.2.3).

3.2.2 Distributions for group latent codes g

The group latent code in our model plays a similar role to that in Copycat model, and its distributions are computed in a similar way. Its prior $p(g)$ is set to the standard normal distribution. To compute the variational posterior $q_\phi(g|r_{1:N})$, we first compute the importance coefficient of each word in the review group, which is

$$\alpha_i^l = \frac{\exp(f_\phi^\alpha(m_i^l))}{\sum_{i'=1}^{N} \sum_{l'=1}^{L_{i'}} \exp(f_\phi^\alpha(m_{i'}^{l'}))}, \quad (2)$$

for the l-th word in review r_i. Here, f_ϕ^α is a 2-layer FFNN with tanh non-linearity, which takes as input the word context states and returns a scalar.

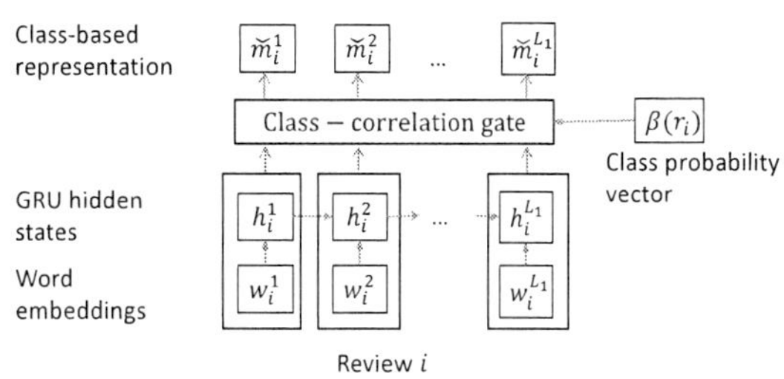

Figure 3: Generation of context states and class-based representations by text representation component.

The mean and log covariance of $q_\phi(g|r_{1:N})$ are then computed by separate affine projections of the intermediate group representation $\hat{h}_g$, which is the weighted sum of the word context states: $\hat{h}_g = \sum_{i=1}^{N} \sum_{l=1}^{L_i} \alpha_i^l m_i^l$.

We can then sample a latent code g from the above posterior distribution. The reparameterization trick (Kingma and Welling, 2013) is applied during sampling to allow backpropagation of the reconstruction error.

3.2.3 Distributions for class latent codes t

The prior for class latent codes is conditioned on the common group latent code g and shared across different classes, i.e., $p_\phi(t_j|g) = \mathcal{N}(t_j; \mu_\phi^t(g), \sigma_\phi^t(g)I)$ for $j = 1, ..., T$, where the mean and log covariance are computed as a linear transformation of g.

The variational posterior for latent code t_j of each class j depends on the common group code g, reviews $r_{1:N}$, and class probabilities $[\beta(r_i)]_{i=1}^N$; it is $q_\phi(t_j|r_{1:N}, [\beta(r_i)]_{i=1}^N, g)$. To compute this posterior of t_j, we also first compute the importance coefficient of each word in each review to the class representation t_j, but now we use class-based word representations instead of word context states as in g:

$$\check{\alpha}_{ji}^l = \frac{\exp(f_\phi^{\check{\alpha}_j}(\check{m}_i^l))}{\sum_{i'=1}^{N} \sum_{l'=1}^{L_{i'}} \exp(f_\phi^{\check{\alpha}_j}(\check{m}_{i'}^{l'}))}. \quad (3)$$

We then compute the intermediate class representation $\hat{h}_{t_j} = \sum_{i=1}^{N} \sum_{l=1}^{L_i} \check{\alpha}_{ji}^l \check{m}_i^l$. The computation of $\hat{h}_{t_j}$ can be viewed as a two-layer filter mechanism to extract class-specific information and key words, and reduce irrelevant and generic information to be represented in class latent codes. First, the class-correlation gate pays attention to key words related to the class of each review. Then, among those key words from different reviews, the importance coefficients $\check{\alpha}_{ji}^l$ pay attention to those related to the class j of interest.

Finally, we apply affine transformations on the concatenation of $\hat{h}_{t_j}$ and g to give the mean and log variance of the variational posterior for t_j. We can sample a latent code t_j from this posterior and generate an assembled code $\mathbf{t} = [t_j]_{j=1}^T$.

3.2.4 Distributions for review latent codes $\mathbf{z}_i$

The prior on the review code z_{ij} corresponding to review r_i and class j is conditioned on the class code t_j and is shared across different reviews, i.e. $p_\phi(z_{ij}|t_j) = \mathcal{N}(z_{ij}; \mu_\phi^z(t_j), \sigma_\phi^z(t_j)I)$ for $j = 1, ..., T$, where the mean and log covariance are computed as a linear transformation of t_j.

To compute the mean and log covariance of variational posterior $q_\phi(z_{ij}|r_i, t_j)$, we perform affine transformation on the concatenation of $h_i^{L_i}$ and t_j. $\mathbf{z}_i = [z_{ij}]_{j=1}^T$ is then sampled from these posteriors.

3.3 The Decoder

The decoder reconstructs the original reviews by computing the distribution $p_\theta(r_i|\mathbf{z}_i, \beta(r_i), r_{-i})$. First, the aggregated latent code $\hat{z}_i$ for each review r_i can be computed as: $\hat{z}_i = \sum_{j=1}^{N} \beta(r_i)_j z_{ij}$. After that, we follow the structure of CopyCat's decoder (Bražinskas et al., 2020b). The decoder takes $\hat{z}_i$ and r_{-i} as input and computes $p_\theta(r_i|\hat{z}_i, r_{-i})$. We use an auto-regressive GRU decoder with the attention mechanism and a pointer generator network.

3.4 Loyalty term

The VAE lower bound in Eq. (1) focuses on reconstructing a review r_i from its latent representation and other reviews r_{-i} of the same group. Because reviews may vary largely, and it is not always possible to reconstruct a review from other reviews, the decoder tends to be creative, and inclines toward generating a new word, instead of copying a word from other reviews. As a result, the generated summaries at test phase often contain many new words and possibly false information that is not present in original reviews. To remedy this problem, inspired by (Bražinskas et al., 2020a), we add a loyalty term $\mathcal{L}_0$ that encourages assigning the probability mass to words that appear in r_{-i}:

$$\mathcal{L}_0(\theta, \phi, r_{1:N}) = \mathop{\mathbb{E}}_{g\sim q_\phi(g|r_{1:N})} \left[\mathop{\mathbb{E}}_{\mathbf{t}\sim q_\phi(\mathbf{t}|r_{1:N}, [\beta(r_i)]_{i=1}^N, g)} \left(\sum_{i=1}^{N} \mathop{\mathbb{E}}_{\mathbf{z}_i\sim q_\phi(\mathbf{z}_i|r_i, \mathbf{t})} \left[\sum_{l=1}^{L_i} \sum_{w\in V(r_{-i})} -p_\theta(w|\mathbf{z}_i, \beta(r_i), r_{-i}, r_i^{1:l-1}) \right] \right) \right],$$

where $V(r_{-i})$ is the vocabulary of all words in r_{-i}. The final loss function is computed as

$$\mathcal{L} = \mathcal{L}_{VAE} + \alpha * \mathcal{L}_0, \quad (4)$$

where α is the trade-off hyperparameter. $\mathcal{L}$ is minimized w.r.t. both the inference network's parameter ϕ and the generative network's parameter θ.

3.5 Summary Generation

At test time, we can generate a summary per class for a new group of reviews $r_{1:N}$. This is equivalent to generating a new review that reflects common information from the reviews $r_{1:N}$. To do so, the latent variables are fixed to their respective means. The steps to generate a summary r_* for a class j from a group of reviews $r_{1:N}$ are as follows:

1. Fix g at the mean of its posterior $q_\phi(g|r_{1:N})$.
2. Fix t_j at the mean of its posterior $q_\phi(t_j|r_{1:N}, [\beta(r_i)]_{i=1}^N, g)$.
3. Fix z_{*j} at the mean of its prior $p_\phi(z_{*j}|t_j)$.
4. Assign $\hat{z}_* = z_{*j}$, and compute the decoder's probability for r_*: $p_\theta(r_*|\hat{z}_*, r_{1:N})$.

4 Experimental Results

4.1 Experimental setup

Our experiment is conducted on a subset of the public dataset of Amazon product reviews (He and McAuley, 2016). In this dataset, each review is written for a particular product, and accompanied by a rating value between 1 and 5. We apply our model to generate summaries for a group of average and low-rating reviews (1 to 3-star rating reviews) belonging to a product according to the classes of issues behind the poor ratings. Following (Bražinskas et al., 2020b), we use reviews from four product categories: Clothing Shoes and Jewelry, Electronics, Health and PersonalCare, and Home and Kitchen. We obtain reviews with 1 to 3-star ratings, and group them by products with each group having no less than 8 reviews. The dataset consists of 773,797 reviews for 54,706 products. From this, we sampled 1000 products for test, and split the remaining products into training/validation sets with a $9:1$ ratio. See Appendix A.3 for more details in data pre-processing, and Appendix A.4 for hyperparameter settings and implementation details of our model.

We created an independent classifier $\beta(.)$ that classifies reviews into 6 classes of possible issues: POOR QUALITY OR DEFECTIVE, SIZING/FIT/STYLE ISSUE, BAD/MISLEADING PRODUCT DESCRIPTION, COMPATIBILITY ISSUE, WRONG ITEM RECEIVED, and OTHERS. Definition for each class is given in Appendix A.2. The classifier produces a class probability for each issue class per review. Using the class probability output of this classifier $\beta(.)$ as input, we train our Class-CopyCat model to generate class-specific summaries for these 6 issue classes from product reviews. At test time, we compute an aggregated probability for each issue class per product by averaging the classifier probability outputs across all reviews for that product, and only generate summaries for classes whose aggregated class probabilities for the product is greater than a threshold of 0.1. This threshold is adjustable. This is meant to filter out those issues that are not supported by the reviews, assuming that there are much more pronounced issues that we want to summarize. Reading class-specific summaries for top issue classes enable users to quickly understand different predominant issues for a product. We note that our model can be applied for any set of topical classes and classifiers. The choice to use the 6 product issue classes is arbitrary, and we could easily choose some other classification (e.g. sentiment, rating, author).

For evaluation, we sampled 100 products and 8 reviews per product from the test set. We obtained gold summaries for these products from 2 external workers. We asked each worker to write a set of gold summaries per product, one for each issue class of the product, provided that the aggregated class probability for the product is greater than 0.1.

Table 2 shows an example of average and low-rating reviews for a product, the gold summaries, and summaries produced by different models. Additional examples are given in Appendix A.1.

4.2 Baseline Models

We prepare 7 baseline models for class-specific summarization.

Abstractive baselines

CopyCat with Class-embedding. We combine CopyCat model for multi-document review summarization (Bražinskas et al., 2020b) with the class-embedding mechanism proposed in (Narayan et al., 2018) for class-specific summarization. Particularly, the class probability vector $\beta(r_i)$ for a review r_i is appended to each word embedding of that review at both encoder and decoder during training. When generating a class-specific summary, the class probability vector at decoder becomes a one-hot encoding of that class.

Collection of CopyCat models. We train one CopyCat model for each issue class. Each class-specific Copycat model is trained only on reviews that are classified into that class (the top class). Class-specific summaries are generated by the corresponding class-specific model.

Collection of MeanSum models. MeanSum is another state-of-the-art multi-review summarization method (Chu and Liu, 2019). This baseline is similar to the second baseline above.

Extractive baselines

Highest probability. The review with highest class probability is used as class-specific summary.

Clustroid. The clustroid review among the set of reviews belonging to a class is used as the class-specific summary. It is the review with the highest

Top issue classes	POOR QUALITY OR DEFECTIVE	COMPATIBILITY ISSUE
Gold summary for each issue	The mount does not hold weight when closed. It doesn't work properly. It bends down.	The mount is not suitable for big TV screens. It does not fit a 42" TV. It should be for 32" or less.
Our class-specific summaries	I am very disappointed in this product. It is hard to get it to hold the weight of the TV, and it will not work.	I bought this for my 42 inch TV. It does not fit the TV. It is too small.
Collection of CopyCat models' summaries	I bought this to use with my Samsung TV. It did not work at all. I tried to adjust the TV but it didn't work. I would not recommend this product to anyone. Very disappointed.	The title of this says it would fit a 49 inch TV, but my TV will not fit. The mount didn't work either. Would not recommend this product for the specific model of TV.
Collection of MeanSum models' summaries	Bought this for my Samsung TV and it did not fit my LG TV. I would not recommend this product to anyone. Don't waste your time and money on this piece of junk. Do not buy!	The end of this mount doesn't work with my Samsung TV. The mount is too wide and there is no space for my TV, which defeats the purpose of being able to mount it in my TV!
Review 1	I would not use this mount for any big tvs . I had a hard time trying to make this work and junked it in the end.	
Review 2	JUNK!!! I have a 65 " Toshiba 91 # bigger than stated but weight is weight. Sags, will not hold weight when closed. Also very hard the hook the tv mount to the wall mount. I am afraid to even pull it out to full length. I am taking it down tomorrow.	
Review 3	don 't work well with heavy lcd tvs. installation was easy, find two stud screw it in. mount my samsung 52 " lcd and just points down, tilt all the way up and as soon as i let go off my hand it just tilt down just cant have the tv parallel to the wall. you get what you pay for.	
Review 4	This mount will not hold a 50 LCD TV. As soon as we placed the tv on the mount it sagged and bent a little. When we tried to angle it it tilted a lot. If you have a 40 or under TV you will be fine.	
Review 5	size of the bracket is too small trying to mount a 55 inch - please reconsider buying this product this product only safe with 15 - 32 inch only not recommended for 55inch tv.	
Review 6	I bought this item for a 42 " TV. It does not fit the TV ! Partially my own fault for not doing a bit more research but it is way to small to holder an older 42 " TV. I used it on a smaller 32 " TV which saved me some trouble but it is a bit of overkill for a smaller TV.	
Review 7	12 inches too narrow for my 37 inch LG TV. This mount should only be used on a 32 inch or less.	
Review 8	The product hung on the wall crooked. Cheap. Don 't buy. Had to return. Waste of time. I guess you get what you pay for.	

Table 2: Examples of reviews, gold summaries, and summaries generated by various models. Generic or redundant information not related to the class is marked in Blue; hallucinating or incorrect information is marked in Red.

ROUGE-L score w.r.t. other reviews in the set.

Lead. We construct the class-specific summary by concatenating leading sentences from reviews belonging to that class. "Lead" baseline has been shown to be a strong baseline for both single- and multi-document summarization (See et al., 2017; Bražinskas et al., 2020b; Chu and Liu, 2019).

Random. A random review belonging to a class is used as the class-specific summary.

See Appendix A.5 for training procedure of our model and those of the abstractive baselines.

4.3 Automatic Evaluation

We measure semantic overlap between generated and gold summaries using ROUGE scores (Lin, 2004). A higher ROUGE score associates with more semantic overlap between pairs of texts. The class-specific gold summaries are used as reference. Table 3 reports ROUGE scores based on F1 on the 100 test products.

Class-Copycat outperforms all the baselines. The summaries of extractive baselines ("Highest probability" , "Clustroid", "Lead" and "Random") are extracted from the subset of reviews that belong to the class of interest only, and therefore, contain a good amount of class-specific information. This results in relatively higher ROUGE scores for these baselines compared to abstractive ones, except for Class-CopyCat. The low ROUGE scores for "CopyCat with Class-embedding" indicate that class-embedding mechanism does not sufficiently extract class-specific information from reviews. Similarly, limiting the training set to only reviews belonging to the class of interest as in "Collection of CopyCat models" and "Collection of MeanSum models" does not allow the models to sufficiently focus on class-related information and omit generic and irrelevant information from reviews, as shown in Table 2 and in Appendix A.1. This results in low ROUGE scores for these two methods, and is confirmed with human evaluation (Sec. 4.4).

Model	R1	R2	RL
Class-CopyCat (ours)	**0.308**	**0.102**	**0.238**
CopyCat w Class-embed	0.186	0.037	0.133
Collection of CopyCat(s)	0.190	0.038	0.141
Collection of MeanSum(s)	0.182	0.034	0.138
Highest probability	0.254	0.092	0.207
Clustroid	0.242	0.085	0.204
Lead	0.258	0.098	0.210
Random	0.213	0.061	0.171

Table 3: ROUGE scores on the 100 test products.

4.4 Human evaluation

We performed human evaluation on 50 products from the test set. Two annotators are asked to rate each summary on a scale of 1 (very poor) to 5 (very good) based on 6 criteria as follows:

Model	Informativeness	Conciseness & non-redundancy	Content support	Opinion consensus	Fluency	Overall
Collection of CopyCat models	2.87	2.69	2.91	3.09	3.83	2.80
Collection of MeanSum models	2.80	2.55	2.63	2.70	3.80	2.54
Class-CopyCat	**3.60**	**4.30**	**3.98**	**3.72**	**4.57**	**3.84**

Table 4: Average scores of human evaluation for six criteria. Score ranges from 1 (very poor) to 5 (very good).

- Informativeness: how well summary covers dominant and repeated issues in the class.
- Content support: how well the content of summaries is supported by input reviews
- Conciseness and non-redundancy: The summary should be concise and not contain unrelated information or unnecessary repetition.
- Opinion consensus: the summary should reflect common opinions expressed in reviews.
- Fluency: summary sentences should be grammatically correct, and easy to understand.
- Overall: based on annotators' judgment.

Class-CopyCat outperforms both reference models by a large margin across all criteria (Table 4). The biggest gain of Class-CopyCat over the two baselines is in conciseness and non-redundancy (4.30 vs 2.55 and 2.69). Examples in Table 2 and Appendix A.1 show qualitatively that our summaries are more concise compared to baselines. The latter contains more generic and irrelevant information (highlighted in blue in the examples).

Class-CopyCat also outperforms the two baselines in terms of content support. Both baselines produce much information not present in original reviews; such information is highlighted in red in Table 2 and Appendix A.1. Our model performs well in this criteria due to the loyalty term introduced in Sec. 3.4. Moreover, since our model often generates more concise and non-redundant summaries from salient class-related information, it has less chance of introducing incorrect information.

As our model focuses on and includes more class-related information, it also does better in informativeness (3.60 vs 2.80 and 2.87). Because class-related key information is often salient and consistent, this also results in better opinion consensus.

4.5 Model Variant Ablation Studies

Here, we compare Class-CopyCat with its variants. The result is shown in Table 5. In "*without class-correlation gate*" variant, we omit the class-correlation gate in Fig. 3, and use word context states directly (in place of class-based representation in Fig. 2) to compute the posterior of the class latent code **t**. In "*class-embedding*" variant, instead of using class-correlation gate, we append the class probability vector $\beta(r_i)$ to each word context state of the review r_i to generate class-based word representations as in (Narayan et al., 2018). In "*without loyalty term*" variant, the loyalty term (Sec. 3.4) is not added to loss function. Finally, in "*without g*" variant, we remove the group latent code g, as we question whether g is still needed, in the presence of the class code t per class per group.

The result in Table 5 shows that each model component indeed contributes to final performance. *Without class-correlation gate*, performance drops most significantly. Using *class-embedding* instead improves ROUGE scores compared to not using any class-based representation, but its performance is still far from using class-correlation gate in the final Class-CopyCat. *Without loyalty term*, the model generates more 'hallucinating' words (eg. product names, models), resulting in lower ROUGE scores. Finally, "*without g*", ROUGE scores reduce slightly. This is because the class latent code t is designed to focus more on keywords for each class and without conditioning on g, it cannot represent differences among various products (eg. pants vs shirt).

Model	R1	R2	RL
Class-CopyCat	**0.312**	**0.107**	**0.216**
Without class-correlation gate	0.272	0.092	0.209
Class-embedding	0.287	0.098	0.212
Without loyalty term	0.282	0.096	**0.216**
Without g	0.304	0.103	0.208
Random	0.213	0.061	0.171

Table 5: Ablation results: ROUGE scores for different model variants using the gold summary dataset.

5 Conclusion

We have proposed a model for generating class-specific summaries from a collection of reviews. Our evaluation results show that our model outperforms many abstractive and extractive baselines, including state-of-the-art models, in term of ROUGE scores that measure the semantic overlap between generated and gold summaries. We also show through human evaluation that generated summaries of our model are highly relevant to the classes of interest, fluent, and representative of common opinion.

References

Samuel Bowman, Luke Vilnis, Oriol Vinyals, Andrew Dai, Rafal Jozefowicz, and Samy Bengio. 2016. Generating sentences from a continuous space. In *Proceedings of The 20th SIGNLL Conference on Computational Natural Language Learning*, pages 10–21.

Arthur Bražinskas, Mirella Lapata, and Ivan Titov. 2020a. Few-shot learning for opinion summarization. In *Proceedings of the 2020 Conference on Empirical Methods in Natural Language Processing (EMNLP)*, pages 4119–4135.

Arthur Bražinskas, Mirella Lapata, and Ivan Titov. 2020b. Unsupervised opinion summarization as copycat-review generation. In *Proceedings of the 58th Annual Meeting of the Association for Computational Linguistics*, pages 5151–5169.

Kyunghyun Cho, Bart van Merriënboer, Caglar Gulcehre, Dzmitry Bahdanau, Fethi Bougares, Holger Schwenk, and Yoshua Bengio. 2014. Learning phrase representations using rnn encoder–decoder for statistical machine translation. In *Proceedings of the 2014 Conference on Empirical Methods in Natural Language Processing*, pages 1724–1734.

Eric Chu and Peter Liu. 2019. Meansum: a neural model for unsupervised multi-document abstractive summarization. In *International Conference on Machine Learning*, pages 1223–1232.

Günes Erkan and Dragomir R Radev. 2004. Lexrank: Graph-based lexical centrality as salience in text summarization. *Journal of artificial intelligence research*, 22:457–479.

Katja Filippova. 2010. Multi-sentence compression: Finding shortest paths in word graphs. In *Proceedings of the 23rd international conference on computational linguistics (Coling 2010)*, pages 322–330.

Hao Fu, Chunyuan Li, Xiaodong Liu, Jianfeng Gao, Asli Celikyilmaz, and Lawrence Carin. 2019. Cyclical annealing schedule: A simple approach to mitigating kl vanishing. In *Proceedings of the 2019 Conference of the North American Chapter of the Association for Computational Linguistics: Human Language Technologies, Volume 1 (Long and Short Papers)*, pages 240–250.

Kavita Ganesan, ChengXiang Zhai, and Jiawei Han. 2010. Opinosis: a graph-based approach to abstractive summarization of highly redundant opinions. In *Proceedings of the 23rd International Conference on Computational Linguistics*, pages 340–348.

Xavier Glorot and Yoshua Bengio. 2010. Understanding the difficulty of training deep feedforward neural networks. In *Proceedings of the thirteenth international conference on artificial intelligence and statistics*, pages 249–256. JMLR Workshop and Conference Proceedings.

Jiatao Gu, Zhengdong Lu, Hang Li, and Victor OK Li. 2016. Incorporating copying mechanism in sequence-to-sequence learning. In *Proceedings of the 54th Annual Meeting of the Association for Computational Linguistics (Volume 1: Long Papers)*, pages 1631–1640.

Ruining He and Julian McAuley. 2016. Ups and downs: Modeling the visual evolution of fashion trends with one-class collaborative filtering. In *Proceedings of the 25th international conference on world wide web*, pages 507–517.

Karl Moritz Hermann, Tomas Kocisky, Edward Grefenstette, Lasse Espeholt, Will Kay, Mustafa Suleyman, and Phil Blunsom. 2015. Teaching machines to read and comprehend. In *Advances in neural information processing systems*, pages 1693–1701.

Masaru Isonuma, Toru Fujino, Junichiro Mori, Yutaka Matsuo, and Ichiro Sakata. 2017. Extractive summarization using multi-task learning with document classification. In *Proceedings of the 2017 Conference on Empirical Methods in Natural Language Processing*, pages 2101–2110.

Chandra Khatri, Gyanit Singh, and Nish Parikh. 2018. Abstractive and extractive text summarization using document context vector and recurrent neural networks. *arXiv preprint arXiv:1807.08000*.

Diederik P Kingma and Jimmy Ba. 2014. Adam: A method for stochastic optimization. *arXiv preprint arXiv:1412.6980*.

Diederik P Kingma and Max Welling. 2013. Auto-encoding variational Bayes. *arXiv preprint arXiv:1312.6114*.

Philippe Laban, Andrew Hsi, John Canny, and Marti A Hearst. 2020. The summary loop: Learning to write abstractive summaries without examples. In *Proceedings of the 58th Annual Meeting of the Association for Computational Linguistics*, volume 1.

Chin-Yew Lin. 2004. Rouge: A package for automatic evaluation of summaries. In *Text summarization branches out*, pages 74–81.

Shuming Ma, Xu Sun, Junyang Lin, and Xuancheng Ren. 2018. A hierarchical end-to-end model for jointly improving text summarization and sentiment classification. In *Proceedings of the 27th International Joint Conference on Artificial Intelligence*, pages 4251–4257.

Zhengjie Miao, Yuliang Li, Xiaolan Wang, and Wang-Chiew Tan. 2020. Snippext: Semi-supervised opinion mining with augmented data. In *Proceedings of The Web Conference 2020*, pages 617–628.

Ramesh Nallapati, Bowen Zhou, Cicero dos Santos, Caglar Gulcehre, and Bing Xiang. 2016. Abstractive text summarization using sequence-to-sequence rnns and beyond. In *Proceedings of The 20th SIGNLL Conference on Computational Natural Language Learning*, pages 280–290.

Shashi Narayan, Shay B Cohen, and Mirella Lapata. 2018. Don't give me the details, just the summary! topic-aware convolutional neural networks for extreme summarization. In *Proceedings of the 2018 Conference on Empirical Methods in Natural Language Processing*, pages 1797–1807.

Evan Sandhaus. 2008. The New York Times annotated corpus. *Linguistic Data Consortium, Philadelphia*, 6(12):e26752.

Abigail See, Peter J Liu, and Christopher D Manning. 2017. Get to the point: Summarization with pointer-generator networks. In *Proceedings of the 55th Annual Meeting of the Association for Computational Linguistics (Volume 1: Long Papers)*, pages 1073–1083.

Yoshihiko Suhara, Xiaolan Wang, Stefanos Angelidis, and Wang-Chiew Tan. 2020. Opiniondigest: A simple framework for opinion summarization. In *Proceedings of the 58th Annual Meeting of the Association for Computational Linguistics*, pages 5789–5798.

Ilya Sutskever, Oriol Vinyals, and Quoc V Le. 2014. Sequence to sequence learning with neural networks. In *Advances in neural information processing systems*, pages 3104–3112.

Oriol Vinyals, Meire Fortunato, and Navdeep Jaitly. 2015. Pointer networks. In *Advances in neural information processing systems*, pages 2692–2700.

Hongli Wang and Jiangtao Ren. 2018. A self-attentive hierarchical model for jointly improving text summarization and sentiment classification. In *Asian Conference on Machine Learning*, pages 630–645.

Li Wang, Junlin Yao, Yunzhe Tao, Li Zhong, Wei Liu, and Qiang Du. 2018. A reinforced topic-aware convolutional sequence-to-sequence model for abstractive text summarization. In *Proceedings of the 27th International Joint Conference on Artificial Intelligence*, pages 4453–4460.

Peilin Yang and Hui Fang. An opinion-aware approach to contextual suggestion.

A Appendices

A.1 Additional examples of reviews and summaries

Table 6 and Table 7 show additional examples of reviews for a product, the gold summaries, and the class-specific summaries produced by different models. Additionally, we also show the class-agnostic summaries produced by 3 opinion summarization models: CopyCat, MeanSum, and Lexrank (Erkan and Radev, 2004). Lexrank is an unsupervised extractive algorithm which selects sentences based on graph centrality. Sentences represent nodes in a graph whose edge weights denote tf-idf similarity.

Top issue classes	POOR QUALITY OR DEFECTIVE	MISLEADING PRODUCT DESCRIPTION
Gold summary for each issue	The stand and the screen angle are not adjustable. The monitor is too bright and the picture looks washed out.	The product did not have HDMI hook as it says on the description.
Our class-specific summaries	I was very disappointed in this monitor. It is not worth the price. The picture is very bright and the stand is not adjustable.	Bad description of the product. It didn't have a HDMI hookup.
Collection of CopyCat models' summaries	I bought this monitor for my husband for Christmas. It was a Christmas gift for Christmas and it was already broken. I would not recommend this monitor to anyone. Very disappointed in the quality of it.	It's not compatible with my monitor, even though it is advertised as a Samsung 46 inch memory. Very disappointed! Don't waste your time and money on this item. Don't buy this.
Collection of MeanSum models' summaries	The monitor is not bright enough to adjust the monitor. I had to send it back because it was a waste of my time and money. Don't waste your money on this one. Do not buy!	What a waste of money, but when I received it in the mail it looked much better. You can't see through the screen. It's not worth the trouble of returning it and returning.
CopyCat's summary	It's a nice monitor, but I had to return it for a refund. Also, the monitor doesn't work with the monitor. I would not recommend this product to anyone. Save your money	
MeanSum's summary	It's a nice looking monitor, but it is not what I expected. I have tried everything to get it to work, but the screen resolution is terrible. I would not recommend this product.	
Lexrank's summary (Erkan and Radev, 2004)	It is the worst monitor i have ever purchased, the stand is not adjustable and their is something wrong with the base. I was unable to adjust the viewing angle and therefore returned the monitor.	
Review 1	Like someone who reviewed this before me... this monitor is too bright. It looks like there is a bright white haze on everything and i do not like it. I just received this monitor and i will be returning it as soon as possible. Very disappointed.	
Review 2	Disappointment. The monitor does not allow you to adjust the screen angle without weakening the stability of the monitor. I sent it back. Amazon did refund full purchase price with no hassle.	
Review 3	Had to return this one. the plugin in the back didn 't work. Pain to get it and it not work, especially since it was a gift.	
Review 4	Picture is dusty looking! the stand is not adjustable. Not worth the low price. You don 't even get what you pay for!	
Review 5	The color is terrible, the contrast does not adjust, unless you look it from one very specific unrealistic angle the picture is washed out	
Review 6	Would be nice to have known it didn 't have hdmi hookup before is wasted money. Worst description of a product features	
Review 7	It is the worst monitor i have ever purchased, the stand is not adjustable and their is something wrong with the base.	
Review 8	I was unable to adjust the viewing angle and therefore returned the monitor. There was nothing in the instructions about this.	

Table 6: Example reviews for a product, the corresponding gold summaries written by human, and the summaries generated by different models. For class-specific summaries, generic or redundant information not related to the class is marked in Blue; hallucinating or incorrect information is marked in Red.

Top issue classes	SIZING/FIT/STYLE ISSUE	POOR QUALITY OR DEFECTIVE
Gold summary for each issue	The size is not true. The pants are too small and super skinny.	The material is shoddy, the stitch quality is terrible. They are not Levi's.
Our class-specific summaries	These pants are too small for me. They are too tight.	These pants are not what I expected. Their quality is very poor. The material is very cheap and the stitch quality is really poor.
Collection of CopyCat models' summaries	These are not true to size, I ordered a large and they are still too tight. I will not be buying these again. I'm a size 6 and these pants are not flattering at all.	These are not the same quality Levi's pants I have ever seen. They are made out of thin material and tear apart easily. I would not recommend these to anyone, especially for the price.
Collection of MeanSum models' summaries	It's a shame because the pants are too small for me. I normally wear a medium, but these pants were way too big for me and I could barely zip them up. Very disappointed.	The stitching on the pants are so stiff that they are uncomfortable. I would not recommend these pants to anyone. I had to return them because they were a waste of my money. Don't buy them.
CopyCat's summary	These are not the relaxed fit for me. I ordered a 34, and they were way too big for my legs. I would not recommend these pants to anyone else in the future.	
MeanSum's summary	These are not true to size. I ordered a large and they were too tight around the waist. I will have to return them. They are not worth the hassle of returning them. I am returning them.	
Lexrank's summary (Erkan and Radev, 2004)	These pants are not real Levi's. Super skinny jeans , more like chick pants guys shouldn't be wearing these, more like a joke cant believe i bought these pants	
Review 1	I bought "Levi 's Men's 513 Slim Straight Jean, Mr Blue, 28Wx32L". Size is good fit. But this item is too small. Same brand, same size is not same.	
Review 2	The jeans missing a loop what the ass ah hold loop in the back poor really poor need to inspect the items before	
Review 3	It is too big it is not the correct size I have another Levi s size 40 and its perfect.	
Review 4	Super skinny jeans, more like chick pants guys shouldn't be wearing these, more like a joke cant believe i bought these pants	
Review 5	I ordered up two sizes after reading that these run tight, but before putting them on I realized they aren't even real. The material is shoddy, the stitch quality is terrible, and the color doesn't resemble the photo online at all! Beware of these pants and hope that you don't get ripped off like I have.	
Review 6	you need legs like broomsticks for these guys to fit. Could barely slip them over my calves without splitting the seams, if you have muscular legs, these are not for you...	
Review 7	These pants aren't what I expected. The quality is really low and I'm pretty sure these pants won't last very long. It 's simply cheap material. The fit is good though.	
Review 8	These pants are not real Levi's. I was comparing the 511's I just bought in store to these ones and they are barely anything alike. The material is not the same. The only place it says Levi is on the button and the back patch. The stitching isn 't the same either.	

Table 7: Example reviews for a product, the corresponding gold summaries written by human, and the summaries generated by different models. For class-specific summaries, generic or redundant information not related to the class is marked in Blue; hallucinating or incorrect information is marked in Red.

A.2 Definition of issue classes

Issue class	Class definition
POOR QUALITY OR DEFECTIVE	Product is defective and does not perform its function, or contains a flaw that results in objectively poor performance and utilization of the product.
COMPATIBILITY ISSUE	Product is incompatible with another product that it is meant to be used with/for.
SIZING/FIT/STYLE ISSUE	Product is either too small/big to fit the customer's use case, without mentioning size incompatibility with another product.
BAD/MISLEADING PRODUCT DESCRIPTION	Product description contains misleading or insufficient information.
WRONG ITEM RECEIVED	Product shipped is different than the one the customer ordered.
OTHERS	Product issues that do not belong to any of the above classes.

Table 8: Definition of the issue classes.

A.3 Data Pre-Processing

We select only the reviews of which the star rating is between 1 to 3, and the length is between 20 to 70 words. These reviews are grouped by products, and only the products that have no less than 8 reviews satisfying the above conditions are selected. In addition, popular products with the number of reviews above the 90th percentile are removed, so that the dataset is not dominated by a small portion of products. During both training and test time, each group of reviews is formed from 8 reviews which are sampled without replacement from the set of reviews belonging to a same product.

A.4 Hyperparamters and Implementation Details

We use similar hyperparameter settings to those used in (Bražinskas et al., 2020b). The word embeddings are shared by both the encoder and decoder; their dimension is set to 200. The vocabulary size is 80000. Both the GRUs at encoder and decoder have the hidden state dimension of 600. The dimension of all the latent variables (g, t and z) is set to 600. Both the FFNNs that are used to compute the importance coefficients toward the posteriors of g and t in Eq. (2) and (3) have a 300-dimensional hidden layer. The decoder's attention network has a 200-dimensional hidden layer with a $\tanh$ non-linearity. The network for computing copy gate in the pointer-generator network also has a 100-dimensional hidden layer with the same non-linearity. The trade-off hyperparameter α in Eq. (4) is set to 2.

A.5 Initialization and Training

The CopyCat model (Sec. 4.6) and its variants (CopyCat with Class-embedding and the collection of class-specific CopyCat models, described in Sec. 4.2), which are used as baselines in our evaluation, are initialized with the CopyCat reference model provided by the authors of CopyCat (Bražinskas et al., 2020b). This reference model was previously trained on a larger dataset (183,103 products and 4,566,519 reviews) consisting of all the reviews with star rating from 1 to 5, unlike our training set which contains only the reviews with star rating from 1 to 3. We find that initializing the above baseline models (the CopyCat model and its variants) with this reference model gives a better performance for these baselines compared to training from scratch with our training set. For our Class-CopyCat model, the word embedding module and the two GRUs are also initialized with the corresponding components of the reference CopyCat model. Other 2D weights are initialized with Xavier uniform initialization (Glorot and Bengio, 2010), and 1D weights are initialized with the scaled normal noise with 0.1 standard deviation.

After initialization, we train each of the Class-CopyCat model, the CopyCat model, the CopyCat with Class-embedding and the collection of class-specific CopyCat models for 5 epoches on our training set of average and poor rating reviews (Sec. 4.1) using Adam optimizer (Kingma and Ba, 2014) with a learning rate of 0.0001. For decoding a summary at test time, length-normalized beam search of size 5 is used. Cycling annealing (Fu et al., 2019) is applied for all the KL terms to mitigate the problem of "posterior collapse" (Bowman et al., 2016).

The MeanSum model and its variants are also pre-trained on the larger dataset of reviews with 1 to 5-star rating before being fine-tuned on our smaller training set of average and poor rating reviews.

Scalable Approach for Normalizing E-commerce Text Attributes (SANTA)

Ravi Shankar Mishra
India Machine Learning
Amazon
rmsam@amazon.com

Kartik Mehta
India Machine Learning
Amazon
kartim@amazon.com

Nikhil Rasiwasia
India Machine Learning
Amazon
rasiwasi@amazon.com

Abstract

In this paper, we present *SANTA*, a scalable framework to automatically normalize E-commerce attribute values (e.g. "*Win 10 Pro*") to a fixed set of pre-defined canonical values (e.g. "*Windows 10*"). Earlier works on attribute normalization focused on fuzzy string matching (also referred as syntactic matching in this paper). In this work, we first perform an extensive study of nine syntactic matching algorithms and establish that 'cosine' similarity leads to best results, showing 2.7% improvement over commonly used Jaccard index. Next, we argue that string similarity alone is not sufficient for attribute normalization as many surface forms require going beyond syntactic matching (e.g. "*720p*" and "*HD*" are synonyms). While semantic techniques like unsupervised embeddings (e.g. word2vec/fastText) have shown good results in word similarity tasks, we observed that they perform poorly to distinguish between close canonical forms, as these close forms often occur in similar contexts. We propose to learn token embeddings using a twin network with triplet loss. We propose an embedding learning task leveraging raw attribute values and product titles to learn these embeddings in a self-supervised fashion. We show that providing supervision using our proposed task improves over both syntactic and unsupervised embeddings based techniques for attribute normalization. Experiments on a real-world attribute normalization dataset of 50 attributes show that the embeddings trained using our proposed approach obtain 2.3% improvement over best string matching and 19.3% improvement over best unsupervised embeddings.

1 Introduction

E-commerce websites like Amazon are marketplaces where multiple sellers can list and sell their products. At the time of product listing, these sellers often provide product title and structured product information (e.g. *color*), henceforth, termed as product attributes[1]. During the listing process, some attribute values have to be chosen from dropdown list (having fixed set of values to choose from) and some attributes are free-form text (allowing any value to be filled). Multiple sellers may express these free-form attribute values in different forms, e.g. "*HD*", "*1280 X 720*" and "*720p*" represents same TV resolution. Normalizing (or mapping) these raw attribute values (henceforth termed as surface forms) to same canonical form will help improve customer experience and is crucial for multiple underlying applications like search filters, product comparison and detecting duplicates. E-commerce websites provide functionality to refine search results (refer figure 1), where customers can filter based on attribute canonical values. Choosing one of the canonical values restricts results to only those products which have the corresponding attribute value. A good normalization solution will ensure that products having synonym surface form (e.g. '720p' vs 'HD') are not filtered out on applying such filters.

Normalization can be considered as a two step process consisting of - a) identifying list of canonical forms for an attribute, and, b) mapping surface forms to one of these canonical forms. Identification task is relatively easier as most attributes have only few canonical forms (usually less than 10), whereas attributes can have thousands of surface forms. Hence, we focus on the mapping task in this paper, leaving identification of canonical forms as a future task to be explored.

Building an attribute normalization system for thousands[2] of product attributes poses multiple

[1] We use the terms 'product attributes' and 'attributes' interchangeably in this paper.

[2] E.g. Xu et al. (2019) have 77K attributes only from 'Sports & Entertainment category'

Proceedings of the 4th Workshop on e-Commerce and NLP (ECNLP 4), pages 101–110
August 5, 2021.

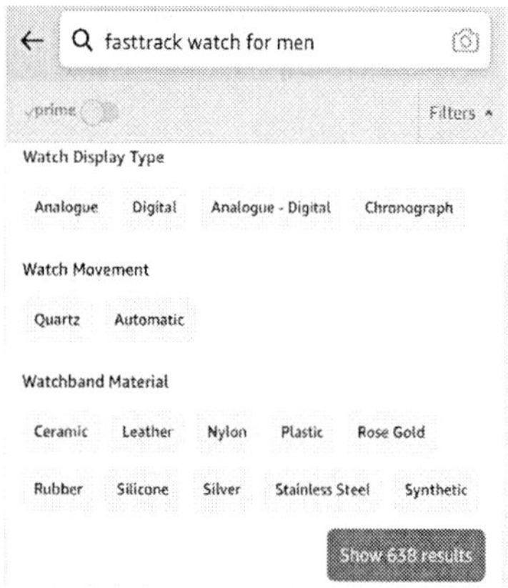

Figure 1: Search filters widget on Amazon.

challenges such as:

- Presence of spelling mistakes (e.g. "*grey*" vs "*gray*", "*crom os*" vs "*chrome os*")
- Requirement of semantic matches (e.g. "*linux*" vs "*ubuntu*", "*mac os*" vs "*ios*")
- Existence of abbreviations ("*polyurethane*" vs "*PU*", "*SSD*" vs "*solid state drive*")
- Presence of multi-token surface forms and canonical forms (e.g. "*windows 7 home*")
- Presence of close canonical forms (e.g. "*windows 8.1*" and "*windows 8*" can be two separate canonical forms)

Addressing these challenges in automated manner is the primary focus of this work. One can use lexical similarity of raw attribute value (surface form) to a list of canonical values and learn a normalization dictionary (Putthividhya and Hu, 2011). For example, lexical similarity can be used to normalize "*windows 7 home*" to "*windows 7*" or "*light blue*" to "*blue*". However, lexical similarity-based approaches won't be able to handle cases where understanding the meaning of attribute value is important (e.g. matching "*ubuntu* to "*linux*" or "*maroon*" to "*red*"). Another alternative is to learn distributed representation (embeddings) of surface forms and canonical forms and use similarity in embedding space for normalization. One can use unsupervised word embeddings (Kenter and De Rijke, 2015) (e.g. word2vec and fastText) for this. However, these approaches are designed to keep embeddings close by for tokens/entities which appear in similar contexts. As we shall see, these unsupervised embeddings do a poor job at distinguishing close canonical attribute forms.

In this paper, we describe SANTA, a scalable framework for normalizing E-commerce text attributes. Our proposed framework uses twin network (Bromley et al., 1994) with triplet loss to learn embeddings of attribute values (canonical and surface forms). We propose a self supervision task for learning these embeddings in automated manner, without requiring any manually created training data. To the best of our knowledge, our work is first successful attempt at creating an automated framework for E-commerce attribute normalization that can be easily extended to thousands of attributes.

Our paper has following contributions : (1) we do a systematic study of nine lexical matching approaches for attribute normalization, (2) we propose a self supervision task for learning embeddings of attribute surface forms and canonical forms in automated manner and describe a fully automated framework for attribute normalization using twin network and triplet loss, and, (3) we curate an attribute normalization test set of 2500 surface forms across 50 attributes and present an extensive evaluation of various approaches on this dataset. We also show an independent analysis on syntactic and semantic portions of this dataset and provide insights into benefits of our approach over string similarity and other unsupervised embeddings. Rest of the paper is organized as follows. We do a literature survey of related fields in Section 2. We describe string matching and embeddings based approaches, including our proposed SANTA framework, in Section 3. We describe our experimental setup in Section 4 and results in Section 5. Lastly, we summarize our work in Section 6.

2 Related Work

2.1 E-commerce Attribute normalization

The problem of normalizing E-commerce attribute values have received limited attention in literature. Researchers have mainly focused on normalizing *brand* attribute, exploring combination of manual mapping curation or lexical similarity-based approaches (More, 2016; Putthividhya and Hu, 2011). More (2016) explored use of manually created key-value pairs for normalizing brand values extracted from product titles. Putthividhya and Hu (2011) explored two fuzzy matching algorithms of Jaccard similarity and Jaro-Winkler distance and found n-gram based Jaccard similarity to be performing better for brand normalization. We use this Jaccard similarity approach as a baseline for comparison.

2.2 Fuzzy String Matching

Fuzzy string matching has been explored for multiple applications, including address matching, names matching (Cohen et al., 2003; Christen, 2006; Recchia and Louwerse, 2013), biomedical abbreviation matching (Yamaguchi et al., 2012) and query spelling correction. Although extensive work has been done for fuzzy string matching, there is no consensus on which technique works best. Christen (2006) explored multiple similarity measures for personal name matching, and reported that best algorithm depends upon the characteristics of the dataset. Cohen et al. (2003) experimented with edit-distance, token-based distance and hybrid methods for matching entity names and reported best performance for a hybrid approach combining TF-IDF weighting with Jaro-Winkler distance. Recchia and Louwerse (2013) did a systematic study of 21 string matching methods for the task of place name matching. While they got relatively better performance with n-gram approaches over commonly used Levenshtein distance, they concluded that best similarity approach is task-dependent. Gali et al. (2016) argued that performance of the similarity measures is affected by characteristics such as text length, spelling accuracy, presence of abbreviations and underlying language. Motivated by these learnings, we do a systematic study of fuzzy matching techniques for the problem of E-commerce attribute normalization. Besides, we use latest work in the field of neural embeddings for attribute normalization.

3 Overview

Attribute normalization can be posed as a matching problem. Given an attribute surface form and a list of possible canonical forms, similarity of surface form with each canonical form is calculated and surface form is mapped to the canonical form with highest similarity or mapped to 'other' class if none of the canonical forms is suitable (refer Figure 2 for illustration). Formally, given a surface form s_i $(i \in [1, n])$ and a list of canonical forms c_j $(j \in [0, k])$, where c_0 is the 'other' class, n is number of surface forms and k is number of canonical forms. The aim is to find a mapping function M such that:

$$M(s_i) = c_j \; where \; i \in [1, n], j \in [0, k] \quad (1)$$

In this paper, we explore fuzzy string matching and similarity in embedding space as matching

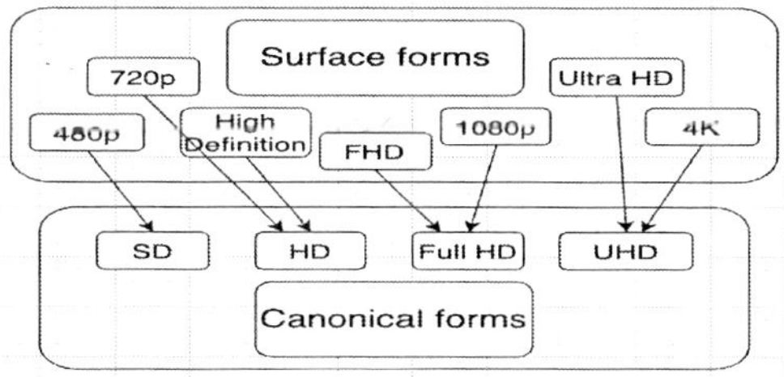

Figure 2: Illustration of Attribute Normalization Task

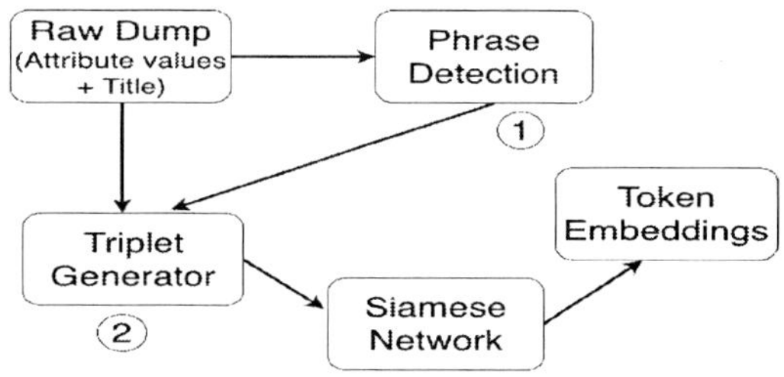

Figure 3: SANTA framework for training embeddings suitable for attribute normalization

techniques. We describe multiple string matching approaches in Section 3.1, followed by unsupervised token embedding approaches in Section 3.2 and our proposed SANTA framework in Section 3.3.

3.1 String Similarity Approach

We study three different categories of string matching algorithms[3] and explore three algorithms in each category[4]:

- **Edit distance-based**: These algorithms compute the number of operations needed to transform one string to another, leading to higher similarity score for less operations. We experimented with six algorithms in this category, a) Hamming, b) Levenshtein, and c) Jaro-Winkler.
- **Sequence-based**: These algorithms find common sub-sequence in two strings, leading to higher similarity score for longer common sub-sequence or a greater number of common sub-sequences. We experimented with three algorithms in this category, a) longest common subsequence similarity, b) longest common substring similarity, and c) Ratcliff-Obershelp similarity.

[3]https://itnext.io/string-similarity-the-basic-know-your-algorithms-guide-3de3d7346227

[4]For algorithms which return distance metrics rather than similarity, we use lowest distance as substitute for highest similarity.

- **Token-based**: These algorithms represent string as set of tokens (e.g. ngrams) and compute number of common tokens between them, leading to higher similarity score for higher number of common tokens. We experimented with three algorithms in this category - a) Jaccard index, b) SorensenDice coefficient, and c) Cosine similarity. We converted strings to character ngrams of size 1 to 5 before applying this similarity.

We used python module textdistance[5] for all string similarity experiments. For detailed definition of these approaches, we refer readers to Gomaa and Fahmy (2013) and Vijaymeena and Kavitha (2016).

3.2 Unsupervised Embeddings

Mikolov et al. (2013) introduced word2vec model that uses a shallow neural network to obtain distributed representation (embeddings) of words, ensuring words that appear in similar contexts are closer in the embedding space. To deal with unseen and rare words, Bojanowski et al. (2017) proposed fastText model that improves over word2vec embeddings by considering sub-words and representing word embeddings as average of embeddings of corresponding sub-words. To learn domain-specific nuances, we trained a word2vec and fastText model using a dump consisting of product titles and attribute values (refer Section 4 for details of this dump). We found better results with using concatenation of title with attribute value as compared to using only title, likely due to including surface form from title and attribute canonical form (or vice versa) in a single context.

3.3 Scalable Approach for Normalizing Text Attributes (SANTA)

Figure 3 gives an overview of learning embeddings with our proposed SANTA framework. We define an embedding learning task using twin network with triplet loss to enforce that embeddings of attribute values are closer to corresponding titles as compared to embeddings of a randomly chosen title from the same product category. To deal with multi-word values, we use a simple step of treating each multi-word attribute value as a single phrase. Overall, we observed 40K such phrases, e.g. "*back cover*", "*android v4.4.2*", "*9-12 month*" and "*wine red*". For both attribute values and product titles, we converted these multi-token phrases to single tokens (e.g. 'back cover' is replaced with 'back_cover').

[5]https://pypi.org/project/textdistance/

We describe details of the embedding learning task and triplet generation in Section 3.3.1, and twin network in Section 3.3.2.

3.3.1 Triplet Generation

There are scenarios when title contains canonical form of attribute value (e.g. "*3xl*" could be size attribute value for a title 'Nike running shoes for men xxxl'). We can leverage this information to learn embeddings that not only capture semantic similarity but can also distinguish between close canonical forms. Motivated by work in answer selection (Kulkarni et al., 2019; Bromley et al., 1994), we define an embedding learning task of keeping surface form closer to corresponding title as compared to a randomly chosen title. We created training data in form of triplets of anchor (q), positive title (a_+) and negative title (a_-), where q is attribute value, a_+ is corresponding product title and a_- is a title selected randomly from product category of a_+. One way to select negatives is to pick a random product from any product category, but that may provide limited signal for embedding learning task (e.g. choosing an Apparel category product when actual product is from Laptop category). Instead, we select a negative product from same product category, which acts as a hard negative (Kumar et al., 2019; Schroff et al., 2015) and improves the attribute normalization results. Selecting products from same category may lead to few incorrect negative titles (i.e. negative title may contain the correct attribute value). We screen out incorrect negatives where anchor attribute value (q) is mentioned in title, reducing noise in the training data.

3.3.2 Twin Network and Triplet Loss

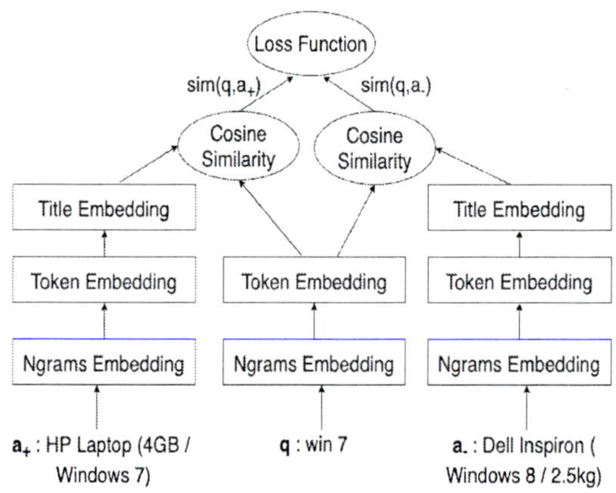

Figure 4: Illustration of Twin network with Triplet loss.

We choose twin network as it projects surface forms and canonical forms in same embedding space and triplet loss helps to keep surface forms closer to the most appropriate canonical form. Figure 4 describes the architecture of our SANTA framework. Given a (q, a_+, a_-) triplet, the model learns embedding that minimize the triplet loss function (Equation 2). Similar to fastText, we represent each token as consisting of sub-words (n-gram tokens). Embedding for a token is created using a composite function on sub-word embeddings, and similarly, embeddings for title are created using composite function on word embeddings. We use averaging of embeddings as composite function (similar to fastText), though the framework is generic and other composite functions like LSTM, CNN and transformers can also be used.

Let E denote the embedding operator and cos represent cosine similarity metric, then triplet loss function is given as:

$$Loss = max\,\{0, M - cos(E(q), E(a_+)) + cos(E(q), E(a_-))\} \tag{2}$$

where M is margin.

The advantage of this formulation over unsupervised embeddings (Section 3.2) is that in addition to learning semantic similarities for attribute values, it also learns to distinguish between close canonical forms, which may appear in similar contexts. For example, the embedding of surface form '720p' will move closer to embedding of 'HD' mentioned in a_+ title but away from embedding of 'Ultra HD' mentioned in a_- title.

4 Experimental Setup

In this section, we describe our experimental setup, including dataset, metrics and hyperparameters of our model. There is no publicly available data set for attribute normalization problem. More (2016) and Putthividhya and Hu (2011) worked on brand normalization problem but the datasets are not published for reuse. Xu et al. (2019) published a dataset collected from AliExpress 'Sports & Entertainment' category for attribute extraction use-case. This dataset belongs to a single category and is restricted to samples where attribute value is present in title, hence limiting its applicability for attribute normalization. To ensure robust learnings, we curate a real-world attribute normalization dataset spread across multiple categories and report all our evaluations on this dataset.

4.1 Training and Test data

We selected 50 attributes across 20 product categories including electronics, apparel and furniture for our study and obtained their canonical forms from business teams. These selected attributes have on average 7.5 canonical values (describing the exact selection process for canonical values is outside the scope of current work). For each of these attributes, we picked top 50 surface forms and manually mapped these values to corresponding canonical forms, using 'other' label when none of the existing canonical forms is suitable. We, thus, obtain a labelled dataset of 2500 samples (50 surface forms each for 50 attributes), out of which 38% surface forms are mapped to 'other' class. Surface forms mapping to 'other' are either junk value (e.g. "*5MP*" for operating system) or coarser value (e.g. "*android*" when canonical forms are "*android 4.1*", "*android 4.2*" etc.). It took 20 hours of manual effort for creating this dataset. We split this data into two parts (20% used as dev set and 80% as test set).

For training, we obtain a dump of $100K$ products corresponding to each attribute, obtaining a dump of $5M$ records (50 attributes X $100K$ products per attribute), having title and attribute values. This data ($5M$ records) is used for training unsupervised embeddings (Section 3.2). For each record, we select one negative example for triplet generation (Section 3.3.1) and use this triplet data (5M records) for learning SANTA model. Kindly note that training data creation is fully automated, and does not require any manual effort, making our approach easily scalable.

4.2 Metric

There are no well-established metrics in literature for attribute normalization problem. One simple approach is to consider canonical form with highest similarity as predicted value for evaluation. However, we argue that an algorithm should be penalized for mapping a junk value to any canonical form. Based on this motivation, we define two evaluation metrics that we use in this work.

4.2.1 Accuracy

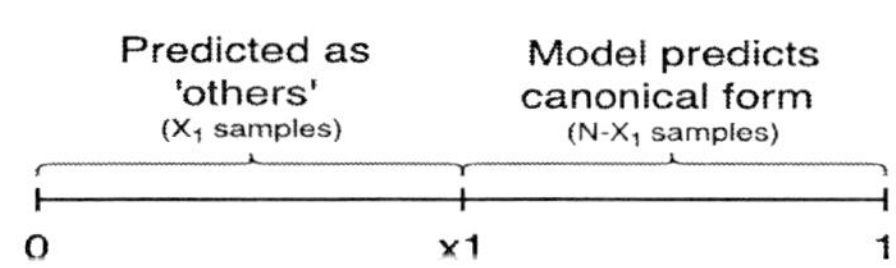

Figure 5: Illustration for Accuracy metric.

We divide predictions on all samples (N) into two sets using a threshold x_1 (see Figure 5). 'Other' class is predicted for samples having score less than x_1 (low similarity to any canonical form) and canonical form with highest similarity is considered for samples having score greater than x_1 (confident prediction). We consider prediction as correct for samples in X_1 set if true label is 'other' and for samples in $N - X_1$ set, if model prediction matches the true label. We define Accuracy as ratio of correct predictions to the number of cases where prediction is made (N in this case). The threshold x_1 is selected based on performance on dev set.

4.2.2 Accuracy Coverage Curve

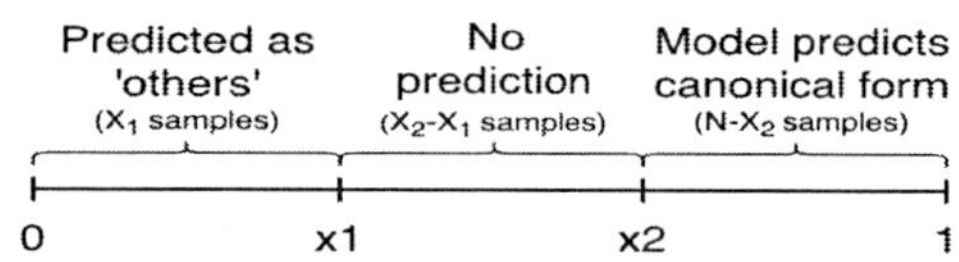

Figure 6: Illustration for Accuracy Coverage metric.

It can be argued that a model is confident about surface forms when prediction score is on either extreme (close to 1 or close to 0). Motivated by this intuition, we define another metric where we divide predictions into three sets using two thresholds x_1 and x_2 (see Figure 6). 'Other' class is predicted for samples having score less than x_1 (low similarity to any canonical form), no prediction is made for samples having score between x_1 and x_2 (model is not confidently predicting any canonical form but confidence score is not too low to predict 'other' class) and canonical form with highest similarity is considered for samples having score greater than x_2. We define Coverage as fraction of samples where some prediction is made ($(X_1 + N - X_2)/N$), and Accuracy as ratio of correct predictions to the number of predictions. For samples in X_1 set, we consider prediction correct if true label is 'other' and for samples in $N - X_2$ set, we consider prediction correct when model prediction matches the true canonical form. The thresholds are selected based on performance on dev set and based on different choice of thresholds, we create Accuracy-Coverage curve for comparison.

4.3 SANTA Hyperparameters

We set the value of M as 0.4, embedding dimension as 200, minimum n-gram size as 2 and maximum n-gram size as 4. We run the training using Adadelta optimizer for 5 epochs, which took approximately 8 hours on a NVIDIA V100 GPU. The parameters to be learned are ngram embeddings

Table 1: Evaluation of String similarity approaches.

STRING SIMILARITY	ACCURACY
EDIT DISTANCE BASED	
HAMMING	51.6
LEVENSHTEIN	61.1
JARO-WINKLER	62.1
SEQUENCE BASED	
LC SUBSEQUENCE	57.6
LC SUBSTRING	64.7
RATCLIFF-OBERSHELP	64.9
TOKEN BASED	
JACCARD INDEX	74.6
SORENSEN-DICE	74.6
COSINE SIMILARITY	**76.6**

($0.63M$ ngrams X 200 embedding dimension = $127M$ parameters). Ngram embeddings are shared across the twin network.

5 Results

We present systematic study on string similarity approaches in Section 5.1, followed by experiments of unsupervised embeddings in Section 5.2. We compare best results from Section 5.1 and Section 5.2 with our proposed SANTA framework in Section 5.3. We study these algorithms separately on syntactic and semantic portion of test dataset in Section 5.4 and perform qualitative analysis based on t-SNE visualization in Section 5.5.

5.1 Evaluation of String Similarity

Table 1 shows comparison of string similarity approaches for attribute normalization. We observe that token based methods performs best, followed by comparable performance of sequence based and edit distance based methods. We believe that token based approaches outperformed other approaches as they are insensitive to the position where common sub-string occurs in the two strings (e.g. matching "*half sleeve*" to "*sleeve half*" for *sleeve type* attribute). Putthividhya and Hu (2011) evaluated n-gram based 'Jaccard index' (token based approach) and 'Jaro-Winkler distance' (character based approach) for brand normalization and got similar observations, obtaining best results with 'Jaccard index'. We observe that 'Cosine similarity' obtains 2.7% accuracy improvement over Jaccard index in our experiments.

5.2 Evaluation of Unsupervised Embeddings

Table 2 shows performance of word2vec and fastText approach. We observe that presence of n-grams information in fastText leads to significant improvement over word2vec, as use of n-grams helps with matching of rare attribute values. However, fastText is not able to match string similarity

Table 2: Comparison of normalization approaches

MODEL	ACCURACY
RANDOM	37.8
MAJORITY CLASS PREDICTION	48.5
JACCARD INDEX	74.6
COSINE SIMILARITY	76.6
WORD2VEC	48.4
FASTTEXT	65.7
SANTA (WITHOUT NGRAMS)	47.4
SANTA (WITH NGRAMS)	**78.4**

baseline (refer Table 1). We believe unsupervised embeddings shows relatively inferior performance for attribute normalization task, as embeddings are learnt based on contexts in product titles, keeping different canonical forms (e.g. "*HD*" and "*Ultra HD*") close by as they occur in similar context.

5.3 Evaluation of SANTA framework

Table 2 shows comparison of SANTA with multiple normalization approaches, including best solutions from Section 5.1 and Section 5.2. To understand the difficulty of this task, we introduce two baselines of a) randomly mapping surface form to one of the canonical forms (termed as 'RANDOM'), and b) predicting the most common class based on dev data (termed as 'MAJORITY CLASS'). We observe 37.8% accuracy with 'RANDOM' and 48.5% accuracy with 'MAJORITY CLASS', establishing the difficulty of the task. SANTA (with ngrams) shows best performance with 78.4% accuracy, leading to 2.3% accuracy improvement over 'Cosine Similarity' (best string similarity approach) and 19.3% over fastText (best unsupervised embeddings). We discuss few qualitative examples for these approaches in appendix.

Figure 7 shows Accuracy-Coverage curve for these algorithms. As observed from this curve, SANTA consistently outperforms string similarity and fastText across all coverages.

5.4 Study on Syntactic and Semantic Dataset

In this section, we do a separate comparison of normalization algorithms on samples requiring semantic and syntactic matching. We filtered test dataset where true label is not 'Others', and manually labelled each surface form as requiring syntactic or semantic similarity. Based on this analysis, we observe that 45% of test data requires syntactic matching, 17% requires semantic matching and remaining 38% is mapped to 'other' class. For current analysis of syntactic and semantic set, we

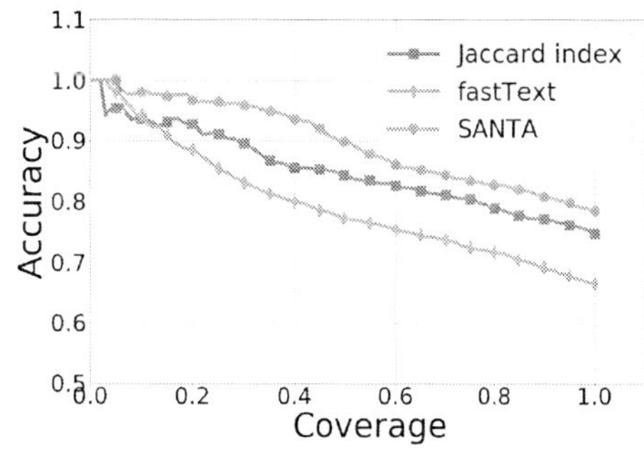

Figure 7: Accuracy-Coverage plot for various Normalization techniques.

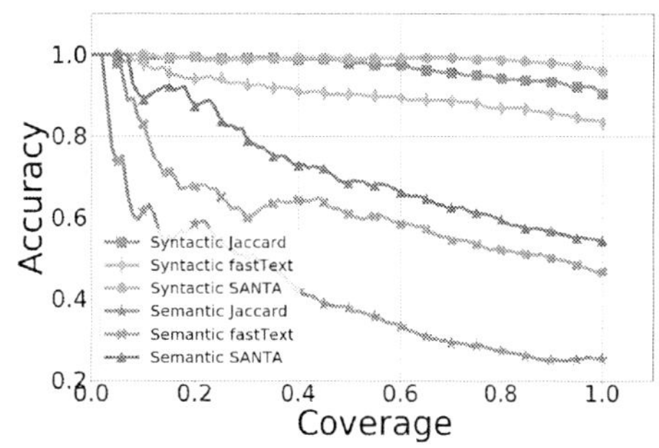

Figure 8: Study of various normalization algorithms on semantic and syntactic dataset

use a special case of metric defined in section 4 (since 'other' class is not present). We set $x_1 = 0$, ensuring that 'other' class is not predicted for any samples of test data. We show Accuracy-Coverage plot for semantic and syntactic cases in Figure 8.

For semantic set, we observe that fastText performs better than string similarity, due to its ability to learn semantic representation. Our proposed SANTA framework, further improves over fastText for better semantic matching with close canonical forms. For syntactic set, we observe comparable performance of SANTA and string similarity. These results demonstrate that our proposed SANTA framework performs well on both syntactic and semantic set.

5.5 Word Embeddings Visualization

For qualitative comparison of fastText and SANTA embeddings, we project these embeddings into 2-dimensions using t-SNE (van der Maaten and Hinton, 2008). Figure 9 shows t-SNE plots[6] for 3 attributes (Headphone Color, Jewelry Necklace type and Watch Movement type). For color attribute, we observe that values based on SANTA have ho

[6] `https://scikit-learn.org/stable/modules/generated/sklearn.manifold.TSNE`

mogenous cohorts of canonical values and corresponding surface forms (e.g. there is a cohort for 'black' color on bottom-right and 'blue' color on top-left of the plot.). However, with fastText, the color values are scattered across the plot without any specific cohorts. Similar patterns are seen with necklace type where SANTA results show better cohorts than fastText. These results demonstrate that embeddings learnt with SANTA are better suited than fastText embeddings to distinguish between close canonical forms.

6 Conclusion

In this paper, we studied the problem of attribute normalization for E-commerce. We did a systematic study of multiple syntactic matching algorithms and established that use of 'cosine similarity' leads to 2.7% improvement over commonly used Jaccard index. Additionally, we argued that attribute normalization requires combination of syntactic and semantic matching. We described our SANTA framework for attribute normalization, including our proposed task to learn embeddings in a self-supervised fashion with twin network and triplet loss. Evaluation on a real-world dataset for 50 attributes, shows that embeddings learnt using our proposed SANTA framework outperforms best string matching algorithm by 2.3% and fastText by 19.3% for attribute normalization task. Our evaluation based on semantic and syntactic examples and t-SNE plots provide useful insights into qualitative behaviour of these embeddings.

References

Piotr Bojanowski, Edouard Grave, Armand Joulin, and Tomas Mikolov. 2017. Enriching word vectors with subword information. *TACL*, 5:135–146.

Jane Bromley, Isabelle Guyon, Yann LeCun, Eduard Säckinger, and Roopak Shah. 1994. Signature verification using a" siamese" time delay neural network. In *NIPS*, pages 737–744.

Peter Christen. 2006. A comparison of personal name matching: Techniques and practical issues. In *Sixth IEEE ICDM-Workshops (ICDMW'06)*, pages 290–294. IEEE.

William W Cohen, Pradeep Ravikumar, and Stephen E Fienberg. 2003. A comparison of string distance metrics for name-matching tasks. In *IIWeb*, pages 73–78.

Najlah Gali, Radu Mariescu-Istodor, and Pasi Fränti. 2016. Similarity measures for title matching. In *2016 23rd ICPR*, pages 1548–1553. IEEE.

Wael H Gomaa and Aly A Fahmy. 2013. A survey of text similarity approaches. *International Journal of Computer Applications*, 68(13):13–18.

Tom Kenter and Maarten De Rijke. 2015. Short text similarity with word embeddings. In *24th ACM CIKM*, pages 1411–1420.

Ashish Kulkarni, Kartik Mehta, Shweta Garg, Vidit Bansal, Nikhil Rasiwasia, and Srinivasan Sengamedu. 2019. Productqna: Answering user questions on e-commerce product pages. In *Companion Proceedings of The 2019 WWW Conference*, pages 354–360.

Sawan Kumar, Shweta Garg, Kartik Mehta, and Nikhil Rasiwasia. 2019. Improving answer selection and answer triggering using hard negatives. In *Proceedings of the 2019 EMNLP-IJCNLP*, pages 5913–5919.

Laurens van der Maaten and Geoffrey Hinton. 2008. Visualizing data using t-sne. *Journal of Machine Learning Research*, 9(86):2579–2605.

Tomas Mikolov, Ilya Sutskever, Kai Chen, Greg S Corrado, and Jeff Dean. 2013. Distributed representations of words and phrases and their compositionality. In *NIPS*, pages 3111–3119.

Ajinkya More. 2016. Attribute extraction from product titles in ecommerce. *arXiv preprint arXiv:1608.04670*.

Duangmanee Pew Putthividhya and Junling Hu. 2011. Bootstrapped named entity recognition for product attribute extraction. In *EMNLP*, pages 1557–1567. Association for Computational Linguistics.

Gabriel Recchia and Max M Louwerse. 2013. A comparison of string similarity measures for toponym matching. In *COMP@ SIGSPATIAL*, pages 54–61.

Florian Schroff, Dmitry Kalenichenko, and James Philbin. 2015. Facenet: A unified embedding for face recognition and clustering. In *CVPR*, pages 815–823.

MK Vijaymeena and K Kavitha. 2016. A survey on similarity measures in text mining. *Machine Learning and Applications: An International Journal*, 3(2):19–28.

Huimin Xu, Wenting Wang, Xinnian Mao, Xinyu Jiang, and Man Lan. 2019. Scaling up open tagging from tens to thousands: Comprehension empowered attribute value extraction from product title. In *Proceedings of the 57th Annual Meeting of the Association for Computational Linguistics*, pages 5214–5223.

Atsuko Yamaguchi, Yasunori Yamamoto, Jin-Dong Kim, Toshihisa Takagi, and Akinori Yonezawa. 2012. Discriminative application of string similarity methods to chemical and non-chemical names for biomedical abbreviation clustering. In *BMC genomics*, volume 13, page S8. Springer.

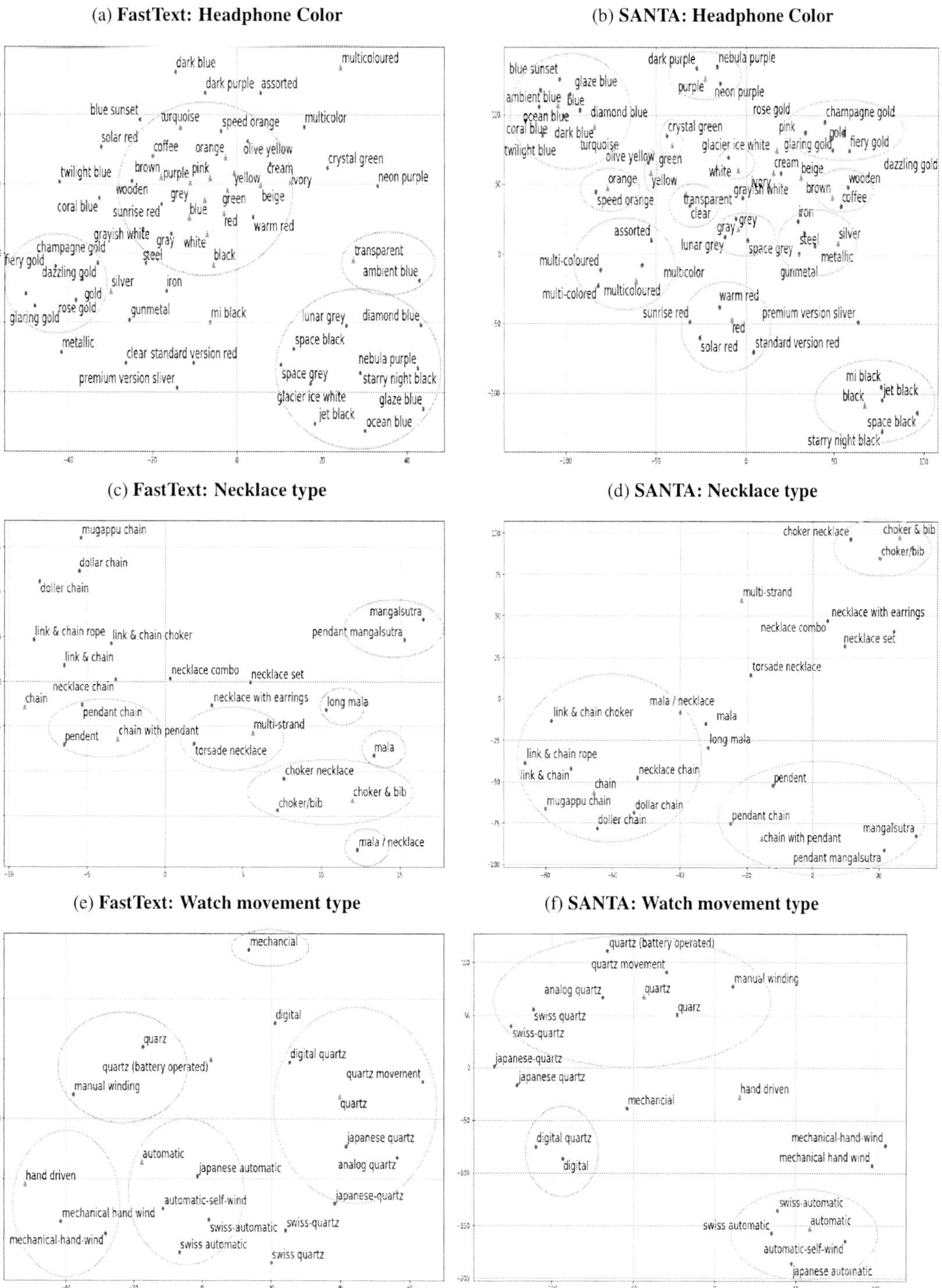

Figure 9: Figure showing t-SNE plot of fastText and SANTA embeddings for three attributes. Surface forms are shown with green dots and canonical forms with red triangles. For better understanding of results, we use green oval selection to show correct homogenous cohorts and red oval selection for incorrect cohorts. This figure is best seen in colors.

7 Appendix

We list few interesting examples in Table 3. It can be observed that string similarity makes correct predictions for cases requiring fuzzy matching (e.g. matching "*multi*" with "*multicoloured*"), but, makes incorrect predictions for examples requiring semantic matching (e.g. incorrectly matching "*cane*" with "*polyurethane*"). With fastText, we get correct predictions for many semantic examples, however, we get incorrect predictions for close canonical forms (e.g. incorrectly mapping "*3 seater sofa set*" to "*five seat*" as "*three seat*" and "*five seat*" occur in similar contexts in title). Our proposed SANTA model does well for most of these examples, but it fails to make correct predictions for rare surface forms (e.g. "*no assembly required, pre-aseembled*").

Surface Form	Actual Canonical Form	Cosine Similarity Prediction	FastText Prediction	SANTA prediction	Comment
multi	multicoloured	multicoloured	green	multicoloured	FastText fails
thermoplastic	plastic	plastic	silicone	plastic	
amd radeon r3	ati radeon	ati radeon	nvidia geforce	ati radeon	
free size	one size	one size	small	one size	
2 years	2 - 3 years	11 - 12 years	3 - 4 years	2 - 3 years	Both String Similarity and fastText fails but SANTA gives correct mapping
elbow sleeve	half sleeve	3/4 sleeve	short sleeve	half sleeve	
cane	bamboo	polyurethane	rattan	bamboo	
product will be assembled	requires assembly	already assembled	d-i-y	require assembly	
3 seater sofa set	three seat	four seat	five seat	three seat	
nokia os	symbian	palm web os	symbian	symbian	String Similarity fails
silicone	rubber	silk	rubber	rubber	
coffee	brown	off-white	brown	brown	
no assembly required, pre-aseembled	already assembled	requires assembly	already assembled	requires assembly	SANTA fails
mechancial	hand driven	hand driven	hand driven	automatic	

Table 3: Qualitative Examples for multiple normalization approaches. Correct predictions are highlighted in green color and incorrect predictions are highlighted in red color.

Multimodal Item Categorization Fully Based on Transformers

Lei Chen[*], Hou Wei Chou[*], Yandi Xia, Hirokazu Miyake
Rakuten Institute of Technology
Boston, MA, USA
{lei.a.chen,houwei.chou,yandi.xia,hirokazu.miyake}@rakuten.com

Abstract

The Transformer has proven to be a powerful feature extraction method and has gained widespread adoption in natural language processing (NLP). In this paper we propose a multimodal item categorization (MIC) system solely based on the Transformer for both text and image processing. On a multimodal product data set collected from a Japanese e-commerce giant, we tested a new image classification model based on the Transformer and investigated different ways of fusing bi-modal information. Our experimental results on real industry data showed that the Transformer-based image classifier has performance on par with ResNet-based classifiers and is four times faster to train. Furthermore, a cross-modal attention layer was found to be critical for the MIC system to achieve performance gains over text-only and image-only models.

1 Introduction

Item categorization (IC) is a core technology in modern e-commerce. Since there can be millions of products and hundreds of labels in e-commerce markets, it is important to be able to map these products to their locations in a product category taxonomy tree efficiently and accurately so that buyers can easily find the products they need. Therefore, IC technology with high accuracy is needed to cope with this demanding task.

Products can contain text (such as titles) and images. Although most IC research has focused on using text-based cues, images of products also contain useful information. For example, in some sub-areas like fashion, the information conveyed through images is richer and more accurate than through the text channel. In this paper, we propose an MIC model entirely based on the Transformer architecture (Vaswani et al., 2017) for achieving a simplification of the model and faster training speed. We conducted experiments on real product data collected from an e-commerce giant in Japan to (a) test the performance of the Transformer-based product image classification, and (b) systematically compare several bi-modal fusion methods to jointly use both text and image cues.

2 Related works

(Zahavy et al., 2016) is a seminal work on MIC where multi-label classification using both titles and images was conducted on products listed on the Walmart.com website. They used a convolutional neural network to extract representations from both titles and images, then designed several policies to fuse the outputs of the two models. This led to improved performance over individual models separately. Since this work, further research has been conducted on MIC such as (Wirojwatanakul and Wangperawong, 2019; Nawaz et al., 2018).

Recently, a MIC data challenge was organized in the SIGIR'20 e-commerce workshop[1]. Rakuten France provided a dataset containing about $99K$ products where each product contained a title, an optional detailed description, and a product image. The MIC task was to predict 27 category labels from four major genres: books, children, household, and entertainment. Several teams submitted their MIC systems (Bi et al., 2020; Chordia and Vijay Kumar, 2020; Chou et al., 2020). A common solution was to fine-tune pre-trained text and image encoders to serve as feature extractors, then use a bi-modal fusion mechanism to combine predictions. Most teams used the Transformer-based BERT model (Devlin et al., 2019) for text feature extraction and ResNet (He et al., 2016) for image feature extraction, including the standard ResNet-

[*] Equal contributor

[1] https://sigir-ecom.github.io/ecom2020/data-task.html

Proceedings of the 4th Workshop on e-Commerce and NLP (ECNLP 4), pages 111–115
August 5, 2021.

152 and the recently released Big Transfer (BiT) model (Kolesnikov et al., 2020). For bi-modal fusion, the methods used were more diverse. Roughly in order of increasing complexity, the methods included simple decision-level late fusion (Bi et al., 2020), highway network (Chou et al., 2020), and co-attention (Chordia and Vijay Kumar, 2020). It is interesting to note that the winning team used the simplest decision-level late fusion method.

In other recent work, a cross-modal attention layer which used representations from different modalities to be the key and query vectors to compute attention weights was studied. In (Zhu et al., 2020), product descriptions and images were jointly used to predict product attributes, e.g., color and size, and their values in an end-to-end fashion. In addition, based on the fact that product images can contain information not clearly aligned with or even contradicting the information conveyed in the text, a special gate was used to control the contribution of the image channel. A similar idea was used in (Sun et al., 2020) on multimodal named entity recognition research on Twitter data.

Although the field has converged on using Transformer-based models for processing text in recent years, ResNet-based image processing is still the dominant approach in MIC research. One immediate difficulty in combining the two types of models is the big gap between the training speeds. Owing to the superior parallel running capability enabled by self-attention in the Transformer architecture, text encoder training is much faster than the image encoder, and the training bottleneck of the MIC system becomes solely the image encoder. In addition, using two different deep learning architectures simultaneously makes building and maintaining MIC systems more complex. One solution is to use Transformers as the encoder of choice for both modalities. Furthermore, a detailed comparison of different fusion methods on large-scale multimodal industry product data is still missing. Our work addresses these two directions of research.

3 Model

Our MIC model is depicted in Figure 1[2]. It consists of feature extraction components using a Transformer on uni-modal channels (i.e., text titles and images), a fusion part to obtain multimodal representations, and a Multi-Layer Perceptron (MLP) head to make final predictions.

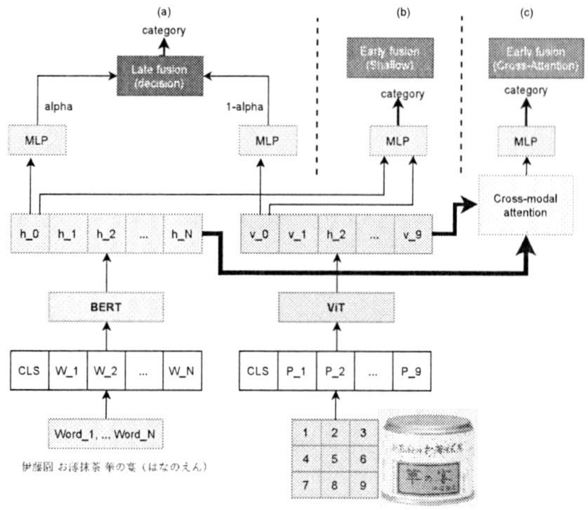

Figure 1: Our Transformer-based MIC system consists of a BERT model to extract textual information and a ViT model to extract visual information. Three different types of multimodal fusion methods are compared, including (a) late fusion, (b) early fusion by concatenating textual and image representations (shallow), and (c) early fusion by using a cross-modal attention. Wide arrows indicate that the entire sequence, e.g., h_0 to h_N, is used in the computation. For illustration we show 3×3 patches for ViT but in our actual implementation a higher P was used.

3.1 BERT text model

We fine-tuned a Japanese BERT model (Devlin et al., 2019) trained on Japanese Wikipedia data. The BERT model encodes a textual product title, $\mathbf{x} = ([CLS], x_1, ..., x_N)$, into text representation sequence $\mathbf{h} = (h_0, h_1, ...h_N)$, where h_i is a vector with a dimension of 768.

3.2 ViT image model

Although originally developed for NLP applications, in recent years the Transformer architecture (Vaswani et al., 2017) has been increasingly applied to the computer vision domain. For example, (Han et al., 2020) is a recent survey paper listing many newly emerging visual models using the Transformer.

Among the many visual Transformer models we used the ViT model (Dosovitskiy et al., 2020), which is a pure Transformer that is applied directly on an image's $P \times P$ patch sequence. ViT utilizes the standard Transformer's encoder part as an image classification feature extractor and adds a MLP head to determine the image labels. The ViT model

[2]The image of the can of tea is from https://item.rakuten.co.jp/kusurinokiyoshi/10016272/

was pre-trained using a supervised learning task on a massive image data set. The size of the supervised training data set impacts ViT performance significantly. When using Google's in-house JFT 300M image set, ViT can reach a performance superior to other competitive ResNet (He et al., 2016) models.

The ViT model encodes the product image. After converting a product image to $P \times P$ patches, ViT converts these patches to visual tokens. After adding a special [CLS] visual token to represent the entire image, the $M = P \times P + 1$ long sequence is fed into a ViT model to output an encoding as $\mathbf{v} = (v_0, v_1, v_2, ...v_M)$, where $M = P \times P$.

3.3 Multimodal fusion

The fusion method plays an important role in MIC. In this paper we compared three methods, corresponding to Figure 1 (a), (b), and (c).

3.3.1 Late fusion

The simplest fusion method is combining the decisions made by individual models directly (Bi et al., 2020; Chou et al., 2020). We used weights α and $1 - \alpha$ to interpolate the probabilities estimated by BERT and ViT models. The α value was chosen using a held-out set.

3.3.2 Early fusion – shallow

The [CLS] token, the first token of every input sequence to BERT and ViT, is used to provide a global representation. Therefore we can concatenate the two encoded [CLS] tokens to create a multimodal output. The concatenated feature vectors are sent to an MLP head for predicting multi-class category labels. This method is called a *shallow fusion* (Siriwardhana et al., 2020).

3.3.3 Early fusion – cross-modal attention

A cross-modal attention layer provides a more sophisticated fusion between text and image channels (Zhu et al., 2020; Sun et al., 2020). Cross-modal attention is computed by combining Key-Value (K-V) pairs from one modality with the Query (Q) from the other modality. In addition, (Zhu et al., 2020) used a gate to moderate potential noise from the visual channel.

Specifically, the multimodal representation $\mathbf{h}'$ is computed from the addition of the self-attention (SA) version of text representation $\mathbf{h}$ and the cross-modal attention version by considering the visual representation $\mathbf{v}$ as

$$\mathbf{h}' = SA(\mathbf{h}, \mathbf{h}, \mathbf{h}) + VG \odot SA(\mathbf{h}, \mathbf{v}, \mathbf{v}), \quad (1)$$

where

$$SA(\mathbf{q}, \mathbf{k}, \mathbf{v}) = \text{softmax}\left(\frac{(W_Q \mathbf{q})(W_K \mathbf{k})^T}{\sqrt{d_k}}\right) W_V \mathbf{v}, \quad (2)$$

$$VG_i = \sigma(W_1 h_i + W_2 v_0 + b), \quad (3)$$

W_Q, W_K, and W_V are trainable query, key, and value parameters, d_k is the dimension of the key vectors, and the visual gate, VG, can be learned from both the local text representations h_i and global visual representation v_0, with W_1, W_2, and b as trainable parameters. The category label prediction $\hat{y}$ is determined as

$$\hat{y} = \text{softmax}\left(W_3 \sum_i h'_i\right), \quad (4)$$

where W_3 is a trainable parameter.

4 Experiment

4.1 Setup

Data set: Our data consisted of about 500,000 products from a large e-commerce platform in Japan, focusing on three major product categories. Our task, a multi-class classification problem, was to predict the leaf-level product categories from their Japanese titles and images. Further details of our data set are shown in the left part of Table 1. We used the macro-averaged F1-score to evaluate model performance.

Models: We compared the following models.

- Text-only: Japanese BERT model[3] fine-tuned on product titles.
- Image-BiT: BiT image model (Kolesnikov et al., 2020) fine-tuned on product images. In particular, we used BiT-M.[4] BiT showed a considerable performance advantage than other conventional ResNet models in the SIGIR'20 MIC data challenge (Chou et al., 2020).

[3] https://huggingface.co/cl-tohoku/bert-base-japanese-whole-word-masking

[4] https://tfhub.dev/google/bit/m-r152x4/1

Root genre	Class size	Train size	Test size	Ma-F1 (BiT)	Ma-F1 (ViT)
Beverages (B)	32	29,269	7,332	**0.666**	0.610
Appliances (A)	280	200,552	50,283	0.574	**0.639**
Men's Fashion (M)	70	228,148	57,077	0.715	**0.733**

Table 1: Summary of our data set obtained from a large e-commerce platform in Japan. Right two columns report image classification macro-F1 values using BiT and ViT models, respectively.

- Image-ViT: ViT image model (Dosovitskiy et al., 2020) fine-tuned on product images. We used ViT-L-16.[5] 16 means that we used 16 × 16 patches when feeding images.

- Fusion: The **late** fusion method described in Section 3.3.1 and depicted in Figure 1 (a), the **early** fusion method described in Section 3.3.2 and depicted in Figure 1 (b), and the **cross-modal** fusion method described in Section 3.3.3 and depicted in Figure 1 (c).

Implementation details: Our models were implemented in PyTorch using a GPU for training and evaluation. The AdamW optimizer (Loshchilov and Hutter, 2017) was used. Tokenization was performed with MeCab.[6]

4.2 Result

Table 1 reports on macro-F1 values for the three genres using the ResNet-based BiT vs. Transformer-based ViT. ViT shows higher performance compared to BiT on two of the three genres. In addition, consistent with the speed advantage reported in (Dosovitskiy et al., 2020), we also observed that the training for ViT is about four times faster than BiT. This is critical for an MIC system deployable in industry since image model training time is the main bottleneck.

Model	F1 (B)	F1 (A)	F1 (M)
Text-BERT	0.718	0.733	0.802
Image-ViT	0.610	0.639	0.733
Fusion-late	0.725	0.709	0.814
Fusion-early	0.714	0.726	0.788
Fusion cross-modal	**0.729**	**0.740**	**0.815**

Table 2: Macro-F1 on the three product genres. Uni-modal models, i.e., BERT text model and ViT image model, and different fusion models are compared.

Table 2 reports on uni-modal model performance, i.e., text-BERT and image-ViT separately, as well as the results of fusing these models in various ways. We found that the early (shallow) fusion method leads to poor model performance. One possible reason is that product images used in e-commerce product catalogs sometimes do not appear to be clearly related to its corresponding titles. For example, a bottle of wine may be packaged in a box and its image only shows the box. We also found that late (decision) fusion does not lead to consistent gains. In the appliance genre, we found that the fused model was worse than the text model. On the other hand, the cross-modal attention fusion method showed consistent gains over both the text and image models separately on all three genres.

5 Discussion

Although various approaches have been explored in MIC research, we found that a MIC system built entirely out of the Transformer architecture was missing. Combining the well-established BERT text model and the newly released ViT image model, we proposed an all-Transformer MIC system on Japanese e-commerce products. From experiments on real industry product data from an e-commerce giant in Japan, we found that the ViT model can be fine-tuned four times faster than BiT and can have improved performance. Furthermore, fusing both text and image inputs in an MIC setup using the cross-modal attention fusion method led to model performance better than each model separately, and we found that this fusion method worked better than late fusion and the early (shallow) fusion of simply concatenating representations from the two modalities.

There are several directions to extend the current work in the future, including (1) considering jointly modeling texts and images in one Transformer model like FashionBERT (Gao et al., 2020), and (2) using self-training to go beyond the limit caused by the size of labeled image data for the image model.

[5]https://github.com/asyml/vision-transformer-pytorch

[6]https://taku910.github.io/mecab/

References

Ye Bi, Shuo Wang, and Zhongrui Fan. 2020. A Multimodal Late Fusion Model for E-Commerce Product Classification. *arXiv preprint arXiv:2008.06179*.

V. Chordia and B.G. Vijay Kumar. 2020. Large Scale Multimodal Classification Using an Ensemble of Transformer Models and Co-Attention. In *Proc. SIGIR'20 e-Com workshop*.

H. Chou, Y.H. Lee, L. Chen, Y. Xia, and W.T. Chen. 2020. CBB-FE, CamemBERT and BiT Feature Extraction for Multimodal Product Classification and Retrieval. In *Proc. SIGIR'20 e-Com workshop*.

Jacob Devlin, Ming-Wei Chang, Kenton Lee, and Kristina Toutanova. 2019. BERT: Pre-training of Deep Bidirectional Transformers for Language Understanding. *arXiv:1810.04805 [cs]*. ArXiv: 1810.04805.

Alexey Dosovitskiy, Lucas Beyer, Alexander Kolesnikov, Dirk Weissenborn, Xiaohua Zhai, Thomas Unterthiner, Mostafa Dehghani, Matthias Minderer, Georg Heigold, and Sylvain Gelly. 2020. An image is worth 16x16 words: Transformers for image recognition at scale. *arXiv preprint arXiv:2010.11929*.

Dehong Gao, Linbo Jin, Ben Chen, Minghui Qiu, Peng Li, Yi Wei, Yi Hu, and Hao Wang. 2020. Fashionbert: Text and image matching with adaptive loss for cross-modal retrieval. In *Proceedings of the 43rd International ACM SIGIR Conference on Research and Development in Information Retrieval*, pages 2251–2260.

Kai Han, Yunhe Wang, Hanting Chen, Xinghao Chen, Jianyuan Guo, Zhenhua Liu, Yehui Tang, An Xiao, Chunjing Xu, and Yixing Xu. 2020. A Survey on Visual Transformer. *arXiv preprint arXiv:2012.12556*.

Kaiming He, Xiangyu Zhang, Shaoqing Ren, and Jian Sun. 2016. Deep residual learning for image recognition. In *Proceedings of the IEEE conference on computer vision and pattern recognition*, pages 770–778.

Alexander Kolesnikov, Lucas Beyer, Xiaohua Zhai, Joan Puigcerver, Jessica Yung, Sylvain Gelly, and Neil Houlsby. 2020. Big Transfer (BiT): General Visual Representation Learning. *arXiv:1912.11370 [cs]*. ArXiv: 1912.11370.

Ilya Loshchilov and Frank Hutter. 2017. Decoupled weight decay regularization. *arXiv preprint arXiv:1711.05101*.

Shah Nawaz, Alessandro Calefati, Muhammad Kamran Janjua, Muhammad Umer Anwaar, and Ignazio Gallo. 2018. Learning fused representations for large-scale multimodal classification. *IEEE Sensors Letters*, 3(1):1–4.

Shamane Siriwardhana, Andrew Reis, Rivindu Weerasekera, and Suranga Nanayakkara. 2020. Tuning "BERT-like" Self Supervised Models to Improve Multimodal Speech Emotion Recognition.

Lin Sun, Jiquan Wang, Yindu Su, Fangsheng Weng, Yuxuan Sun, Zengwei Zheng, and Yuanyi Chen. 2020. RIVA: A Pre-trained Tweet Multimodal Model Based on Text-image Relation for Multimodal NER. In *Proceedings of the 28th International Conference on Computational Linguistics*, pages 1852–1862.

Ashish Vaswani, Noam Shazeer, Niki Parmar, Jakob Uszkoreit, Llion Jones, Aidan N. Gomez, \Lukasz Kaiser, and Illia Polosukhin. 2017. Attention is all you need. *Advances in neural information processing systems*, 30:5998–6008.

Pasawee Wirojwatanakul and Artit Wangperawong. 2019. Multi-Label Product Categorization Using Multi-Modal Fusion Models. *arXiv preprint arXiv:1907.00420*.

Tom Zahavy, Alessandro Magnani, Abhinandan Krishnan, and Shie Mannor. 2016. Is a picture worth a thousand words? A Deep Multi-Modal Fusion Architecture for Product Classification in e-commerce. *arXiv preprint arXiv:1611.09534*.

Tiangang Zhu, Yue Wang, Haoran Li, Youzheng Wu, Xiaodong He, and Bowen Zhou. 2020. Multimodal Joint Attribute Prediction and Value Extraction for E-commerce Product. *arXiv preprint arXiv:2009.07162*.

Textual Representations for Crosslingual Information Retrieval

Bryan Zhang
Amazon.com
bryzhang@amazon.com

Liling Tan
Amazon.com
lilingt@amazon.com

Abstract

In this paper, we explored different levels of textual representations for cross-lingual information retrieval. Beyond the traditional token level representation, we adopted the subword and character level representations for information retrieval that had shown to improve neural machine translation by reducing the out-of-vocabulary issues in machine translation. Additionally, we improved the search performance by combining and re-ranking the result sets from the different text representations for German, French and Japanese.

1 Introduction

Cross-lingual information retrieval (CLIR) systems commonly use machine translation (MT) systems to translate the user query to the language of the search index before retrieving the search results (Fujii and Ishikawa, 2000; Pecina et al., 2014; Saleh and Pecina, 2020; Bi et al., 2020).

Traditionally, information retrieval and machine translation systems convert search queries to tokens and n-grams level textual representation (Jiang and Zhai, 2007; McNamee and Mayfield, 2004; Leveling and Jones, 2010; Yarmohammadi et al., 2019). Modern neural machine translation (NMT) systems have shown that subwords and character representations with flexible vocabularies outperform fixed vocabulary token-level translations (Sennrich et al., 2016; Lee et al., 2017; Kudo and Richardson, 2018; Wang et al., 2019). This study explores the shared granularity of textual representations between machine translation and cross-lingual information retrieval.

Textual representations of varying granularity encode queries differently, resulting in more diverse and robust search retrieval. Potentially, subwords and character-level representations are less sensitive to irregularities in noisy user-generated queries, e.g. misspellings and dialectal variants.

Tokens:	*americium ist ein chemisches element ...*
Subwords:	*_am er ic ium _ist _ein _chemische s _ element ...*
Characters:	*a m e r c i u m _ i s t _ e i n _ c h e m i s c h e s _ e l e m e n t*

Table 1: Example of a Pre-processed Document with Different Text Representations

2 Related Work

Neural machine translation had shown to outperform older paradigm of statistical machine translation models significantly and even "*achieved human parity in specific machine translation tasks*" (Hassan et al., 2018; Läubli et al., 2018; Toral, 2020). Moving from fixed token-level vocabulary to a subword representation unlocks open vocabulary capabilities to minimize out-of-vocabulary (OOV) issues[1].

Byte-Pair Encoding (BPE) is a popular subword algorithm that splits tokens into smaller units (Sennrich et al., 2016). This is based on the intuition that smaller units of character sequences can be translated easily across languages.

For instance, these smaller units appear when handling compound words via compositional translations, such as

For instance, subword units can better handle compound words via compositional German to English translations, ***schoko**lade* → *chocolate* and ***schoko**-creme* → *chocolate cream*. Suwbords can also cope with translations where we can easily copy or translate part of the source tokens or translate cognates and loanwords via phonological or morphological transformations, e.g. *positiv* →

[1]Although subwords allow more flexibility than tokens in creating unseen words, most NMT systems cannot support a genuinely open vocabulary thus a backoff token <unk> is often used during inference to represent subwords that is not seen in the training data.

Proceedings of the 4th Workshop on e-Commerce and NLP (ECNLP 4), pages 116–122
August 5, 2021.

positive and *negativ* (German) $\rightarrow$ *negative*.

While BPE reduces the OOV instances, it requires the input to be pre-tokenized before applying the subword compression. Alternatively, Kudo and Richardson (2018) proposed a more language-agnostic approach to subword tokenization directly from raw string inputs using unigram language models.

Completing the whole gamut of granular text representations, Lee et al. (2017) explored character-level neural machine translations that do not require any form of pre-processing or subword or token-level tokenization. They found that multilingual many-to-one character-level NMT models are more efficient and can be as competitive as or sometimes better than subwords NMT models. Moreover, character-level NMT can naturally handle intra-sentence code-switching. In the context of CLIR, they will be able to handle mixed language queries. Following this, Wang et al. (2019) found that using byte-level BPE vocabulary is 1/8 the size of a full subword BPE model. A multilingual NMT (many-to-one) setting achieves the best translation quality, outperforming subwords models and character-level models.

While finer granularity of text representations was exploited for machine translation, to our best knowledge, information retrieval studies have yet to study the impact of using these subword representations on traditional information retrieval systems (Robertson, 2004; Robertson and Zaragoza, 2009; Aly et al., 2014). However, many previous works have leapfrogged to using fully neural information retrieval systems representing text with underlying various subword representations and neural dense text representation.

Often, these neural representations are available in multilingual settings in which the same neural language model can encode texts in multiple languages. Jiang et al. (2020) explored using the popular multilingual Bidirectional Encoder Representations from Transformers (BERT) model to learn the relevance between English queries and foreign language documents in a CLIR setup. They showed that the model outperforms competitive non-neural traditional IR systems on a few of the sub-tasks.

Alternatively, previous researches have also used a cascading approach to machine translation and traditional IR where (i) the documents are translated to the foreign languages with neural machine translation and/or (ii) the foreign queries are translated before retrieval from the source document index (Saleh and Pecina, 2020; Oard, 1998; McCarley, 1999).

Saleh and Pecina (2020) compared the effects of statistical machine translation (SMT) and NMT in a cascaded traditional CLIR setting. They found that the better quality translations from NMT outperforms SMT and translating queries to the source document language that achieved better IR results than using foreign language queries on an index of translated documents.

Although fully neural IR systems are changing the paradigm of information retrieval, traditional IR (e.g. TF-IDF or BM25) approaches remain very competitive and can still outperform neural IR systems for some tasks (Boytsov, 2020; Jiang et al., 2020). In this regard, we follow up on the cascading approach to machine translation and information retrieval on traditional IR systems. This study fills the knowledge gap of understanding the effects of subword representation in traditional IR indices.

3 Experiments

We report the experiments on different textual representations on traditional IR in a cross-lingual setting using a large-scale dataset derived from Wikipedia Sasaki et al. (2018).

Sasaki et al. (2018) focused their work on a supervised re-ranking task using relevance annotations. We use those annotations from the same Wikipedia dataset to perform the typical retrieval task. The dataset was designed so that the English queries are expected to retrieve the Wikipedia documents in the foreign languages, and the foreign documents with the highest relevance are annotated with three levels of relevance. Formally, the ground truth data is a set of tuples: (English query, q, foreign document, d and relevance judgement r, where $r \in \{0, 1, 2\}$).[2]

Lang	#Docs	#Tokens	#Subwords	#Chars
DE	2.08	344	580	2,086
FR	1.89	289	405	1,508
JA	1.07	510	475	734

Table 2: Corpus statistics on Wikipedia documents in dataset from Sasaki et al. (2018). (All numbers are in units of one million)

We note that the Wikipedia documents in the dataset are not parallel (i.e. not translations of

[2]Note that a single English query can be mapped to multiple documents with varying relevance judgements

each other) but they are comparable in nature depending on the varying amounts of contributions available on the official Wikipedia dumps across different languages. For our study, we use the German, French and Japanese document collections and report retrieval performance of English queries translated to these languages.[3]

The Wikipedia corpus came pre-tokenized, so we had to detokenize the documents[4](Tan, 2018) before putting them through the subword tokenizer. We used pre-trained SentencePiece subword tokenizers used by the OPUS machine translation models(Tiedemann and Thottingal, 2020)[5]. Additionally, we emulated the typical pre-processing steps for character-level machine translation and split all individual characters by space, replacing the whitespaces with an underscore character.

Table 2 shows the corpus statistics of the number of documents, tokens, subwords, and characters for the respective languages. Although Latin alphabetic languages benefit from the extra information produced by splitting the tokens into subwords, Japanese presents an opposite condition. Japanese became more compact when represented by the subwords in place of the tokens. The examples in Table 1 show an instance of a sentence pre-processed in different levels of granularity. The underscore in the subword sequence represents a symbolic space and is usually attached to the following subword unit, whereas the whitespace represents the unit boundary between the subwords.

The English queries were translated using the same OPUS machine translation models.[6] Although these machine translation models are open source and free to use under a permissive CC-BY license, it takes a significant amount of GPU computation and major changes to the HuggingFace API (Wolf et al., 2020) to efficiently translate the query samples parallelized inference. We will release the modified code for parallel GPU inference and translation outputs for the data used in this experiment for future convenience to improve the replicability of this paper.

3.1 Information Retrieval System

We use the Okapi BM25 implementation in `PyLucene` as the retrieval framework with hyperparameter setting ($k_1 = 1.2, b = 0.75$) (Manning et al., 2008). We consider the top 100 documents ($top_k = 100$) in the search ranking as search results for each query.

3.1.1 Building index for the documents

For each foreign language, we created an index for the documents with 5 *TextField* as follows:

- **`id`**: the unique index of the document
- **`surface`**: the raw text of the document
- **`tokens`**: the document after tokenization
- **`subword`**: the document in SentencePiece subwords
- **`char`**: the document in characters

3.1.2 Querying the document index

During retrieval, each translated query is first processed into its respective text representations (tokens, subwords or characters) and parsed using Lucene's built-in query parser and analyzer. Additionally, we tried to improve the search results by combining and re-ranking the result sets from the different text representations.

3.1.3 Search result expansion

Our intuition is that queries of more granular text representation can improve the robustness of the retrieval and potentially override the textual noise (e.g., misspellings are handled better for some languages). Hence, we attempt to expand the list of possible candidate documents by combining the search results from the token and the subword representations.

Given a query q and its token q_{token} and subword $q_{subword}$ representations, we obtained two sets of search results from their respective indices R_{tokens} and $R_{subword}$. We concatenated R_{tokens} and $R_{subword}$, and remove the repeated candidates that appear in both sets from $R_{subword}$ as illustrated in Figure 1.

[3]We use the raw dataset from `http://www.cs.jhu.edu/~kevinduh/a/wikiclir2018/` for the document indices.

[4]`https://github.com/alvations/sacremoses`

[5]`https://huggingface.co/Helsinki-NLP`

[6]We use the `opus-mt-en-de`, `opus-mt-en-fr`, and `opus-mt-en-jap` models, their BLEU and ChrF scores (Papineni et al., 2002; Popović, 2015) can be found on https://huggingface.co/Helsinki-NLP (Tiedemann and Thottingal, 2020; Tiedemann, 2020)

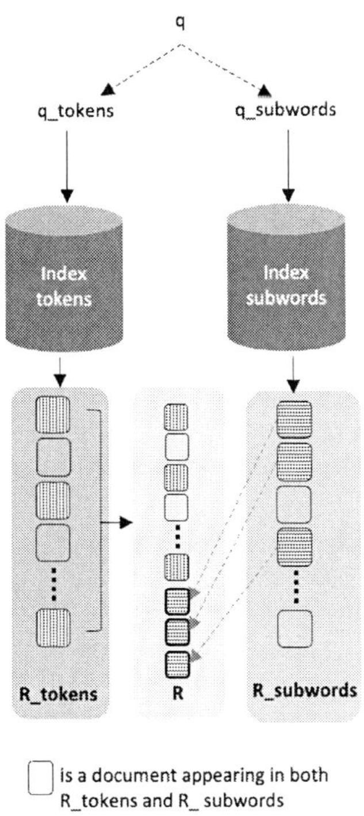

Figure 1: Search Results Expansion

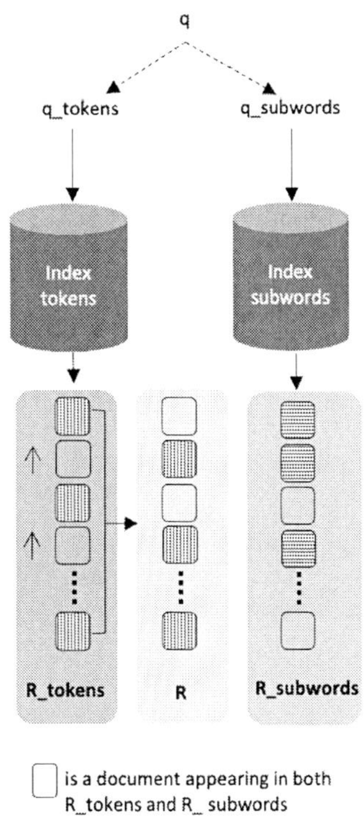

Figure 2: Search Results Re-ranking

3.1.4 Search result re-ranking

Aside from expanding the search results, we tried a re-ranking technique. We presumed that if different representations retrieve a document from a single query, it is more relevant than the documents that appear solely from one representation. Thus, we boosted the rank of the documents (D_{shared}) that are retrieved both in R_{tokens} and $R_{subword}$ from the same query. After boosting the rank of such documents (D_{shared}) by 1: $d \in D_{shared}$, $rank_{new}(d) = rank_{original}(d) - 2$, we re-rank the token-based search result, as illustrated in Figure 2 to get the final search result R.

3.2 Evaluation Metrics

We choose the following ranking metrics to evaluate the retrieval performance of the different text representations of query translation. Those ranking metrics are Mean Reciprocal Ranking **(MRR)**, Mean Average Precision **(MAP)**, normalized Discounted Cumulative Gain **(nDCG)**;

- MRR measures the ranking of the first document that is relevant to a given query in the search result.
- MAP evaluates the rankings of top 100 documents that are relevant to a given query in the search result.
- nDCG calibrates the ranking and relevance score of all the documents that are relevant to a given query in the search result. We compute nDCG@16 for the top-16 search results respectively.

4 Results

Table 3, 4 and 5 show the result for the CLIR experiments on the translated English queries and the German, French, and Japanese documents of different textual representations. For all the German and French setups, the token level representation achieved the best MAP, MMR, and NDCG scores, followed by subwords at significantly lower performance. Character-level representation performs the words at a magnitude $10\hat{4}$ times worse than token-level results.

We expected a margin between the token and subword level performance but the stark difference was surprising. Although machine translation can exploit the sequential nature of the open vocabulary with the subwords representation, traditional information retrieval methods disregard the other textual representation to a lesser extent. However, for

Metric	Token	Subword	Characters	Expansion	Re-ranking
MAP	**0.31299**	0.10072	0.00031	0.30432	0.30688
MRR	0.39938	0.12783	0.00033	0.39956	**0.40368**
nDCG	**0.40410**	0.13461	0.00021	0.13461	0.00021

Table 3: Results of CLIR Experiments on Translated English Queries on ***German*** Wikipedia

Metric	Token	Subword	Characters	Expansion	Re-ranking
MAP	**0.30330**	0.06931	0.00035	0.29859	0.29898
MRR	0.37866	0.08492	0.00039	**0.37872**	0.37830
nDCG	**0.36810**	0.09153	0.00060	0.36397	0.36537

Table 4: Results of CLIR Experiments on Translated English Queries on ***French*** Wikipedia

Metric	Token	Subword	Characters	Expansion	Re-ranking
MAP	**0.00039**	0.00036	0.00024	0.00036	0.00024
MRR	**0.00038**	0.00037	0.00025	0.00037	0.00025
nDCG	**0.00076**	0.00054	0.00022	0.00074	0.00075

Table 5: Results of CLIR Experiments on Translated English Queries on ***Japanese*** Wikipedia

Japanese, we see that the subword representation performs very similarly to the tokens counterparts.

For German and French documents, the intuition behind the poor performance of the character-level representation can be attributed to the meaningless and arbitrary nature of the unordered bag of characters. Whereas in Japanese, with its mix of syllabic and logographic orthography, the individual characters can potentially encode crucial semantic information.

We can see that both search result expansion and re-ranking techniques can improve the final search results for some languages. Table 3, 4 and 5 show that the search result expansion technique improves MRR for all three languages compared with the token-based retrieval baseline, and it improves both MRR and MAP for Japanese. The re-ranking technique achieves the highest MRR for both German and Japanese. Improvement in the MRR indicates that those two techniques can improve the ranking of the first relevant document appearing in the search results, which can be beneficial for cross-lingual e-commerce search systems. Neither the expansion nor the re-ranking technique achieves a better nDCG score, which is consistent with our expectation of improving the accuracy and robustness of retrieval with minimal changes to the relevance score that affects nDCG.

5 Conclusion

We explored the different granularity of textual representations in a traditional IR system within the CLIR task by re-using the subword representation from the neural machine translation systems. Our experiments in this paper provide empirical evidence for the underwhelming impact of subwords in traditional IR systems for Latin-based languages as opposed to the advancements that subword representation has made in machine translation.[7] In some scenarios, it is possible to achieve better CLIR performance by combining and expanding retrieval results of token and subword representations.

We conducted the experiments in this study using well-formed queries and documents. Our intuition is that a combination of the different textual representations can improve the robustness of the indexing and retrieval systems in realistic situations with noisier data (e.g. queries spelling or translations errors). For future work, we want to explore similar experiments with noisy e-commerce search datasets.[8]

[7] The processed datasets, code to generate the translations and evaluations will be made available under an open source license upon paper acceptance.

[8] We note that many open-source CLIR experiments are constrained to Wikipedia document searches. Although the lesson learned from these experiments can impact industrial e-commerce applications, the lack of open source e-commerce IR datasets limited the results reported in this study.

References

Robin Aly, Thomas Demeester, and Stephen Robertson. 2014. Probabilistic models in IR and their relationships. *Inf. Retr.*, 17(2):177–201.

Tianchi Bi, Liang Yao, Baosong Yang, Haibo Zhang, Weihua Luo, and Boxing Chen. 2020. Constraint translation candidates: A bridge between neural query translation and cross-lingual information retrieval.

Leonid Boytsov. 2020. Traditional ir rivals neural models on the ms marco document ranking leaderboard.

Atsushi Fujii and Tetsuya Ishikawa. 2000. Applying machine translation to two-stage cross-language information retrieval. In *Envisioning Machine Translation in the Information Future*, pages 13–24, Berlin, Heidelberg. Springer Berlin Heidelberg.

Hany Hassan, Anthony Aue, Chang Chen, Vishal Chowdhary, Jonathan Clark, Christian Federmann, Xuedong Huang, Marcin Junczys-Dowmunt, William Lewis, Mu Li, Shujie Liu, Tie-Yan Liu, Renqian Luo, Arul Menezes, Tao Qin, Frank Seide, Xu Tan, Fei Tian, Lijun Wu, Shuangzhi Wu, Yingce Xia, Dongdong Zhang, Zhirui Zhang, and Ming Zhou. 2018. Achieving human parity on automatic chinese to english news translation.

Jing Jiang and ChengXiang Zhai. 2007. An empirical study of tokenization strategies for biomedical information retrieval. *Inf. Retr.*, 10(4-5):341–363.

Zhuolin Jiang, Amro El-Jaroudi, William Hartmann, Damianos Karakos, and Lingjun Zhao. 2020. Cross-lingual information retrieval with BERT. In *Proceedings of the workshop on Cross-Language Search and Summarization of Text and Speech (CLSSTS2020)*, pages 26–31, Marseille, France. European Language Resources Association.

Taku Kudo and John Richardson. 2018. SentencePiece: A simple and language independent subword tokenizer and detokenizer for neural text processing. In *Proceedings of the 2018 Conference on Empirical Methods in Natural Language Processing: System Demonstrations*, pages 66–71, Brussels, Belgium. Association for Computational Linguistics.

Samuel Läubli, Rico Sennrich, and Martin Volk. 2018. Has machine translation achieved human parity? a case for document-level evaluation. In *Proceedings of the 2018 Conference on Empirical Methods in Natural Language Processing*, pages 4791–4796, Brussels, Belgium. Association for Computational Linguistics.

Jason Lee, Kyunghyun Cho, and Thomas Hofmann. 2017. Fully character-level neural machine translation without explicit segmentation. *Transactions of the Association for Computational Linguistics*, 5:365–378.

Johannes Leveling and Gareth J. F. Jones. 2010. Subword indexing and blind relevance feedback for english, bengali, hindi, and marathi ir. *ACM Transactions on Asian Language Information Processing*, 9(3).

Christopher D Manning, Prabhakar Raghavan, Hinrich Schütze, et al. 2008. *Introduction to information retrieval*, volume 1. Cambridge university press Cambridge.

J Scott McCarley. 1999. Should we translate the documents or the queries in cross-language information retrieval? In *Proceedings of the 37th Annual Meeting of the Association for Computational Linguistics*, pages 208–214.

Paul McNamee and James Mayfield. 2004. Character n-gram tokenization for european language text retrieval. *Information Retrieval*, 7(1-2):73–97.

Douglas W Oard. 1998. A comparative study of query and document translation for cross-language information retrieval. In *Conference of the Association for Machine Translation in the Americas*, pages 472–483. Springer.

Kishore Papineni, Salim Roukos, Todd Ward, and Wei-Jing Zhu. 2002. Bleu: a method for automatic evaluation of machine translation. In *Proceedings of the 40th Annual Meeting of the Association for Computational Linguistics*, pages 311–318, Philadelphia, Pennsylvania, USA. Association for Computational Linguistics.

Pavel Pecina, Ondřej Dušek, Lorraine Goeuriot, Jan Hajič, Jaroslava Hlaváčová, Gareth J.F. Jones, Liadh Kelly, Johannes Leveling, David Mareček, Michal Novák, Martin Popel, Rudolf Rosa, Aleš Tamchyna, and Zdeňka Urešová. 2014. Adaptation of machine translation for multilingual information retrieval in the medical domain. *Artificial Intelligence in Medicine*, 61(3):165 – 185. Text Mining and Information Analysis of Health Documents.

Maja Popović. 2015. chrF: character n-gram F-score for automatic MT evaluation. In *Proceedings of the Tenth Workshop on Statistical Machine Translation*, pages 392–395, Lisbon, Portugal. Association for Computational Linguistics.

Stephen Robertson. 2004. Understanding inverse document frequency: On theoretical arguments for idf. *Journal of Documentation*, 60:2004.

Stephen E. Robertson and Hugo Zaragoza. 2009. The probabilistic relevance framework: BM25 and beyond. *Found. Trends Inf. Retr.*, 3(4):333–389.

Shadi Saleh and Pavel Pecina. 2020. Document translation vs. query translation for cross-lingual information retrieval in the medical domain. In *Proceedings of the 58th Annual Meeting of the Association for Computational Linguistics*, pages 6849–6860, Online. Association for Computational Linguistics.

Shota Sasaki, Shuo Sun, Shigehiko Schamoni, Kevin Duh, and Kentaro Inui. 2018. Cross-lingual learning-to-rank with shared representations. In *Proceedings of the 2018 Conference of the North American Chapter of the Association for Computational Linguistics: Human Language Technologies, Volume 2 (Short Papers)*, pages 458–463, New Orleans, Louisiana. Association for Computational Linguistics.

Rico Sennrich, Barry Haddow, and Alexandra Birch. 2016. Neural machine translation of rare words with subword units. In *Proceedings of the 54th Annual Meeting of the Association for Computational Linguistics (Volume 1: Long Papers)*, pages 1715–1725, Berlin, Germany. Association for Computational Linguistics.

Liling Tan. 2018. Sacremoses: Python implementations of moses statistical machine translation pre-processing tools. https://github.com/alvations/sacremoses.

Jörg Tiedemann. 2020. The Tatoeba Translation Challenge – Realistic data sets for low resource and multilingual MT. In *Proceedings of the Fifth Conference on Machine Translation (Volume 1: Research Papers)*. Association for Computational Linguistics.

Jörg Tiedemann and Santhosh Thottingal. 2020. OPUS-MT — Building open translation services for the World. In *Proceedings of the 22nd Annual Conferenec of the European Association for Machine Translation (EAMT)*, Lisbon, Portugal.

Antonio Toral. 2020. Reassessing claims of human parity and super-human performance in machine translation at wmt 2019.

Changhan Wang, Kyunghyun Cho, and Jiatao Gu. 2019. Neural machine translation with byte-level subwords. *arXiv preprint arXiv:1909.03341*.

Thomas Wolf, Lysandre Debut, Victor Sanh, Julien Chaumond, Clement Delangue, Anthony Moi, Pierric Cistac, Tim Rault, Remi Louf, Morgan Funtowicz, Joe Davison, Sam Shleifer, Patrick von Platen, Clara Ma, Yacine Jernite, Julien Plu, Canwen Xu, Teven Le Scao, Sylvain Gugger, Mariama Drame, Quentin Lhoest, and Alexander Rush. 2020. Transformers: State-of-the-art natural language processing. In *Proceedings of the 2020 Conference on Empirical Methods in Natural Language Processing: System Demonstrations*, pages 38–45, Online. Association for Computational Linguistics.

Mahsa Yarmohammadi, Xutai Ma, Sorami Hisamoto, Muhammad Rahman, Yiming Wang, Hainan Xu, Daniel Povey, Philipp Koehn, and Kevin Duh. 2019. Robust document representations for cross-lingual information retrieval in low-resource settings. In *Proceedings of Machine Translation Summit XVII Volume 1: Research Track*, pages 12–20, Dublin, Ireland. European Association for Machine Translation.

Detect Profane Language in Streaming Services to Protect Young Audiences

Jingxiang Chen
Amazon Prime Video
jxchen@amazon.com

Kai Wei
Amazon Alexa
kaiwe@amazon.com

Xiang Hao
Amazon Prime Video
xianghao@amazon.com

Abstract

With the rapid growth of online video streaming, recent years have seen increasing concerns about profane language in their content. Detecting profane language in streaming services is challenging due to the long sentences appeared in a video. While recent research on handling long sentences has focused on developing deep learning modeling techniques, little work has focused on techniques on improving data pipelines. In this work, we develop a data collection pipeline to address long sequence of texts and integrate this pipeline with a multi-head self-attention model. With this pipeline, our experiments show the self-attention model offers 12.5% relative accuracy improvement over state-of-the-art distilBERT model on profane language detection while requiring only 3% of parameters. This research designs a better system for informing users of profane language in video streaming services.

1 Introduction

Streaming services such as Netflix and Prime Video have dramatically changed the media habits of young people, with six-in-ten primarily watching television today with streaming services (Pew, 2017). The increased exposure of online content has raised concerns about profane language appeared in these contents (Chen et al., 2012; Phan and Tan, 2017; Obadimu et al., 2019). Exposure to profane language can increase aggressive thoughts, angry feelings, physiological arousal, and aggressive behavior (Bushman, 2016; Phan and Tan, 2017) .

Profane language is a type of language that includes dirty words, swearing, and obscenity contents. Previous research has focused on developing automated techniques to detect profane language in user generated contents on social media. For example, there have been growing interests in detecting hate speech and racism on Twitter (Xiang et al., 2012; Badjatiya et al., 2017; Lozano et al., 2017). Some recent works have also studied offensive contents in Youtube (Alcântara et al., 2020). However, few studies have focused on profane language detection in streaming services that host movies and TV shows.

Recent works have shown the importance of data techniques such as pre-processing and augmentation in improving machine learning models. For example, there has been research on applying transfer learning or semi-supervised learning for learning word embedding and addressing insufficient data issues in tasks with limited sample sizes (Howard and Ruder, 2018; d'Sa et al., 2020). In addition, using text pre-processing methods such as text normalization, lowercasing, lemmatizing, tokenizing and multiword grouping can help increase sentiment, topic and polarity classification accuracy (Satapathy et al., 2017; Camacho-Collados and Pilehvar, 2017). However, few studies have focused on improving data techniques to better handle long sequence of text appeared in streaming videos. Research on addressing data issue have primarily focused on improving data quantity, rather than quality. Also, our problem has its novelty in that the data sets of most previous studies are on written text, which can have a different distribution from the spoken-form video captions.

In this work, we study the problem of profane language with a specific online video streaming service, Amazon Prime Video (PV), as an example. Specifically, we develop a data pipeline that can be integrated sentence level model to automatically predict the level of profanity in video titles according to their caption contents. We collect data from both the targeted service and public data set, and augment training data by merging multiple data sources. Our experiments show that this data collection pipeline that can be used to address long

Proceedings of the 4th Workshop on e-Commerce and NLP (ECNLP 4), pages 123–131
August 5, 2021. ©2021 Association for Computational Linguistics

sequence of text and help non-hierarchical models to achieve state-of-the-art performance. Using this pipeline, we train a multi-head self-attention model on embedding pre-trained on PV caption dataset, and show this simple self-attention model (with 2 million parameters) can outperform the pre-trained distilBERT model (with 66 million parameters) that is fine-tuned on the same dataset by 9% accuracy.

2 Related Work

Profane language is a type of language that includes dirty words, swearing, and obscenity contents. Previous research in this area has primarily focused on detecting profane language in social media. For example, a recent work studied the diffusion of profanity in Sina Weibo, one of the largest Chinese social media platforms (Song et al., 2020). Research on abusive and hate speech detection (a close related research area to profane language detection) has focused on developing automatic techniques to identify racists and sexist on Twitter (Badjatiya et al., 2017; Lozano et al., 2017), Reddit (Chandrasekharan et al., 2017; Mohan et al., 2017), and Youtube (Obadimu et al., 2019). However, few studies have focused on detecting profane language in video stream services such as Netflix, Hulu, and Prime Video.

Research on this area has also shifted from using traditional machine learning methods to using deep learning methods. For example, while early work uses traditional machine learning classifiers, such as logistic regression, support vector machine, and tree-based methods (Xiang et al., 2012; Warner and Hirschberg, 2012), there has been a growing interest in applying LSTM, CNN, and BERT (Bidirectional Encoder Representations from Transformers) for detecting racism, sexism, hate, or offensive content (Badjatiya et al., 2017; Founta et al., 2019; Basile et al., 2019; Mozafari et al., 2019). However, one of the limits of these deep learning method is its capacity of working memory. This is because processing long texts (even for BERT) will quadratically increasing memory and time consumption and slicing the text by a sliding window or simplifying transformers, suffer from insufficient long-range attentions or need customized CUDA kernels (Ding et al., 2020). Due to this issue, these prior methods are not directly applicable for detecting profane language in video stream services since the video captions are often very long, with an average length of hundreds of sentences per video.

3 Data

Our data collection pipeline aims to address two challenges. First, there is no labeled data for profane language detection task in streaming service. To address this challenge, we collect data from a popular streaming service, design an annotation guideline, and hire human annotators to label the levels of profanity in video titles. Then, we augment training data by collecting additional labeled contents from a publicly available database. Last, we perform pre-processing on the collected data to improve its quality. Second, the title caption is so long that it is very challenging for a model to learn from context. To address this challenge, we develop a pipeline for creating sentence-level profanity labels using domain knowledge and title-level labeling information. We provide details about our data collection pipeline in the sections below.

3.1 Data Collection and Annotation

Figure 1 below shows the overall steps of our data collection and pre-processing technique pipeline. Specifically, we collected 150k titles that occupy the top streaming volume from Prime Video, a stream service that hosts movie and television shows. The titles include popular movies and TV shows in the most recent decades from global marketplaces, with duration ranging from 10 minutes to 3 hours (with 70% as TV). The titles are diverse and come from 200 genres such as kids cartoon, drama, romance, and horror. Their caption lengths range from a few sentences to thousands with average at about 700 sentences. We randomly sampled 5,260 titles from them for annotation.

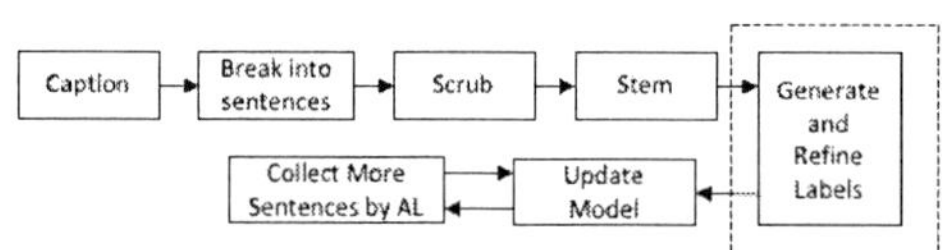

Figure 1: Data Collection and Pre-processing Pipeline

We develop codebook based on standard policy from movie and TV series rating associations, including Motion Picture Association of America (MPAA) and TVPG (TV Parental Guidelines Monitoring Board). In the codebook, we define the level of profanity in video titles based on their captions used. In total, the codebook includes 92 keywords and instructs on how the usage of them can lead to profanity. Some keywords always have malicious meaning while others depend on their contexts. Based on the keyword frequency and the context severity, each title has a label from one of the following categories: None (all age), Mild (7+ kids), Moderate (13+ kids), Strong (16+ young adults), Severe (18+ adults), indicating the severity of profane language. For example, the singular instance use of disparaging slurs in the captions of a movie, such as Fag or Faggot in racism context, is rated as strong; and more than singular use of disparaging slurs is rated as severe.

A total of 15 human annotators are recruited to label the video captions. When annotating the captions of a video, the annotators go through the context of each keyword and decide whether the keyword is profane or not. After checking all such keywords in the entire caption, they make the final decision on the severity of the video title based on the counts and severity of the keywords appeared in the captions of a video. The maximum severity across all keywords in the captions of a video is used as the title-level rating. Throughout the whole annotation process, we randomly audit their labeling results to ensure the labeling quality.

3.2 Training Data Augmentation

Considering the small sample size collected in the above process, we add additional training data by collecting labeled data from the MPAA database according to the reason code description. We name the technique as *data augmentation* in this paper. For example, a video title may be rated as R due to strong language based on the reason code in MPAA database. In particular, we first select all the titles that is either G rating (suitable for all ages) or have profane language in the reason code. Then, we convert the rating from the MPAA standard to our rating category following a pre-defined mapping (i.e., G to None, PG to Mild, PG-13 to Moderate, NR/R/NC-17 to Severe). Note that MPAA does not have a rating corresponding to Strong (i.e., 16+ young adults) level. We clean the labels by comparing the rating with IMDB user votes when available, filter out mismatches. In total, we collected 5,010 additional labeled titles and combined them with the training data collected in Section 3.1.

3.3 Generating Sentence Labels

To generate sentence level labels, we use a keyword approach to scope relevant sentences in a video given its title level labels. Specifically, we use pre-defined keywords that express profanity to determine whether a given sentence is relevant to profanity. In total, there are 92 unique keywords. Some keywords always have malicious meaning while others depend on their contexts. For simplicity, we name the first class as *unambiguous* keywords and the second as *ambiguous* keywords. To identify them, we define the precision of a certain keyword w_i as the positive rate (i.e., the proportion of titles labeled as above all age) of training titles that contain w_i. We categorize a keyword to be unambiguous as long as its precision exceeds a given threshold ϵ ($\epsilon = 0.95$ for our case considering the chances that annotators may miss certain keywords and mislabel contain titles as all age). We ask domain experts to confirm the categorization results.

We then use a build-in sentence tokenizer from *python* package *NLTK* to break captions, which mainly relies on punctuation. We label the sentences that contain unambiguous keywords as positive (i.e., profane), and those do not as negative. This is because unambiguous keywords are profane in regardless of their context. In addition, we only cover the candidates from the pre-defined keywords, as recommended by domain experts.

The generated labels can have noise due to the unavoidable imperfection of the generation process. Inspired by knowledge distillation (Hinton et al., 2015), we train an intermediate classifier to generate the probability scores on sentences and save the predicted probability as a soft target to alleviate label noise. Such a new target contains the knowledge transferred from the intermediate classifier, and can be more robust than the original binary label. For example, it can help correct some labelling noises caused by limited rule coverage. As an example, the sentence *this guy sucks* is more likely to have a high score even if the previous rules do not cover it precisely than other similar expressions such as *he sucks* and *it sucks*. In this way, labelling it with a prediction score can be better than with zero. In practice, the intermediate classifier we use is a multi-head attention model, which will be introduced in Section 4.

3.4 Reduce Labeling Noise

We find that the model trained above still performs not very well on sentences with certain keywords, which may be caused by labeling noise. To address the issue, we apply the idea of active learning and manually label sentences picked by model predictions. First, we pick all the sentences that are

Severity	Count	Perc	# Sents	# Words
None	4061	55.9%	306	2634
Mild	971	13.4%	530	4812
Moderate	801	11.0%	720	5013
Strong	221	3.0%	720	5013
Severe	1216	16.7%	1071	8848

Table 1: Statistics of the training titles: number and percentage of titles at each rating, and the average number of sentences and words per each caption.

Severity	Count	Perc	# Sents	# Words
None	1036	35.4%	371	3161
Mild	398	13.6%	624	5301
Moderate	897	30.7%	703	5680
Strong	482	16.5%	851	6792
Severe	113	3.9%	1022	8772

Table 2: Statistics of the evaluation titles.

predicted as positive in none titles and those containing keywords from negatively predicted titles (i.e. all sentences of that title are predicted as negative). Second, we calculate the frequency n_i of each keywords from this sentence pool, and pick the top K ambiguous ones. Third, we randomly pick N sentences for manual labeling (N=2k for our case). In particular, we sample $N \cdot n_j / \sum_{i=1}^{K} n_i$ for each keyword j in the top K words obtained above. Finally, we label those N sentences, replicate them by T times to increase the weights (T=5 in practice), and combine them with the old training set for retraining. The newly added data helps correct the model at the boundary region.

3.5 Data Description

Table 1 and 2 present the overall statistics of training and evaluation data. Among these categories, None category has the shortest captions on average because many of the videos are kids cartoons or mini shows, which are often very short. In addition, the training and evaluation caption lengths are close to each other at each rating. However, there is a shift between the rating distributions of training and evaluation set. For example, the MPAA titles have more None labels than PV video dataset. The underlying reason can be: 1) MPAA may have less restrictive policy in labeling; and 2) PV video dataset may contain movies with larger diversity, and hence not dominated by None titles. The training set also has less Strong and more Severe titles because MPAA titles do not have Strong according to the rate mapping that we use.

4 Experiments

We integrated several models to our data pipeline and conducted experiments at both title level and sentence level. For the title level methods, we include xgboost and logistic regression, and deep learning methods such as an augmented version of the hierarchical attention network. We will introduce more details of these methods below. For the sentence level methods, we apply DistilBERT, rule based method that is used to create labels, and a sentence level multi-head attention model with and without the knowledge distillation soft target step. The purpose is to check whether the model learns the context information well, and whether the soft target helps. For each method, we have also fitted the model with only the 2.6k titles from prime video to study the effects of augmented data from MPAA.

4.1 Title Level Models

TF-IDF with traditional ML First, we use term frequency-inverse document frequency (TF-IDF, Leskovec et al. (2014)) to extract features and build models on them. We calculate the TF-IDF weights for unigrams and bigrams that have total frequencies greater than 5 and are contained by less than 90% of the titles (i.e., removing stop words). We try two classifiers logistic regression with L_2 penalty and xgboost (Chen and Guestrin, 2016), with unigram features alone (TI1 and TI3 in Table 3 and Table 4) or with both unigram and bigram features together (TI2 and TI4 in Table 3 and Table 4). For the logistic model, a multi-class cross-entropy loss is used for multi-category rating prediction.

Hierarchical Attention Network In addition, to capture the contextual information better, we propose an adjusted Hierarchical Attention Network (HAN, Yang et al. (2016)) on title level data. To enable HAN to take sentence level information, we propose generating 2k synthetic titles accordingly. Specifically, each title only contains the labelled sentence at a random position s_i and has other sentences as empty strings. Then, we fit the model with the synthetic titles and the old training set together. We include the 2k manually labelled sentences in the training set.

4.2 Sentence Level Models

DistilBERT We apply DistilBERT (Sanh et al., 2019) to the generated sentences, a distilled version of BERT that is 40% lighter but 60% faster and can preserve over 95% of BERT's performances in downstreaming tasks. We fine tune the pretrianed DistillBERT on our sentence level data with generated labels. We do not apply token stemming because the model was pretrained on the raw corpus in a self-supervised fashion, using the BERT base model as a teacher.

Multi-Head Self-Attention Model We modify the self-attention model (Lin et al., 2017) to predict sentence-level profanity by introducing multi-head attention and soft target. The architecture of the model is presented in Figure 2. The model first converts each word ($\boldsymbol{w}_i$) of a n-length sentence into a vector with GloVE (Pennington et al., 2014) trained on the training captions of the 150k PV captions. Then the output is fed into a bidirectional GRU (BiGRU) layer with ReLU as the activation function. We find a BiGRU performs slightly better than a bidirectional LSTM in practice. This layer aims at capturing the long-term word dependency. The output of the BiGRU units, denoted as $\boldsymbol{h}_i$, is then passed into an m-head self-attention layer that allows attending different keywords of a sentence in a flexible way. The n-length weights of the j-th attention head are calculated via

$$\boldsymbol{a}_j = \mathrm{softmax}(\tanh(\boldsymbol{\alpha}_j \cdot H^T + \boldsymbol{b}_j)),$$

for $j = 1, ..., m$, where $H = [\boldsymbol{h}_1, ..., \boldsymbol{h}_n]$ and ($\boldsymbol{\alpha}_j$, $\boldsymbol{b}_j$) are the coefficients. The elements of the vector (i.e. a_{1j}, ... , a_{nj}) represent how important each word is to determine the label of the sentence for the j-th attention head. The output of the attentions, $\boldsymbol{S}_j$ for $j = 1, ..., m$, is calculated by taking the weighted average as:

$$\boldsymbol{S}_j = \sum_{i=1}^{n} a_{ij} \cdot \boldsymbol{h}_i$$

The m outputs are concatenated with a fully connected with fully connected layer with a *sigmoid* activation function built on the top of it. The loss function is the cross-entropy but with label using the soft target, denoted as q_i, as described in the second to the last step in generating sentence labels. In this way, the corresponding loss can be written as $L(\boldsymbol{p}, \boldsymbol{q}) = \sum_i q_i \log p_i$ where p_i is the output of the fully connected layer.

The predictions at sentence level are used to generate the title level labels. We calculate the frequencies of each keywords within the title by summing the scores of positive sentences that contain them. Then we accumulate the counts of keywords at each

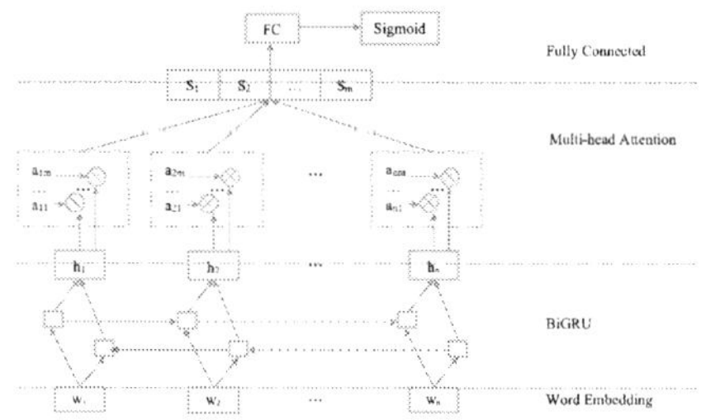

Figure 2: Sentence Level Multi-head Attention Model.

severity level following the standard policy that operators refer to. Such accumulated numbers are used to map the titles to the level of profanity. For example, over 10 times usage of non-aggressive coarse language and less than 2 times usage of disparaging slurs make the title labeled as strong.

4.3 Experiment Setup

For logistic regression, we choose the regularization parameter from $\{0, 1, 5, 10\}$. For xgboost, we tune the learning rate from $\{0.01, 0.05, 0.1\}$, max depth from $\{3, 6, 9\}$, number of estimators from $\{100, 200, 300\}$. For the multi-head self-attention model, we initialize the layer weights with Xavier uniform initializer and the bias with zeros. As to the hyper-parameter tuning, we use random search by selecting learning rate from $\{0.01, 0.001, 0.0001\}$ with decay rate of 0.9, RNN hidden size from $\{64, 128, 256\}$, attention output size from $\{64, 128, 256\}$, attention head number from $\{1, 3, 5\}$, and number of attention and dense layers from $\{1, 2\}$.

4.4 Evaluation Metric

We are interested in evaluating performance in terms of both binary classification (i.e. whether a video contains any profane language) and multi-class classification(i.e. levels of profane language in a video). For both, we use precision and recall as our primary metrics. In addition, it is important to control the chance of predicting a contain title as None because it is more risky to present an adult level video to kids than vice versa. In this way, we define a secondary metric in binary case as the recall at precision at 80%, 90%, and 97% for None titles, i.e. maximize the coverage of None titles at a given None precision level.

5 Results

In this section, we present our experiment results for detecting the presence of profane language and the level of profane language for video titles.

5.1 Detecting Presence of Profane Language

Table 3 shows the model performance on detecting the presence of profane language in video title. Overall, models built based on the proposed pipeline of generating sentence labels (GSL) achieve better performance than those without it. Also, data augmentation helps in both methods with and without GSL (i.e., the best without DA always gets lower accuracy by over 3%). Among the method with GSL, multi-head attention model built on internally trained GloVE achieves the best accuracy and recall at precision of 97% and 80%. The comparison between intermediate and the final self-attention shows the marginal effect of the soft target. As to DistilBERT fine-tuned on PV data, it achieves the best recall at 90% precision but has the accuracy lower than the self-attention model trained on PV data by 3%. We also performed error analysis and found that DistilBERT prediction seems to do better at making inferences on semantic meaning, i.e., sentences that even do not contain keywords may still be predicted as positive if the expression is rude. However, DistilBERT does not perform well on ambiguous keywords; for example, it mis-classifies many negative sentences with *suck* as positive.

Compared to models built without generating sentence labels (w/o GSL), models built with GSL achieve better accuracy and recall at different precision threshold. This suggests that generating sentence labels can help improve model prediction on detecting the presence of profane language in video title. Within models built without GSL, the HAN model with data augmentation performs the best at recall at 97% precision, and the xgboost with both uni-gram and bi-gram features is the best among the traditional methods.

5.1.1 Error Analysis

The error analysis on the estimated word-level weights of HAN shows that title models assign high weights not only to the keywords related to profane language but also to those connected to other content descriptors like violence, such as *kill*, *police*, *liar* and *shoot*. The underlying reason can be that a severe title usually also contains elements such as violence and sexuality, and hence the existence of those corresponding words can be highly correlated. This can dilute the weights that are supposed to be given to the language keywords.

Method	Model	Acc (%)	R97	R90	R80
w/o GSL	TI1	78.3	36.1	54.5	67.6
	TI2	75.5	34.4	53.2	65.6
	TI3	85.2	53.1	78.1	96.8
	TI4	87.2	58.8	81.2	97.3
	HAN	85.5	58.9	74.6	89.1
	Best w/o DA	82.3	49.5	78.1	92.1
w/ GSL	Rule Based	87.7	76.3	-	-
	Intermediate	88.2	76.6	82.6	95.4
	DistilBERT	86.2	78.3	**86.4**	94.8
	Best w/o DA	87.4	76.9	81.7	88.4
	Self-Attn	**90.6**	**80.1**	84.1	**97.9**

Table 3: Overall Performance of detecting profane language: accuracy (Acc) and recall (Rec) at different precision thresholds (97%, 90%, and 80%). Among these methods, w/o GSL refers to the prediction method that use all captions to predict whether profane language presents in title-level without generating sentence level labels; and w/o GSL refers to the method with generating sentence level labels. TI1-TI4 represent the four baselines introduced in the experiment section. Best w/o DA means the best model that only uses 2.6k titles from targeted streaming services in training.

We also performed qualitative analysis to understand why the self-attention model built with GSL outperforms all the other models in both accuracy and recalls at all given precision levels. There can be two reasons. First, the soft target created by the intermediate model is more robust than the rule based target especially for the positives that go beyond the rule's coverage. Second, the manually labelled sentences picked from active learning results can help reinforce the weak signal for certain keywords. In particular, we find the model performs significantly better than others in the top five frequent words (*hel, jerk, suck, piss, ho*) picked by active learning. In addition, it is not surprising that the intermediate model outperforms the rule based slightly. The main difference comes from sentences with ambiguous keywords. The model can correct certain labelling issues by applying the average scores calculated by its fitted weights on these keywords and their neighbors. The best sentence model without data augmentation performs a bit worse than the rule based, which can be caused by smaller coverage of certain keywords in training.

In addition, the attention layer localizes the keywords well by assigning them with larger weights. In Figure 3, we pick both positive and negative sentences with certain ambiguous keywords when one-head attention is used. We print their scores as well as the attention weights (scaled to 10) on each word. The model learns the context in the Bi-GRU

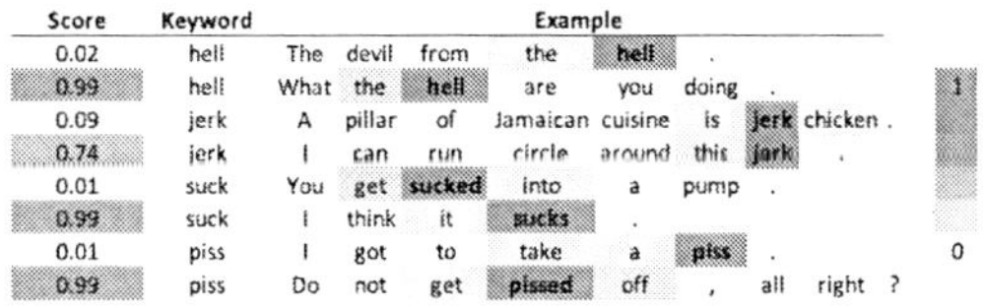

Figure 3: Sentence classification examples: confidence score and weight coefficients (scale to 10) at the attention layer at one head. According to the label, sentence 2, 4, 6 and 8 contain profane language.

Method	Model	Acc (%)	Prec (%)	Rec (%)
	TI1	31.2	42.1	78.8
	TI2	35.6	45	79.1
w/o	TI3	54.7	75.5	92.5
	TI4	53.4	73.2	89.8
	HAN	55.8	73.7	**92.9**
	Best w/o DA	38.2	64.4	81.8
	Rule Based	76.3	89.8	78.4
w/ GSL	DistilBERT	71.2	86.3	79.4
	Best w/o DA	72.2	87.7	79.8
	Self-Attn	**80.1**	**93.6**	80.2

Table 4: Overall performance of detecting levels of profane language: accuracy, precision and recall.

layer by passing the neighboring information to the keyword location, and thus equip the same keyword with different output vectors. For example, our observation shows the output vector $\boldsymbol{h}$ (Figure 2) for word *hell* are quite different between *The devil from the hell* and *What the hell are you doing*. In this way, the fully connected layer learns such difference made by context and predicts different scores.

5.2 Detecting the Level of Profane Language

Table 4 shows the overall model performance on detecting the level of profanity. The self-attention model achieves the best accuracy and precision, and it beats the rule based by 3% in accuracy, mainly due to a higher precision at Mild and Moderate level (the rule misses a certain amount of those titles due to the lack of coverage). Also, we find DistilBERT performs a bit worse than the rule based approach due to its suboptimal performance on ambiguous keywords. As to the methods without GSL, HAN achieves the best performance and recall even higher than the self-attention model built with GSL. This shows that it can be beneficial to build hierarchical models to predict title-level profane language from its long video captions when the proposed pipeline is not available. The reason why the HAN has a better None recall at the top severe level is that it tends to be more conservative

Label \Pred	None	Mild	Moderate	Strong	Severe
None	829	**116**	**78**	9	4
Mild	14	197	**179**	8	0
Moderate	3	16	844	32	2
Strong	2	0	40	433	7
Severe	1	0	1	37	74

Table 5: Confusion matrix of multi-category rating prediction.

in predicting a higher rate.

We also find that none of the traditional models built without GSL performs well. In particular, they tend to overestimate the proportion of the severe level and underestimate that of the Moderate and Strong levels, possibly misled by the distribution shift between training and evaluation. In addition, the title level methods trained without data augmentation give significantly worse performance, indicating sample size is crucial when predicting the level of profane language in video title.

5.2.1 Error Analysis

The confusion matrix of our model is reported in Table 5. The main errors come from overrating some None and Mild titles, as the bold numbers show. Error analysis finds that some errors at Mild vs Moderate are caused by the shift of keyword frequency distribution from training to evaluation. For example, the words *crap* and *blow* are more often in evaluation set when used as negative words. In addition, the difference between Mild and Moderate can be quite subtle even to human operators. A deeper analysis shows a certain amount of errors on None titles may be caused by possible annotation mistakes, especially on the boundary of Mild and Moderate. A better way to evaluate the model performance can be using the distance between prediction and label to measure the loss (e.g., misclassifying Moderate as None should be worse than as Mild).

6 Conclusion

In this paper, we presented a data collection pipeline to generate the high quality sentence-level label for profane language detection in a streaming service. This pipeline included specific knowledge distillation and active learning ideas to refine such labels. We applied data augmentation, collected training data from both the targeted streaming service and public open source, and applied a workflow to fill the gap caused by the rating policy inconsistency. We built a multi-head self-attention model for sentence level detection and aggregated the detections to title level for rating prediction. The experiment showed the proposed model outperformed all the baselines including the hierarchical attention network and DistilBERT, and also beat the rules that created the labels. In addition, the output attention weights showed success in locating the right keywords. Future research directions include the exploration on how the proposed pipeline will help detect more general profanity defined in multimodality, such as visual and audio.

Acknowledgements

We thank the anonymous reviewers for their feedback and insights in improving the work.

References

Cleber Alcântara, Viviane Moreira, and Diego Feijo. 2020. Offensive video detection: Dataset and baseline results. In *Proceedings of The 12th Language Resources and Evaluation Conference*, pages 4309–4319.

Pinkesh Badjatiya, Shashank Gupta, Manish Gupta, and Vasudeva Varma. 2017. Deep learning for hate speech detection in tweets. In *Proceedings of the 26th International Conference on World Wide Web Companion*, pages 759–760.

Valerio Basile, Cristina Bosco, Elisabetta Fersini, Nozza Debora, Viviana Patti, Francisco Manuel Rangel Pardo, Paolo Rosso, Manuela Sanguinetti, et al. 2019. Semeval-2019 task 5: Multilingual detection of hate speech against immigrants and women in twitter. In *13th International Workshop on Semantic Evaluation*, pages 54–63. Association for Computational Linguistics.

Brad J Bushman. 2016. Violent media and hostile appraisals: A meta-analytic review. *Aggressive behavior*, 42(6):605–613.

Jose Camacho-Collados and Mohammad Taher Pilehvar. 2017. On the role of text preprocessing in neural network architectures: An evaluation study on text categorization and sentiment analysis. *arXiv preprint arXiv:1707.01780.*

Eshwar Chandrasekharan, Umashanthi Pavalanathan, Anirudh Srinivasan, Adam Glynn, Jacob Eisenstein, and Eric Gilbert. 2017. You can't stay here: The efficacy of reddit's 2015 ban examined through hate speech. *Proceedings of the ACM on Human-Computer Interaction*, 1(CSCW):1–22.

Tianqi Chen and Carlos Guestrin. 2016. Xgboost: A scalable tree boosting system. In *Proceedings of the 22nd acm sigkdd international conference on knowledge discovery and data mining*, pages 785–794.

Ying Chen, Yilu Zhou, Sencun Zhu, and Heng Xu. 2012. Detecting offensive language in social media to protect adolescent online safety. In *2012 International Conference on Privacy, Security, Risk and Trust and 2012 International Confernece on Social Computing*, pages 71–80. IEEE.

Ming Ding, Chang Zhou, Hongxia Yang, and Jie Tang. 2020. Cogltx: Applying bert to long texts. *Advances in Neural Information Processing Systems*, 33.

Ashwin Geet d'Sa, Irina Illina, Dominique Fohr, Dietrich Klakow, and Dana Ruiter. 2020. Label propagation-based semi-supervised learning for hate speech classification. In *Insights from Negative Results Workshop, EMNLP 2020.*

Antigoni Maria Founta, Despoina Chatzakou, Nicolas Kourtellis, Jeremy Blackburn, Athena Vakali, and Ilias Leontiadis. 2019. A unified deep learning architecture for abuse detection. In *Proceedings of the 10th ACM Conference on Web Science*, pages 105–114.

Geoffrey Hinton, Oriol Vinyals, and Jeff Dean. 2015. Distilling the knowledge in a neural network. *arXiv preprint arXiv:1503.02531.*

Jeremy Howard and Sebastian Ruder. 2018. Universal language model fine-tuning for text classification. *arXiv preprint arXiv:1801.06146.*

Jure Leskovec, Anand Rajaraman, and Jeffrey David Ullman. 2014. *Mining of Massive Datasets*, 2nd edition. Cambridge University Press, USA.

Zhouhan Lin, Minwei Feng, Cicero Nogueira dos Santos, Mo Yu, Bing Xiang, Bowen Zhou, and Yoshua Bengio. 2017. A structured self-attentive sentence embedding. *arXiv preprint arXiv:1703.03130.*

Estefanía Lozano, Jorge Cedeño, Galo Castillo, Fabricio Layedra, Henry Lasso, and Carmen Vaca. 2017. Requiem for online harassers: Identifying racism from political tweets. In *2017 Fourth International Conference on eDemocracy & eGovernment (ICEDEG)*, pages 154–160. IEEE.

Shruthi Mohan, Apala Guha, Michael Harris, Fred Popowich, Ashley Schuster, and Chris Priebe. 2017. The impact of toxic language on the health of reddit communities. In *Canadian Conference on Artificial Intelligence*, pages 51–56. Springer.

Marzieh Mozafari, Reza Farahbakhsh, and Noël Crespi. 2019. A bert-based transfer learning approach for hate speech detection in online social media. In *International Conference on Complex Networks and Their Applications*, pages 928–940. Springer.

Adewale Obadimu, Esther Mead, Muhammad Nihal Hussain, and Nitin Agarwal. 2019. Identifying toxicity within youtube video comment. In *International Conference on Social Computing, Behavioral-Cultural Modeling and Prediction and Behavior*

Representation in Modeling and Simulation, pages 214–223. Springer.

Jeffrey Pennington, Richard Socher, and Christopher D Manning. 2014. Glove: Global vectors for word representation. In *Proceedings of the 2014 conference on empirical methods in natural language processing (EMNLP)*, pages 1532–1543.

Pew. 2017. About 6 in 10 young adults in u.s. primarily use online streaming to watch tv. *Pew Research Center*.

Quang Anh Phan and Vanessa Tan. 2017. Play with bad words: A content analysis of profanity in video games. *Acta Ludica-International Journal of Game Studies*, 1(1):7–30.

Victor Sanh, Lysandre Debut, Julien Chaumond, and Thomas Wolf. 2019. Distilbert, a distilled version of bert: smaller, faster, cheaper and lighter. *arXiv preprint arXiv:1910.01108*.

Ranjan Satapathy, Claudia Guerreiro, Iti Chaturvedi, and Erik Cambria. 2017. Phonetic-based microtext normalization for twitter sentiment analysis. In *2017 IEEE international conference on data mining workshops (ICDMW)*, pages 407–413. IEEE.

Yunya Song, K Hazel Kwon, Jianliang Xu, Xin Huang, and Shiying Li. 2020. Curbing profanity online: A network-based diffusion analysis of profane speech on chinese social media. *New Media & Society*, page 1461444820905068.

William Warner and Julia Hirschberg. 2012. Detecting hate speech on the world wide web. In *Proceedings of the second workshop on language in social media*, pages 19–26. Association for Computational Linguistics.

Guang Xiang, Bin Fan, Ling Wang, Jason Hong, and Carolyn Rose. 2012. Detecting offensive tweets via topical feature discovery over a large scale twitter corpus. In *Proceedings of the 21st ACM international conference on Information and knowledge management*, pages 1980–1984.

Zichao Yang, Diyi Yang, Chris Dyer, Xiaodong He, Alex Smola, and Eduard Hovy. 2016. Hierarchical attention networks for document classification. In *Proceedings of the 2016 conference of the North American chapter of the association for computational linguistics: human language technologies*, pages 1480–1489.

Exploring Inspiration Sets in a Data Programming Pipeline for Product Moderation

Justine Winkler[1], Simon Brugman[1], Bas van Berkel[2], Martha Larson[1]
[1]Radboud University, Netherlands
[2]bol.com, Netherlands
m.larson@cs.ru.nl

Abstract

We carry out a case study on the use of data programming to create data to train classifiers used for product moderation on a large e-commerce platform. Data programming is a recently-introduced technique that uses human-defined rules to generate training data sets without tedious item-by-item hand labeling. Our study investigates methods for allowing product moderators to quickly modify the rules given their knowledge of the domain and, especially, of textual item descriptions. Our results show promise that moderators can use this approach to steer the training data, making possible fast and close control of classifiers that detect policy violations.

1 Introduction

Text classifiers play an important role in filtering inappropriate products on e-commerce platforms. Product moderators are dependent on classifiers that have been trained on up-to-date labeled data in order to keep pace with policy changes and new instances of inappropriate products. For example, Amazon had to take fast action to remove offensive T-shirts during the 2020 US election (Bryant, 2020) and overpriced items and fake cures during the COVID-19 pandemic (BBC, 2020). In this paper, we carry out a case study at a large e-commerce platform. We investigate an approach that allows moderators to rapidly steer the creation of labeled training data, thereby enabling close control of moderation classifiers.

Our approach makes use of a recently-introduced technique called *data programming* (Ratner et al., 2016), which generates classifier training data on the basis of rules that have been specified by domain experts (platform moderators). Data programming eliminates the need to individually hand-label training data points. We propose a feedback loop that selects subsets of data, called *inspiration sets*, that are used by moderators as the basis for updating an initial or existing set of rules. We investigate whether inspiration sets can be selected in an unsupervised manner, i.e., without ground truth.

The contribution of our case study is insight into how to support moderators in updating the rules used by a data programming pipeline in a real-world use scenario requiring fast control (i.e., imposing time constraints). Our study is carried out in collaboration with professional moderators at bol.com, a large European e-commerce company. In contrast to our work, most papers on product moderation, such as Arnold et al. (2016), do not obviously take an inside perspective. Most previous studies of data programming, such as Ehrenberg et al. (2016), have looked at user control, but not at *fast* control, i.e., the ability to update rules quickly in order to steer the training data.

Because of the sensitive nature of the work of the platform moderators, our case study is written with a relatively high level of abstraction. We cannot reveal the exact statistics of inappropriate items on the platform. The rules formulated by the moderators are largely based on keywords occurring in the text of product descriptions, but it is not possible to state them exactly. Nonetheless, we find that we are able to report enough information to reveal the potential of inspiration sets for fast control of inappropriate products on e-commerce platforms. This paper is based on a collaborative project with bol.com. Further analysis and experimental results are available in the resulting thesis (Winkler, 2020).

2 Related Work

Most work on product moderation (Martin et al., 2018; Xu et al., 2019; Mackey and Kalyanam, 2017) focuses on products sold on social media. In contrast, we study an e-commerce platform from the inside. Like social media moderation, we face the challenge of lexical variation of keywords, cf. Chancellor et al. (2016).

Our study is related to work investigating applications of data programming to a specific problem.

Proceedings of the 4th Workshop on e-Commerce and NLP (ECNLP 4), pages 132–139
August 5, 2021.

Such work includes examples from the medical domain (Callahan et al., 2019; Dutta and Saha, 2019; Dutta et al., 2020; Fries et al., 2019; Saab et al., 2019, 2020), multi-task learning (Ratner et al., 2018, 2019a,b), information extraction (Ehrenberg et al., 2016), and learning discourse structure (Badene et al., 2019). Like our work, such work often adjusts the Snorkel framework (Ratner et al., 2017) for the task at hand.

Previous work has proposed a variety of methods for giving users (who are in our case the product moderators) control over classifiers by making use of a pipeline that allows them to provide feedback about training data labels and classification results. In WeSAL (Nashaat et al., 2018, 2020) user feedback improves the labels that sets of rules assign to data points. In contrast, our focus is on feedback that allows moderators to improve the rules directly. In this respect, our work is related to DDLite (Ehrenberg et al., 2016), which was, to our knowledge, the first to discuss how rules in a data programming pipeline can be improved using sampled data as feedback. Socratic Learning (Varma et al., 2017a,b) considered the issue of users implicitly focusing on subsets of data when they formulate rules, limiting the ability of the data programming pipeline to generalize to data outside of these subsets.

We are working under time-constrained conditions. There are two constraints. First, our moderators are given a limited amount of time to formulate the initial rules. They formulate the rules themselves based solely on their domain expertise and experience, which allows them to work quickly. In contrast, in work such as Ehrenberg et al. (2016) and Ratner et al. (2018), users consult labeled data to formulate the initial rules. Second, our moderators have limited time to *revise* the initial rules. In this step, they consult data in the form of inspiration sets. Wu et al. (2018) investigate time constraints, but focuses on supervised feedback, whereas we also investigate unsupervised approaches.

We consider the work of Cohen-Wang et al. (2019) to be the existing work closest to ours. This work investigates intelligent ways of sampling data points for rule improvement. Our inspiration sets are based on these strategies. A key difference is that Cohen-Wang et al. (2019) simulate their human experts and we work with real domain experts.

category	**train set**	**dev set**	**test set**
fur	7633	406 (69)	760 (113)
illegal wildlife	7426	312 (9)	627 (20)
magnetic balls	2316	340 (5)	688 (10)
weapon knives	1266	210 (17)	421 (28)
smoking-drug	1071	172 (10)	342 (21)
1-use plastic	7364	454 (124)	931 (250)

Table 1: Number of data points in our data sets. For sets with ground truth, the number of points with the positive label, i.e., "inappropriate", is in parentheses.

3 Approach

In this section, we describe the data programming pipeline and also our experiment with *inspiration sets*, which investigates the potential for fast control of training data for moderation classifiers.

3.1 Policy-based Monitoring Categories

The platform policy of the company we study has five dimensions. It excludes products (1) that are illegal (2) whose production or consumption causes harm (3) that do not match customer expectations (4) that technically fall outside of what the platform can handle (5) that project hate or discrimination. Each dimension contains concrete categories. For example, under (2) there is a category ("single-use plastic"), which contains single-use plastic cups, straws, and cotton swabs that are excluded based on European guidelines. Each of the categories is monitored independently using a classifier, which must detect not only the re-occurring items, but also novel items that are in violation of the platform policy. In this work, we select six typical categories to study: *fur*, *illegal wildlife related*, *magnetic balls* (small enough to be swallowed by children), *weapon-grade knives*, *smoking-drug-related*, and *single-use plastic*.

3.2 Data Programming

Figure 1 shows our data programming pipeline. When moderating a product category, product moderators first carry out a "scope" step that identifies the products related to that category (cf. *scoping query*). Then, they carry out a "scan" step that identifies products that violate the policy. The goal of our study is to investigate the usefulness of this pipeline for quickly generating training data to train a classifier that will support the product moderators in carrying out the "scan" step, with a focus on understanding the potential of inspiration sets.

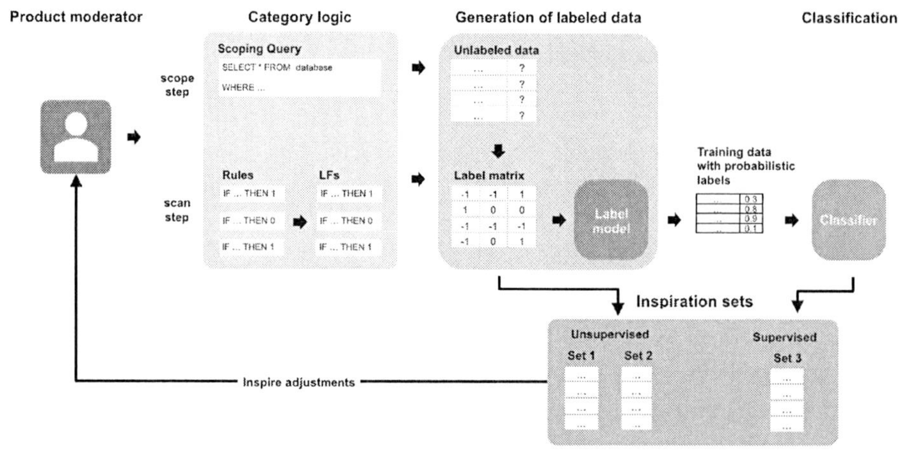

Figure 1: Top row: Our data programming pipeline. Bottom row (red box): Inspiration sets used for fast control.

Data programming (Ratner et al., 2016) is a method that leverages multiple weak supervision signals provided by people who are experts in a domain. The signals take the form of rules, expressed in the form of *labeling functions* (LFs). Given a training data point, an LF either returns a suggested label (0 for "appropriate" or 1 for "inappropriate") or abstains, meaning that it assigns no label. In our study, LFs involve the content of product metadata and keywords in the textual descriptions of products, e.g., `|IF brand == 'brand123' THEN inappropriate ELSE abstain|`. In practice most LFs return only (0, abstain) or (1, abstain). The LFs are applied to the data that was selected in the "scope" step (cf. "Unlabeled data" in Figure 1) to generate a label matrix in which each data point may have multiple, contradictory labels.

In our study, moderators were asked to create rules based on their knowledge of the product categories and their moderation experience. Note that the same moderator was responsible for one category throughout our experiment. They had a limited amount of time (60 min. per category). The time limits in our study were determined in consultation with bol.com's product quality team to simulate real-world settings. This led to an initial set of LFs for each category (number of LFs per category: fur 14, illegal wildlife related 6, magnetic balls 5, weapon-grade knives 5, smoking-drug-related 15, single-use plastic 13).

The label matrix created by the rules is then transformed into labeled data. Ratner et al. (2016) demonstrate that provided a fixed number LFs, a probabilistic labeling model is able to recover a set of labels and corresponding probabilities that can be used to train a classifier (cf. "Training data" and "Classifier" in Figure 1). Snorkel (Ratner et al., 2017) is the first end-to-end system that applies the data programming paradigm. Our case study builds on Snorkel. (More technical details of our setup are in Appendix A.)

3.3 Inspiration Sets

We test three different ways of sampling data points to create the inspiration sets consisting of products (cf. Figure 1, bottom). These sets are shown to the moderators to allow them to revise the rules.

Set 1: Abstain-based strategy Randomly drawn from training data not yet covered by an LF.

Set 2: Disagreement-based strategy Randomly drawn from training data on which LFs disagreed.

Set 3: Classifier-based strategy Development data points with largest classifier error.

Set 1 and Set 2 are loosely based on strategies introduced by Cohen-Wang et al. (2019). These strategies are particularly interesting for a real-world setting because they are *unsupervised*, meaning that they are based on information included in the label matrix and do not require ground truth or classifier training. Set 3 is a *supervised* set. It provides product moderators with information about errors that are made by classifiers. This strategy is touched upon, but not implemented, by Cohen-Wang et al. (2019). Recall that Cohen-Wang et al. (2019) uses a simulated human expert, whereas in our experiment, human domain experts inspect the inspiration sets and revise the rules. We used a sim-

	fur	**illegal wildlife**	**magnetic balls**	**knives**	**smoking-drug related**	**single-use plastic**
initial	**0.80**	0.02	0.08	0.03	0.31	0.57
Set 1	0.78	0.19	0.49	0.03	0.31	**0.64**
Set 2	0.78	0.00	**0.65**	0.03	**0.36**	0.57
Set 3	0.77	**0.24**	0.59	**0.17**	0.23	0.57

Table 2: Data quality results: Label model performance (F_2 measure) on the test set.

ple logistic regression classifier for the supervision of Set 3 (see Appendix A.3 for more details).

Each inspiration set contains the number of data points available, up to a maximum of 100. The moderators had a limited amount of time (30 min. per set) to inspect the inspiration sets and add, remove, or change rules in their initial set of rules. Note that in our setting, each inspiration set was drawn once and not updated after the moderator changed one rule.

4 Results and Discussion

We analyze how the inspiration sets impact the quality of our data. Table 1 summarizes the data that we use. The ground truth was created by our domain experts. Table 2 presents our results in terms of data quality. Results are reported using the F_2 measure due to the importance of recall in our use case. Data points whose "inappropriate" label is generated as having a probability > 0.5 are considered positive. Note that scores in Table 2 do not directly reflect the ultimate performance of the classifier, which to a certain extent can leverage data with low F_2 scores.

Our results suggest two findings that have, to our knowledge, not been previously documented. First, professional content moderators do not necessarily need labeled sample data to write rules for a data programming pipeline, but instead come quite far relying only on domain knowledge and experience (cf. "initial" in Table 2). Second, when revising their initial set of rules, moderators do not necessarily need an inspiration set created using supervision. Instead, a 30-min. session with an unsupervised inspiration set (Set 1 or Set 2) can improve data quality. The exception is *fur* where F_2 is already 0.8, and inspiration sets make the data slightly worse. The category *knives* starts out with extremely low quality data, and inspiration sets do not help much, except for a small, but expensive boost by Set 3, our supervised set. The moderator had only basic experience with this category.

We also found that for most categories, a considerable amount of training data (31-56%) received only abstains (see Appendix B for more details). This observation is consistent with previous work, e.g., that of Cohen-Wang et al. (2019), which has noted that LF sets rarely reach complete coverage. In general, a small number of rules tend to cover a large portion of the data.

The majority of rules had a low precision, and a small number of rules had high recall. Possible reasons are that product moderators tried not to miss out on inappropriate products, or that they had set of specific data points in mind during LF definition, as suggested by Varma et al. (2017a). We also noticed that moderators added and changed, but did not delete rules. In fact, we only observed a single case of a rule being deleted. More research is necessary to understand if this reflects high confidence in the initial choices, or a default thinking pattern, as studied by Adams et al. (2021). Finally, we observe it is important not to assume that each newly added rule yields improvement: rule interactions are also important. A more detailed analysis of the changes brought about by the inspiration sets for two representative cases is included in Appendix C.

5 Conclusion and Outlook

Our case study has shown our data programming pipeline can generate labeled data for moderation classifiers in a fraction of the time needed for hand labeling (90 min. vs. a week or more of effort). We have seen that moderators can create effective rules based on their domain knowledge and experience, plus a short exposure to an unsupervised inspiration set. Labeling data by hand in order to create supervised inspiration sets may not be worth the effort. Our observations suggest that it is important that moderators not only write rules, but also continue moderating so that they can gain expertise and also be able to update rules quickly in response to changes in the domain, i.e., a new type of offensive clothing items, as in Bryant (2020).

We hope that our work will inspire research on data programming in domains in which fast response to inappropriate products or content is needed. Future research could seek to understand the ability of moderators to predict the interaction of rules and why they seem hesitant to discard rules once they have created them.

References

Gabrielle S. Adams, Benjamin A. Converse, Andrew H. Hales, and Leidy E. Klotz. 2021. People systematically overlook subtractive changes. *Nature*, 592(7853):258–261.

Patrick Arnold, Christian Wartner, and Erhard Rahm. 2016. Semi-automatic identification of counterfeit offers in online shopping platforms. *Journal of Internet Commerce*, 15(1):59–75.

Sonia Badene, Kate Thompson, Jean-Pierre Lorré, and Nicholas Asher. 2019. Data programming for learning discourse structure. In *Proceedings of the 57th Annual Meeting of the Association for Computational Linguistics*, pages 640–645.

BBC. 2020. Coronavirus: Amazon removes overpriced goods and fake cures. 28 February 2020 (Accessed 6 May 2021).

Miranda Bryant. 2020. Amazon removes shirts with derogatory slogan about Kamala Harris. *The Guardian*. 19 Aug 2020 (Accessed 6 May 2021).

Alison Callahan, Jason A. Fries, Christopher Ré, James I. Huddleston, Nicholas J. Giori, Scott L. Delp, and Nigam Haresh Shah. 2019. Medical device surveillance with electronic health records. *npj Digital Medicine*, 2(94).

Stevie Chancellor, Jessica Annette Pater, Trustin Clear, Eric Gilbert, and Munmun De Choudhury. 2016. #thyghgapp: Instagram content moderation and lexical variation in pro-eating disorder communities. In *Proceedings of the 19th ACM Conference on Computer-Supported Cooperative Work & Social Computing*, pages 1201–1213.

Benjamin Cohen-Wang, Stephen Mussmann, Alexander Ratner, and Christopher Ré. 2019. Interactive programmatic labeling for weak supervision. In *Workshop on Data Collection, Curation, and Labeling for Mining and Learning*.

Pratik Dutta and Sriparna Saha. 2019. A weak supervision technique with a generative model for improved gene clustering. In *2019 IEEE Congress on Evolutionary Computation*, pages 2521–2528.

Pratik Dutta, Sriparna Saha, Sanket Pai, and Aviral Kumar. 2020. A protein interaction information-based generative model for enhancing gene clustering. *Scientific Reports*, 10(665).

Henry R. Ehrenberg, Jaeho Shin, Alexander Ratner, Jason A. Fries, and Christopher Ré. 2016. Data programming with DDLite: Putting humans in a different part of the loop. In *Proceedings of the Workshop on Human-In-the-Loop Data Analytics*.

Jason A. Fries, Paroma Varma, Vincent S. Chen, Ke Xiao, Heliodoro Tejeda, Priyanka Saha, Jared Dunnmon, Henry Chubb, Shiraz Maskatia, Madalina Fiterau, et al. 2019. Weakly supervised classification of aortic valve malformations using unlabeled cardiac MRI sequences. *Nature Communications*, 10(3111).

Tim K. Mackey and Janani Kalyanam. 2017. Detection of illicit online sales of fentanyls via Twitter. *F1000Research*, 6:1937.

Rowan O. Martin, Cristiana Senni, and Neil C. D'Cruze. 2018. Trade in wild-sourced African grey parrots: Insights via social media. *Global Ecology and Conservation*, 15:e00429.

Mona Nashaat, Aindrila Ghosh, James Miller, and Shaikh Quader. 2020. WeSAL: Applying active supervision to find high-quality labels at industrial scale. In *Proceedings of the 53rd Hawaii International Conference on System Sciences*, pages 219–228.

Mona Nashaat, Aindrila Ghosh, James Miller, Shaikh Quader, Chad Marston, and Jean-Francois Puget. 2018. Hybridization of active learning and data programming for labeling large industrial datasets. In *2018 IEEE International Conference on Big Data*, pages 46–55.

Alexander Ratner, Stephen H. Bach, Henry Ehrenberg, Jason Fries, Sen Wu, and Christopher Ré. 2017. Snorkel: Rapid training data creation with weak supervision. In *Proceedings of the Very Large Data Bases Endowment*, volume 11, pages 269–282.

Alexander Ratner, Christopher M. De Sa, Sen Wu, Daniel Selsam, and Christopher Ré. 2016. Data programming: Creating large training sets, quickly. In *Advances in Neural Information Processing Systems*, volume 29, pages 3567–3575.

Alexander Ratner, Braden Hancock, Jared Dunnmon, Roger Goldman, and Christopher Ré. 2018. Snorkel metal: Weak supervision for multi-task learning. In *Proceedings of the Second Workshop on Data Management for End-To-End Machine Learning*.

Alexander Ratner, Braden Hancock, Jared Dunnmon, Frederic Sala, Shreyash Pandey, and Christopher Ré. 2019a. Training complex models with multi-task weak supervision. In *Proceedings of the AAAI Conference on Artificial Intelligence*, volume 33, pages 4763–4771.

Alexander Ratner, Braden Hancock, and Christopher Ré. 2019b. The role of massively multi-task and weak supervision in software 2.0. In *Proceedings of the Conference on Innovative Data Systems Research*.

Khaled Saab, Jared Dunnmon, Roger Goldman, Alexander Ratner, Hersh Sagreiya, Christopher Ré, and Daniel Rubin. 2019. Doubly weak supervision of deep learning models for Head CT. In *International Conference on Medical Image Computing and Computer-Assisted Intervention*, pages 811–819.

Khaled Kamal Saab, Jared Dunnmon, Christopher Ré, Daniel L. Rubin, and Christopher Lee-Messer. 2020. Weak supervision as an efficient approach for automated seizure detection in electroencephalography. *npj Digital Medicine*, 3(59).

Paroma Varma, Bryan He, Dan Iter, Peng Xu, Rose Yu, Christopher De Sa, and Christopher Ré. 2017a. Socratic learning: Correcting misspecified generative models using discriminative models. *arXiv preprint arXiv:1610.08123*.

Paroma Varma, Dan Iter, Christopher De Sa, and Christopher Ré. 2017b. Flipper: A systematic approach to debugging training sets. In *Proceedings of the 2nd Workshop on Human-In-the-Loop Data Analytics*.

Justine Winkler. 2020. Snorkeling for beginners: Applying data programming to product moderation in e-commerce. Master's thesis, Radboud University, Nijmegen, Netherlands.

Sen Wu, Luke Hsiao, Xiao Cheng, Braden Hancock, Theodoros Rekatsinas, Philip Levis, and Christopher Ré. 2018. Fonduer: Knowledge base construction from richly formatted data. In *Proceedings of the 2018 International Conference on Management of Data*, pages 1301–1316.

Qing Xu, Jiawei Li, Mingxiang Cai, and Tim K. Mackey. 2019. Use of machine learning to detect wildlife product promotion and sales on Twitter. *Frontiers Big Data*, 2:28.

A Technical details of our setup

A.1 Snorkel

The technical details of the setup we used are as follows: we make use of the official implementation of the Snorkel system. This implementation consolidates work from various publications (Ratner et al., 2017, 2019a) even though the repository name is "snorkel". We used version 0.9.0[1]. There, the label model is optimized using Stochastic Gradient Descent (SGD) on the matrix-completion formulation as in (Ratner et al., 2019a) as opposed to interleaving SGD and Gibbs sampling in (Ratner et al., 2017). In general in data programming, the label model needs two inputs: the dependency structure of the LFs and the class balance of the dependent variable (i.e. $p(Y)$). By default, this implementations assumes the LFs to be conditionally independent and that the class balance is uniformly distributed.

A.2 Gold labels

For each category of inappropriate items, the product moderator that was specialized in that category labeled the development, validation and test data.

A.3 Classifier

For each category of inappropriate items, we trained a binary classifier. In line with the official Snorkel introduction tutorial[2], we utilized a simple Logistic Regression classifier. We used categorical cross-entropy loss and an Adam optimizer with a learning rate of 0.01. Note that in this work, we use the classifier for selecting the items in the inspiration Set 3. More details on the whole pipeline can be found in (Winkler, 2020).

B Properties of the label matrix

In our experiments, inspiration sets inspired the product moderators to adjust their initial set of rules. We translated these rules into LFs in Python. Figure 2 illustrates the impact of the changes to the LFs across all categories of inappropriate items. The leftmost bar of each group represents the coverage of the initial LF sets.

In general, we notice that inspiration sets have an impact on the coverage of the LFs, but that they fall far short from allowing us to achieve full coverage. We also notice, however, that there is a general trend towards inspiration sets increasing the coverage, reflected by a decrease in the fraction of the data set that is assigned 0 labels. This happened in most categories with Set 1 and Set 3 and in half of the categories with Set 2. The strongest coverage increase happened using Set 1.

After the adjustments, for most categories, the LFs within each set seemed to be more coordinated with respect to the data points that they labeled. This can be seen in the increase in the percentage of each data set with multiple labels per sample. However, note that overall, most data points that received a label, received a label from only one LF.

[1] https://github.com/snorkel-team/snorkel/releases/tag/v0.9.0

[2] https://github.com/snorkel-team/snorkel-tutorials/blob/93fc77718b608c5709d4eb8b90b7de7683ba4c15/spam/01_spam_tutorial.ipynb

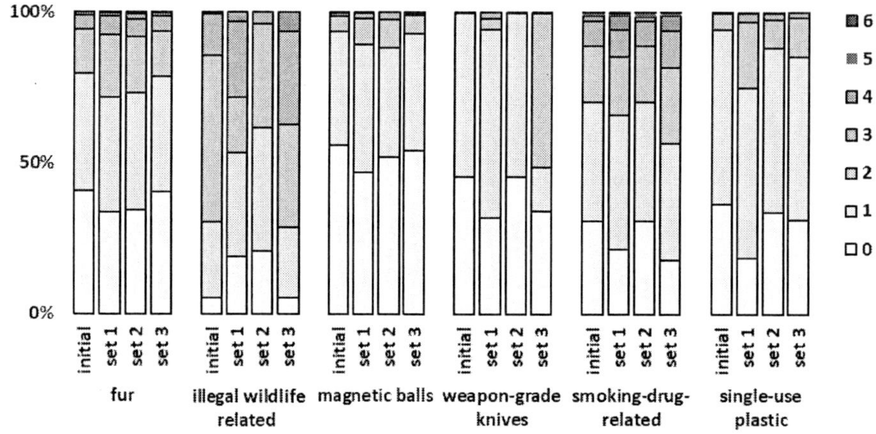

Figure 2: This figure shows the sizes of training data set fractions that received a certain number of labels per sample. Results are shown for the all versions (initial or adjusted using an inspiration set: Set 1, Set 2 or Set 3) of each monitor.

LF Index	Change	Polarity	Coverage	Overlaps	Conflicts	% gain in F_2
0	A	[1]	0.01	0.00	0.00	18.37
1	A	[0]	0.04	0.02	0.00	1.96
2	A	[0]	0.32	0.08	0.03	16.67
3	/	[1]	0.08	0.04	0.03	-21.21
4	A	[0]	0.08	0.03	0.01	0.00
5	A	[0]	0.03	0.02	0.01	0.00
6	N	[0]	0.11	0.04	0.01	1.96
7	N	[1]	0.01	0.00	0.00	0.00

Table 3: This table contains the characteristics of the individual LFs for magnetic balls after they have been adjusted with the inspiration Set 1.

C Individual rule characteristics

In the main paper, we mentioned several observations we made regarding the sets of rules that were created by the professional moderators.

- A small number of rules tend to cover a large portion of the data.
- Moderators added and changed, but did not delete rules (except one rule upon one occasion).
- We cannot not assume that each newly added rule yields improvement.

We based these observations on characteristics that we computed on the training and validation sets in each category. The statistics of these training and validation sets are provided in Table 5.

After translating the rules into LFs, we computed the following characteristics:

- **LF index**: a running index of each rule (Labeling Function) in the set.
- **Change** indicates whether the rules were adjusted (A), newly added (N) or not changed (/) as a result of considering the inspiration set.
- **Polarity**: the polarity that the rule assigns to the training set data points. If the value is [0], then the rule either assigned "appropriate" or abstained. If the value is [1], then the rule either assigned "inappropriate" or abstained. If the value is then the rule always abstained.
- **Coverage**: the fraction of the training set data points to which the LF assigned a label (i.e., did not abstain).
- **Overlaps**: the fraction of the training set on which the rule assigned a label and at least one other rule did as well (i.e., the rule and at least one other rule did not abstain).
- **Conflicts**: the fraction of the training set on which the labels suggested by multiple rules disagree.

LF Index	Change	Polarity	Coverage	Overlaps	Conflicts	% gain in F_2
0	/	[1]	0.02	0.01	0.01	4.35
1	/	[0]	0.06	0.04	0.01	0.00
2	/		0.00	0.00	0.00	0.00
3	/		0.00	0.00	0.00	0.00
4	/		0.00	0.00	0.00	0.00
5	A	[0]	0.69	0.23	0.05	0.53
6	A	[0]	0.14	0.13	0.00	-0.41
7	A	[0]	0.01	0.01	0.00	0.00
8	/	[0]	0.01	0.01	0.00	0.00
9	/	[0]	0.01	0.00	0.00	0.00
10	/	[1]	0.01	0.01	0.01	-0.36
11	/	[0]	0.06	0.04	0.00	0.00
12	/	[0]	0.00	0.00	0.00	0.00
13	A	[1]	0.11	0.06	0.05	73.21
14	N	[0]	0.00	0.00	0.00	0.00

Table 4: This table contains the characteristics of the individual LFs for single-use plastic after they have been adjusted with the inspiration Set 1.

category	**training set**	**validation set**
fur	7633	400 (55)
illegal wildlife related	7426	318 (10)
magnetic balls	2316	324 (7)
weapon-grade knives	1266	210 (18)
smoking-drug-related	1071	173 (12)
single-use plastic	7364	445 (118)

Table 5: Number of data points in our training and validation sets. These were the data sets on which we computed the LF characteristics. For convenience, we repeat the sizes of the training data here. Note that the validation sets are disjoint from the development and test sets used in the main paper. For these validation sets, the number of points with the positive label, i.e., "inappropriate", is in parentheses.

- **% gain in F_2**: the relative improvement in the F_2 score of the labeled data generated by the label model contributed by the individual rule.

Note that Polarity, Coverage, Rules, and Overlap are all calculated on the training data set, and "% gain in F_2" is calculated on the validation set.

We chose two representative categories that show the variation of the gain, and provide example analyses for each. The category magnetic balls is in Table 3 and single-use plastic is in Table 4. The analysis uses the rules adjusted after consulting the inspiration Set 1.

Enhancing Aspect Extraction in Hindi

Arghya Bhattacharya, Alok Debnath and **Manish Shrivastava**
Language Technologies Research Center (LTRC),
Kohli Center for Information Systems (KCIS),
International Institute of Information Technology, Hyderabad (IIIT-H)
{arghya.b, alok.debnath}@research.iiit.ac.in
m.shrivastava@iiit.ac.in

Abstract

Aspect extraction is not a well-explored topic in Hindi, with only one corpus having been developed for the task. In this paper, we discuss the merits of the existing corpus in terms of quality, size, sparsity, and performance in aspect extraction tasks using established models. To provide a better baseline corpus for aspect extraction, we translate the SemEval 2014 aspect-based sentiment analysis dataset and annotate the aspects in that data. We provide rigorous guidelines and a replicable methodology for this task. We quantitatively evaluate the translations and annotations using inter-annotator agreement scores. We also evaluate our dataset using state-of-the-art neural aspect extraction models in both monolingual and multilingual settings and show that the models perform far better on our corpus than on the existing Hindi dataset. With this, we establish our corpus as the gold-standard aspect extraction dataset in Hindi.

1 Introduction

Recent literature has seen an increase in the amount of work being done in fine-graining downstream NLP tasks. One common method of fine-grained analysis is the use of aspect information. An aspect term is an entity of interest which identifies a unique aspect of a predefined topic or domain (Pontiki et al., 2014). For example, in the *restaurant* domain, *service* and *seasoning* are aspects. While aspect extraction (AE) has been often seen as a subtask of fine grained aspect-based sentiment analysis (ABSA), recent advances in literature have established it as an independent task which can be used in other downstream tasks as well, such as summarization (Fremann and Klementiev, 2019) and topic-specific information retrieval such as opinion mining (Asghar et al., 2019).

Aspect extraction (as a subtask of aspect-based sentiment analysis) datasets and models have been developed for multiple languages. ABSA has been a shared task in SemEval 2014 (Pontiki et al., 2014), 2015 (Nakov et al., 2015), 2016 (Pontiki et al., 2016), and as a part of the overall task of sentiment analysis on Twitter in SemEval 2017 (Rosenthal et al., 2017). These tasks have garnered a lot of attention in various languages including Arabic, Chinese, Dutch, French, Russian, Spanish and Turkish. Each monolingual dataset consisted of one or two domains with each language having anywhere between 4,000 to 9,000 sentences overall (including the train and test split). For Indian languages, there has been some work in developing a dataset for aspect extraction in Hindi (Akhtar et al., 2016) and Telugu (Regatte et al., 2020).

Limited work has been done on improving the state of AE and ABSA in Hindi beyond the development of a singular dataset, namely Akhtar et al. (2016). Existing evaluations show that existing sequence tagging models (both general and specific to AE) have performed very poorly on this dataset when their performance is compared to English AE as well as in similar sequence tagging tasks in Hindi such as named entity recognition (NER) and event detection.

In this paper, we thoroughly analyze the existing dataset for AE in Hindi and explain the reason for the poor model performance. We then propose the creation of a parallel corpus, by manually translating the SemEval-2014 ABSA corpus (Pontiki et al., 2014). We provide detailed guidelines and challenges faced during the creation of this resource. We show that our dataset performs much better than the existing dataset for Hindi using baseline as well as state-of-the-art neural models for AE. Finally, we leverage the SemEval-2014 corpus to perform zero-shot and fine-tuned aspect extraction in Hindi using multilingual BERT with baseline and SoTA neural models in the dataset we have created.

Therefore, the main contributions of this paper

Proceedings of the 4th Workshop on e-Commerce and NLP (ECNLP 4), pages 140–149
August 5, 2021. ©2021 Association for Computational Linguistics

are:

- providing an in-depth qualitative and quantitative analysis of the existing Hindi AE dataset,
- creating a new resource for aspect extraction in Hindi by translating the SemEval 2014 corpus into Hindi[1],
- providing detailed guidelines and challenges associated with the creation of this corpus, as well as explaining the quality of the translations and annotations, and
- evaluating the new dataset using state-of-the-art neural sequence labeling models for aspect extraction in Hindi in monolingual and multilingual settings using transfer learning.

We establish that our corpus is a more robust and representative corpus for aspect extraction in Hindi, and its parallel nature can be exploited for a large number of downstream tasks including review translation, cross-lingual opinion mining, and aspect-based sentiment analysis.

2 Dataset Development

As discussed in Section 1, Akhtar et al. (2016) is the only corpus for aspect term extraction and aspect-based sentiment analysis in Hindi. In this section, we discuss the inadequacy of this corpus by analyzing the data qualitatively, statistically and through experiments using established aspect extraction models. We also detail the process of creating a parallel aspect extraction datset from the English gold standard dataset (Pontiki et al., 2014). This resource can be treated as an individual Hindi aspect extraction dataset or can be considered a parallel resource for the aspect extraction task.

The annotation format used for the existing dataset and the dataset being created is the Begin-Inside-Outside or `BIO` sequence labeling format (Ramshaw and Marcus, 1999). This format annotates each word with a corresponding label where a word labeled `B` denotes the first word of an aspect, `I` denotes any word within the aspect span and `O` denotes the words outside the aspect span.

2.1 Analyzing Existing Datasets

In this section, we aim to prove based on a qualitative and statistical analysis of the Hindi ABSA dataset for AE, and compare it to the SemEval-2014 English ABSA dataset. Some of the metrics for comparison include the number of sentences, number of aspects, ratios of `B`s, `I`s, and `O`s and the number of marked sentences (sentences with one or more aspects). We explain how these comparisons explain the quality of the dataset for this task as well. We also show a quantitative performance analysis of these datasets on baseline model as well as the state-of-the-art models in sequence tagging and aspect term extraction in Section 3.1.

The Akhtar et al. (2016) dataset consists of $5,147$ sentences, and a total of $4,509$ aspect terms. The combined SemEval-2016 dataset shows a similar trend, with $6,092$ sentences and $6,072$ aspect terms. However, on a closer analysis of the dataset, detailed in Table 1, we see three prominent distinguishing factors:

1. While the percentage of marked sentences (sentences with one or more aspects) is higher in the Hindi dataset than in the English one, there is a noticeable difference between the average number of aspects per sentence (both for marked sentences and overall).
2. The percentage of `I`s in the Hindi dataset (3.26%, $3,135$ out of $96,140$ words) are higher than the English dataset (2.96%, $2,564$ in $86,552$ words), while the number of `B`s in the Hindi dataset are lower. This implies that in multi-word aspects are far more common in Hindi than they are in English. Further, the percentage of `O`s is higher in the Hindi dataset as well, so there are not as many words which are aspect terms either.
3. The data in Hindi corpus is from *12* different domains, with some domains having less than 50 sentences. So, not only is there a large variety in topics and aspects per topic, there is also a high disparity in the number of samples per topic. In contrast, the English dataset is derived from only two different domains, with over 2000 sentences per domain.

This disparity in the number of aspects per topic as well as the noticeable difference in the number of multi-word aspect terms implies that corpus developed by Akhtar et al. (2016) is sparse with very few examples of the syntactic features, aspects and their categories.

[1] `https://drive.google.com/file/d/1wrCHi3VbQjosvhmpfS577TXZL-O6UbUo/view?usp=sharing`

<sentence id="lap_271"> स्वाइप अल्टीमेट में 8 मेगापिक्सल कैमरा पीछे की तरफ और 2 **एमपी** कैमरा आगे की तरफ दिया गया है। </sentence>	<sentence id="mob_771"> **20MP** रियर स्नैपर इष्टतम प्रकाश की स्थितियों के तहत महान छवियों को लेता है और कम प्रकाश के तहत भी अच्छी तरह से प्रदर्शन करता है। </sentence>
<sentence id="lap_77"> मुझे लगा था कि ये सिर्फ मेरे ही **कम्प्यूटर** में है परंतु नहीं ये समस्या बहुत से, हजारों-लाखों एचपी/कॉम्पैक नोटबुक/लैपटॉप में है। </sentence>	<sentence id="lap_249"> इस Chip **Computer** में ऑलविनर एसओसी का इस्तेमाल किया गया है जो सस्ता होने के साथ-साथ पावरफुल भी है। </sentence>
<sentence id="mob_162"> एस60 में 5 इंच की एचडी आईपीएस स्क्रीन दी गई है साथ में 64 बिट 1.2 गिगा **क्वॉड कोर** क्वॉलकॉम स्नैपड्रैगन 410 **प्रोसेसर**, 2 **जीबी** रैम और माली 450 एमपी जीपीयू। </sentence>	<sentence id="mob_667"> **Quad Core Processor**, 1 **GB** RAM, परफॉरमेंस अच्छी है। </sentence>

Figure 1: Some examples of inconsistent samples in the Hindi dataset. The words in bold face are the same in both examples, transliterated into Devnagari on the left and left Romanized on the right in different training samples.

Further qualitative analysis of the data reveals discrepancies in the data creation methodology, particularly surrounding technical terms which do not have commonly used translations. Terms such as 'computer', 'megapixel', 'quad core' and 'processor' have been transliterated in some examples and have been left Romanized in others. Given the low number of examples per category, this inconsistency contributes to the data sparsity. Figure 1 shows a few examples of such inconsistencies.

Finally, we see examples of incorrect annotation which also contributes to the dataset quality in terms of performance in machine learning models. These incorrect annotations include incorrect spacing between words in the original review text, incomplete aspect annotation where the last character of the last word of the aspect was not a part of the aspect span, and subword level aspects due to stemming, lemmatization and dehyphenation.

There are two available task performance measures for the term of aspect extraction in the Hindi dataset:

- Akhtar et al. (2016) analyzed aspect term extraction using the `BIO` annotation using conditional random fields (CRFs) for sequence labelling. They report an average F1 score of just 41.07%. The CRFs used were heavily feature engineered to use features such as semantic orientation, local context tagging and bigram specific features.

- Akhtar et al. (2020) performed joint modeling and end-to-end aspect extraction on both the Hindi as well as the Pontiki et al. (2014) English dataset. They reported a maximum F1 score of 83.36% for the English dataset using an end-to-end architecture, while the maximum F1 score for Hindi using the same architecture was 52.03%. Other experiments also show this vast disparity.

These discrepancies show that even heavily feature-engineered statistical models as well as neural models do not perform well on the existing Hindi dataset and the neural models seem to perform a lot better on the SemEval 2014 dataset. An aspect term extraction task comparison for various models can be found in table 3 for a number of models described in section 3.1.

Table 3 shows that the discrepancies noted by Akhtar et al. (2020) continue to hold across multiple neural models. The difference between the F1 scores between the two datasets is nearly 40% for all three models, with the maximum F1 score in the Hindi dataset being a mere 38.21% for the DeCNN model. We conclude through this thorough analysis that the Akhtar et al. (2016) dataset is inadequate as a benchmark dataset for aspect extraction in Hindi.

2.2 Constructing the Parallel Corpus

We construct a parallel corpus by translating the SemEval 2014 English aspect based sentiment analysis dataset of restaurant and laptop reviews (Pontiki et al., 2014). The dataset constructed by this translation can be used as an independent Hindi dataset, or can be used such that it leverages the English dataset for aspect extraction. By using the guidelines provided below, we are able to preserve the diversity of syntactic constructions from the original dataset, making the quantitative comparisons more representative.

The final dataset constructed by this methodology consists of 5989 sentences with 5864 aspects. Not all the sentences could be translated based on our guidelines which aim at maintaining naturalness and fluency. The guidelines pertaining to the translation and aspect extraction have been discussed below, followed by the methodology of annotation. The comparative statistics of this dataset can be found in 1, when compared to Akhtar et al. (2016) and Pontiki et al. (2014).

Annotation Guidelines The guidelines for creating this parallel corpus were twofold, translating the dataset into Hindi and identifying the aspect terms in the translations.

The translation methodology adopted for this task had to account for fluency, accuracy and style. Not only did the translated reviews had to be as semantically similar to the original review as possible, but they also had to be faithful to the style of restaurant and technology reviews in Hindi. In order to achieve a natural translation true to this style, we propose the following translation guidelines.

1. For proper nouns and other names in English, such as locations, company names and other named entities, annotators were asked to directly use Roman script. For example: *Brooklyn, 2nd Street, Sony*. We found that proper nouns in both domains indicated a property of the main topic and rarely that of an aspect, so using Roman script could aid in attribute extraction without being a problem in aspect extraction or other downstream tasks.

2. For common nouns without Hindi translations, or with very obscure translations which are not commonly used, annotators were asked to transliterate these nouns into Hindi. This was done in order to maintain consistency in the use of technical terms which could act as aspects in the Hindi sentence, while maintaining the domain-specific naturalness and fluency of the translated sentence. Word such as *keyboard, bluetooth, monitor, sake* and *soy sauce* were transliterated into Hindi.

3. Aspect descriptions often contain idiomatic constructions or other compositional phrases. Translators were asked to simplify these phrases to their meaning rather than translate word for word. Therefore, for phrases such as '*on the nose*' was translated to *yathaarth* (meaning 'obvious') rather than *naak ke upar* (literally meaning 'on or over the nose')

4. For common nouns with gender and number inflections, annotators were asked to transliterate the root word (as mentioned in rule (2)) but use the Hindi inflection markers. As English pronouns and nouns are not gender marked, the default male inflection is used whenever applicable.

5. For all other words, aspects and aspect descriptions, translate into Hindi using the most commonly used words given the appropriate context. In the case where the context is so scarce that there is no way to translate the sentence in a way that preserves meaning, do not translate the sentence.

After the translation, a different group of annotators were asked to identify aspect terms. Aspect term identification guidelines were the same as those used in the SemEval-2014 ABSA task[2] (Pontiki et al., 2014). The annotators were asked to annotate all single or multiword terms which were a particular aspect of the target entity (i.e. 'Restaurant' or 'Laptop').

Annotation Methodology Each sentence in the Pontiki et al. (2014) dataset was translated by four translators, two undergraduate and two graduate students. All translators are bilingual speakers of Hindi and English and are between the ages of 18 and 22. The translated sentences were then provided to two other annotators for the aspect extraction task. These annotators were in the same age group and of the same composition in terms of expertise in Hindi and English.

Translation was performed in two phases: *aspect-aware* and *aspect-blind* translations. In aspect-aware translation, the translator were provided the aspect terms while translating the sentence and were to retain as many aspects in the translated sentence as possible while maintaining the rules of translation mentioned above. In the aspect-blind translation, the translators were provided just the sentence to translate with no additional instructions. This two-phase translation was done to determine the fluency and naturalness of the translations with respect to one another with and without the constraint of maintaining aspects. The dataset contains the most fluent version of the annotations and those which maintain the most aspects from the source sentences in the SemEval dataset.

These translated sentences were provided to the final annotators, who were asked to identify the aspects in these sentences based on the guidelines provided above. This was compared to a direct translation of the extracted aspects in the source sentence (which were provided in the dataset).

Challenges in Annotation Some of the main challenges in translating the data are detailed below.

[2]http://alt.qcri.org/semeval2014/task4/data/uploads/semeval14_absa_annotationguidelines.pdf

Metrics	Akhtar et al. (2016)	Pontiki et al. (2014)	Our Dataset
Total # Sentences	5417	**6092**	5989
Total # Aspects	4509	**6072**	5864
Total # Tokens	96140	86552	**104618**
% Sentences marked with Aspects	**61.5%**	57.7%	57.9%
Avg. # of aspects per sentence	0.81	**0.99**	0.98
Avg. # of aspects per marked	1.32	**1.72**	1.69
% of `B`s	4.69%	**7.01%**	5.60%
% of `I`s	**3.26%**	2.96%	2.80%
% of `O`s	**92.15%**	90.22%	91.60%
No. of Domains	**12**	2	2

Table 1: Some basic comparative statistics between the aspect extraction and aspect based sentiment analysis datasets. We see that while the Hindi dataset has lower number of samples, fewer aspects, lower ratio of aspects per sentence and lower number of sentences with aspects. Interestingly, however, these words have been added to a much larger number of domains in Hindi and there are higher number of words with the `I` and `O` tags.

1. The most common problem in translation was semantically compositional constructions such as idiomatic phrases. Phrases such as "*boy oh boy*", "*don't look down your nose*" etc. were descriptive of a given aspect in the corpus, but could not be easily translated due to a lack of natural corollaries for these phrases in Hindi.

2. Constructions with puns and aspects embedded in the compositional constructions were the biggest challenge to the translation. For example: '*But that wasn't the icing on the cake: a tiramisu that resembled nothing I have ever had*' had the aspect '*icing on the cake*' which is both literal and metaphorical in this sentence. In the final version of the data, these sentences have not been included due to very high disparity between the translations and the difficulty in extracting aspects.

3. Elided references were a concern for translators. For example, a sentence such as '*A cheap eat for NYC, but not for dosa.*' uses the term '*eat*' to refer to a '*place to eat*' which is also an aspect in this sentence. A direct translation forces this elision to be explicit, which also changes the aspect term.

4. Hindi syntax has relatively free word order, which affords fragmentation of noun and verb phrases by adjectives and adverbs respectively. The aspect-aware and aspect-blind translations often differed in such cases, as the aspect-aware translation is not fragmented, but is also generally unnatural according to the annotators. For example, the phrase "*everything bagel with lox spread*" has the annotated aspect *bagel with lox spread*, but gets translated to *lauks spred ke saath evarithing begal* (where the word "everything" fragments the aspect term).

5. Certain aspect terms translate only based on context, which is not always provided in the data. An example of this is ... *mine was well done and dry* without a subject in reference, where the term *well done* can have different translations in different contexts (such as a well-done steak versus an actual compliment).

Due to these challenges in dataset annotation and the lack of context to make an informed translation which was natural and fluent, some sentences and aspects could not be translated into Hindi. Therefore the Hindi dataset has a few fewer sentences that the English dataset. The final translated dataset consists of 5,989 sentences with 5,864 aspect terms.

2.3 Dataset Analysis

In this section, we show some basic statistical analyses of the dataset including the annotator performance in translation and aspect term extraction. For translation performance, we compare the ROUGE-L scores across the translators, while for the annotation task, we use the Fleiss' Kappa metric.

We evaluate these translation based on the ROUGE-L metrics as the average review length is no more than 15 words, and most words have only one (or very few) variations in translation. Given

Comparison	ROUGE-L	Fleiss' Kappa
Aspect-aware	0.8994	0.8961
Aspect-blind	0.8722	0.9244
Overall	0.8960	0.9130

Table 2: The average ROUGE-L and Fleiss' Kappa score in the translation and annotation tasks respectively.

the stringent translation/transliteration guidelines, lack of extensive vocabulary in the descriptions and less number of words per sentence, the ROUGE-L metric is a decent approximation of the translation quality provided by the annotators. The ROUGE-L metric also accounts for the relative free-word order nature and constituent rearrangement (Lin and Och, 2004).

ROUGE-L is the comparison of the longest common subsequence between two translated phrases. Given the translations X of length m and Y of length n, the ROUGE-L score is given by:

$$R_{lcs} = \frac{\text{LCS}(X,Y)}{m} \quad (1)$$

$$P_{lcs} = \frac{\text{LCS}(X,Y)}{n} \quad (2)$$

$$F_{lcs} = \frac{(1+\beta^2)R_{lcs}P_{lcs}}{R_{lcs}+\beta^2 P_{lcs}} \quad (3)$$

where $\beta = \frac{P_{lcs}}{R_{lcs}}$ when $\frac{\partial F_{lcs}}{\partial R_{lcs}} = \frac{\partial F_{lcs}}{\partial P_{lcs}}$. This value is an F-measure. In Table 2 we show the comparison between the ROUGE-L scores of the aspect-aware and aspect-blind translations, by taking a weighted average over the entire dataset based on the number of words in the source and target sentence. We also show the score of the translation with the highest ROUGE-L score with the rest of the translations which has been used in the dataset.

Aspect extraction is treated as a sequence labeling task and is evaluated using the Fleiss Kappa metric (Fleiss and Cohen, 1973). Fleiss' Kappa is a multiclass inter-annotator agreement score which is computed as follows:

$$\kappa = \frac{\bar{P} - \bar{P}_e}{1 - \bar{P}_e} \quad (4)$$

where $P - P_e$ is the actual degree of agreement achieved and $1 - P_e$ is the degree of agreement above chance. Given N tokens to be annotated and n annotators, with k categories to annotate the data. We first calculate the proportion of annotations in the jth domain as:

$$p_j = \frac{1}{Nn}\sum_{i=1}^{N} n_{ij}\,, \quad 1 = \sum_{j=1}^{k} p_j \quad (5)$$

We then calculate P_i, the degree of agreement with the ith annotator as:

$$P_i = \frac{1}{n(n-1)}\sum_{j=1}^{k} n_{ij}(n_{ij}-1) \quad (6)$$

$$= \frac{1}{n(n-1)}\left[\left(\sum_{j=1}^{k} n_{ij}^2\right) - n\right] \quad (7)$$

Finally we calculate $\bar{P}$ and $\bar{P}_e$ as:

$$\bar{P} = \frac{1}{N}\sum_{i=1}^{N} P_i \quad (8)$$

$$\bar{P}_e = \sum_{j=1}^{k} p_j^2 \quad (9)$$

The Fleiss' Kappa scores of the aspect-aware, aspect-blind and overall translations are provided in table 2. The high Fleiss' Kappa scores indicate the confidence in the aspect identification guidelines.

Note that the ROUGE-L score of the aspect-aware translation is higher than the overall as well as the aspect-blind translations, as translators often resorted to word-for-word translations in order to preserve each and every aspect of the sentence with its associated semantic information. Note that ROUGE-L is the weighted average of the F-measure taken over all the sentences in the dataset, weighted based on the number of words in the source and target sentences. For the overall ROUGE score, the weighted average was taken over the dataset, weighted based on the number of words in the sentence which gave the highest comparative score for each translation.

Another important insight into the corpus is the difference in aspect coverage between the aspect-aware and the aspect-blind translations. As mentioned in 2.2, aspect-blind translations often dropped aspects due to constraints in syntactic representation or incoherent translation due to sentence semantics, such as due to complex idiomatic phrases. The difference in aspect coverage was seen in about 6% of the corpus, specifically, 358 sentences overall.

3 Evaluating the Dataset

In this section, we detail the evaluation of our translated aspect extraction dataset. We evaluate our dataset using multiple monolingual and multilingual models. The monolingual models are trained and tested on the individual language datasets while the multilingual models involve the use of transfer learning from the SemEval-2014 dataset to the dataset we have created.

3.1 Monolingual Aspect Extraction

We evaluate our dataset against the existing Hindi dataset and the SemEval 2014 dataset using the following baselines:

- **CRF**: We use a conditional random field with basic features[3] such as word form and POS tag.
- **BiLSTM**: We use a vanilla BiLSTM as a baseline model for aspect extraction as it is an established baseline in seq2seq tasks (Liu et al., 2015).
- **BiLSTM-CRF**: We use a BiLSTM to encode the input sentence and a conditional random field for the sequence labeling. This is a commonly used baseline for sequence tagging tasks (Huang et al., 2015).

We also use the following neural models for our analysis:

- **BiLSTM-CNN-CRF**: The state-of-the-art in neural named entity recognition. The architecture uses both character and word level features in a CNN and BiLSTM respectively, and using a CRF for sequence labeling tasks (Reimers and Gurevych, 2017). We use a slightly modified version where word embeddings are generated by concatenating character embeddings, as done by Prabhu et al. (2019) for event detection in Hindi.
- **DeCNN**: The commonly adopted model for aspect extraction specifically, this model uses a combination of general and domain based embeddings in multiple convolutional layers and a fully connected layer with softmax for label prediction (Xu et al., 2018).
- **Seq2Seq4ATE**: This model is a sequence-to-sequence model for aspect terms extraction. The model uses a BiGRU encoder and a position aware attention variant of gated unit networks as a decoder with softmax for label prediction (Ma et al., 2019).

For consistency, in all the above mentioned models, we use the FastText embeddings for word as well as character embeddings for both English and Hindi (Bojanowski et al., 2017; Mikolov et al., 2018; Grave et al., 2018). For the English dataset, we use the Pontiki et al. (2014) train-test split (3045 training to 800 test sentences and 2000 training to 676 test sentences in the 'Laptop' and 'Restaurant' domains respectively). For the Hindi dataset, we use a train-test split of 4062 train to 1355 test sentences based on Akhtar et al. (2020). For the LSTM based models, we use 128 unit LSTM layers, with a hidden size of 1024, and a dropout of 0.4 over 50 epochs. For the CNN based model, we use a 128 filter network with a kernel size of 5 and hidden embeddings of size 100 and dropout of 0.4 over 50 epochs.

We find that the Seq2Seq4ATE model is the best performing model for this task across the datasets. We see that the model performance on our dataset is close to that on the English dataset. While the human aspect extraction baseline shows that there is a lot more work to be done in this task, our dataset provides an adequate baseline for this task, similar to those in the SemEval Aspect Extraction subtask (Pontiki et al., 2014).

3.2 Leveraging Parallel Data

As mentioned in section 2, the corpus we have developed aims to be a parallel corpus, which allows us to use language invariant, transfer learning based models for aspect extraction in Hindi. We use the BERT mutilingual sentence embeddings (Devlin et al., 2018) as the sentence representations for the English and Hindi on the (a) BiLSTM, (b) BiLSTM-CNN-CRF and (c) the Seq2Seq4ATE models, mentioned in Section 3.1. The BERT multilingual embeddings have been used for a variety of tasks in Hindi including machine comprehension (Gupta and Khade, 2020) and named entity recognition (Pires et al., 2019), among other sequence labeling tasks. Pires et al. (2019) showcases the model efficacy in using monolingual corpora for zero-shot code-mixed tasks as well, which would be useful for our corpus.

[3] https://sklearn-crfsuite.readthedocs.io/en/latest/tutorial.html

Model	Akhtar et al. (2016)	Pontiki et al. (2014)	Our Dataset
Baselines			
CRF	22.08	**54.97**	47.07
BiLSTM	20.71	**61.01**	54.77
BILSTM-CRF	34.71	**62.61**	50.26
Neural SoTA Models			
BiLSTM-CNN-CRF	36.56	**73.03**	67.08
DeCNN	38.21	**77.67**	68.35
Seq2Seq4ATE	35.04	**78.86**	68.61

Table 3: F1 scores of established models on the monolingual aspect extraction task.

Training	Model	F1-score
Baseline	BiLSTM	41.06
	BiLSTM-CNN-CRF	54.92
	Seq2Seq4ATE	43.51
Zero-shot	BiLSTM	40.72
	BiLSTM-CNN-CRF	56.16
	Seq2Seq4ATE	42.08
Fine-tuned	BiLSTM	57.37
	BiLSTM-CNN-CRF	62.12
	Seq2Seq4ATE	**66.28**

Table 4: F1-score of the models by leveraging English aspect extraction data using M-BERT. The baseline score is based on using Hindi for training as well as testing.

We design three experiments for evaluating our dataset using M-BERT, which are detailed below.

1. *M-BERT baseline* where we train and test on the Hindi sentences and aspects from our dataset directly, using the M-BERT embeddings. This has been done to establish a baseline for our experiments that follow for leveraging the English data.

2. *Zero shot aspect extraction for Hindi* where we train using the English dataset and evaluate the model performances on the Hindi data, in order to estimate how much aspect information can be extracted about aspect representation in this data which can be applied on the Hindi dataset directly.

3. *Fine tuned aspect extraction for Hindi* where we train the models on the Hindi and a small part of the English dataset and test on the translated Hindi test set. In this experiment, we augment the training data and therefore showcase the use of the English representation of aspect terms in the dataset. This is done with the motivation to boost the token representation of English tokens, as the Hindi data contains English tokens in the form of proper nouns. These tokens are aspects in a part of the corpus and therefore introducing this experiment improves the representation and extraction of these aspect tokens.

Table 4 provides the F1-scores of the various models described above. We use the pretrained BERT Mulitilingual cased model. The best performing model is the fine-tuned Seq2Seq4ATE model with an F1 of 66.28. We also see that the zero-shot performance of the BiLSTM-CNN-CRF is better than the baseline, and that fine-tuning using English data definitely helps the model.

4 Conclusion

In this paper, we detailed the state of aspect extraction in Hindi by thoroughly analyzing and evaluating the currently available baseline dataset for this task. By understanding the flaws in that dataset, we explain its inadequacy in terms of lack of uniformity, high domain sparsity and incorrect aspect annotations. We further compare its performance with existing models to show that it performs very poorly as compared to the existing English dataset.

We then explain the mechanism of creating a SemEval style corpus for aspect extraction in Hindi, by translating the English SemEval 2014 aspect based sentiment analysis corpus. We provide a detailed list of guidelines in order to make this task as replicable as possible. We also focus on maintaining the naturalness and fluency of the translations using transliteration wherever necessary. Our translation and annotation methodology is evaluated on the ROUGE-L and Fleiss' Kappa metrics respectively.

We use this dataset to show performance on basline statistical and neural sequence labeling models, as well as the current state-of-the-art models in neural aspect extraction such as DeCNN and Seq2Seq4ATE. We show that while the published Hindi dataset does not perform nearly as well, we provide comparable results to those models. Since we have a parallel corpus, we also leverage the English data for improving aspect extraction in Hindi using multilingual BERT.

Future work in this direction includes developing an aspect based sentiment analysis corpus which can be trained and tested in a multilingual manner and fine-tuning multilingual BERT for few-shot and zero-shot sequence labeling tasks.

Acknowledgements

We would like to thank the annotators of the corpora, Mukund Chaudhary, Mashrukh Islam, Ishaan Sanjeev Upadhyay, and KV Aditya Srivatsa, who took time out and volunteered to help out with this project. We would also like to thank the anonymous reviewers for their insightful comments which aided in improving this contribution.

References

Md Shad Akhtar, Asif Ekbal, and Pushpak Bhattacharyya. 2016. Aspect based sentiment analysis in hindi: resource creation and evaluation. In *Proceedings of the Tenth International Conference on Language Resources and Evaluation (LREC'16)*, pages 2703–2709.

Md Shad Akhtar, Tarun Garg, and Asif Ekbal. 2020. Multi-task learning for aspect term extraction and aspect sentiment classification. *Neurocomputing*.

Muhammad Zubair Asghar, Aurangzeb Khan, Syeda Rabail Zahra, Shakeel Ahmad, and Fazal Masud Kundi. 2019. Aspect-based opinion mining framework using heuristic patterns. *Cluster Computing*, 22(3):7181–7199.

Piotr Bojanowski, Edouard Grave, Armand Joulin, and Tomas Mikolov. 2017. Enriching word vectors with subword information. *Transactions of the Association for Computational Linguistics*, 5:135–146.

Jacob Devlin, Ming-Wei Chang, Kenton Lee, and Kristina Toutanova. 2018. Bert: Pre-training of deep bidirectional transformers for language understanding. *arXiv preprint arXiv:1810.04805*.

Joseph L Fleiss and Jacob Cohen. 1973. The equivalence of weighted kappa and the intraclass correlation coefficient as measures of reliability. *Educational and psychological measurement*, 33(3):613–619.

Lea Frermann and Alexandre Klementiev. 2019. Inducing document structure for aspect-based summarization. In *Proceedings of the 57th Annual Meeting of the Association for Computational Linguistics*, pages 6263–6273.

Edouard Grave, Piotr Bojanowski, Prakhar Gupta, Armand Joulin, and Tomas Mikolov. 2018. Learning word vectors for 157 languages. In *Proceedings of the International Conference on Language Resources and Evaluation (LREC 2018)*.

Somil Gupta and Nilesh Khade. 2020. Bert based multilingual machine comprehension in english and hindi. *arXiv preprint arXiv:2006.01432*.

Zhiheng Huang, Wei Xu, and Kai Yu. 2015. Bidirectional lstm-crf models for sequence tagging. *arXiv preprint arXiv:1508.01991*.

Chin-Yew Lin and Franz Josef Och. 2004. Automatic evaluation of machine translation quality using longest common subsequence and skip-bigram statistics. In *Proceedings of the 42nd Annual Meeting of the Association for Computational Linguistics (ACL-04)*, pages 605–612.

Pengfei Liu, Shafiq Joty, and Helen Meng. 2015. Fine-grained opinion mining with recurrent neural networks and word embeddings. In *Proceedings of the 2015 Conference on Empirical Methods in Natural Language Processing*, pages 1433–1443.

Dehong Ma, Sujian Li, Fangzhao Wu, Xing Xie, and Houfeng Wang. 2019. Exploring sequence-to-sequence learning in aspect term extraction. In *Proceedings of the 57th Annual Meeting of the Association for Computational Linguistics*, pages 3538–3547.

Tomas Mikolov, Edouard Grave, Piotr Bojanowski, Christian Puhrsch, and Armand Joulin. 2018. Advances in pre-training distributed word representations. In *Proceedings of the International Conference on Language Resources and Evaluation (LREC 2018)*.

Preslav Nakov, Torsten Zesch, Daniel Cer, and David Jurgens. 2015. Proceedings of the 9th international workshop on semantic evaluation (semeval 2015). In *Proceedings of the 9th International Workshop on Semantic Evaluation (SemEval 2015)*.

Telmo Pires, Eva Schlinger, and Dan Garrette. 2019. How multilingual is multilingual bert? In *Proceedings of the 57th Annual Meeting of the Association for Computational Linguistics*, pages 4996–5001.

Maria Pontiki, Dimitrios Galanis, Haris Papageorgiou, Ion Androutsopoulos, Suresh Manandhar, Mohammad Al-Smadi, Mahmoud Al-Ayyoub, Yanyan Zhao, Bing Qin, Orphée De Clercq, et al. 2016. Semeval-2016 task 5: Aspect based sentiment analysis. In *10th International Workshop on Semantic Evaluation (SemEval 2016)*.

Maria Pontiki, Dimitris Galanis, John Pavlopoulos, Harris Papageorgiou, Ion Androutsopoulos, and Suresh Manandhar. 2014. SemEval-2014 task 4: Aspect based sentiment analysis. In *Proceedings of the 8th International Workshop on Semantic Evaluation (SemEval 2014)*, pages 27–35, Dublin, Ireland. Association for Computational Linguistics.

Suhan Prabhu, Pranav Goel, Alok Debnath, and Manish Shrivastava. 2019. A language invariant neural method for timeml event detection. In *Proceedings of International Conference on NLP (ICON)*.

Lance A Ramshaw and Mitchell P Marcus. 1999. Text chunking using transformation-based learning. In *Natural language processing using very large corpora*, pages 157–176. Springer.

Yashwanth Reddy Regatte, Rama Rohit Reddy Gangula, and Radhika Mamidi. 2020. Dataset creation and evaluation of aspect based sentiment analysis in telugu, a low resource language. In *Proceedings of The 12th Language Resources and Evaluation Conference*, pages 5017–5024.

Nils Reimers and Iryna Gurevych. 2017. Reporting score distributions makes a difference: Performance study of lstm-networks for sequence tagging. In *Proceedings of the 2017 Conference on Empirical Methods in Natural Language Processing*, pages 338–348.

Sara Rosenthal, Noura Farra, and Preslav Nakov. 2017. Semeval-2017 task 4: Sentiment analysis in twitter. In *Proceedings of the 11th international workshop on semantic evaluation (SemEval-2017)*, pages 502–518.

Hu Xu, Bing Liu, Lei Shu, and S Yu Philip. 2018. Double embeddings and cnn-based sequence labeling for aspect extraction. In *Proceedings of the 56th Annual Meeting of the Association for Computational Linguistics (Volume 2: Short Papers)*, pages 592–598.

Combining semantic search and twin product classification for recognition of purchasable items in voice shopping

Dieu-Thu Le
Amazon.com, Inc.
deule@amazon.com

Verena Weber
Amazon.com, Inc.
wverena@amazon.com

Melanie Bradford
Amazon.com, Inc.
neunerm@amazon.com

Abstract

The accuracy of an online shopping system via voice commands is particularly important and may have a great impact on customer trust. This paper focuses on the problem of detecting if an utterance contains actual and purchasable products, thus referring to a shopping-related intent in a typical Spoken Language Understanding architecture consisting of an intent classifier and a slot detector. Searching through billions of products to check if a detected slot is a purchasable item is prohibitively expensive. To overcome this problem, we present a framework that (1) uses a retrieval module that returns the most relevant products with respect to the detected slot, and (2) combines it with a twin network that decides if the detected slot is indeed a purchasable item or not. Through various experiments, we show that this architecture outperforms a typical slot detector approach, with a gain of +81% in accuracy and +41% in F1 score.

1 Introduction

Spoken Language Understanding (SLU) constitutes the backbone of voice-controlled devices such as Amazon Alexa or Google Assistant. SLU is typically divided into two sub-tasks, intent classification (IC) and slot filling (SF). IC determines the user's intent and slot filling (SF) extracts the semantic constituents. For instance, if a user says $buy\ batteries$, IC should classify the intent as $BuyItem$ and SF should label the utterance as $buy|Other\ batteries|ItemName$. The slot in this example is *ItemName* and the slot value is *batteries*. This constitutes a way to map the utterance on a semantic space. Throughout this paper the term carrier phrase denotes all tokens that are not part of the slot, e.g. *buy* in the previous example.

In typical SLU architectures, the final confidence score is obtained through multiplication of the two scores from the IC and the SF model. For each utterance, the model produces n-best hypotheses ranked by the final confidence score. One hypothesis consists of an intent and slot labels.

Problem statement - The complexity for both IC and SF tasks is continuously increasing due to the growth of voice-controlled device functionalities. Investigations have revealed that the model tends to put more weight on the carrier phrase than the slot value. This bias implies that particular slot labels are assigned based on the carrier phrase rather than the slot value. Since with a rising amount of functionalities carrier phrases can be identical across functionalities and the correct class then solely depends on the slot value. Label confusions are particularly observed for Shopping intents, e. g. *BuyItem*. For example, $how\ much\ is$ {*toilet paper*} / $was\ kostet$ {*Klopapier*} is a request that falls into the realm of Shopping functionalities because the user could actually purchase this item through the device. In contrast, if the user asks $how\ much\ is$ {*Ronaldo*} $worth$ / $was\ kostet$ {*Ronaldo*} the request needs to be processed by QA functionalities. Note that in German the two sentences have an identical pattern $How\ much\ is$ {*slot_value*} / $wie\ viel\ kostet$ {*slot_value*} while the carrier phrase slightly differs in English.

Shopping functionalities in a voice-controlled device have a particular importance due to their high potential impact on customer trust and experience. If a user has the feeling they could accidentally buy something, this may reduce trust in the system and drive customers away. On the contrary, not recognizing Shopping intents is equally harmful as users will not shop with the device anymore.

Contribution and approach - In this paper, we focus on solving the problem of label confusions, where detected slots are mistaken as *ItemName*,

Proceedings of the 4th Workshop on e-Commerce and NLP (ECNLP 4), pages 150–157
August 5, 2021.

hence are routed to Shopping (false accept) and the other way around, when an item name is not identified as *ItemName*, hence are not correctly handled as Shopping (false reject). In order to correctly determine if an item is purchasable or non-purchasable, one needs to match the *ItemName* candidates to products sold on the respective platform. If the item is similar (enough) to products in the product catalog, it is purchasable.

A straightforward way of solving this problem is to search through the whole Shopping catalog to identify if the detected slot is found within the catalog or not through simple string or substring matching. However, this approach has two main drawbacks: First, it is extremely expensive to search through the full catalog for all slot candidates and is therefore prohibitive in real applications. Second, the approach is not precise and does not utilize meaning at all. Take the non-purchasable *ItemName* candidate *lamborghini* as an example. A Lamborghini cannot be purchased on e-commerce platforms and is therefore non-purchasable in this context. String or substring matching however returns matches like *lego lamborghini, toy lamborghini* from the product catalog and as such would indicate that a lamborghini could be bought through the device. Instead, we need an approach that is able to detect the difference between a *lego lamborghini* and a *lamborghini*.

To improve the accuracy of the detected slots with respect to the *ItemName* entities, we propose to combine a retrieval module with a Twin Product Classifier. Instead of searching through all billions of possible products, this approach uses a twin network (Bromley et al., 1994; Reimers and Gurevych, 2019a) to compare the candidate slot only with the semantically most similar products returned by the retrieval module from the product catalog. By looking at negative (non-purchasable) and positive (purchasable) examples of *ItemName* candidates and their matched (retrieved) items from the product catalog, the twin network learns to pull together pairs that result in a correct match (positive) and push apart pairs that are not a match (negative). The Twin Product Classifier can be used as a signal to adjust the final confidence scores for the n-best hypotheses from IC-SF.

This framework overcomes the problem of high numbers of false accept and false reject for Shopping functionalities in voice-controlled devices, while taking into account the efficiency and speed requirement for a real world application.

2 Related Work

Pre-trained transformer (Devlin et al., 2018; Liu et al., 2019) models have proven successful in many language applications including Spoken Language Understanding (SLU) (Radfar et al., 2020; Chen et al., 2019; Do and Gaspers, 2019). Transformers are typically used to create an embedding of input tokens that is then fed to a downstream task. However, as explained in more detail by Reimers and Gurevych (2019a), transformer models such as BERT are unsuitable for semantic similarity search as well as for unsupervised tasks like clustering. Reimers and Gurevych (2019a) therefore proposed Sentence-BERT (SBERT). SBERT is a modification of the pretrained BERT network based on a twin network to derive semantically meaningful sentence embeddings that can be compared via cosine similarly.

In e-commerce, product retrieval plays a key role and is a well-researched topic (Lu et al.; Ahuja et al., 2020). E-commerce systems typically perform two steps: a retrieval and a ranking step. In the retrieval step relevant products are retrieved from the product catalog. In the second step, the retrieved products are ranked by relevance with respect to the query. Semantic search (Huang et al., 2020; Nigam et al., 2019; Johnson et al., 2017; Huang et al., 2013) is state-of-the-art for product retrieval and replaced previously prevalent keyword matching (Schütze et al., 2008).

In this paper we propose a product retrieval stage in the context of SLU to retrieve potential matches for tokens labelled as *ItemName* by the SF model (*ItemName* candidate) from a product catalog. We then replace the ranking stage with a similarity-based classification to identify if the ItemName *candidate* is indeed a purchasable item or not. The goal of this approach is to reduce false accepts and false rejects for voice commerce functionalities as explained in Section 1.

3 Twin Product Classifier

In order to solve the problem of deciding if an *ItemName* candidate is purchasable or non-purchasable, we leverage information from the product catalog and employ a twin network to differentiate between these two categories. Figure 1 illustrates the general architecture of the proposed approach, which consists of two main components: (1) the catalog

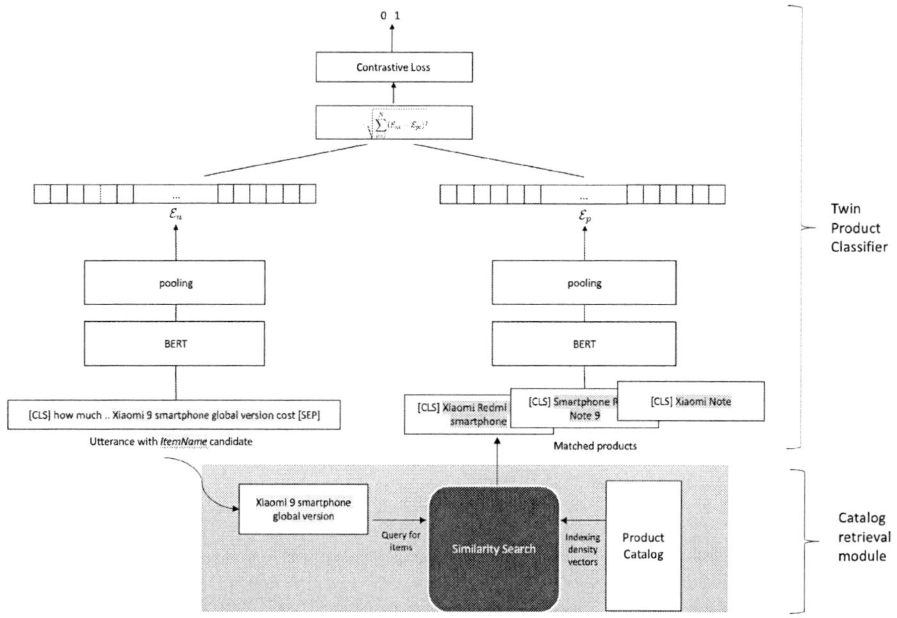

Figure 1: The general architecture of the Twin Product Classifier

retrieval module and (2) the Twin Product Classifier. In the retrieval module, the detected *ItemName* candidate will be matched with similar items indexed from the product catalog in order to find the best matching items with respect to the candidate. After that, we employ a twin network architecture (Bromley et al., 1994) and pass the original utterance on the left side and the set of matching items on the right side. Instead of learning to classify the inputs, twin networks aim at learning to differentiate between two inputs, i.e., to learn the similarity between them and to identify pairs that don't match. The similarity between these two parts (the original utterance vs. the matching items) will be computed. After that, the twin network is trained using a contrastive loss to learn to differentiate between pairs of utterances and matching catalog items to finally decide if the given item name is purchasable, i.e., could be matched with items from the product catalog.

Let u be an input utterance and c_u be the *ItemName* candidate that this utterance contains. Our task is to decide if u should be classified as a Shopping intent or not based on checking if c_u is a purchasable product. Note that the candidate c_u is provided by the n-best hypotheses from the IC-SF architecture described in the previous section. From the product catalog, we retrieve a set of products $p = \{p_1, p_2, .., p_k\}$ that are semantically most similar to c_u, with $p \in \mathbf{P}$ where $\mathbf{P}$ denotes the product catalog. u and p are passed through the twin network, which yields two embeddings $\mathcal{E}_u$ and $\mathcal{E}_p$ respectively. We define a pair of utterance u and matched products p to be positive if the *ItemName* candidate c_u contained in u can be potentially found in the product catalog $\mathbf{P}$ and negative if c_u is a non-purchasable item.
Once p is retrieved from the catalog, we compute the distance between $\mathcal{E}_u$ and $\mathcal{E}_p$ using the Euclidean distance and the contrastive loss $\mathcal{L}$:

$$\begin{aligned}\mathcal{L}(u,p) = y * d(\mathcal{E}_u, \mathcal{E}_p)^2 + (1-y) \\ * \max(\tau - d(\mathcal{E}_u, \mathcal{E}_p), 0)^2\end{aligned} \tag{1}$$

where y denotes the output, which is 0 for negative samples and 1 for positive samples. The distance d is computed as:

$$d(\mathcal{E}_u, \mathcal{E}_p) = \sqrt{\sum_{i=1}^{N} (\mathcal{E}_{ui} - \mathcal{E}_{pi})^2} \tag{2}$$

N is the embedding size and τ the margin parameter which determines the minimum distance a pair should have in order to be classified as negative. The final loss is the sum of both positive and negative loss. Contrastive loss has been shown to be very effective for training twin networks (Radenovic et al., 2017; Reimers and Gurevych, 2019b), which pulls together similar pairs and push dissimilar pairs apart. The gradient of the constrastive loss is computed as:

$$\nabla\mathcal{L}(u,p) = \begin{cases} d(\mathcal{E}_u, \mathcal{E}_p) & y = 1 \\ min(d(\mathcal{E}_u, \mathcal{E}_p) - \tau, 0) & y = 0 \end{cases} \quad (3)$$

In practice, to accelerate the training process and improve the performance, we employ online contrastive loss, which selects only hard positive and hard negative samples in each mini-batch. In particular, the distance between each pair is computed and the loss is only added for pairs with the smallest or biggest distances.

With the aim of finding the best set of matching products p for an *ItemName* candidate c_u, we argue that the top products returned by fast semantic search provide essential information to the twin network to learn the similarity between c_u and p for purchasable items and generalize on unseen items. Keyword exact match search is usually faster using a reverse indexing system, but is limited since it cannot find items that are differently spelled, written or semantically close.

We use FAISS (Johnson et al., 2017), a library that has shown to be fast and efficient in similarity search for billion-scale data sets. FAISS takes embedded catalog vectors as inputs and starts the indexing process, which involves clustering the data into different clusters represented by their centroids - which are used as inverted file or index. When a query vector comes in, the most suitable cluster found based on its similarity with the centroids is returned together with the top K nearest items. FAISS is implemented for running both in CPU and GPU, supporting single and multi-GPUs together with batch processing. The encoding and indexing of $\mathbf{P}$ is done once completely offline and could be stored in memory for instant RAM search of incoming *ItemName* candidates c_u.

Integration of the Twin Product Classifier into the SLU system

Finally, the integration of the Twin Product Classifier in the whole SLU architecture is displayed in Figure 2. It illustrates the previous SLU architecture (IC-SF) on the left and the added Twin Product Classifier on the right. The IC-SF component illustrated on the left side is an independent part that one can integrate together with the twin product classifier proposed here. The flow would be as follows: the utterance is first encoded using character, positional and catalog embeddings. The catalog embedding is a fixed-size real vector for each token that indicates if the token or a substring of the token is present in one of the catalogs. Note that the product catalog used for generating the catalog embedding is a superset of the product catalog used in the Twin Product Classifier (see next Section 4.2). This first-stage embedding is then fed through a tinyBERT encoder block. The resulting encoding is then passed to the respective decoders, the SF and the IC decoder. Since the model as is has difficulties to distinguish between purchasable and non-purchasable items, we pass the utterances with *ItemName* candidates in the n-best hypothesis through the Twin Product Classifier. Dependent on the classifier feedback, the Shopping IC-SF score can be adjusted accordingly.

4 Data

4.1 Product catalog

We replace the full product catalog with the top product search queries to reduce the size and improve the matching between c_u and $p \in \mathbf{P}$. The product catalog entries contain too many details that a user would usually not include in their request, e.g *Samsung Galaxy Book Pro 15.6" — i5 11th Gen, 8GB Memory, 512GB SSD — Mystic Blue — (NP950XDB-KB2US) 2021* versus just *Samsung Galaxy Book Pro*. Moreover, the actual product catalog has a size and granularity that is not needed to detect if an item is purchasable or not. The top one million search queries already cover a wide variety of products and product categories that are representative of the full product catalog. Note that the this catalog is a subset of the catalog used for the catalog embedding in IC-SF. For simplicity, we will refer to the one million product search queries as product catalog.

4.2 Training and test data

We use a dataset with positive and negative examples to train the classifier. One example contains *(utterance, ItemName candidate, product matches, class label)*. The *ItemName* candidate is produced by the IC-SF architecture. The catalog matches are retrieved via semantic search from the product catalog using the *ItemName* candidate as a query. The data was collected and annotated over the time span of one year. All data is in German and anonymized such that users are not identifiable.

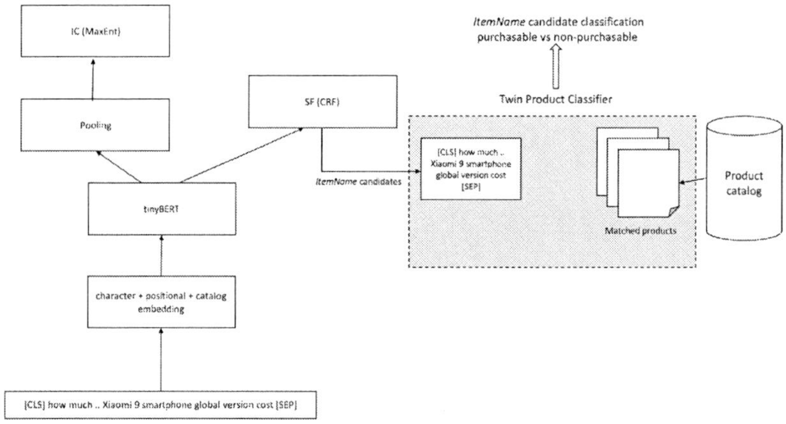

Figure 2: Integrating the Twin Product Classifier into the SLU system

To create positive and negative examples, we use all utterances for which any slot in the n-best hypotheses from IC-SF is an *ItemName* slot. The hypothesized slot is recorded as *ItemName* candidate. If the ground-truth annotation of the utterance is Shopping, the utterance serves as positive example. If the ground-truth annotation is not Shopping, we use it as a negative example. Table 1 shows that we have slightly more negative than positive examples in our dataset.

Table 2 displays the sequence length distribution for utterance, *ItemName* candidate and product matches when split by white space. While the utterances tend to be rather short sentences (on average only 5.8 tokens), the slot value can take up a substantial portion of the request itself, on average 2.2 tokens out of 5.8. For each *ItemName* candidate an average of about 19 product matches is retrieved from the product catalog using semantic search.

Dataset	Share unique *ItemName* cand.	Share positive
train	35 %	41 %
test	51 %	41 %

Table 1: Dataset statistics.

	Utterance	Item name candidate	Product matches
mean	5.8	2.2	19.0
std	2.5	1.6	8.8
min	1.0	1.0	10.0
25 %	4.0	1.0	11.0
50 %	5.0	2.0	18.0
75 %	7.0	3.0	24.0
max	53.0	30.0	85.0

Table 2: Sequence length distribution when split by white space for training set. Displays min, max, mean, std and standard quantiles of number of tokens in sequence.

5 Results

5.1 Experimental setup

BERT model for Twin network - For the BERT embedding block shown in Figure 1, we use a pretrained German BERT model, gbert-base (Chan et al., 2020; Devlin et al., 2018), fine-tuned on annotated data sampled from live traffic. For fine-tuning we use a dataset of 1.5 million live traffic utterances. Shopping utterances as well as Shopping false rejects are upsampled moderately in this dataset. The BERT model is fine-tuned in a multi-task fashion to predict two binary targets: (1) is the utterance a Shopping utterance or not, (2) is the utterance a Shopping false reject or not. Later we discard the classification layer and only use the fine-tuned BERT for the purposes of this paper.
Retrieval module - We see that semantic search works well for numbers (e.g., *hundred liter* matches *100 liter*) and different variants of a product (*i. phone x.* matches *i phone x, i phone xs*, *öl* matches *öle*). The results are quite as expected: the matches for shoppable items are usually more relevant, whereas the matches for negative examples are not immediate matches (e.g., *porsche* is matched with *porges, porsche shoes, porsche lego, porsche knife, porsche book, porsche watch*).
Twin network setup - For the implementation of

the classifier, we use the sentence transformer package[1] to setup the experiments. In each experiment, we set the number of epochs to four, the batch size for the contrastive loss is 64 and the margin τ is 0.5. We experiment with two more loss functions, multiple negatives ranking loss and multi-task learning loss. The multiple negatives ranking loss is defined as follows: Let $\{u_i, p_i\}$ be all positive pairs in our training data. Multiple negative ranking loss will generate all $\{u_i, p_j\}$ for $\forall i \neq j$ and compute the negative log-likelihood (Reimers and Gurevych, 2019b). The multi-task learning loss combines both contrastive loss and multiple negatives ranking loss by alternating between both in each batch. For experiments with the multiple negatives ranking loss and the multi-task learning loss we use a batch size of 128 together with a max sequence length of 50.

5.2 Experimental results

We design the experiments to (1) quantify the effect of the number the retrieved products, (2) compare the effect of adding the Twin Product Classifier to the original IC-SF classifier outputs. Finally, we conduct a couple of experiments using different loss functions such as multiple negatives ranking and multi-task learning and compare them to the contrastive loss, as well as cosine, Manhattan and Euclidean distance measurement in the twin network.

First of all, we compare our proposed system to the baseline, which takes the utterance as input and the hypothesis ranked first to classify if the utterance has a Shopping intent. In this baseline, the catalog is used to produce a catalog embedding to encode the utterance, but no product classifier is used. The results of this experiment are reported in Table 3.

We see a significant improvement in both accuracy (+81.6%) and F1 score (+42.2%) when adding the product classifier compared to the baseline using only intent and slot classifier with catalog embeddings as input. We observe a slight decrease in recall of -11.6% compared to an increase of +97.7% in precision. This is due to the fact that the dataset created for training and testing as described in Section 4 contains many more false accept samples than false reject samples. This is the case since the dataset was created by pulling and annotating utterances where any of the hypothesis in the n-best from IC-SF was Shopping and contained an *ItemName* slot, hence entails that IC-SF Shopping false accepts are much better represented in the dataset than IC-SF Shopping false rejects. This is hard to circumvent since annotating random samples from the overall live traffic only yields few IC-SF Shopping false rejects. Therefore, creating a dataset with many false reject samples is challenging due to the annotation limits.

Metrics	Twin Product Classifier
Accuracy	+81.58%
F1	+42.27%
Precision	+97.67%
Recall	-11.55%

Table 3: Relative difference between the baseline and Twin Product Classifier. Note that the IC-SF architecture is evaluated here on a binary task similar to the Twin Product Classifier. The IC-SF classification is evaluated as correct if the first hypothesis is a Shopping intent.

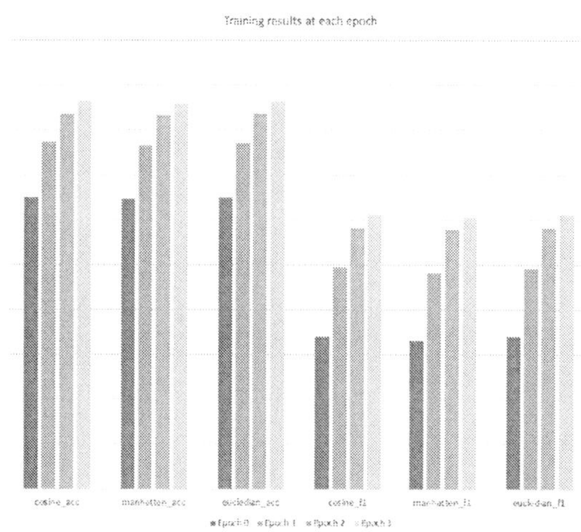

Figure 3: Performance on validation set in terms of Accuracy & F1 at each epoch using cosine, Manhattan and Euclidean distance.

We quantify the effect of the number of retrieved products in the retrieval module by comparing the results of the classifier when using only the first matched item vs. using the top five matched items. As expected, retrieving more relevant products instead of using only the first matched product gives a much better result with a gain of +14.95% in accuracy and +10.88% in precision. Interestingly, we also see a small increase in recall when using only one matched product. This can be explained by the

[1]https://github.com/UKPLab/sentence-transformers/

fact that when using only one matched item, it is likely to classify more items as purchasable (positive) and get a few more false accepts since the first matching item might not reflect the full characteristics of the *ItemName* candidate. An example we often observe is when a user searches for a Lamborghini (which is not purchasable on e-commerce platforms), the returned matches are Lamborghini toys, legos, etc. Retrieving more matching items helps to better characterize and hence to give better accuracy for purchasable items.

Metrics	Cosine similarity	Manhattan distance	Euclidean distance
Accuracy	+14.95%	+14.92%	+14.95%
F1	+10.69%	+10.84%	+10.88%
Precision	+23.30%	+24.95%	+23.88%
Recall	-3.65%	-4.88%	-3.85%

Table 4: Relative difference between the system using the first matching product and the top five matching products

In the next experiment, we further extend the left side of the twin network with the whole utterance, instead of using only the *ItemName* candidate. We see a big gain in both accuracy (+8.5%) and F1 (+9.72%) (Table 5). In this case, the whole utterance is proven to contain important information for deciding if the intent is related to Shopping or not. Hence extending the comparison between *itemName* candidates and matched products with the whole utterance information is beneficial.

Metrics	Cosine similarity	Manhattan distance	Euclidean distance
Accuracy	+8.53%	+8.49%	+8.54%
F1	+9.79%	+9.64%	+9.72%
Precision	+18.72%	+18.11%	+18.26%
Recall	+1.17%	+1.56%	+1.44%

Table 5: Relative difference between the system using only the *ItemName* candidate vs. using the whole utterance in training the classifier

Next, we quantify the effect of different similarity and distance measures for computing the contrastive loss (Table 6). Taking the cosine similarity as the baseline, we compute the relative changes when using the Manhattan distance and Euclidean distance. From the experimental results, we do not see much difference overall with respect to using different distance measures. Euclidean distance gives a slightly better result though.

Finally, we evaluate the impact of using different loss functions for our approach. We compare online contrastive loss with multiple negatives ranking loss and the multi-task loss. The results are reported in Table 7. We see that using the multiple negatives ranking loss function as well as the multi-task loss function gives much lower performance than the contrastive loss. The multiple negatives ranking loss function is usually more useful in the information retrieval use case, when one has more positive pairs. Overall, the contrastive loss function has shown to yield the best performance for this use case.

Metrics	Manhattan distance	Euclidean distance
Accuracy	-0.03%	+0.01%
F1	-0.11%	+0.00%
Precision	+0.50%	-0.14%
Recall	-0.70%	+0.10%

Table 6: Relative difference when using different distance metrics (with cosine similarity as the baseline)

Metrics	Negative ranking	Multi-task loss
Accuracy	-30.02%	-12.64%
F1	-32.33%	-13.21%
Precision	-50.74%	-22.56%
Recall	+6.23%	-1.69%

Table 7: Relative difference when using alternative loss functions compared to online contrastive loss

We also report the performance (Accuracy and F1) at each epoch measured on a validation set that has same size and class distribution as the test set for the three different distance metrics, where we see steady improvement at each epoch (Figure 3).

6 Conclusion

We have presented an architecture with a retrieval module and a twin product classification module to verify if a detected *ItemName* slot from the SF model contains a purchasable item or not. The experimental results have shown the effectiveness of the framework to increase accuracy by +81% for purchasable item detection. For the retrieval module, we have experimented with different numbers of matching products returned by semantic search. We showed that using the top five most relevant product names yields the best results. Moreover, adding the whole utterance in the twin network and using an online contrastive loss function resulted in the best performance. This approach can be leveraged in a voice-based shopping system to decrease the number of false rejects and false accepts and thereby improve customer experience.

References

Aman Ahuja, Nikhil Rao, Sumeet Katariya, Karthik Subbian, and Chandan K Reddy. 2020. Language-agnostic representation learning for product search on e-commerce platforms. In *Proceedings of the 13th International Conference on Web Search and Data Mining*, pages 7–15.

Jane Bromley, Isabelle Guyon, Yann LeCun, Eduard Säckinger, and Roopak Shah. 1994. Signature verification using a "siamese" time delay neural network. In *Advances in Neural Information Processing Systems*, volume 6. Morgan-Kaufmann.

Branden Chan, Stefan Schweter, and Timo Möller. 2020. German's next language model. *arXiv preprint arXiv:2010.10906*.

Q. Chen, Z. Zhuo, and W. Wang. 2019. Bert for joint intent classification and slot filling. *arXiv:1902.10909*.

Jacob Devlin, Ming-Wei Chang, Kenton Lee, and Kristina Toutanova. 2018. Bert: Pre-training of deep bidirectional transformers for language understanding.

Quynh Ngoc Thi Do and Judith Gaspers. 2019. Cross-lingual transfer learning for spoken language understanding. In *ICASSP 2019-2019 IEEE International Conference on Acoustics, Speech and Signal Processing (ICASSP)*, pages 5956–5960. IEEE.

Jui-Ting Huang, Ashish Sharma, Shuying Sun, Li Xia, David Zhang, Philip Pronin, Janani Padmanabhan, Giuseppe Ottaviano, and Linjun Yang. 2020. Embedding-based retrieval in facebook search. In *Proceedings of the 26th ACM SIGKDD International Conference on Knowledge Discovery & Data Mining*, pages 2553–2561.

Po-Sen Huang, Xiaodong He, Jianfeng Gao, Li Deng, Alex Acero, and Larry Heck. 2013. Learning deep structured semantic models for web search using clickthrough data. In *Proceedings of the 22nd ACM international conference on Information & Knowledge Management*, pages 2333–2338.

Jeff Johnson, Matthijs Douze, and Hervé Jégou. 2017. Billion-scale similarity search with gpus. *CoRR*, abs/1702.08734.

Yinhan Liu, Myle Ott, Naman Goyal, Jingfei Du, Mandar Joshi, Danqi Chen, Omer Levy, Mike Lewis, Luke Zettlemoyer, and Veselin Stoyanov. 2019. Roberta: A robustly optimized bert pretraining approach. *arXiv preprint arXiv:1907.11692*.

Hanqing Lu, Youna Hu, Tong Zhao, Tony Wu, Yiwei Song, and Bing Yin. Graph-based multilingual product retrieval in e-commerce search.

Priyanka Nigam, Yiwei Song, Vijai Mohan, Vihan Lakshman, Weitian Ding, Ankit Shingavi, Choon Hui Teo, Hao Gu, and Bing Yin. 2019. Semantic product search. In *Proceedings of the 25th ACM SIGKDD International Conference on Knowledge Discovery & Data Mining*, pages 2876–2885.

Filip Radenovic, Giorgos Tolias, and Ondrej Chum. 2017. Fine-tuning CNN image retrieval with no human annotation. *CoRR*, abs/1711.02512.

Martin Radfar, Athanasios Mouchtaris, and Siegfried Kunzmann. 2020. End-to-end neural transformer based spoken language understanding. *arXiv preprint arXiv:2008.10984*.

Nils Reimers and Iryna Gurevych. 2019a. Sentence-BERT: Sentence embeddings using Siamese BERT-networks. In *Proceedings of the 2019 Conference on Empirical Methods in Natural Language Processing and the 9th International Joint Conference on Natural Language Processing (EMNLP-IJCNLP)*, pages 3982–3992, Hong Kong, China. Association for Computational Linguistics.

Nils Reimers and Iryna Gurevych. 2019b. Sentence-BERT: Sentence embeddings using Siamese BERT-networks. In *Proceedings of the 2019 Conference on Empirical Methods in Natural Language Processing and the 9th International Joint Conference on Natural Language Processing (EMNLP-IJCNLP)*, pages 3982–3992, Hong Kong, China. Association for Computational Linguistics.

Hinrich Schütze, Christopher D Manning, and Prabhakar Raghavan. 2008. *Introduction to information retrieval*, volume 39. Cambridge University Press Cambridge.

Improving Factual Consistency of Abstractive Summarization on Customer Feedback

Yang Liu, Yifei Sun, Vincent Gao
Amazon, Inc.
{yngliun, sunyifei, vincegao}@amazon.com

Abstract

E-commerce stores collect customer feedback to let sellers learn about customer concerns and enhance customer order experience. Because customer feedback often contains redundant information, a concise summary of the feedback can be generated to help sellers better understand the issues causing customer dissatisfaction. Previous state-of-the-art abstractive text summarization models make two major types of factual errors when producing summaries from customer feedback, which are *wrong entity detection* (WED) and *incorrect product-defect description* (IPD). In this work, we introduce a set of methods to enhance the factual consistency of abstractive summarization on customer feedback. We augment the training data with artificially corrupted summaries, and use them as counterparts of the target summaries. We add a contrastive loss term into the training objective so that the model learns to avoid certain factual errors. Evaluation results show that a large portion of WED and IPD errors are alleviated for BART and T5. Furthermore, our approaches do not depend on the structure of the summarization model and thus are generalizable to any abstractive summarization systems.

1 Introduction

In order to improve customer order experience, most e-commerce stores allow customers to submit reviews or feedback via their post-order communication channels. Such customer feedback, usually in the form of short paragraphs of free texts, contains information reflecting the issues that customers experienced in their purchases. This information can be shared with sellers to bring their awareness on the problems in their products. However, customer feedback often include other contents that are irrelevant to the product issues. Such redundant information requires extra efforts for sellers to fully understand the customers major concerns, and sometimes even causes confusion.

Source: (...) I ordered this mouse for my new laptop. However, when I received it, I could see many scratches on the product. It looks like it has been used before. (...) **Reference Summary**: The mouse delivered has many scratches. It looks like it has been used. **Model Summary**: The laptop came with many scratches, looks like it has been used.
Source: (...) I checked the serial number and found it doesn't match the one on the website. This phone is not defective. I question the source of this product (...) **Reference Summary**: The phone serial number doesn't match the one on the website but the phone is not defective. **Model Summary**: This phone is defective and the serial number doesn't match the one on the website.

Table 1: Examples of the two major factual errors: WED (upper) and IPD (lower).

To reduce the redundancy, a concise summary of customer feedback can be provided where the information is concentrated on the product issues while other irrelevant contents are filtered out. Such summary allows sellers to quickly capture and comprehend the problems, and thus they can address buyer dissatisfaction more efficiently.

The problem of generating summaries from customer feedback is modeled as a text summarization task (Nallapati et al., 2016; Allahyari et al., 2017; Gao et al., 2020) in the natural language processing (NLP) domain. Abstractive summarization models with transformer-based architecture have achieved success in a variety of summarization tasks (Lewis et al., 2020; Raffel et al., 2020; Zhang et al., 2020; Bao et al., 2020). Hence, we harnessed the recent state-of-the-art (SOTA) abstractive summarization models, BART (Lewis et al., 2020) and T5 (Raffel et al., 2020), and fine tuned the models for our specific summarization task. We aim to utilize summarization models to produce the summary that can correctly describe the product issues presented in customer feedback. However, from human evalu-

Proceedings of the 4th Workshop on e-Commerce and NLP (ECNLP 4), pages 158–163
August 5, 2021.

ation results, we observed that the summary generated by these abstractive summarization models sometimes contains the information that is inconsistent with facts in the input text. Such factual inconsistencies have also been observed in previous studies (Cao et al., 2018; Kryscinski et al., 2019, 2020). More specifically, we analyzed 75 inconsistent summaries obtained from human evaluations on more than 600 model-generated summaries. We found that around 70% factual inconsistent summaries [1] follow two error patterns: *wrong entity detection* (WED) and *incorrect product-defect description* (IPD). The error of WED often occurs in the cases where the feedback text involves multiple entities but the models fail to detect the primary entity. For IPD, the generated summary contains the product-defect description that contradicts with the original description in the customer feedback. Table 1 shows the examples [2] of the two types of factual errors.

In this work, we propose a set of methods in order to improve the factual consistency of abstractive summarization on customer feedback. We first introduce specific factual errors into each target summary to generate their negative counterpart. We then use such pair of consistent and inconsistent summaries with a contrastive loss term added in the training objective to enhance the model's robustness against the two major factual errors.

Our contributions are two folds. First, The proposed approaches with corrupted summary generation and contrastive loss augmentation do not pose requirements on the achitecture of the summarization model. Thus, they can be applied to any abstraction-based summarization model to improve the model faithfulness. Second, we test the proposed approaches on SOTA summarization algorithms such as BART and T5. Our approaches show large benefits in reducing the common factual errors in customer-feedback summarization.

2 Related Work

There have been increasing research attentions on improving the factual consistency of abstractive summarization models. Lots of priors work focused on different ways of adding external signals or constraints to enhance the summary generation. Cao et al. (2018) built a dual-attention framework so that the summary generation is conditioned on both the source document and extracted key information. Li et al. (2018) incorporated the entailment knowledge by utilizing entailment-aware encoder and decoder. With using the textual entailment, Falke et al. (2019) re-ranked the candidates summaries to select the summary that's better aligned with the source document. Dou et al. (2020) studied different external signals, including key sentences, keywords and relations, and used them in addition to the input text to guide the summary generation. Mao et al. (2020) constrained certain tokens to require them to be present in the summary. Similarly, Yuan et al. (2020) add constraints on the model to include certain attribute words in the product summarization. Zhu et al. (2021) integrated information extraction and graph attention network into transformer-based seq2seq framework.

To identify and correct the unfaithful summaries, Wang et al. (2020) proposed to use a question answering framework to check the faithfulness of the summary while Dong et al. (2020) built a factual correction model that leverages knowledge learned from question answering models. Kryscinski et al. (2020) trained a BERT-based model to classify whether the summary is factual consistent. Cao et al. (2020) and Zhu et al. (2021) developed factual corrector based on BART (Lewis et al., 2020) and UniLM (Dong et al., 2019), as a post-processor to rectify factual errors from the upstream summarization model. They corrupted the reference summaries with artificial errors and used them as the negative samples for training the correctors. In our work, we also generate corrupted summaries as the negative counterparts of the target summaries. The difference is that, instead of building a separate corrector model, we directly engineer the training objective of the summarization model. By leveraging contrastive learning (Schroff et al., 2015; Khosla et al., 2020), we define contrasive losses to guide the output summary away from certain factual errors.

3 Proposed Approaches

Our error analysis of customer-feedback summarizaton showed that most of the factual errors belong to two error types: WED and IPD. Hence, in our proposed approaches, we first apply rule-based transformations and introduce synthetic factual errors of the two error patterns into the target summaries. We then modify the training objective by

[1] The rest of the unfaithful summaries are due to miscellaneous factual errors that are hard to cluster.

[2] Due to confidentiality, all customer feedback examples in this paper are composed by the authors.

Source: (...) I've bought cheese from this store for many times, and they were very good. So I think other products must be good too. Then I ordered several bottles of milk. But they are clearly expired (...) **Reference Summary**: Milk delivered is expired. **Corrupted Summary**: Cheese delivered is expired.
Source: (...) The eggs I purchased have bad smells. They don't look like fresh eggs. (...) **Reference Summary**: Eggs have bad smells, and don't look like fresh eggs. **Corrupted Summary**: Eggs have good smells, and don't look like fresh eggs.

Table 2: Examples of corrupted summaries. We replace the primary entity in the first example and switch the description in the second example.

adding the contrastive loss so as to guide the model to avoid those mistakes.

3.1 Synthetic Factual Errors

We augment the training data by applying two types of corruption methods on the target summary. The corruptions are designed to mimic the factual errors we observed. In the first method, we replace the named entities in the target summary with the other random entities of the same type in the source document. If no such replacement entity can be found in the source document, we randomly pick one from the top 50 appeared entities in our dataset. We used Spacy toolkit (Honnibal et al., 2020) for the named entity extraction. In the second method, we use predefined rules to transform the product-defect description in the target summary. We detect the adjectives describing the product defect and switch their sentiment. There are two ways that we change the description. One is by adding negation word *not* before the adjective. For example, we alter *"product is broken"* to *"product is not broken"*. If word *not* is already presented, we will remove it instead. The other way is by switching a descriptive word to the one with opposite meaning, such as changing *"opened"* to *"sealed"*. Table 2 shows some examples of the corrupted summaries.

3.2 Training Objective

For each training sample, we now have a triplet (d, s_+, s_-) consisting of the source document d, target summary s_+, and corrupted summary s_-. The summarization model takes d as the input and generates the output o. Our training objective is to drive the model output o to resemble s_+ while at the same time avoiding the factual errors presented in s_-. Inspired by contrastive learning (Schroff et al., 2015; Khosla et al., 2020), we compare different contrastive loss functions for model training.

Direct Contrast Compared to the ordinary loss function for summarization, we add an extra term that takes into account the informration from corrupted summary:

$$\mathcal{L}_{DC} = \mathcal{L}(s_+, o) - \alpha * \mathcal{L}(s_-, o)$$

where $\mathcal{L}(s_+, o)$ is the cross entropy loss between s_+ and o, $\mathcal{L}(s_-, o)$ is the cross entropy loss between s_- and o, and α is a tunable hyperparameter controlling the impact from the second term. The loss function will purely focus on the difference between s_+ and s_- if $\alpha = 1.0$. Thus, we generally use small value for α to ensure the model will produce fluent summary.

Constrained Negative Here, we add a margin term M to constrain the value of $\mathcal{L}(s_-, o)$:

$$\mathcal{L}_{CN} = \mathcal{L}(s_+, o) + \alpha * \max\Big(M - \mathcal{L}(s_-, o), 0\Big)$$

For easy negatives with $\mathcal{L}(s_-, o) > M$, their effects won't be taken into account during training as the model can confidently distinguish them from positive samples.

Constrained Contrast We augment the ordinary loss function for summarization with a constrained contrastive term:

$$\mathcal{L}_{CC} = \mathcal{L}(s_+, o) + \alpha * \max\Big(\mathcal{L}(s_+, o) + M - \mathcal{L}(s_-, o), 0\Big)$$

In this formula, the model is not only trained towards predicting correct labels but also deviating from certain factual errors extracted from the contrast between the negative and positive samples.

4 Experiments

4.1 Dataset

We collected 10,000 samples of negative customer feedback from the post-order communication channels of e-commerce stores. We asked subject matter experts to generate summary for each customer feedback text with emphasis on extracting the information related to product issues. The summary is required to contain the (1) primary item names and (2) descriptions about the product defects associated with the items, if they are presented in the customer feedback. We use the human-produced summary as the target summary in model training. The train/test split ratio is 85:15.

Model	ROUGE-1	ROUGE-2	ROUGE-L
BART$_{+corruption, \mathcal{L}_{DC}}$	+0.30	+0.36	+0.49
BART$_{+corruption, \mathcal{L}_{CN}}$	+0.54	+0.01	+0.59
BART$_{+corruption, \mathcal{L}_{CC}}$	**+0.83**	**+1.12**	**+0.68**
T5$_{+corruption, \mathcal{L}_{DC}}$	+0.05	-0.19	+0.04
T5$_{+corruption, \mathcal{L}_{CN}}$	+0.20	+0.08	+0.25
T5$_{+corruption, \mathcal{L}_{CC}}$	**+0.45**	**+0.71**	**+0.43**

Table 3: Impact of our approaches on ROUGE scores. The reported numbers are relative changes of ROUGE scores compared to the ordinary fine-tuned BART and T5 models, respectively[4].

4.2 Model

We use two recently proposed abstractive summarization models, BART (Lewis et al., 2020) and T5 (Raffel et al., 2020), for customer-feedback summarization. We adopt the pretrained models from the HuggingFace implementation [3] and fine tune the models on our training dataset. Both models share the same training parameters including learning rate as 5e-5, $\alpha = 0.05$ in $\mathcal{L}_{DC}$, $(\alpha = 0.5, M = 2.0)$ in $\mathcal{L}_{CN}$, and $(\alpha = 0.5, M = 5.0)$ in $\mathcal{L}_{CC}$.

4.3 Evaluation metrics

We employ the ROUGE-1, ROUGE-2, and ROUGE-L scores (Lin, 2004) to ensure that our proposed methods do not degrade the fluency and continuity of the generated summary. These ROUGE scores measure the accuracy based on unigrams, bigrams, and longest subsequences.

We rely on the human evaluation to examine the factual consistency of the model output. We ask human annotators to classify the faithfulness of generated summary into *consistent* and *inconsistent* based on whether there are inaccurate or contradictory facts. We then compare the summary consistency before and after implementing the proposed methods.

5 Results

5.1 ROUGE Scores

We report the changes of ROUGE scores[4] in Table 3. Results show that the models trained with our correction methods generally have improvements on the ROUGE scores compared to the original BART and T5 models. Higher scores imply that the summaries from the corrected models are better aligned with the target summaries. In addition, using $\mathcal{L}_{CC}$ as the loss function turns out to produce the highest ROUGE scores for both BART and T5. Thus, for human evaluation, we will focus on the summaries produced by the models trained with $\mathcal{L}_{CC}$.

Model	Error Type	% Corrected
BART	WED	63.6
	IPD	50.0
T5	WED	46.7
	IPD	42.1

Table 4: Percentage of corrected WED and IPD errors for BART and T5. Comparisons are made between the ordinary models and the models trained with $\mathcal{L}_{CC}$.

Model	% Consis. to Inconsist.
BART	1.2
T5	2.1

Table 5: Percentage of cases where the summaries from the ordinary models are factual consistent but become inconsistent after our methods are applied.

5.2 Human Evaluation and Analysis

The human evaluation included 124 examples for BART and 600 examples for T5, all of which were randomly sampled from the test set. Table 4 shows the effect of our approaches on correcting the two major factual errors. As the results show, a large portion of the WED and IPD errors are corrected. Over 63% WED and 50% IPD mistakes from ordinary BART are rectified. For T5, our methods are able to correct around 46% WED and 42% IPD errors. It implies our models perform more robustly on the cases that can potentially lead to WED and IPD.

One remaining question is whether our approaches would degrade the originally faithful summaries. In Table 5, we report the percentage of cases where the summaries from the ordinary mod-

[3]https://huggingface.co/transformers/

[4]Absolute ROUGE scores are not shown due to confidentiality.

Source: (...) I bought this expensive TV that's supposed to have good screen and built-in wifi connection. But this one runs with lots of lagging, not as advertised on the website. (...)
Original: Screen runs with lots of lagging, not as advertised.
After: TV runs with lots of lagging, not as advertised.

Source: (...) The packaging is heavily damaged and opened, though the product inside is not broken. The seller should be careful on the packaging next time (...)
Original: The packaging is heavily damaged and opened. Product is broken.
After: The packaging is heavily damaged and opened. The product inside is not broken.

Table 6: Examples of error corrections using our methods.

els are consistent but become inconsistent after using our methods. We can see that most of the summaries remain consistent from our models. Furthermore, our analysis shows that the overall amounts of inconsistent summaries are reduced by 44.1% for BART and 31.6% for T5, which indicates the effectiveness of our methods.

Table 6 shows several input texts and summaries from the models before and after using our methods. In the first example, our model is able to pick up the correct entity from multiple entities in the source document, where the ordinary model fails. In the second example, the summary from the ordinary model contains contradicting description against the source document but our model captures the correct information.

6 Conclusion

In conclusion, we study the error patterns in the customer-feedback summaries generated by BART and T5. We propose to augment the training data with artificially corrupted summaries and use contrastive learning methods to enhance the model faithfulness. Human analysis shows that significant portion of WED and IPD errors from BART and T5 are reduced. Because our methods do not involve modifying the model structure, they can also be applied to other abstractive summarization frameworks.

References

Mehdi Allahyari, Seyedamin Pouriyeh, Mehdi Assefi, Saeid Safaei, Elizabeth D Trippe, Juan B Gutierrez, and Krys Kochut. 2017. Text summarization techniques: a brief survey. *arXiv preprint arXiv:1707.02268*.

Hangbo Bao, Li Dong, Furu Wei, Wenhui Wang, Nan Yang, Xiaodong Liu, Yu Wang, Jianfeng Gao, Songhao Piao, Ming Zhou, et al. 2020. Unilmv2: Pseudo-masked language models for unified language model pre-training. In *International Conference on Machine Learning*, pages 642–652. PMLR.

Meng Cao, Yue Dong, Jiapeng Wu, and Jackie Chi Kit Cheung. 2020. Factual error correction for abstractive summarization models. In *Proceedings of the 2020 Conference on Empirical Methods in Natural Language Processing (EMNLP)*, pages 6251–6258.

Ziqiang Cao, Furu Wei, Wenjie Li, and Sujian Li. 2018. Faithful to the original: Fact aware neural abstractive summarization. In *Proceedings of the AAAI Conference on Artificial Intelligence*, volume 32.

Li Dong, Nan Yang, Wenhui Wang, Furu Wei, Xiaodong Liu, Yu Wang, Jianfeng Gao, Ming Zhou, and Hsiao-Wuen Hon. 2019. Unified language model pre-training for natural language understanding and generation. *arXiv preprint arXiv:1905.03197*.

Yue Dong, Shuohang Wang, Zhe Gan, Yu Cheng, Jackie Chi Kit Cheung, and Jingjing Liu. 2020. Multi-fact correction in abstractive text summarization. In *Proceedings of the 2020 Conference on Empirical Methods in Natural Language Processing (EMNLP)*, pages 9320–9331.

Zi-Yi Dou, Pengfei Liu, Hiroaki Hayashi, Zhengbao Jiang, and Graham Neubig. 2020. Gsum: A general framework for guided neural abstractive summarization. *arXiv preprint arXiv:2010.08014*.

Tobias Falke, Leonardo FR Ribeiro, Prasetya Ajie Utama, Ido Dagan, and Iryna Gurevych. 2019. Ranking generated summaries by correctness: An interesting but challenging application for natural language inference. In *Proceedings of the 57th Annual Meeting of the Association for Computational Linguistics*, pages 2214–2220.

Shen Gao, Xiuying Chen, Zhaochun Ren, Dongyan Zhao, and Rui Yan. 2020. From standard summarization to new tasks and beyond: Summarization with manifold information. *arXiv preprint arXiv:2005.04684*.

Matthew Honnibal, Ines Montani, Sofie Van Landeghem, and Adriane Boyd. 2020. spaCy: Industrial-strength Natural Language Processing in Python.

Prannay Khosla, Piotr Teterwak, Chen Wang, Aaron Sarna, Yonglong Tian, Phillip Isola, Aaron Maschinot, Ce Liu, and Dilip Krishnan. 2020. Supervised contrastive learning. *Advances in Neural Information Processing Systems*, 33.

Wojciech Kryscinski, Nitish Shirish Keskar, Bryan McCann, Caiming Xiong, and Richard Socher. 2019. Neural text summarization: A critical evaluation. In *Proceedings of the 2019 Conference on Empirical*

Methods in Natural Language Processing and the 9th International Joint Conference on Natural Language Processing (EMNLP-IJCNLP), pages 540–551.

Wojciech Kryscinski, Bryan McCann, Caiming Xiong, and Richard Socher. 2020. Evaluating the factual consistency of abstractive text summarization. In *Proceedings of the 2020 Conference on Empirical Methods in Natural Language Processing (EMNLP)*, pages 9332–9346.

Mike Lewis, Yinhan Liu, Naman Goyal, Marjan Ghazvininejad, Abdelrahman Mohamed, Omer Levy, Veselin Stoyanov, and Luke Zettlemoyer. 2020. Bart: Denoising sequence-to-sequence pre-training for natural language generation, translation, and comprehension. In *Proceedings of the 58th Annual Meeting of the Association for Computational Linguistics*, pages 7871–7880.

Haoran Li, Junnan Zhu, Jiajun Zhang, and Chengqing Zong. 2018. Ensure the correctness of the summary: Incorporate entailment knowledge into abstractive sentence summarization. In *Proceedings of the 27th International Conference on Computational Linguistics*, pages 1430–1441.

Chin-Yew Lin. 2004. Rouge: A package for automatic evaluation of summaries. In *Text summarization branches out*, pages 74–81.

Yuning Mao, Xiang Ren, Heng Ji, and Jiawei Han. 2020. Constrained abstractive summarization: Preserving factual consistency with constrained generation. *arXiv preprint arXiv:2010.12723*.

Ramesh Nallapati, Bowen Zhou, Cicero dos Santos, Caglar Gucehre, and Bing Xiang. 2016. Abstractive text summarization using sequence-to-sequence rnns and beyond. In *Proceedings of The 20th SIGNLL Conference on Computational Natural Language Learning*, pages 280–290.

Colin Raffel, Noam Shazeer, Adam Roberts, Katherine Lee, Sharan Narang, Michael Matena, Yanqi Zhou, Wei Li, and Peter J Liu. 2020. Exploring the limits of transfer learning with a unified text-to-text transformer. *Journal of Machine Learning Research*, 21:1–67.

Florian Schroff, Dmitry Kalenichenko, and James Philbin. 2015. Facenet: A unified embedding for face recognition and clustering. In *Proceedings of the IEEE conference on computer vision and pattern recognition*, pages 815–823.

Alex Wang, Kyunghyun Cho, and Mike Lewis. 2020. Asking and answering questions to evaluate the factual consistency of summaries. In *Proceedings of the 58th Annual Meeting of the Association for Computational Linguistics*, pages 5008–5020.

Peng Yuan, Haoran Li, Song Xu, Youzheng Wu, Xiaodong He, and Bowen Zhou. 2020. On the faithfulness for e-commerce product summarization. In *Proceedings of the 28th International Conference on Computational Linguistics*, pages 5712–5717.

Jingqing Zhang, Yao Zhao, Mohammad Saleh, and Peter Liu. 2020. Pegasus: Pre-training with extracted gap-sentences for abstractive summarization. In *International Conference on Machine Learning*, pages 11328–11339. PMLR.

Chenguang Zhu, William Hinthorn, Ruochen Xu, Qingkai Zeng, Michael Zeng, Xuedong Huang, and Meng Jiang. 2021. Enhancing factual consistency of abstractive summarization. *North American Chapter of the Association for Computational Linguistics (NAACL) 2021*.

SupportNet: Neural Networks for Summary Generation and Key Segment Extraction from Technical Support Tickets

Vinayshekhar Bannihatti Kumar **Mohan Yarramsetty** **Sharon Sun** **Anukul Goel**
Amazon Web Services
Seattle, WA, USA
{vinayshk, ymohank, sharosun, anukul}@amazon.com

Abstract

We improve customer experience and gain their trust when their issues are resolved rapidly with less friction. Existing work has focused on reducing the overall case resolution time by binning a case into predefined categories and routing it to the desired support engineer. However, the actions taken by the engineer during case analysis and resolution are altogether ignored, even though it forms the bulk of the case resolution time. In this work, we propose two systems that enable support engineers to resolve cases faster. The first, a guidance extraction model, that mines historical cases and provides technical guidance phrases to the support engineers. These phrases can then be used to educate the customer or to obtain critical information needed to resolve the case and thus minimize the number of correspondences between the engineer and customer. The second, a summarization model that creates an abstractive summary of a case to provide better context to the support engineer. Through quantitative evaluation we obtain an F1 score of 0.64 on the guidance extraction model and a BertScore (F1) of 0.55 on the summarization model.

1 Introduction

It is of paramount importance to AWS Support organization to reduce the resolution time of customer cases to ensure their business runs seamlessly without any downtime. We have a unique challenge in that the customers' issues can be deeply technical and require technically skilled agents to resolve it. There is a rapid increase in the number of users of the services offered by our cloud company and it is important to improve tooling for Support Engineers (SEs) in order to scale. A significant portion of customers' cases are business critical and time-sensitive.

Cases are created by customers for several reasons such as guidance about a specific service or troubleshooting when a production service is down. A typical customer creates a case with a title of the case (case title) and a detailed correspondence on their issue as a part of the case (communication text). The agents then have to read this case, understand the customer's problem and suggest ways for them to resolve the issues. This requires the agents to spend a lot of time to completely read the case and then guide the customer to solve the problem. We have developed two systems that can use the inputs from the customer in the form of case text (case title + communication text) to speed up the agent's time to resolve a case. The first system is a summarization system that presents the customers problem to the agent to give them a head start in tackling the case. The second system provides them snippets from similar historical cases to reduce the time the agent takes to respond to the customer.

Prior work in the domain of customer support has focused on improving the time to resolve a case by improving routing and detecting the customer problems into one of several predefined categories (Gupta et al., 2013; Hui and Jha, 2000; Muni et al., 2017; Molino et al., 2018). While these methods reduce average total time to resolve issues throughout the case journey, they do not focus on reducing the active handle time by SEs, i.e., the time a SE has to invest to understand and respond to the customer. In our work, we address this gap by introducing two novel solutions as previously described.

SEs often look to similar previously resolved cases when beginning to tackle a new case according to a few internal studies. A previous similar case provides them troubleshooting resources, hints on root causes, and guidance material that they reuse on the new case. These resources from

Proceedings of the 4th Workshop on e-Commerce and NLP (ECNLP 4), pages 164–173
August 5, 2021.

previous similar cases have been found to reduce the handle time by SEs, but it takes time for agent to browse through the results. Hence, we built a knowledge mining system based on NLP that allows SEs to efficiently look up historical cases without having to read the whole case.

Typical technical cases contain many conversations, and reading through them is a time-consuming process. In order to solve this problem, a system was introduced - State of the Case (SOC) - where SEs update a summary of the current state of a case. These updates are made manually by SEs while they hand the case back to the customer or to another internal team. In addition to serving as a smooth transition between SEs throughout the case lifecycle, the SOC of a case was intended to serve as its expert summary view, eliminating the vagueness and jargon that may be present in customers' case text. However, the additional manual effort to fill SOC resulted in a low adoption rate of 9.8% over time. We introduce the solution in Section 3.2 automating SOC generation based on customer communications. Table 1 provides a simulated example of the data we have. The SEs can use the SOC to get a head start in solving the case.

Customer case text **Case Title:** Server down because of full volume **Case description:** We had our server go down this evening because the @gig volume of our EC@ server full. To avoid this in the future, I have two questions: - How can we know the amount of free space left in the Ec@ volume? - Is there a way we can setup alerts to monitor free usage? Thank you for your help in this matter. Have a good day, Instance ID(s): How can we track the storage / volume usage of our EC@ instances
State of Case(SOC) Case Summary: how can we track the free space remaining on the volume of an EC2 server ?@- how do we set up alerts at certain thresholds to know to act?

Table 1: The customer can describe their problem in several different ways. The state of the case summarizes the customer issue into something that is actionable.

We show that the summary version that a SE would write in SOC can be automatically generated using the state-of-the-art encoder (Bert (Devlin et al., 2018))-decoder (GPT-2 (Radford et al., 2019)) models with cross attention. We compare this model against recent baseline models such as Bart (Lewis et al., 2019) and on traditional encoder decoder models using LSTMs. We present findings that support using this model in production when compared to a more memory efficient model such as LSTM. Any conditional generation task requires a parallel dataset on which the model is trained on. Our dataset on the other hand has labeled data for the encoder text as well. This allows us to introduce a classification loss on the encoder to obtain better encoder representations that can be fed to the decoder. This also allows us to jointly train an encoder and a decoder with a simultaneous multi-task objective. We perform this novel experiment to show the efficacy of training the encoder with a cross entropy loss function while the decoder is trained using Maximum Likelihood Estimation (MLE).

Thus, the contribution of this work can be summarized as follows:

1. We present a model that is capable of mining technical guidance phrases from support cases.

2. We present a summarization model that generates a concise summary of customer problems from the communication text. We also compare several summarization models and discuss the potential impact of productionizing our model. In addition, we performed multi-task learning on the encoder to determine if it can improve decoder's performance.

3. We present the results from a human subject study to show the usefulness of our solution. Initial results suggest that the SEs considered the summary generated by our model as a good starting point to solve a case.

2 Related Work

As mentioned earlier, Molino et al. (2018) built systems that could categorize case issues into predefined categories. They also suggest predefined templates to SE. Specific details of the case are not taken into picture while suggesting these templates to make them more appropriate. Our summary model on the other hand ingests the context of the case and generates a personalized problem

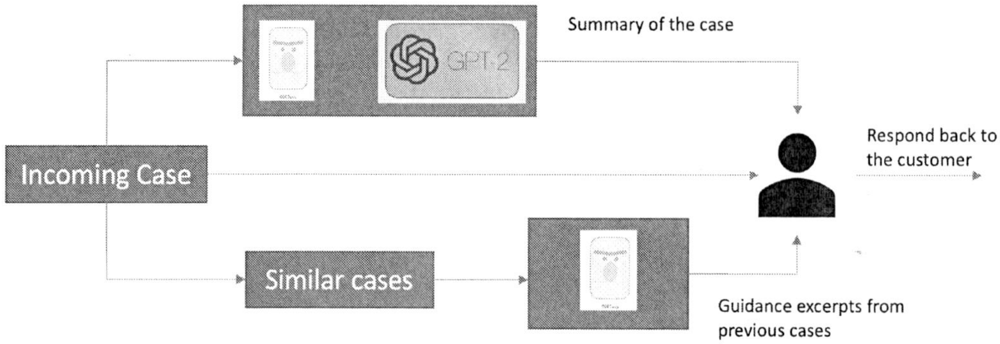

Figure 1: (a) Component 1 reads the contents of the incoming case and sends a summary to the support agent to get a head start. (b) Component 2 reads the contents of the historical cases and provides guidance excerpts for the agents to respond back to the customer.

template that a SE can use to update the state of case.

Prior work (Godse et al., 2018; Chess et al., 2007; Brittenham et al., 2007; Pathak and Khandelwal, 2017) has looked at providing better Information Technology Service Management (ITSM) to their customers by building resources that help the customers diagnose their own issue and find a solution for it. However, customers usually try to self-diagnose their issues before cutting a case. Hence, our solution focuses on helping the SE and improve their efficiency.

Other work (Gupta et al., 2013; Hui and Jha, 2000; Muni et al., 2017) has looked at the use of the support case text along with other metadata to classify the intent of the case and improve routing. We on the other hand analyze the case text to provide assistance to SE in their day-to-day tasks.

3 System and Model Overview

Figure 1 shows the overall architecture of the proposed system. There are two major components that we propose in this work. The first one uses a Bert and GPT-2 model to allow the SE to get a head start in solving the case. The second component runs on the case text of previously solved cases to provide the SE with guidance phrases. They can use the predicted guidance phrases to understand how the case can be solved and to also construct a response back to the customer.

In this section, we provide details of the models that were built in these components and the steps that we took to train them.

3.1 Guidance Extraction Model

Support cases that we receive from customers are filled with jargon rich text that takes highly skilled agents to read and understand. In order to train the models that can understand this text, we need large amounts of supervised data that is very expensive to obtain as it requires expert annotations. However, we can train large Language Models (LMs) with the vast amounts of self-supervised case text that enables the models to understand this jargon filled technical domain.

Following Lee et al. (2020); Beltagy et al. (2019) we continue the pre-training of the model presented by Devlin et al. (2018) . We continue the pre-training of the Bert model for another 60,000 steps on the support cases that we have received in the period of 2019 – 20. We call this model SupportBert. We show that this model outperforms the Bert base model trained on English Wikipedia and the Book corpus (Zhu et al., 2015) on our guidance phrase prediction task. We follow the standard procedure of fine-tuning this model on a labeled dataset of guidance excerpts. More about this dataset is presented in Section 4. We try several variants of the models while pre-training and the details of the experiments are presented in Section 5.

3.2 Summarization Model

We use a Seq2Seq (Sutskever et al., 2014) model with the cross attention as our baseline model. We use a Bert encoder and a GPT-2 decoder to summarize the case content. For every word W_i that belongs to the case description and the communication text, we pass that word through the

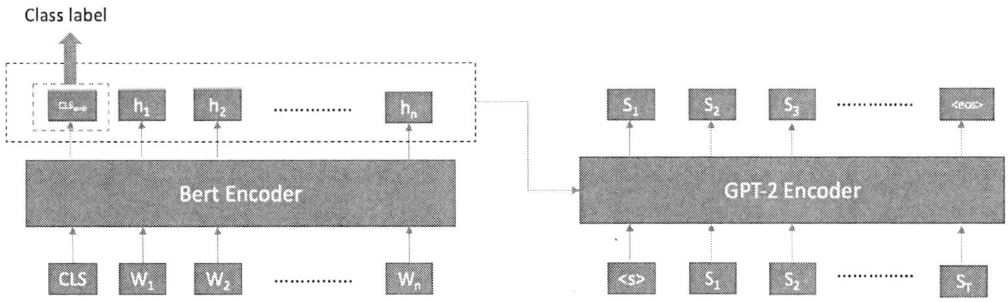

Figure 2: The complete setup of our summary model is shown above. We use the output of the GPT-2 decoder as a summary of the case description fed into the Bert Encoder. For the multi-task experiment we use the class label to add more gradients to the encoder.

Bert encoder to obtain the contextualized representations of the case content. We use Maximum Likelihood Estimation (MLE) to train the decoder on the case summary $(S_1...S_{T'})$. The case summaries entered by SEs on historical cases are used to train our model. Here S_i represents every word of the summary at a time step t'. T' represents the overall length of the summary. Our overall architecture is shown in Figure 2.

We first pass the words(W_i) into the Support-Bert model to get a contextualized representation of every word(h_{enc}).

$$h_{enc}^T = Bert\_encoder(W_1, W_2....W_N) \quad (1)$$

We then use these hidden states as the keys to the cross-attention units of the GPT-2 decoder. At each stage of the GPT-2 decoder we will see a probability distribution on the vocabulary(P_t^V).

$$P_t^V = GPT\_2(h_{enc}^T, S_{1...t}) \quad (2)$$

We use the SOC described in Table 1 for training the decoder with MLE. We want to maximize the log likelihood of the probability of the true word, in other words we want to minimize the negative log likelihood of the probability of the true word.

$$loss_t = -logP(W_t^{true}) \quad (3)$$

Total decoder loss is averaged cross entropy loss at each time step of the decoder.

$$\text{loss}_{decoder} = \frac{1}{T_{decoder}} \sum_{t=1}^{T_{decoder}} loss_t \quad (4)$$

During inference, we use the words generated by the decoder till time t and the Bert embeddings to produce the word at time $t+1$.

$$S_{t+1} = \arg\max_V [\text{softmax}(GPT\_2(h_{enc}^T, S_t))] \quad (5)$$

3.2.1 Multi-task training

In this variant of the summarization model, we also predict the issue category of the case text along with generating the summary. We have a unique corpus that has a label for the encoder text to train the encoder and SOC text to train the decoder. This enables us to jointly train the encoder and the decoder with both these loss functions. The encoder receives gradients from not only the MLE objective of the decoder but also the cross-entropy loss from issue categorization (241 pre-defined categories). Multi-task learning has shown to improve the performance of the Bert base model (Liu et al., 2019). However, each task head during this training phase is trained independently as parallel labels are not available. Also, there is a lack of a public corpus that enables us to jointly train the encoder on a classification task and the decoder on a text generation task. Our corpus allowed us to perform this experiment.

$$\text{loss}_{encoder} = \sum_{i=0}^{241} P(X)log(Q(X)) \quad (6)$$

$$\text{loss} = \text{loss}_{encoder} + \text{loss}_{decoder} \quad (7)$$

4 Datasets

4.1 Guidance Extraction

For the purpose of guidance extraction we asked annotators to label paragraphs from support cases as Technical Guidance (**T.G**) and Educational Guidance (**E.G**). Using this paragraph labeled case dataset, we want to identify if a paragraph is a guidance or not. As a first step we will combine both these guidance into one bucket and classify if a paragraph is a guidance para-

# Examples	# T.G	# E.G
2050	109	88

Table 2: The number of different types of guidance present in our guidance extraction dataset.

# Train	# Test	# Categories
104892	5000	241

Table 3: Number of training and testing samples used for the summary model. Total categories column indicates the number of categories that the encoder text could be classified into. This was used for training the encoder in a multi-task setup.

graph or not. The statistics of this dataset is shown in Table 2.

4.2 Summarization Dataset

We used an internally available parallel corpus for training our summarization model. Our dataset contains the case subject, first communication and the **Subject Matter Experts (SMEs)** annotated customer problem. We show the dataset statistics in Table 3. We use the case title and the first communication as the input to the model. The model summarizes the customer problem.

5 Experiments:

5.1 Guidance Extraction Model

5.1.1 Experimental setup:

The majority baseline would produce an F1 score of 0.13 if recall is set to 1 by predicting everything as guidance phrase. This shows that the dataset is highly skewed and it is not easy to get good performance with random guessing. Since the number of examples in the test set is not very high (20% of all annotated data in Table 2), we decided to perform a 5-fold validation and average the model performance. For each fold of data, we stop training after 3 epochs similar to (Devlin et al., 2018). We then use the 20% test set for each fold to calculate the accuracy of the model prediction with the ground truth annotation. In order to control for variance, we repeat the experiment 5 different times and average the results. We compared the following 4 variants of the model:

Off the shelf Bert (OSB): We used Bert-base model that was trained on English Wikipedia and the Book Corpus and then fine-tuned the model against our own dataset. During fine-tuning, we used a batch size of 16, max length of 512, learning rate of 5e-5 with weight decay ($\epsilon = 1e-8$).

Model	P	R	F1
OSB	0.665	0.6114	0.6116
PB	0.7178	0.6268	0.6456
PBK	0.6576	0.5386	0.5636
BUL	0.6742	0.6204	0.6306

Table 4: Performance of different guidance extraction models. These performance results have been averaged with 5-fold validation and 5 different runs to control for variance.

Bert – Pre-trained with support case data (PB): Since the language in support cases is wildly different from that of Wikipedia and the Bookcorpus, we continued the pre-training of the Bert model on a corpus of support cases. We used a total of 236,354 cases to continue pretraining the Bert model. We then fine-tuned this Bert model with the same experimental setup as **OSB**.

Bert Pre-trained with Keywords in inputs (PBK): We observed that there were a lot of technical terms in our dataset that have a different contextual meaning (e.g. VPC, route). Hence, we hypothesized that we should add technical keywords to our model's vocabulary. To facilitate this, we trained a new WordPiece model (Wu et al., 2016) on our corpus of support cases. There were 1662 tokens in Bert's vocabulary after adding these words. The rest of the training pipeline was similar to **PB**.

Bert model with under sampling Limit Increase Cases (BUL): When our customers want to add more resources to their existing account they create a Limit Increase Case with us. These cases follow a very generic template (canned email) that might not be very useful to the model. In order to test this hypothesis, we under sampled those cases and re-ran the pre-training and fine-tuning experiment without adding additional keywords.

5.1.2 Experiments Discussion

From Table 4, we see that the best performing model on the guidance phrase dataset is the PB model. This observation is consistent with several other works (Beltagy et al., 2019; Lee et al., 2020). We see that the model performance significantly drops when we add the custom keywords. This is because the word embeddings for these words are trained from scratch while the word embeddings of the Bert base vocabulary have already been tuned. We do see a 2% increase in F1 by under sampling limit increase cases but the performance is still lower than the PB model.

5.2 Summary Model

5.2.1 Experimental Setup

We train the encoder-decoder model for 3 epochs on the training data mentioned above. For the encoder we use a Bert base model. The decoder is the GPT-2 model from OpenAI. The keys to the self-attention units of the GPT-2 decoder are the final hidden states of the Bert encoder. We used a batch of 16, max length of 512, Adam (Kingma and Ba, 2014) optimizer learning rate of $5e-5$ with weight decay of ($\epsilon = 1e-8$). We experiment with several variants of the encoder-decoder model. They are discussed below:

LSTM Based encoder-decoder (LSTM): We implement an LSTM based encoder-decoder model with attention (Sutskever et al., 2014; Bahdanau et al., 2014). There are 512 units in both the encoder and the decoder with 2 layers. We use an Adam optimizer with learning rate of 0.3.

Bert encoder with GPT-2 decoder (BG): We implement a Bert encoder with a GPT-2 decoder. The final hidden states of the Bert base encoder act as the key to the self-attention blocks (Vaswani et al., 2017) of the GPT-2 module.

Pre-trained Bert encoder with GPT-2 decoder (PBG): This model is similar to the **BG** model. But we used the pre-trained Bert model from Section 5.1.1.

Bert encoder with GPT-2 decoder + encoder loss (BGE): This model is similar to the **BG** above. But we also include a multi-task objective that classifies the input text into one of the 241 categories. We want to evaluate if there is any advantage to either the text generation phase or the classification phase by performing this multi-task learning.

Pre-trained Bert encoder with GPT-2 decoder + encoder loss (PBGE): This model is a combination of the PBG model and BGE model. We pre-train the Bert model and use the multi-task loss to get better representations of the input text.

5.2.2 Experiments Discussion

Since Rouge is considered as the industry standard metric for summary tasks (Zhang et al., 2020; Lewis et al., 2019), we compare different models based on ROUGE-L (Lin, 2004) metric. This comparison is consistent with all the other text generation metrics presented in Table 5. We observe that the best performing model is the BG model. The performance is almost the same as the PBG model. However, when we compare the models using BertScore (P, R, F1) (Zhang et al., 2019) we see that PBG model slightly outperforms the BG model. BertScore has been found to have more correlation with human judgment. Further human evaluation is required to get the nuanced differences between the BG model and the PBG model. Several works have investigated the use of multi-task learning for classification (Liu et al., 2019, 2017) and have found that training the model with several losses increases model performance. In our case we see that the multi-task objective deteriorates the model text generation metrics. We hypothesize that both the encoder and the decoder try to modify the Bert representations to suit their task at hand leading to this degradation in the performance. We also looked at the outputs from the Bart (Lewis et al., 2019) model, but observed that the Bart model did not perform abstraction and merely copied the words from the customer text in the decoder response.

We also investigate if we can achieve higher performance on the encoder classification if we train with the multi-task objective. From Figure 3 we see that all the models achieve a similar test performance after 3 epochs of training. However, it is interesting to see that the classifier achieves better performance in the initial steps of training with both the PBGE and the BGE models. The comparison is made with respect to taking an off the shelf Bert model and training with the encoder objective described in Section 3.2.1.

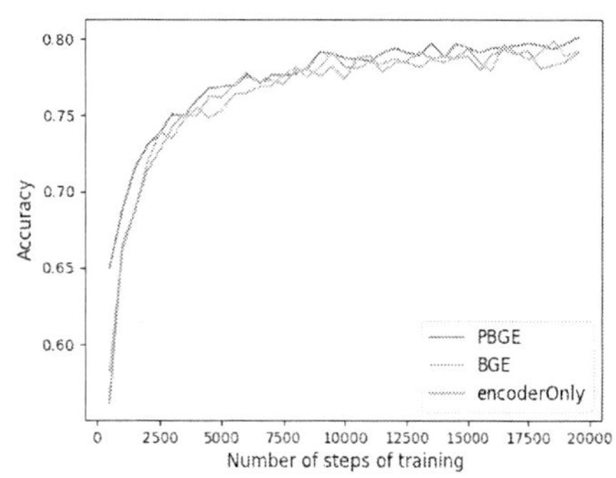

Figure 3: Comparisons of different encoder classifier accuracies against the number of steps the model is trained on.

Model	Bleu-1	Bleu-4	Cider	ROUGE	DIST-1	DIST-2	DIST-3	P	R	F1
PBGE	0.130	0.063	0.190	0.225	0.043	0.170	0.319	0.529	0.512	0.515
LSTM	0.066	0.032	0.062	0.113	0.015	0.119	0.228	0.479	0.415	0.439
BGE	0.131	0.066	0.206	0.294	0.045	0.211	0.415	0.556	0.527	0.535
BG	0.143	0.080	0.220	0.401	0.064	0.275	0.470	0.568	0.539	0.546
PBG	0.132	0.074	0.227	0.436	0.062	0.271	0.470	0.580	0.535	0.551

Table 5: Comparison of all the models. Based on the ROUGE score we see that the BG model performed as well as the PBG model. The results obtained from BertScore(P, R, F1) closely resembles that of our human evaluation

The performance of a simple model like LSTM is not close to the transformer based model. Even though the LSTM models can give a significant gain in inference time while deploying the model in production, from the model performance above we can see that we need to have infrastructure in place to productionize the transformer based models for our use case. The transformer based models took a total time of 15 minutes to decode the test set of 5000 examples which adds an average latency time of 180ms to summarize each example.

Another important metric that one should look at is the number of distinct phrases that the Seq2Seq model is able to generate. Seq2Seq models are known to suffer from the dull response problem (Gupta et al., 2019a). If the DIST-* metrics are high, that shows that the model is able to generate more diverse outputs when presented with different input scenarios (Li et al., 2015; Gupta et al., 2019a). From the table we can see that the DIST-3 metric which captures the number of unique trigrams is highest for the BG model. The next closest model is the PBG model. We also observe that adding encoder loss does not improve the distinct scores.

5.2.3 Human Evaluation

Since the PBG model had the best BertScores and was pre-trained on support cases we used the summaries from this model for human evaluation. While automatic evaluation metrics captures many aspects of the ground truth with the generated text they have been criticized for the lack of semantic understanding (Gupta et al., 2019b; Sulem et al., 2018). In order to evaluate the efficacy of the summaries generated by our models and to validate its usefulness, we conducted a human subject study with the 2 subject matter experts. We randomly sampled 50 cases from the test set and asked them to provide feedback on the accuracy of the summary and if the summary generated would form a good starting point to write the summary of the current case. We observed that 23/50 were considered as a useful summary from both the SEs. 10/50 were considered as not useful by both. The other 17 had mixed ratings. If we consider a summary useful if either of the individual annotated it as useful, then 40/50 were useful summaries.

5.2.4 Qualitative Analysis:

We show some of the summaries generated by our model in Table 6. As we can see from the model generations, the model has learned to predict the technical language of our domain. In row 1 and 2 of Table 6 we see that the model has learned to predict the customers' problem well based on the communication text. This is because of the knowledge from the historical cases where in other customers had similar problem. We can also see from example 3 that the model has learned to associate CPU spikes with Internet Information Server. When we manually inspected a few samples (e.g. row 4) from the human subject study and spoke to our participants, we found that the model was penalized because it tried to generate a very specific customer problem that might not make sense semantically. We leave the introduction of semantic knowledge into these models as future work.

6 Application of the models to Support Businesses

Extraction of guidance phrases from case text of previous cases can provide quick tips to SEs and make it easier for them while working on a case. Every SE is required to write a reply to the customer with the steps they can take to resolve the issue. These guidance phrases will help them reuse the text enabling them to spend less time on the reply email.

The summary models we have built can be used in a variety of SE tasks. We can use the automated summary to provide the context of the

Customer Text	Ground truth	Generated Summary
Transfer t3 instance from one account to anotherIIello, There is a t@.large reserved instance in account @ and we would like to transfer it to the other account that we have	Cx would like assistance on transferring the t2.large Reserved instance from account @ to account @	Cx wants to transfer instance from one account to another
Server down because of full volumeHello, Our Servers went down this evening because the volume of our EC@ server was completely full. I have a couple of questions to avoid this in the future: - How do I know the amount of free space left in the Ec@ volume? - How do I setup alarms to monitor free usage? Have a good day,	how can we track the free space remaining on the volume of an EC2 server?@- how do we set up alerts at certain thresholds to know to act?	Customer wants to know how to monitor the disk usage of the EC2 instance
Performance issue cpu spikesWe have noticed CPU spikes on an instance that is running an IIS site up to @We stopped the site and cpu is still spiking up to @ when running with few services installed. Issue occurs only when our monitoring services are running @am to @pm. I need help trying to understand what is causing this spike with http. Instance ID(s): i-@f@e@a Timestamp (YYYY-MM-DD HH:MM:SS UTC): @/@/@	We would need help with monitoring http traffic going in/out of the box and more details about cpu load by process name.	Customer experienced high CPU spikes on an instance that is running on IIS and wanted to know the cause
Chat: S@ access denied I am getting an error with IAM user or role experiencing the issue: arn:aws:iam::@:role/ with this role. Not sure what the problem is. Could you help?	Cx was facing ""lambda access error: lambda: GetAccountSettings"" error and needed assistance with the same	Customer was getting access denied error while trying to access S3 bucket via IAM user

Table 6: Examples of a few qualitative results produced by our model. Please note we have simulated the queries in the table to preserve customer privacy.

case to the next SE who picks up the case. When presenting similar cases to the SE, we can provide the summaries to let them quickly identify if the case is useful. The summaries that we generate can also be used as a starting point when the SEs are tasked with completing the SOC.

7 Conclusion

It is important for us to scale the support business with our rapid user growth. We describe two components of a system that aims to reduce the time spent by SE in resolving a support case. The aim of this work is to promote research at the intersection of NLP and support business. Using our models, we were able to achieve an F1 score of 0.64 on the guidance extraction problem and BertScore (F1) of 0.55 on the summarization problem. These promising results shows us that they can be deployed in production, create impact and help SEs in their day-to-day tasks. We hope this contribution can lead to better tools that can improve the tooling necessary for support agents to provide a rich customer experience.

References

Dzmitry Bahdanau, Kyunghyun Cho, and Yoshua Bengio. 2014. Neural machine translation by jointly learning to align and translate. *arXiv preprint arXiv:1409.0473.*

Iz Beltagy, Kyle Lo, and Arman Cohan. 2019. Scibert: A pretrained language model for scientific text. *arXiv preprint arXiv:1903.10676.*

Peter Brittenham, R Russell Cutlip, Christine Draper, Brent A Miller, Samar Choudhary, and Marcelo Perazolo. 2007. It service management architecture and autonomic computing. *IBM Systems Journal*, 46(3):565–581.

David M Chess, James E Hanson, John A Pershing, and Steve R White. 2007. Prospects for simplifying itsm-based management through self-managing resources. *IBM Systems Journal*, 46(3):599–608.

Jacob Devlin, Ming-Wei Chang, Kenton Lee, and Kristina Toutanova. 2018. Bert: Pre-training of deep bidirectional transformers for language understanding. *arXiv preprint arXiv:1810.04805*.

Neha Atul Godse, Shaunak Deodhar, Shubhangi Raut, and Pranjali Jagdale. 2018. Implementation of chatbot for itsm application using ibm watson. In *2018 Fourth International Conference on Computing Communication Control and Automation (ICCUBEA)*, pages 1–5. IEEE.

Narendra Gupta, Mazin Gilbert, and Giuseppe Di Fabbrizio. 2013. Emotion detection in email customer care. *Computational Intelligence*, 29(3):489–505.

Prakhar Gupta, Vinayshekhar Bannihatti Kumar, Mukul Bhutani, and Alan W Black. 2019a. Writerforcing: Generating more interesting story endings. *arXiv preprint arXiv:1907.08259*.

Prakhar Gupta, Shikib Mehri, Tiancheng Zhao, Amy Pavel, Maxine Eskenazi, and Jeffrey P Bigham. 2019b. Investigating evaluation of open-domain dialogue systems with human generated multiple references. *arXiv preprint arXiv:1907.10568*.

Siu Cheung Hui and G Jha. 2000. Data mining for customer service support. *Information & Management*, 38(1):1–13.

Diederik P Kingma and Jimmy Ba. 2014. Adam: A method for stochastic optimization. *arXiv preprint arXiv:1412.6980*.

Jinhyuk Lee, Wonjin Yoon, Sungdong Kim, Donghyeon Kim, Sunkyu Kim, Chan Ho So, and Jaewoo Kang. 2020. Biobert: a pre-trained biomedical language representation model for biomedical text mining. *Bioinformatics*, 36(4):1234–1240.

Mike Lewis, Yinhan Liu, Naman Goyal, Marjan Ghazvininejad, Abdelrahman Mohamed, Omer Levy, Ves Stoyanov, and Luke Zettlemoyer. 2019. Bart: Denoising sequence-to-sequence pre-training for natural language generation, translation, and comprehension. *arXiv preprint arXiv:1910.13461*.

Jiwei Li, Michel Galley, Chris Brockett, Jianfeng Gao, and Bill Dolan. 2015. A diversity-promoting objective function for neural conversation models. *arXiv preprint arXiv:1510.03055*.

Chin-Yew Lin. 2004. Rouge: A package for automatic evaluation of summaries. In *Text summarization branches out*, pages 74–81.

Pengfei Liu, Xipeng Qiu, and Xuanjing Huang. 2017. Adversarial multi-task learning for text classification. *arXiv preprint arXiv:1704.05742*.

Xiaodong Liu, Pengcheng He, Weizhu Chen, and Jianfeng Gao. 2019. Multi-task deep neural networks for natural language understanding. *arXiv preprint arXiv:1901.11504*.

Piero Molino, Huaixiu Zheng, and Yi-Chia Wang. 2018. Cota: Improving the speed and accuracy of customer support through ranking and deep networks. In *Proceedings of the 24th ACM SIGKDD International Conference on Knowledge Discovery & Data Mining*, pages 586–595.

Durga Prasad Muni, Suman Roy, Yeung Tack Yan John John Lew Chiang, Antoine Jean-Marie Viallet, and Navin Budhiraja. 2017. Recommending resolutions of itil services tickets using deep neural network. In *Proceedings of the Fourth ACM IKDD Conferences on Data Sciences*, pages 1–10.

Ramesh C Pathak and Pankaj Khandelwal. 2017. A model for hybrid cloud integration: With a case study for it service management (itsm). In *2017 IEEE International Conference on Cloud Computing in Emerging Markets (CCEM)*, pages 113–118. IEEE.

Alec Radford, Jeffrey Wu, Rewon Child, David Luan, Dario Amodei, and Ilya Sutskever. 2019. Language models are unsupervised multitask learners. *OpenAI blog*, 1(8):9.

Elior Sulem, Omri Abend, and Ari Rappoport. 2018. Bleu is not suitable for the evaluation of text simplification. *arXiv preprint arXiv:1810.05995*.

Ilya Sutskever, Oriol Vinyals, and Quoc V Le. 2014. Sequence to sequence learning with neural networks. *Advances in neural information processing systems*, 27:3104–3112.

Ashish Vaswani, Noam Shazeer, Niki Parmar, Jakob Uszkoreit, Llion Jones, Aidan N Gomez, Łukasz Kaiser, and Illia Polosukhin. 2017. Attention is all you need. In *Advances in neural information processing systems*, pages 5998–6008.

Yonghui Wu, Mike Schuster, Zhifeng Chen, Quoc V Le, Mohammad Norouzi, Wolfgang Macherey, Maxim Krikun, Yuan Cao, Qin Gao, Klaus Macherey, et al. 2016. Google's neural machine translation system: Bridging the gap between human and machine translation. *arXiv preprint arXiv:1609.08144*.

Jingqing Zhang, Yao Zhao, Mohammad Saleh, and Peter Liu. 2020. Pegasus: Pre-training with extracted gap-sentences for abstractive summarization. In *International Conference on Machine Learning*, pages 11328–11339. PMLR.

Tianyi Zhang, Varsha Kishore, Felix Wu, Kilian Q Weinberger, and Yoav Artzi. 2019. Bertscore: Evaluating text generation with bert. *arXiv preprint arXiv:1904.09675*.

Yukun Zhu, Ryan Kiros, Rich Zemel, Ruslan Salakhutdinov, Raquel Urtasun, Antonio Torralba, and Sanja Fidler. 2015. Aligning books and movies: Towards story-like visual explanations by watching movies and reading books. In *Proceedings of the IEEE international conference on computer vision*, pages 19–27.

Product Review Translation: Parallel Corpus Creation and Robustness towards User-generated Noisy Text

Kamal Kumar Gupta, Soumya Chennabasavraj,[†], Nikesh Garera[†] and Asif Ekbal
Department of Computer Science and Engineering, Indian Institute of Technology Patna, Patna, India
[†]Flipkart, India
kamal.pcs17,asif@iitp.ac.in
[†]soumya.cb,nikesh.garera@flipkart.com

Abstract

Reviews written by the users for a particular product or service play an influencing role for the customers to make an informative decision. Although online e-commerce portals have immensely impacted our lives, available contents predominantly are in English language- often limiting its widespread usage. There is an exponential growth in the number of e-commerce users who are not proficient in English. Hence, there is a necessity to make these services available in non-English languages, especially in a multilingual country like India. This can be achieved by an in-domain robust machine translation (MT) system. However, the reviews written by the users pose unique challenges to MT, such as misspelled words, ungrammatical constructions, presence of colloquial terms, lack of resources such as in-domain parallel corpus etc. We address the above challenges by presenting an English–Hindi review domain parallel corpus. We train an English-to-Hindi neural machine translation (NMT) system to translate the product reviews available on e-commerce websites. By training the Transformer based NMT model over the generated data, we achieve a score of 33.26 BLEU points for English-to-Hindi translation. In order to make our NMT model robust enough to handle the noisy tokens in the reviews, we integrate a character based language model to generate word vectors and map the noisy tokens with their correct forms. Experiments on four language pairs, *viz.* English-Hindi, English-German, English-French, and English-Czech show the BLUE scores of 35.09, 28.91, 34.68 and 14.52 which are the improvements of 1.61, 1.05, 1.63 and 1.94, respectively, over the baseline.

1 Introduction

In the era of exponentially rising internet users, contents over social media, e-commerce portals are increasing rapidly. In recent times, there has been a phenomenal growth in the number of e-commerce users, especially during this COVID pandemic situation. However, the contents in such e-commerce portals are mostly in English, limiting the scope of these services to only a section of the society who can read and/or write in English. India is a multilingual country with 22 officially spoken languages. The number of internet users in India has increased dramatically in the last few years with the widespread usage of low-cost android phones. Users find it very difficult to understand the English contents written in these service portals. Hence, there is a great demand to translate these contents from English to Indian languages. As the manual translation is both time-consuming and cost-sensitive, building an automated machine translation (MT) system that could translate these enormous amounts of reviews will be of great interest. However, there are several challenges for this, such as the non-availability of in-domain parallel training corpus, noisy nature of the text, ungrammatical constructions, and the mixing of more than one language (i.e. code-mixed contents) (ref. Table 1). Product reviews are user generated content where writing inconsistencies are common as shown in Table 1. It is possible to make mistakes in writing words in a sentence due to various reasons, for example, weak grasp on the language, fast writing, writing just to convey the message without concerning more about the sentence formation etc.

Type of noise	Example
Emoji	Face unlock works well. even in dim light
Char Repetiton	full package bestttttt phone
Capital letter	NICE PHONE IN LOW BUDGET.
Misspell	Awsome prodct....loved it
Punctuation Irregularity	phone gives best photos!! awesome feeling
Article missing	It is best earphone I got with phone
Starting noun pronoun missing	was a nice product i got
Code Mixed	Good product. lekin price bahot high hai

Table 1: Various noise present in product review sentences

In our current work, we take up English-to-Hindi translation as there are 57.09% Hindi

Proceedings of the 4th Workshop on e-Commerce and NLP (ECNLP 4), pages 174–183
August 5, 2021. ©2021 Association for Computational Linguistics

1. Source	the performence of the phone is bad.
Reference	फोन की परफॉर्मेंस खराब है। (phone of performance bad is.)
Output	फोन का परफ्यूम खराब है। *(phone of perfume bad is.)*
2. Source	The content is a disgrce to the page.
Reference	Der Inhalt ist eine Schande für die Seite.
Output	Der Inhalt ist eine Abneigung gegen die Seite.
3. Source	current procedure is more transpatent
Reference	la procédure courante est plus transparente .
Output	la procédure courante est plus transcriptive .

Table 2: Sample outputs for **1** En→Hi, **2.** En→De and **3.** En→Fr translation in presence of noisy input tokens.

speakers in India[1]. These two languages are morphologically and syntactically distant to each other, posing challenges to build a robust NMT system. We crawl the English review sentences (electronic gadgets) from the e-commerce websites. After pre-processing (ref. Section 3.2) and filtering (ref. Section 3.3), we translate the English sentences into Hindi language using our in-house English-Hindi translation system[2]. The generated Hindi output sentences are given to the professionals who are experts in Hindi and English languages. The language experts post-edit the Hindi output as per the guidelines (ref. Section 3.5) provided to them. In addition, we also crawl monolingual Hindi sentences (ref. Section 3.6) from electronics gadgets' description websites. These sentences are back-translated[3] (Sennrich et al., 2016a) using the Hindi-to-English translation model trained over the post-edited parallel corpus.

Neural machine translation (NMT) (Bahdanau et al., 2015; Vaswani et al., 2017) is the dominant translation technology nowadays, and adapting this to the noisy text is very crucial due to the phenomenal growth in social media. Since NMT models learn from a fixed number of source and target vocabulary during training, any noisy word during the inference becomes an out-of-vocabulary (OOV) token because it does not belong to the NMT model's training vocabulary. It is not possible to train an NMT model with all the noisy versions of a correct token. In this case, models treat noisy tokens as OOV tokens and either miss their translation in the output sentence or translate them incorrectly. Incorrect translation of noisy tokens affects the translation quality of the whole output sequence. It affects the translation output and degrades the output quality. For example, English-to-Hindi (En–to–Hi) NMT model has one token *performance* as a part of its source vocabulary during training. As shown in example 1 in Table 2, a noisy version *performence* appears in the input sentence which is incorrectly translated as 'परफ्यूम' *perfume* instead of 'परफॉर्मेंस' *performance*. Similarly, in examples 2 and 3, we can see that *disgrce* and *transpatent* are the noisy tokens in the English to German (En–to–De) and English to French (En–to–Fr) models, respectively, and both of these noisy tokens are incorrectly translated by their respective translation models.

To handle the noisy tokens as source input, we integrate a similarity based token replacement model before word segmentation at inference time where the word vectors of noisy input tokens are matched with the correct and seen tokens in the source vocabulary, and replaced with the highest similar token. We use a character based language model to generate the word vectors and map the noisy and correct version of tokens in vector space. The generation of the word vectors depends on the characters present in that word.

The remainder of the paper is organized as follows. In Section 2, we discuss the related work. Section 5 presents the approaches of training the character language model, word vector generation model, and handling of noisy source input tokens at inference time. Section 6 presents the details regarding the dataset used and the experimental setup. Results and analysis of our approach are discussed in Section 7. Finally, Section 8 concludes the work with future research directions.

2 Related Work

Machine translation with noisy text is, itself, a very challenging task. Noisy tokens (misspelled words) pose great challenges to develop the Neural Machine Translation (NMT) models (c.f. Table 2) (Michel and Neubig, 2018). In the literature, there are a few existing works that focus on handling the noisy text by increasing the robustness of the translation model. An MTNT (machine translation of noisy text) test-bed was introduced in (Michel and Neubig, 2018) that discussed the challenges of noisy contents. It has been also observed that even small noise in the input sentence can degrade the translation quality of the NMT model significantly (Belinkov and Bisk, 2018; Karpukhin et al., 2019). To improve the robustness of the translation model, they introduced synthetic errors like character swapping, replacement and drop in the corpus. Synthetic noise using back-translated corpus was also inserted in the original corpus to introduce the NMT model with noise at train-

[1]https://en.wikipedia.org/wiki/List_of_languages_by_number_of_native_speakers_in_India

[2]This system has BLEU of 55.67 for judicial domain

[3]Translating monolingual target data using target→source NMT model.

Sr.	English Sentence (crawled)	Hindi Sentence (corrected)
1.	rounded corners make griping the phone very well .	राउंडेड कोर्नर फोन को बहुत ही अच्छी पकड़ देते हैं । (raunded kornar phon ko bahut hee achchhee pakad dete hain)
2.	one of the best phone ever at this price .	इस कीमत में अब तक के सबसे अच्छे फोन में से एक । (is keemat mein ab tak ke sabase achchhe phon mein se ek .)
3.	but this is Apple and Apple is like that only	लेकिन यह ऐप्पल है और ऐप्पल ऐसा ही होता है (lekin yah aippal hai aur aippal aisa hee hota hai)
4.	At first I want to say Thank u flipkart.	सबसे पहले मैं थैंक यू फ्लिपकार्ट कहना चाहता हूं। (sabase pahale main thaink yoo phlipakaart kahana chaahata hoon.)
5.	Rear camera image quality is very good.	रियर कैमरा इमेज क्वालिटी बहुत अच्छी है। (riyar kaimara imej kvaalitee bahut achchhee hai)

Table 3: Samples from the generated English-Hindi parallel corpus

ing time (Vaibhav et al., 2019; Anastasopoulos et al., 2019).

Since it is difficult for the NMT model to see all the noisy variants of a correct token at training time, the model hence treats the noisy tokens as the unseen tokens. Word segmentation is a popular method that deals with the unseen tokens. Byte-pair-encoding (BPE) (Sennrich et al., 2016b) segments the words based on the rare character combinations. In BPE, a word is converted into the subword units based on the fixed learned list of less frequent character combinations. Subword regularization (SR) (Kudo, 2018) was introduced as a more diverse word segmentation method which segments the words based on a unigram language model. For these segmentation models, it is difficult to capture all the noisy versions at training time. So before segmentation, we use a character based language model that maps the noisy and correct versions of tokens together in a vector space as shown in Figure 1. It helps to replace the noisy token with its correct form before inference.

There has not been any significant attempt to translate the product reviews, *except* the one proposed in (Berard et al., 2019) that addressed the translation of English to French. In contrast, we develop product review translation system for English-Hindi. English and Hindi are morphologically and syntactically distant languages, which pose more challenges for machine translation. Further, Hindi is a resource-poor language for which we do not have sufficient resources and tools, even for the generic domain.

3 Parallel Corpus Creation

3.1 Crawling reviews and challenges in pre-processing

We crawl English product reviews from the e-commerce portal, Flipkart. Product reviews are user generated contents and contain various noises (inconsistencies) as shown in Table 1.

3.2 Pre-processing

We remove the emojis from the English sentence by providing their unicode range using regular expressions. Any character having repetition of more than 2 times is trimmed and then checked for its compatible correct word using spell-checker[4], and a list provided by Facebook[5] (Edizel et al., 2019). Writing the complete sentence in upper case is also very common in user generated content (i.e. *NICE PHONE IN LOW BUDGET*). Normalization is done to convert all such instances into the lower case. Since we focus on the product reviews data, we make the first character of brand's name[6] (Google, Moto, Nokia etc.) as capital. After the pre-processing steps as mentioned above (emoji removal, character repetition, casing etc.), we found that approximately 62.3% sentences from the total crawled sentences are corrected.

3.3 Filtering Standard vs. Non-standard Sentences

We prepare the translation model to deal with the noises as mentioned in Section 3.1. Some sentences in reviews are written in Roman script[7]. We consider these sentences as non-standard sentences. Before generating the target counterpart of the source sentences, we filter out the non-standard sentences using an autoencoder based NMT model. We use Sockeye toolkit (Hieber et al., 2018) to train our model, and the hyperparameters used are mentioned in Section 6.2. Steps involved in the filtering process are as follows:

- Apply 30,000 BPE merge operations using subword technique(Sennrich et al., 2016b) over 21.2 million English monolingual data (Bojar et al., 2014).

[4]https://pypi.org/project/pyspellchecker/

[5]https://github.com/facebookresearch/moe/tree\/master/data

[6]https://en.wikipedia.org/wiki/List_of_mobile_phone_brands_by_country

[7]We do not focus on the sentences written in the Roman script (Hindi words written in Roman script (English letters)).

System	Parallel samples	BLEU	TER
Base	13,000	33.26	46.49
Base+BT	48,000	37.79	41.35

Table 4: BLEU and TER scores for English–to–Hindi NMT system over review domain corpus

- Train an English–to–English system. Here, the source and target are identical.
- After training, infer the English sentence from the crawled product reviews and generate an English hypothesis.
- Calculate the similarity between the input sentence and the inferred hypothesis using BLEU score.
- If BLEU < 40 then the sentence will be filtered out. We consider 40 BLEU point as a threshold because BLEU in the range 30-40 is considered as "understandable to good translations"[8].

The objective of training the autoencoder is to generate an output sequence very similar to the input sequence. Model would not be able to regenerate a source input properly if it is not trained on the similar kind of samples.

On an average from the total crawled reviews, 15 to 20 % reviews were filtered out as the non-standard sentences which were dropped and not considered further. After this filtering, there were still some sentences left, having grammar and spelling inconsistencies. These sentences have been considered as noisy sentences. Noise handling techniques as discussed in Section 5 are used to train the model to translate the noisy sentences.

3.4 Gold Corpus Creation by Human Post-editing

After pre-processing and filtering, we obtain 16,138 standard English sentences. Instead of translating sentences from scratch, we use an in-house English-Hindi machine translation system developed for the judicial domain. The model is trained for English-Hindi translation using judicial data (English-Hindi), and additional English-Hindi corpus (Kunchukuttan et al., 2018)[9]. The sentences generated from this automatic translation are post-edited by human experts. The experts are post-graduates in linguistics and have good command in Hindi and English both. The experts read the English sentences and its Hindi translation. They were instructed to make the correction in the sentences, if required. Some guidelines for making the corrections in the data are mentioned in Section 3.5. The human corrected parallel corpus is divided into training, development and test set consisting of 13000, 599 and 2,539 parallel sentences, respectively. Vocabulary size of English and Hindi training data is 9,331 and 8,367 tokens respectively. We also crawl Hindi sentences and back-translate them into English. In Table 4, 'Base+BT' shows the size of those samples. Section 3.6 describes the generation process of that synthetic (back-translated) data.

3.5 Guidelines for the Gold Corpus Creation

Guidelines for making the corrections (ref. Section 3.4) to generate the review domain parallel corpus are as follows:

- Source and target sentence should carry the same semantic structure.
- Product name should be transliterated.
- User friendly vocabulary selection at Hindi (target) side. Too many complicated Hindi words which are not in much use should be avoided. Transliteration of an English word can also be used in the Hindi side because in India, people generally use Hinglish (mix of Hindi and English words) vocabulary, e.g. 'time', 'face recognition', 'premium' etc.
- If hyphen, slash, dot etc. symbols occur in the source side then the same pattern should be preserved at the translated side too.
- Literal translation can be avoided sometimes. For example, adjectives and nouns like terrible, great etc. which carry extreme intensity should be translated into understandable simple words as घटिया (ghatiya), शानदार (shaanadaar) respectively which preserve the sense and intensity.

A few samples from the generated parallel English-Hindi corpus are shown in Table 3.

3.6 Crawling Hindi Reviews and Back-translating into English

We crawl 35,000 monolingual Hindi sentences from the various websites[10][11][12] which provide Hindi descriptions of electronic gadgets. Since these are commercial websites, we randomly gave 3,000 sentences out of all the

[8] https://cloud.google.com/translate/automl/docs/evaluate

[9] It achieves a 55.67 BLEU (En-to-Hi) on our in-house judicial domain test set

[10] https://www.digit.in/hi/reviews/

[11] https://hindi.gadgets360.com/reviews

[12] https://www.91mobiles.com/hi/tech/

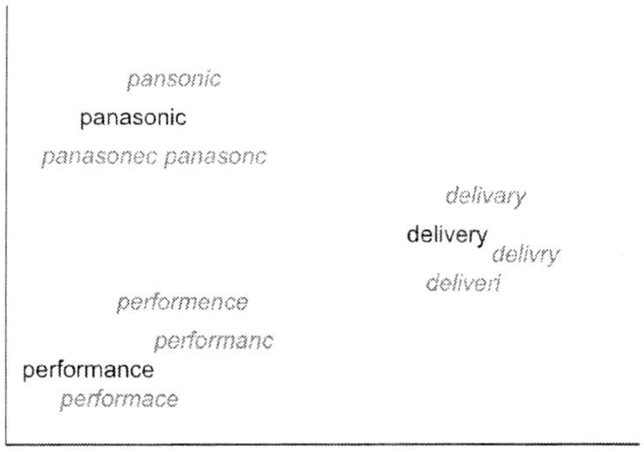

Figure 1: Mapping the noisy and correct forms of tokens close to each other in a vector space

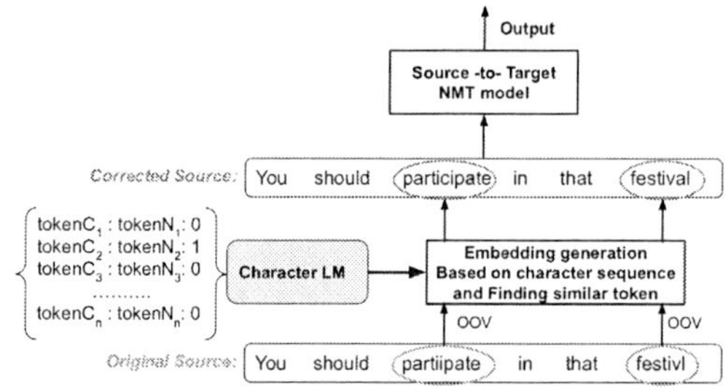

Figure 2: Token correction at inference time using character sequence based word embedding. *tokenC* and *tokenN* are the correct and noisy tokens respectively paired together for training. *0* and *1* denotes the similar and non-similar token pairs respectively.

crawled Hindi sentences as a sample to our language experts to read, and they found them to be in-domain, relevant, correct in the sense of syntax and semantics, and hence useful for our use-case. We build a Hindi–to–English NMT model to back-translate the crawled Hindi sentences. We use IIT Bombay Hindi-English general domain parallel corpus (Kunchukuttan et al., 2018) to train a Hindi–to–English NMT model, and then fine-tune it over the human corrected review domain parallel corpus. The fine-tuned Hindi–to–English NMT model is used to back-translate the crawled 35,000 monolingual Hindi sentences into English. This back-translated (BT) English-Hindi synthetic parallel corpus is augmented with the original 13,000 parallel sentences. Table 4 gives the statistics about the dataset. A new system Base+BT model from English–to–Hindi is trained using the human corrected+back-translated corpus. We will make the human corrected and back-translated parallel corpus available on request for the research purpose [13].

4 Training NMT over Human Corrected Corpus

We train an English–to–Hindi baseline model using the human corrected corpus as mentioned in Table 4. We use the Sockeye framework (Hieber et al., 2018) for training the Transformer neural network based NMT. We splitted the words into subwords (Sennrich et al., 2016b) using BPE technique. We perform 4,000 BPE merge operations. Our model contains 6-6 encoder-decoder layers, 512 hidden size and word embedding size, learning rate as 0.0002 and min batch size as 3800 tokens. We used early stopping over the validation set.

After training over the human corrected corpus, we perform testing over the review domain test set and achieves 33.26 BLEU points and name it as 'Base'- the baseline model. In addition to it, we also add the back-translated synthetic corpus into human corrected corpus, and train the NMT model over it. We call it as the 'Base+BT' model that yields 37.79 BLEU points.

5 Handling Noisy Tokens

In this section, we describe the methodology used in our work. Figure 2 presents the overall process of our proposed method. It consists of various steps like character language model (LM) training, word vector (embedding) generation, and finally noisy token replacement at inference time. Section 5.1 and Section 5.2 describe the steps in details.

5.1 Training Character LM and Word Vector Generation

A word consists of a sequence of characters. Each character is represented as a one-hot vector and a sequence of such vectors is passed through two different Long Short Term Memory (LSTM) (Hochreiter and Schmidhuber, 1997) layers. It generates the embedding vector of that particular word. As a training model, chars2vec[14] is utilized for embedding generation and character sequence learning. To be more specific, we deal with a neural network taking two sequences of one-hot vectors representing two different words as an input, creating their embeddings with one chars2vec model, calculating the norm of the difference between these embedding vectors and feeding it into the last layer of the network with the sigmoid activation function. The output of the neural network is a number that ranges

[13]https://www.iitp.ac.in/~ai-nlp-ml/resources/data/review-corpus.zip

[14]https://github.com/IntuitionEngineeringTeam/chars2vec

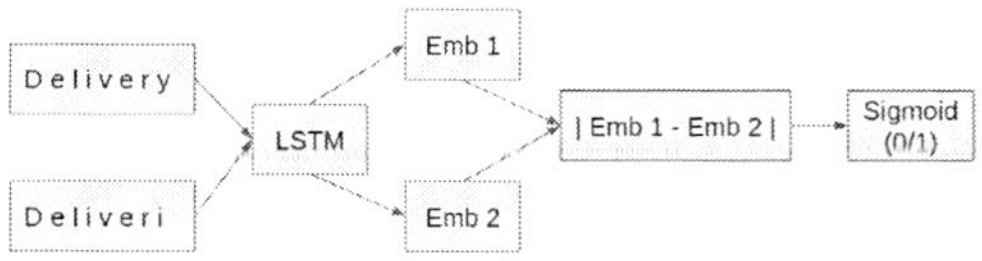

Figure 3: Training the character based language model

from 0 to 1 because of the sigmoid as an output function. The network is trained to capture the similarity between the noisy and its non-noisy version. For similar word pairs, i.e. for noisy and its equivalent version, we use *0* as a class label. On the other hand, we use *1* to denote the non-similar word pairs. For example, *panasonic* and *pansonic* are similar pairs while *panasonic* and *panorama* are non-similar. As shown in Figure 3, we are trying to reduce the distance of two embeddings *Emb1* and *Emb2* of two similar tokens so that they can be mapped as close as possible in vector space. This is why the label of similar pairs is *0* and the training objective is to reduce the distance between *Emb1* and *Emb2* close to *0*.

As shown in the Figure 1, our objective is to map the correct and noisy versions of a token as close as possible in vector space. To train the character LM, we prepare the training data by creating noisy versions of tokens in the source vocabulary set *trainX*. The labelled training data can be generated by taking a multitude of words and then performing various changes (e.g. character drop and replacement) upon them to obtain the noisy versions of those words. These new noisy words, so produced by injecting character errors in one original word, would naturally be similar to this original word, and such pairs of words would have the label 0. As an example, two noisy versions *performnce* and *performence* are generated using character drop and character replacement, respectively, from the original source vocabulary word *performance*. So [(performance, performnce) : 0] and [(performance, performence) : 0] are two similar training pairs with label *0*. It is to be noted that on a source token we apply at most two character operations to generate the similar pairs. To generate non-similar pairs with label *1*, with token from the source vocabulary, we randomly pair the shuffled tokens, for example: [(performance, product) : 1] and [(performance, smartphone) : 1]. These training pairs are used to train and save the character LM model which learns the parameter in the process of mapping the similar word embeddings closer. Now this model is used to generate the vector representation of the source vocabulary tokens and tokens in the input sentence at inference time.

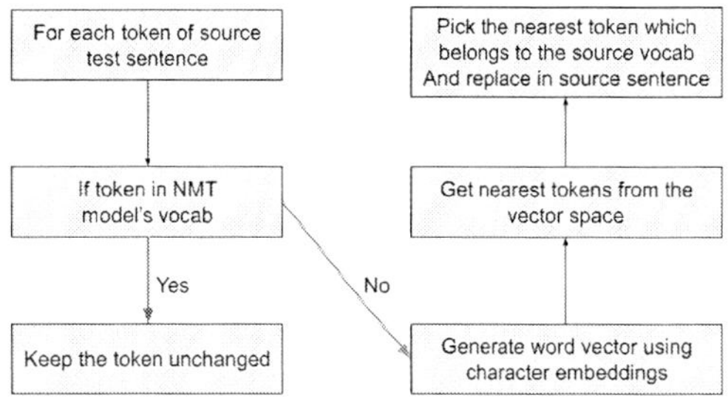

Figure 4: Flowchart of the noisy token replacement

5.2 Noisy Token Replacement

As discussed in Section 5.1, a trained model is saved which is used to generate the vector representation (embedding) of each word in the training source vocabulary. The vector representation is generated based on the characters in those words. Let us have a vector space S which contains the vector representation $trainV_i$ of training source vocabulary token $trainX_i$. Here, $trainV_i$ is generated using the trained chars2vec model based on the characters appearing in the token $trainX_i$.

Now at the time of inference, each test input sentence $input_i$ consists of *len* tokens and $j =$ *1, ..., len*. Here, we assume that if a noisy token or say a noisy version of a word appears in the test input sentence then it will not be a part of the training source vocabulary $trainX$. As shown in Figure 4, for each token $inferX_{ij}$ in the test input sentence $input_i$, we find if $inferX_{ij}$ belongs to the source train vocabulary $trainX$ then we keep that token as it is in source input sentence. If $inferX_{ij}$ does not belong to the source train vocabulary $trainX$, we find the most similar token from the vocabulary list $trainX$ using the cosine similarity. Now $inferX_{ij}$ will be replaced with the most similar token from $trainX$. Finally, the corrected (replaced) source sequence segmented by the subword model will be fed to the NMT model for the translation.

6 Dataset and Experimental Setup

In this section, we present the details of the datasets used in our experiments and the various setups.

6.1 Dataset

We perform experiments with four different translation directions which are English–to–Hindi (En–to–Hi), English-German (En–to–De), English–to–Czech (En–to–Cs) and English–to–French (En–to–Fr). Among these language pairs, English-Hindi is a low-resource and less-explored, and distant language pair.

	Train	Dev	Test
En-Hi (Reviews)	13,000	599	2,539
En-Hi (WMT14)	1,561,840	520	2,507
En-De (WMT14)	1,264,825	1,057	2,000
En-Cs (IWSLT17)	105,924	483	1,080
En-Fr (IWSLT17)	230,912	883	1,466
En-Fr (MTNT18)	36,014	852	1,020

Table 5: Size of train, dev and test sets for different language pairs

For English–to–Hindi translation, we use the IIT Bombay English-Hindi parallel corpus[15]. For English–to–Hindi, we also perform experiments over the generated review domain parallel corpus. For English–to–German, we use Europarl corpus from WMT 2014[16] (Bojar et al., 2014). We use the IWSLT17 dataset for English–to–Czech and English–to–French[17]. We also use the MTNT[18] dataset for English–to–French translation. Table 5 presents the statistics of training, development and test sets.

6.2 Experimental Setup

In order to build our machine translation systems, we use the Sockeye[19](Hieber et al., 2018) toolkit. Our training set-up is described below. The tokens of training, evaluation and validation sets are segmented into the subword units using the BPE technique (Gage, 1994) proposed by (Sennrich et al., 2016b). We perform 20,000 join operations. We use 6 layers at encoder and decoder sides each, 8-head attention, hidden layer of size 512, embedding vector of size 512, learning rate of 0.0002, and the minimum batch size of 3800 tokens.

6.3 Noise Injection in the Test Sets

For the experiment, we introduce noise in the En-Hi, En-De, En-Fr and En-Cs test sets to make them noisy and suitable for testing the models' performance in the noisy environment. We introduce two kinds of noise in the source test sequence: **1.** character drop and **2.** character replacement. In character drop, we randomly drop any character from a source token and in character replacement, we replace the characters randomly with some other characters.

7 Result and Analysis

We evaluate the models using BLEU, and these results are shown in Table 6. We also perform experiments using the word segmentation approaches, viz. BPE (Sennrich et al., 2016b) and subword regularization (Kudo, 2018). For English–to–Hindi review domain translation, proposed method yields 35.09 BLEU points which significantly outperforms synthetic noise, SR and BPE with a difference of 0.82, 1.61 and 1.83 BLEU points, respectively. We also perform experiments for En–to–Hi translation using benchmark newstest2014 as the test set. We achieve 0.96 and 1.29 BLEU improvements over subword regularization (SR) (Kudo, 2018) and byte-pair-encoding BPE (Sennrich et al., 2016b), respectively. We also evaluate the performance for En–to–De translation and achieve 1.05 and 1.07 BLEU improvements over SR and BPE, respectively. For En–to–Cs, we use the IWSLT17 testset, and the evaluation yields 1.94 and 2.48 BLEU improvements over SR and BPE, respectively. For En–to–Fr, we evaluate over two datasets, IWSLT17 and MTNT18. The MTNT is a noisy testset for En-Fr translation. For the MTNT testset, our model yields 1.55 and 2.18 BLEU improvements over SR and BPE, respectively. For IWSLT testset, En–to–Fr translation using our approach achieves the 1.63 and 1.57 BLEU improvements over SR and BPE, respectively.

	Proposed	Synthetic Noise (Vaibhav et al., 2019)	SR (Kudo, 2018)	BPE (Sennrich et al., 2016b)
En–to–Hi (Reviews)	35.09	34.27	33.48	33.26
En–to–Hi (newstest2014)	14.64	14.08	13.68	13.35
En–to–De (newstest2014)	28.91	28.22	27.86	27.84
En–to–Cs (IWSLT17)	14.52	13.65	12.58	12.04
En–to–Fr (MTNT18)	23.01	22.87	21.46	20.83
En–to–Fr (IWSLT17)	34.68	33.62	33.05	33.11

Table 6: Evaluation results of the proposed method in terms of BLEU score for different translation pairs. Here, **SR:** Subword regularization, **BPE:** Byte pair encoding

We also perform experiments by adding synthetic noise in the training corpus (Vaibhav et al., 2019) which is a noise handling technique. For En–to–Hi, En–to–De, En–to–Fr and En–to–Cs, our proposed method achieves 0.96, 1.05, 1.63 and 1.94 BLEU improvement, respectively, over the synthetic noise model (Vaibhav et al., 2019). We perform statistical significance tests[20] (Koehn, 2004), and found that the proposed model attains significant performance gain with 95% confidence level (with p=0.013 which is < 0.05). For En–to–Fr over MTNT18 testset, we achieve only 0.14 BLEU improvement over the synthetic noise model (Vaibhav et al., 2019) which is not a

[15]http://www.cfilt.iitb.ac.in/iitb_parallel/

[16]http://www.statmt.org/wmt14/translation-task.html

[17]`https://wit3.fbk.eu/`

[18]`https://www.cs.cmu.edu/~pmichel1/mtnt/`

[19]https://github.com/awslabs/sockeye

[20]`https://github.com/moses-smt/mosesdecoder/blob/master/scripts\/analysis/bootstrap-hypothesis-difference-significance.pl`

En–to–Hi (newstest2014)	20%	25%	30%	40%
Subword Regularization (SR)	14.37	13.68	10.31	9.81
Proposed	14.84	14.54	12.86	11.27
En–to–De (newstest2014)				
Subword Regularization (SR)	27.24	26.18	24.83	23.48
Proposed	28.53	27.34	26.08	25.22
En–to–Fr (IWSLT17)				–
Subword Regularization (SR)	33.14	32.26	29.24	28.37
Proposed	34.45	33.29	31.07	30.35

Table 7: Performance evaluation in terms of BLEU scores by increasing the % of noisy tokens

significant improvement.

7.1 Quantitative Analysis

We evaluate the performance of our approach in the presence of varying amount of noisy tokens. We inject the noise (character drop and character replacement) in 20%, 25%, 30% and 40% tokens in source input sentences for En-Hi, En-De and En-Fr testsets. Table 7 shows the change in the BLEU scores by increasing the count of noisy tokens. As we increase the number of noisy source tokens for three translation tasks, *viz.* En–to–Hi, En–to–De and En–to–Fr, we observe a decrease in BLEU score in both the models (proposed and SR). But our proposed method preserves the robustness significantly as compared to the SR model.

7.2 Human Evaluation

We perform the qualitative analysis of outputs using human evaluation. We took 250 random samples from English-Hindi review test set. It is given to 3 language experts (postgraduate in linguistics and have experiences for the translation task) to rate the outputs on the basis of adequacy and fluency and assign the scores in the range of 0 to 4 *(0: incorrect, 1: almost incorrect, 2: moderately correct, 3: almost correct and 4: correct)*. Table 8 shows the average ratings for the En-Hi translation.

We also calculate the inter-annotator-agreement scores (IAA) using Fleiss's Kappa. The scores for "En–to–Hi (proposed)" translation are found to be 87.2 and 86.8 for adequacy and fluency rating, respectively. The "En–to–Hi(SR)" translation shows the scores of 89.5 and 84.0 for adequacy and fluency, respectively. We also present a few output samples and error analysis in the appendix **A**.

8 Conclusion

In this paper, we have developed a robust NMT model for product review translation that can handle noisy input text. Because of the absence of an in-domain parallel corpus, we introduce a parallel English-Hindi corpus for product review domain. We crawl the user reviews of electronic gadgets from e-commerce sites written into English language. These are

	Adequacy Range: 0-4	Fluency Range: 0-4
En–to–Hi (Proposed)	2.65	2.81
En–to–Hi (SR)	2.47	2.68
En–to–Hi (BPE)	2.37	2.61

Table 8: Human evaluation for English–to–Hindi translation

pre-processed; passed through an in-house judicial domain NMT system; and a part of this dataset is post-edited by the language experts. It is also observed that product reviews which are user generated content contain noisy tokens which are a challenge to handle in any MT system. Due to the limitation of fixed vocabulary size at training time, it is not possible for the NMT models to see all the noisy variants of input tokens. We have integrated a token replacement approach during the inference time. We trained a character based language model which generates the vector representation of the tokens present in the source vocabulary based on the characters present in that word. The token replacement approach finds the most similar token from the source vocabulary for each noisy input token at inference time to replace it with the correct token.

We perform experiments over a variety of language pairs, such as En–to–Hi, En–to–De, En–to–Fr and En–to–Cs. and using the proposed approach, we achieve 35.09, 28.91, 34.68 and 14.52 BLEU points respectively. We also observe the behaviour of the proposed method by varying the % (20, 25, 30 and 40%) of noisy tokens at the input side. The proposed method significantly outperforms the baseline in the presence of different quantities of noisy tokens. Human evaluation shows that our model achieves good fluency and adequacy levels.

Acknowledgement

Authors gratefully acknowledge the unrestricted research grant received from the Flipkart Internet Private Limited to carry out the research. Authors thank Muthusamy Chelliah for his continuous feedbacks and suggestions to improve the quality of work; and to Anubhav Tripathee for gold standard parallel corpus creation and translation quality evaluation.

References

Antonios Anastasopoulos, Alison Lui, Toan Q. Nguyen, and David Chiang. 2019. Neural machine translation of text from non-native speakers. In *Proceedings of the 2019 Conference of the North American Chapter of the Association for*

Computational Linguistics: Human Language Technologies, Volume 1 (Long and Short Papers), pages 3070–3080, Minneapolis, Minnesota. Association for Computational Linguistics.

Dzmitry Bahdanau, Kyunghyun Cho, and Yoshua Bengio. 2015. Neural Machine Translation by Jointly Learning to Align and Translate. In *Proceedings of the 3rd International Conference on Learning Representation (ICLR 2015)*.

Yonatan Belinkov and Yonatan Bisk. 2018. Synthetic and natural noise both break neural machine translation. In *International Conference on Learning Representations*.

Alexandre Berard, Ioan Calapodescu, Marc Dymetman, Claude Roux, Jean-Luc Meunier, and Vassilina Nikoulina. 2019. Machine translation of restaurant reviews: New corpus for domain adaptation and robustness. In *Proceedings of the 3rd Workshop on Neural Generation and Translation*, pages 168–176, Hong Kong. Association for Computational Linguistics.

Ondřej Bojar, Christian Buck, Christian Federmann, Barry Haddow, Philipp Koehn, Johannes Leveling, Christof Monz, Pavel Pecina, Matt Post, Herve Saint-Amand, et al. 2014. Findings of the 2014 Workshop on Statistical Machine Translation. In *Proceedings of the ninth workshop on statistical machine translation (WMT 2014)*, pages 12–58.

Bora Edizel, Aleksandra Piktus, Piotr Bojanowski, Rui Ferreira, Edouard Grave, and Fabrizio Silvestri. 2019. Misspelling oblivious word embeddings. *ArXiv*, abs/1905.09755.

Philip Gage. 1994. A new algorithm for data compression. *C Users Journal*, 12(2):23–38.

Felix Hieber, Tobias Domhan, Michael Denkowski, David Vilar, Artem Sokolov, Ann Clifton, and Matt Post. 2018. The sockeye neural machine translation toolkit at AMTA 2018. In *Proceedings of the 13th Conference of the Association for Machine Translation in the Americas (Volume 1: Research Papers)*, pages 200–207, Boston, MA.

Sepp Hochreiter and Jürgen Schmidhuber. 1997. Long short-term memory. *Neural computation*, 9(8):1735–1780.

Vladimir Karpukhin, Omer Levy, Jacob Eisenstein, and Marjan Ghazvininejad. 2019. Training on synthetic noise improves robustness to natural noise in machine translation. In *Proceedings of the 5th Workshop on Noisy User-generated Text (W-NUT 2019)*, pages 42–47, Hong Kong, China. Association for Computational Linguistics.

Philipp Koehn. 2004. Statistical significance tests for machine translation evaluation. In *Proceedings of the 2004 Conference on Empirical Methods in Natural Language Processing*, pages 388–395, Barcelona, Spain. Association for Computational Linguistics.

Taku Kudo. 2018. Subword regularization: Improving neural network translation models with multiple subword candidates. In *Proceedings of the 56th Annual Meeting of the Association for Computational Linguistics (Volume 1: Long Papers)*, pages 66–75, Melbourne, Australia. Association for Computational Linguistics.

Anoop Kunchukuttan, Pratik Mehta, and Pushpak Bhattacharyya. 2018. The IIT Bombay English-Hindi parallel corpus. In *Proceedings of the Eleventh International Conference on Language Resources and Evaluation (LREC 2018)*, Miyazaki, Japan.

Paul Michel and Graham Neubig. 2018. MTNT: A testbed for machine translation of noisy text. In *Proceedings of the 2018 Conference on Empirical Methods in Natural Language Processing*, pages 543–553, Brussels, Belgium. Association for Computational Linguistics.

Rico Sennrich, Barry Haddow, and Alexandra Birch. 2016a. Improving Neural Machine Translation Models with Monolingual Data. In *Proceedings of the 54th Annual Meeting of the Association for Computational Linguistics (ACL 2016) (Volume 1: Long Papers)*, pages 86–96.

Rico Sennrich, Barry Haddow, and Alexandra Birch. 2016b. Neural machine translation of rare words with subword units. In *Proceedings of the 54th Annual Meeting of the Association for Computational Linguistics (Volume 1: Long Papers)*, pages 1715–1725, Berlin, Germany.

Vaibhav Vaibhav, Sumeet Singh, Craig Stewart, and Graham Neubig. 2019. Improving robustness of machine translation with synthetic noise. In *Proceedings of the 2019 Conference of the North American Chapter of the Association for Computational Linguistics: Human Language Technologies, Volume 1 (Long and Short Papers)*, pages 1916–1920, Minneapolis, Minnesota. Association for Computational Linguistics.

Ashish Vaswani, Noam Shazeer, Niki Parmar, Jakob Uszkoreit, Llion Jones, Aidan N Gomez, Łukasz Kaiser, and Illia Polosukhin. 2017. Attention is all you need. In *Advances in neural information processing systems*, pages 5998–6008.

A Comparing Output Samples and Error Analysis

Table 9 shows some examples to illustrate the performance of the proposed model. In example A, we translate an English sentence

A. En→Hi Source	Names of other partiipating lawmkers were to be released in coming days .
Reference	सहभागिता करने वाले अन्य विधि - निर्माताओं के नाम आने वाले दिनों में जारी किए जाएँगे । (sahabhaagita karane vaale any vidhi - nirmaataon ke naam aane vaale dinon mein jaaree kie jaenge)
Output (Subword Regularization)	आने वाले दिनों में अन्य दलों के नाम जारी किए जाने थे। (aane vaale dinon mein any dalon ke naam jaaree kie jaane the)
Corrected Source	names of other participating lawmakers were to be released in coming days .
Output (Proposed)	आगामी दिनों में अन्य भाग लेने वाले विधिनिर्माता के नाम जारी किए जाने थे। (aagaamee dinon mein any bhaag lene vaale vidhinirmaata ke naam jaaree kie jaane the)
B. En→De Source	the European Commission's sixth report prsents very valuable conclusions .
Reference	der Sechste Bericht der Europäischen Kommission bietet sehr wertvolle Schlußfolgerungen .
Output (Subword Regularization)	der Sechste Bericht der Europäischen Kommission ist sehr wertvoll .
Corrected Source	the European Commission ' s sixth report presents very valuable conclusions .
Output (Proposed)	der Sechste Bericht der Europäischen Kommission enthält sehr wertvolle Schlußfolgerungen .
C. En→Hi Source	The new featurs of the phone lok nice.
Reference	फोन के नए फीचर अच्छे लगते हैं। (phon ke nae pheechar achchhe lagate hain.)
Output (Subword Regularization)	फोन के नए सौदे बहुत ही अच्छे थे। (phon ke nae saude bahut hee achchhe the)
Corrected Source	The new features of the phone lock nice.
Output (Proposed)	फोन के नए फीचर अच्छे से लोक होते हैं। (phon ke nae pheechar achchhe se lok hote hain.)

Table 9: Output samples for English→Hindi and English→German translation

into Hindi. The two tokens, *partiipating* and *lawmkers* are noisy and appear as OOV candidates for the trained NMT model. The SR model is not able to recognize those tokens and misses their translations in the output sentence. Our proposed method of replacing the tokens using character LM finds the two most similar tokens *participating* and *lawmakers* as the correct tokens and update the source English sentence which results in the correct Hindi sentence as the output. Similarly, in example B, for English–to–German translation, *prsents* appears as noisy as well as OOV token, which is eventually replaced by its correct version *presents* in the proposed method.

Example C shows one limitation of the spell correction method. There are two misspelled tokens *featurs* and *lok* in the source sentence. Using the proposed method, *features* and *lock* tokens appear as the replaced correct tokens respectively. *features* is the correct replacement for *featurs* but *lock* is not the correct replacement for *lok*. It should be *look* as the correct token. But, *lok*, *lock* and *look* tokens contain almost similar character combinations which make them appear closer to each other in the vector space. So our method may struggle in case of very small length (character count) noisy tokens.

Author Index

Association for Computational Linguistics
209 N. Eighth Street
Stroudsburg, Pennsylvania 18360

ISBN 978-1-7138-3373-4